Contesting Public Sector Reforms

Contesting Public Sector Reforms

Critical Perspectives, International Debates

Edited by

Pauline Dibben, Geoffrey Wood and
Ian Roper

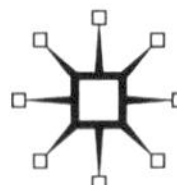

First published 2004 by
PALGRAVE MACMILLAN
Houndmills, Basingstoke, Hampshire RG21 6XS and
175 Fifth Avenue, New York, N. Y. 10010
Companies and representatives throughout the world

PALGRAVE MACMILLAN is the global academic imprint of the Palgrave Macmillan division of St. Martin's Press, LLC and of Palgrave Macmillan Ltd. Macmillan® is a registered trademark in the United States, United Kingdom and other countries. Palgrave is a registered trademark in the European Union and other countries.

ISBN 1–4039–0430–8 hardback

This book is printed on paper suitable for recycling and made from fully managed and sustained forest sources.

A catalogue record for this book is available from the British Library.

Library of Congress Cataloging-in-Publication Data
Contesting public sector reforms : critical perspectives, international debates / edited by Pauline Dibben, Geoffrey Wood, and Ian Roper.
      p. cm.
   Includes bibliographical references and index.
   ISBN 1–4039–0430–8 (cloth)
      1. Public administration. 2. Administrative agencies–Management.
3. Organizational change. 4. Public-private sector cooperation.
5. Public administration–Case studies. 6. Administrative agencies–Management–Case studies. 7. Organizational change–Case studies. 8. Public-private sector cooperation–Case studies. I. Dibben, Pauline, 1965– II. Wood, G. (Geoffrey) III. Roper, Ian, 1964–

JF1351.C65 2004
352.3'67–dc22   2003067590

10   9   8   7   6   5   4   3   2   1
13   12   11   10   09   08   07   06   05   04

Printed and bound in Great Britain by
Antony Rowe Ltd, Chippenham and Eastbourne

To Vicky, Caroline, Peter, Shaun, and Coralie

Contents

Conclusion

List of Tables

List of Figures

List of Contributors

Bruce Baker is a Lecturer in the African Studies Centre at Coventry University. He is currently researching state and non-state policing in Africa. His publications include *Escape from Domination in Africa: Political Disengagement and its Consequences* and *Taking the Law into Their Own Hands: Lawless Law Enforces in Africa.*

Patrick Bond, a political economist, is a professor at the University of the Witwatersrand Graduate School of Public and Development Management in Johannesburg, and Visiting Professor at York University, Department of Political Science, in Toronto. Bond has authored/edited several books, and a dozen policy papers for the South African government from 1994–2002.

Pauline Dibben is a Senior Lecturer at Middlesex University. She has published widely in the area of both Public Sector Management and Human Resource Management. Her current research interests include local government, transport and social exclusion, and social movement unionism. Pauline is a member of the University's Transport Management Research Centre, and is Deputy Director of the Work, Employment and Organisation Research Centre.

Robert Gregory is an Associate Professor of Public Policy and Administration in the School of Government, Victoria University of Wellington. His main fields of interest are state sector reform, particularly issues of accountability and responsibility, organisational behaviour, and public policy-making theory.

Jenny Harrow is Professor of Voluntary Sector Management, Cass Business School, City University. Her research interests focus on voluntary sector/governmental relations and management development in these sectors, and she is active in charity trusteeship. She was formerly Professor in Management, South Bank University Business School and chair of its Centre for Government and Charity Management.

Paul Higgins is a Lecturer at Middlesex University. He teaches and researches in public sector management and employment relations. His current research interests are public sector reform, and particularly the issues of performance measurement and inspection. Paul is also a member of the Chinese Management Centre at Middlesex University where he is conducting a comparative study of student approaches to learning.

Phil James is Professor of Employment Relations at Middlesex University. He has researched extensively in the field of industrial relations in both the private and public sectors. Phil is Director of the university's Work, Organisation and Employment Research Centre and a member of the executive committee of the Institute of Employment Rights.

J. Rogers Hollingsworth is Professor of Sociology and History at the University of Wisconsin. Awarded honorary degrees by the University of Uppsala (Sweden) and by Emory University, he is the author and editor of numerous books and articles on comparative political economy. One of his major research interests is the study of how organisational and institutional factors influence different types of innovations. His recent publications include *Contemporary Capitalism: The Embeddedness of Institutions* (with Robert Boyer, 1997); *Governing Capitalist Economies* (with Philippe Schmitter and Wolfgang Streeck, 1994); *The Governance of the American Economy* (with John Campbell and Leon Lindberg, 1991); and *Advancing Socio-Economics: An Institutionalist Perspective* (with Karl H. Müller and Ellen Jane Hollingsworth, 2002). He is past President and also Honorary Fellow of the Society for the Advancement of Socio-Economics.

Professor Jonathan Liu is Professor of Chinese Management at Middlesex University. His research interests lie in interdisciplinary management issues, productivity and quality management. He has co-authored books and papers relating to the managerial pursuit of excellence in developing and training the work force in Chinese and western organisations.

Zsuzsanna Lonti is Senior Lecturer in Human Resource Management and Industrial Relations at Victoria University of Wellington. Her research focuses primarily on public sector management practices. Prior to entering academia she worked in various policy positions in the governments of Ontario, Canada and Hungary.

Ronaldo Munck is Professor of Political Sociology and Director of the Globalisation and Social Exclusion Unit at the University of Liverpool. He has written widely on Latin America and labour/development issues. His most recent books include: *Labour and Globalisation: The New Great Transformation*; *Contemporary Latin America* and *Globalisation and Social Exclusion: A Transformationalist Perspective*.

Ian Roper is a Senior Lecturer at Middlesex University. He teaches and researches in the area of employment relations, in which he has published. He has a particular interest in the area of public sector reform and the effects of re-regulating work, both in terms of collective bargaining and the labour process.

Anil Verma is Professor of Industrial Relations and Human Resource Management at the University of Toronto where he holds a joint appointment at the Rotman School of Management and the Centre for Industrial Relations. His primary research interests are in the area of management responses to unionisation, participative forms of work organisation, wage and employment outcomes, and the contribution of workplace innovations to organisational effectiveness and performance. He has served as President of the Canadian Industrial Relations Association and on the Executive Board of the International Relations Association, and is on the Advisory Committee on Labour Statistics, Canada. He has published over 60 articles in research journals and books, and is a member of the editorial board of several journals. He has co-edited seven books including: *Unions in the 21st Century: An International Perspective*; *Restructuring Work and the Life Course*; *Contract and Commitment: Employment Relations in the New Economy*.

Axel van den Berg is Professor of Sociology at McGill University. His current research focuses on the sociology of labour markets, the sociology of aesthetic judgement, the relation between sociology and economics and contemporary sociological theory. Recent work includes *The Immanent Utopia: From Marxism on the State to the State of Marxism*; *Politics versus Markets: A Note on the Uses of Double Standards*, in Raymond Breton and Jeffrey Reitz, eds; *Globalisation and Society: Processes of Differentiation Examined*; *La théorie du choix rationnel contre les sciences sociales? Bilan des débats contemporains*, special theme issue of Sociologie et Sociétés', Vol. XXXIV, No. 1, Spring 2002 (with André Blais); and *The Social Sciences and Rationality: Promise, Limits and Problems* (with Hudson Meadwell).

Malcolm Wallis is based at the University of Durban Westville. He has published widely on the issue of bureaucracy, and his research interests include the management of development in developing countries.

Madam Jane Wang is a senior administrator for the Study Tours Programme at Middlesex University Business School. Madam Wang was formerly with the Ministry of Communications of the Peoples' Republic of China. Her main research interests include investigating policy reforms and their impact on the Public and State Administrative Systems in the People's Republic of China.

Geoffrey Wood is Professor of Comparative Human Resource Management at Middlesex University. He is currently Overseas Research Associate of the University of the Witwatersrand, and has served as Commissioned Researcher for the South African Truth and Reconciliation Commission. He has authored/co-authored/edited six books, and over 60 articles in peer-reviewed journals. His current research interests include trade union renewal, the disjunctures between HR theory and practice, human resource development in the shipping and textile industries, neo-corporatism, and maritime industrial policy. He has published extensively on HR issues in comparative contexts.

Acknowledgements

The author and publishers are grateful to the Review of International Political Economy and Taylor and Francis for permission to reprint the article by J. Rogers Hollingsworth, originally published as: 'New Perspectives on the Spatial Dimensions of Economic Coordination: Tensions Between Globalisation and Social Systems of Production' by J. Rogers Hollingsworth, *Review of International Political Economy*, (1998) Vol. 5 No. 3 pp. 482–507 http://www.tandf.co.uk/journals/routledge/09692290.html

1
Introduction: Public Sector Management and the Neo-liberal Hegemony: a Critical and International Perspective

Pauline Dibben, Ian Roper and Geoffrey Wood

This volume is written at a time when the growth of neo-liberal policy prescriptions has led to a general 'paring down' and 'hollowing out' of the state. This began with solitary voices calling for a minimal state, operating merely as a 'nightwatchman' in a Western context (Hayek, 1944), but has subsequently expanded into becoming the guiding principle for the role of the state in a much wider sense. The neo-liberal hegemony emerged as the most influential prescription from the debates tracing the breakdown of the post-war consensus in the Anglo-Saxon countries during the 1970s (Dunleavy and O'Leary, 1987; Mishra, 1984) but has now expanded its ambitions. The neo-liberal view of this post-war consensus has ironically, given its critical approach during this period, now become orthodoxy and has lost its critical status. The doctrines of Hayek (1944), Friedman (1962) and others have now been institutionalised within the very international financial institutions – that were paradoxically, almost exclusively set up along Keynesian lines – that set the terms for the development of nations. A re-evaluation of the impact of this neo-liberal orthodoxy on the redefined role of the 'public sector' is therefore both timely and important. In contrast to the tendency of the neo-liberal approach, that tends to separate economy from the 'less rational' discourses of politics and society, an appropriate evaluation of the public sphere under neo-liberal regimes requires a greater integration of disciplines.

In many countries, the paring back of the state has been coupled with deregulation, privatisation of state assets, and internal marketisation. However, growing doubts have emerged about the effectiveness, and even the efficiency, of deregulation, privatisation and marketisation (Clarke and Pitelis, 1993; Vickers and Yarrow, 1988; Lane, 1995). Questions are now being raised about the responsibility of the State in the light of market failures resulting from private contracts, political, social and economic exclusion, and both local and global inequality.

Rather than proactively ensuring economic growth with equality and equity, the priorities of the public sector have shifted towards an emphasis on value-for-money, 'flexibility' and 'efficiency'. It is also notable that whilst there has apparently been some convergence in ideological terms, this has often translated to a divergence in practice, so that the persistence of relatively interventionist modes of operation in parts of northern Europe stand in sharp contrast to the under-resourced and disempowered states found in many areas of the developing world. All of these developments have translated into far-reaching changes in the manner in which the public sector is administered and managed. The exact nature and consequences of such changes has been the subject of intense debate (Osborne and Gaebler, 1992; Pollitt, 1993; Pollitt and Bouckaert, 2001; Osborne, 2001; Lane, 2001).

Against this background, this volume critically evaluates the role of the public sector, through taking a critical approach in the traditions of political economy. The introduction of neo-liberal reforms over recent years, and their far-reaching implications arguably necessitate such an approach, rather than one that takes a 'neutral' stance (see for example Hughes, 2002; McLaughlin, 2002). A critical analysis of current debates in *Part One*, and the discussion of practical issues in *Part Two* thus form the setting for a series of studies in *Part Three* of a range of countries and regions. The book incorporates theoretical and practical components, and is explicitly international in focus, with a specific emphasis on different regions that include both developed and developing countries. Indeed, on balance, the focus here is on developing countries due to their relative neglect in the literature on public sector management. Due to the coverage of both current issues and debates but also attention to regional studies, it seeks to provide a useful stimulus for discussion of public sector management in individual regions, but at the same time offers the opportunity for comparison and contrast.

This book broaches this subject at a critical juncture when there is a growing realisation about the implications that these developments have had for countries across the world. There is also an explicit acknowledgement within the various chapters of this volume that action needs to be taken to defend, but also to reform or even re-interpret the public sphere, in order to both protect the needs of the vulnerable, and work towards fair treatment, social justice and equity.

In addressing these concerns, there are a number of important and topical themes which run through the book. These are necessarily overlapping, but can be summarised as follows:

1. In a climate dominated by the pervasiveness of minimal government, what is meant by 'publicness', and what remains distinctive about the public sector?

2. How has the long-term trend in the pursuit for efficiency (mainly through an enhanced role for market-based solutions) affected the capacity of the public sector to fulfil its remit (the equitable provision of socially necessary services for defined needs)?
3. How viable is the discourse of New Public Management? How has it been translated into practice, and how transferable is it from the Anglo-Saxon world to other regions and circumstances?
4. How does 'governance' affect the interactions that take place within and between institutions vertically and horizontally, locally and globally?
5. What has been the experience of reform on key stakeholders: employees, service users, public service unions, citizens, taxpayers and other interested groupings.
6. How has public sector 'reform' changed the balance between efficiency, accountability and democracy?

These themes represent significant challenges to the public sector and therefore provide common strands that link the chapters together. The aim of this book is not only to shed light on these challenges, but also to hint at possible ways forward and alternative policy options.

This book thus addresses a gap in the literature on two levels. Firstly, it bridges the gap between, on the one hand, the theoretical debates on the subject of the role and reform of the public sector; and on the other hand, the practical outcomes emanating from these debates, including the implications of 'reform' in both developed and developing countries and regions. Secondly, the above is achieved through a consciously critical perspective and the focus is much wider than merely the internal workings of institutions. For the purpose of this book, therefore, the term 'public sector' includes both micro and macro elements. Thus, there is reflection on both the internal dynamics within public sector institutions and also the political and economic context within which they operate. The book does not confine itself simply to the traditional elements that make up the welfare state, since the 'public sector' encompasses all of the various programmes that governments at different levels run by means of taxation, public resource allocation, income redistribution and public regulation (Lane, 1997). However it does restrict itself to those functions that contribute to the general welfare of citizens. So there is consideration, for example, of the effects of reforming water supply in one context, but not about the effects on military or judicial aspects of the state.

In contrast to this text, much existing work on the public sector tends to be either regional or issue based, or tackles a specific element of public sector management. With regard to texts that focus on specific countries or regions, there are those that cover, for example, Europe and Britain, Latin America and Australasia.[1] Others take a comparative approach, but, (for example in the case of Pollitt and Bouckaert, 2000) the focus often tends to be on countries and regions within the developed world.[2] However, the New Public Management (NPM) model is arguably more oriented toward the cost cutting, tax reducing concerns of northern states, rather than the capacity building and developmental concerns of the southern states. This is acknowledged in Minogue *et al.*'s (1998) contribution, which usefully covers developing countries, but does not, conversely try to examine the situation of developed countries in any depth. The aim of this volume is to make a balanced attempt toward addressing both types regions. Other books in the field of public sector management often take an issue based approach, and investigate either generic management areas such as strategy, quality, marketing, or employee relations in the public sector.[3] These tend to be distinct from other texts that examine specific aspects of public service provision, such as health, housing, education or support services for the vulnerable. Still other groups of texts focus on public sector management from a 'policy outcome' angle, such as the role of policy networks, para-governmental organisations, or the market. More general works on public administration either tend to be introductory,[4] or take a more critical approach that can be theoretically and conceptually rich (as acknowledged by our reference to them), but can tend to include a somewhat disparate collection of themes, or draw on works written over a long time period.[5] As the chapter outline below explains, this book provides a critical, but contemporary analysis of international developments.

Chapter outline

The book is divided into three main sections, examining in turn broader theoretical debates, practical issues, then regional studies. This is followed by a concluding chapter that reflects on the defence and future development of the public sphere.

Part one

The first part of this book begins with an analysis, and critique, of the underpinning logic of the public sector reform agenda. The start point for this is a critique of public choice theory. This is necessary in order to situate the discussion of the more topical New Public Management (NPM) in its wider context. This is then followed by an overview of debates around the *concept* of NPM, its *outcomes* and its *relationship* with democracy in a variety of settings. Having raised a number of potential concerns with recent developments in the public sector, and having drawn attention to the significance – and extent – of private sector 'capture' of the functions of the public sector, the final chapter in this section then examines, from an institutionalist perspective, whether it is possible to tame the market in order for a functioning public sphere to remain.

Thus, the book begins, in chapter 2, by examining the predominant theoretical paradigm underpinning the neo-liberal public sector reform agenda, namely that of Public Choice theory. In this chapter, Axel van den Berg scrutinises Public Choice on its own terms, taking issue with the inconsistency in which public officials' utility maximising behaviour *in practice*, is unfavourably compared to the notion, *in theory*, that private sector entrepreneurs would deal with similar resource allocation decisions more effectively because of the existence of perfectly competitive markets.

Chapter 3 then analyses what is meant by 'new public management' (NPM). Pauline Dibben and Paul Higgins examine the origins and validity of NPM in terms of three types of relationships. The first of these, between the public sector and the private sector, is often characterised as marketisation. Particular attention is paid here to the dynamics of power relationships, and the increasing dominance of the private sector within the reform package. The transformation of the employment relationship in NPM can, on the other hand, be perceived as dominated by managerialism, with implications for role ambiguity and work intensification. Thirdly, the relationship between public sector organisations and the 'public' that it is intended to serve, while often using the language of citizenship, still seems to be dominated by the philosophy of consumerism. Their conclusion reflects on the implications that these three relationships have for the most vulnerable in society.

Concerns can also be raised about the implications of NPM for democracy, and in chapter 4 Bruce Baker examines the relevance of this debate to developing countries. Baker argues that NPM and democratisation have different motivations, since the aim of NPM is to save money, and 'key stakeholders' are not those who rely on the services provided. This does not fit well, for example, with concerns to promote equality, accountability and comprehensive provision of essential state services. Baker questions, in particular, whether NPM is a valid approach in developing countries and suggests that there are some differences in how, for example, privatisation and managerialism have been applied in developing countries. Attempts to impose NPM on developing countries have ignored both internal constraints in doing this and the lack of involvement that citizens have in determining the agenda.

Chapter 5 concludes the section by asking whether it is possible to tame the market from an institutionalist perspective. J. Rogers Hollingsworth highlights the significance that 'institutions' – in the wider sense – have on the development of the public sphere in society, how these institutions shape and distort tendencies towards convergence and the implications that this may have on our understanding of the development of contemporary public sector management. Questions are raised as to what level, and by what means, economic activity is actively co-ordinated, and although a distinction is drawn between different types of system, it is argued that active co-ordination between these systems is required. Hollingsworth rejects the 'globalisation/convergence' thesis, although it is conceded that nation-states are tending to have diminished activity compared to regional and global levels. In summary, a key argument is that collective co-ordination is needed in order to 'tame the market'.

Part two

The second part of the book moves the discussion forward through examining various aspects of the experience of 'reform', and critically evaluates the way in which the state has impacted upon both its citizens (the users of public services) and its workforce (the providers). In doing this, attention is paid first of all to the important, but contentious, issue of ethics in the public sector. This is then followed by a discussion of how neo-liberal reform has affected the adequacy of service provision for service users and for those who provide the services, examining recent trends and issues regarding industrial relations and the nature of work organisation.

In starting this section, Geoffrey Wood, in chapter 6, outlines changes in how public sector ethics have been interpreted. Tensions are drawn out between the rights of the individual and the need to promote equity and fairness, and the dual aspects of ethics within the state and in its dealings with wider society. Wood discusses issues such as the distinction between ethics and morals, and the state's role in relation to the 'freerider problem'. Wood analyses the role of the state, and refers to how ethical frames of reference such as utilitarianism, communitarianism and postmodernism have influenced the agenda on its role, size and spatial orientation. Within this context, Wood discusses how ethical standpoints relate to internal organisational functions, the managerial revolution and the attendant idea that professionals are 'unethical' and therefore need to be made more accountable. However, it is argued that this ignores the economic sphere. Ethical concerns emerge, however, with outsourcing core state functions such as law and health. Moreover, it can be argued that marketisation undermines 'publicnesss', understood as the common good of society, realising shared concerns, securing equality and openness, and representation and impartiality. The chapter therefore concludes by suggesting that there should be a move towards a 'new public ethics'.

In chapter 7, Jenny Harrow reflects on the changing nature of service provision, examining this in terms of both mechanisms and values, and arguing that the focus on services delivery may be seen as a relatively neglected part of, or a latecomer to, the NPM debates. This neglect has been due to the erroneous assumption that once core reforms had taken place, associated service deficiencies and problems would be self-righting. With regard to the mechanisms of service provision, Harrow pays particular attention to the variable institutional mix and the nature of involvement of both private and voluntary sectors. The involvement of the private sector is often referred to broadly as privatisation, and public/private partnerships (PPPs) are often seen as exemplar. However, there are issues around cost transfer, and doubts as to its efficacy, with possible negative implications for the voluntary sector. In examining the values of service provision, attention is drawn to tensions in respect of equity and business values, the impact of modernisation, and the notion of consumerism. Moreover, it is suggested that accountability does not fit well with 'patchwork' service provision. The chapter concludes by suggesting that marketisation does not lead to stability, and that therefore there is a need for a different kind of reform for the public sector.

Chapters 8 and 9 seek to explain the key themes emerging in respect of industrial relations in the public sector and the work organisation. In chapter 8, Philip James examines developments in the area of industrial relations, focusing on the important issue of collective bargaining. James examines recent developments in Britain, which is widely seen as a country where the process of public sector reform has been one of the most dramatic. In examining the situation in Britain, attention is drawn to the role that public sector industrial relations plays in the economy as a whole, the trends in coverage of collective bargaining in the public sector, and the ways in which changes in the structure of bargaining have acted to increase the autonomy of local trade unions and employers. James questions the notion that collective bargaining in the public sector has 'converged' with practices in the private sector; and that public sector industrial relations in Europe has emulated practices in Britain.

Chapter 9 concludes this section. In this chapter, Ian Roper examines the organisation of work, taking the issue of quality as the starting point to examine how new managerial initiatives can potentially impact upon the labour process. A particular focus on empirical research in British local government provides the springboard to highlight the implications of transforming work through imposing commercial definitions of quality in an inherently non-commercial environment. This tension creates distortions that variously lead to a tendency toward 'management by stress', work standardisation and 'work intensification'.

Part three

There have been significant variations, over recent years, in the drivers for reform of the public sector, the ways in which reforms have been made, and the key impacts of these reforms. Therefore, the third part of this book examines the impact of these developments in both developed and in less developed countries. Each chapter tackles pertinent aspects of the current and recent political, economic and social climate, but also critically examines those characteristics of the recent public sector reform agenda that are of key relevance to the particular country or region examined. This provides the context for an examination of the rhetoric and form of public sector management, embracing such areas as deregulation, privatisation and managerial style. The final two chapters are reflective and summative: the penultimate one reflecting more broadly on developing countries and the final one proposing a way forward more generally.

In chapter ten Zsuzsanna Lonti and Anil Verma examine the experience of public sector reform in Canada. Beginning by outlining the structure of the Canadian state and the drivers for reform, Lonti and Verma discuss the influence of global competition, the national debt, technology, expectations, and an ideological shift in favour of a declining role for government. However it is noted that this ideological shift has not been as great as in the UK, the United States, or New Zealand. Drawing on recent empirical research conducted by the authors, some positive, as well as negative, implications of reforms are discussed, with particular attention being paid to the implications of the reforms for public sector workers.

In contrast, the next country to be examined is New Zealand, which is generally considered to have been the vanguard of NPM reform (see, for example, Schick, 1998; Polidano *et al.*, 1998). In chapter 11, Bob Gregory outlines how the radical restructuring of the New Zealand state sector that occurred in the 1980s and early 1990s was an integral part of a wider programme of neo-liberal economic and social policy change that has rested uneasily with the country's egalitarian tradition. Relationships between the reconfigured state in New Zealand and its citizens are now more fraught and less trusting, which has changed the characteristics of public sector employment, the nature of work and of working relationships in the public sector. While there is a need to remedy flaws in the current architecture of the New Zealand state sector, this will not be easily achieved.

Following the reflection on these two contrasting countries, in chapter 12, Geoffrey Wood carries out a broader analysis of the situation in Europe, examining whether there has been integration around NPM, or alternatively whether there has been a broadening of the existing 'social model'. Several archetypes are identified: the Rhineland model, the semi-peripheral 'Fordist' model, the transitional model, the Anglo-American model, the regional or industrial districts model, and the French model. Each has been affected to a greater or lesser extent by neo-liberal practices. In terms of current and future direction, on the one hand it can be argued that convergence has been primarily led by institutions such as the EU, and is leading to the diffusion of a broad social model. On the other hand, it can be argued that national level institutions remain resilient against both global capitalism and transnational bodies such as the EU. The chapter concludes by suggesting that the preservation of the public domain in Europe depends on the vitality of national and residual (neither government nor market) institutions and the development of policy that preserves and develops the social gains of the past.

The second part of this third section examines the situation in developing countries, beginning with chapter 13 which focuses on China, a country characterised by long feudal traditions, a recent communist history and the immersion into 'the socialist market economy'. Jonathan Liu and Jane Wang draw attention to the historical development of the civil service, which dates from the 3rd Century BC, and the significance of Western influence on recruitment and training. They indicate that, rather than the simple transposing of Western public sector management reform, a hybrid system seems to be developing that will not be a mere cloning of Western types, and may yet, therefore, avoid some of the weaknesses in the civil service that earlier chapters have indicated.

Chapter 14, by Patrick Bond, examines the situation in South Africa, and draws attention to the impact of neo-liberal reforms. Bond focuses on the privatisation of water provision in South Africa and uncovers the respective roles of national and municipal government, supranational organisations such as the World Bank, water companies, and progressive civil society organisations, leading to unambiguously negative outcomes for the most needy of the water companies' 'customers'. Bond draws particular attention to the potential role of activists in the light of the apparent technical and eco-social contradictions inherent in applying NPM techniques via the private sector.

In chapter 15, attention moves to Latin America. Ronaldo Munck explains how the 'first generation' of state reform in Latin America occurred under the aegis of the neo-liberal Washington Consensus. Designed to minimise state 'interference' with the workings of the free market, it has left a legacy of problems now being addressed by a 'second generation' state reform programme. A key issue, from a Latin American perspective, is how the international drive towards 'state reform' (variously defined) can assist or hinder the consolidation of democracy in the region after the period of military dictatorships.

The previous six chapters examined trends and characteristics of public sector management in each of the six regions. In chapter 16, Malcolm Wallis reflects on the situation facing the public sector in developing countries. Attention is drawn to issues around diversity, and in particular the colonial legacy of states, size, political diversity, and the degree of government intervention. This is then followed by an examination of the relevance of poverty, governance, the balance between states and markets, decentralisation and development, and capacity building. On the latter aspect, Wallis emphasises, in particular, the topical issues of donor-driven development and technology assisted development. Wallis concludes by emphasising that public sector management must continue to see itself as part of a wider project concerned with the role of states in development.

In the final chapter, the preceding debates are drawn together, providing the opportunity for some reflection on emergent issues but also some speculation on the possible way forward. In this chapter, Geoffrey Wood and Ian Roper tackle the central theme of the book, in pointing toward the need for the revitalisation of the public sphere. In doing so, they reject the calls for minimalism, and argue for the reconstitution of the public sphere in a way that renews accountability and social inclusion.

Notes

1. See for example books by Flynn and Strehl (1996) and Naschold and Arnkil (1996) for Europe, Maidment and Thompson (1994), Isaac-Henry *et al.* (1997), Horton and Farnham (1999), Greenwood *et al.* (2001) for Britain. Also, Buxton and Philips (1999) and Corbett (1996) for Latin America and Australia respectively.
2. See, for example, Nolan (2001).
3. For strategic management, see for example Joyce (1999), Nutt and Backoff (1992), Smith (1994). For Total Quality Management see Kirkpatrick and Martinez-Lucio (1995), Morgan and Muratroyd (1994). For employee relations in the public sector/services see Bach *et al.* (2000), Dell' Arringa *et al.* (2001), White and Corby (1999).
4. See for example Rose and Lawton (1999), Flynn (2002), and Hughes (2002).
5. Useful texts here include the series on public sector management by Bourn (1995) and the three volumes by Osborne (2001).

Part One

Public Sector Reform: Theoretical Debates

2
Public Choice, the Public Sector and the Market: the Sound of One Hand Clapping?

Axel van den Berg

> At the time Adam Smith wrote *The Wealth of Nations*, the world of government, politics and the state that he knew…was riddled with special privileges, monopolies, interferences with trade…the discipline of economics may have been traumatized by this condition of political life at its birth (Almond 1991: 467).

As one of its major advocates simply puts it, Public Choice theory 'is in essence the use of economic tools to deal with the traditional problems of political science' (Tullock, 1987: 1040). But what exactly is at stake comes out more clearly in the rather less innocuous-sounding definition given by Dennis Mueller in his authoritative 'Bible' of Public Choice:

> Public choice can be defined as the economic study of nonmarket decision making, or simply the application of economics to political science…The basic behavioral postulate of public choice, as for economics, is that man is an egoistic, rational utility maximizer (Mueller, 2003: 1–2).[1]

Public Choice is in fact part of a much larger movement seeking to apply the methods of economics to all other social sciences, a movement spearheaded by Gary Becker, Mancur Olson and many others. The movement's credo is most forcefully expressed in Becker's famous call for an economic approach to everything:

> …the economic approach is a comprehensive one that is applicable to all human behaviour, be it behaviour involving money prices or imputed shadow prices, repeated or infrequent decisions, emotional or mechanical ends, rich or poor persons, men or women, adults or children, brilliant or stupid persons, patients or therapists, businessmen or politicians, teachers or students.

> [...]
> I am saying that the economic approach provides a valuable unified framework for understanding *all* human behaviour...If this argument is correct, the economic approach provides a united framework for understanding behaviour that has long been sought by and eluded Bentham, Comte, Marx, and others. (Becker, 1976: 8, 14.)

Now, these are of course fighting words, particularly since they were aimed primarily at sociologists who had long considered their discipline to be an *alternative* to the utilitarianism of the economists, from Comte to Durkheim and Parsons. Predictably, it did not take long for the defenders of the old disciplinary territory to mount a counter-offensive against the 'economic imperialism' (Buckley and Casson, 1993) of Becker *et al.*, and their attempts at 'colonisation' (Fine, 1999) of the other social sciences (see Block, 1990; Etzioni, 1988; Fligstein, 2001; Friedland and Robertson, 1990; Ingham, 1996; Michaels *et al.*, 1990; Smelser, 1992; Zafirovski, 1998). It is safe to say that within sociology at least, the economic approach, or even the rational choice approach more broadly conceived, has remained an embattled minority position at best (see, for example, Abell, 1992; Coleman, 1990; Goldthorpe, 2000; Hechter, 2004; Hechter and Kanazawa, 1997).

Not so in political science. Here Public Choice has been enormously successful, having become if not the dominant then at least the largest single school of thought in the discipline, and claiming to be capable of tackling the entire range of issues within it. It is now confidently proclaimed to be the 'new theory of politics which is more rigorous, more realistic, and better tested than the older orthodoxy' (Tullock, 1987: 1041). By the 'older orthodoxy' Tullock means the assumption that governments, and especially democratically elected ones, are primarily in the business of maximising the public interest. The two works that delivered the first serious blows to this orthodoxy from an economic point of view were Joseph Schumpeter's *Capitalism, Socialism and Democracy* (Schumpeter, 1950), originally published in 1942, and Kenneth Arrow's *Social Choice and Individual Values* (Arrow, 1963), originally published in 1951. Schumpeter, writing against the backdrop of a rising tide of apparently popularly supported totalitarianism, famously dissected the 'classical' doctrine of democracy as a naive and possibly dangerous conflation of the 'public interest' and majority rule. Instead he advocated a more realistic view of 'democracy' as a method for making decisions by means of a competitive struggle between conflicting interests. Arrow, no less famously, showed that under plausible assumptions about individuals' preferences no conceivable democratic voting system may satisfy a reasonable set of criteria for aggregating individual preferences into a collective choice, a finding 'to be taken as proof that democracy is either an illusion or a fraud' (Tullock, 1987: 1042).

But these were only the *precursors* of Public Choice proper. Conventionally the major work launching Public Choice, as such, is taken to be Anthony Downs' *Economic Theory of Democracy* (Downs, 1957). Other classics in the tradition include Mancur Olson's *Logic of Collective Action* (Olson, 1965) and his later *Rise and Decline of Nations* (Olson, 1982), William Riker's *Theory of Political Coalitions* (Riker, 1962), Gordon Tullock's *The Politics of Bureaucracy* (Tullock, 1965), James Buchanan and Tullock's *The Calculus of Consent* (Buchanan and Tullock, 1962), and William Niskanen's *Bureaucracy and Representative Government* (Niskanen, 1971). Each of these has helped to set research agendas and spawn large literatures, on topics as diverse as voting turnout, coalition formation, party politics, voting rules and constitutions, interest groups and rent-seeking, the growth of bureaucracy, collective action problems and public goods, the 'political business cycle,' and public finance. One cannot help but be impressed by both the range of issues addressed and the sheer size of the various literatures more or less closely associated with the Public Choice label. It is also worth noting that as it has grown, the Public Choice approach has become increasingly varied not only in terms of the topics addressed but also in terms of the theoretical assumptions and models used. In fact, there seems to be a secular tendency towards ever more complex – and arguably less purely 'economic' – models, as the earlier ones turn out to run into various empirical and/or logical problems (for useful surveys, see Miller, 1997, and especially the comprehensive and massive Mueller, 2001; 2003).

But for all its apparent success, Public Choice has not gone unchallenged even within political science. There is now also a large and growing literature forcefully criticising the Public Choice approach and/or debating its alleged merits and shortcomings (see especially Green and Shapiro, 1994; Friedman, 1996; Mansbridge, 1990; Monroe, 1991; Schweers Cook and Levi, 1990; Udehn, 1996; see also van den Berg and Meadwell, forthcoming). The usual criticisms – as well as the Public Choice theorists' responses – tend to be the same as those repeated, *ad nauseam*, by the critics and defenders of rational choice theory more generally. The critics take Public Choice to task for attributing empirically unwarranted motives to political actors, and in particular for not recognising the crucial differences between 'economic man' and 'political man.' In politics, they contend, power and norms rather than self-interest motivate behaviour, and 'institutions' (which usually means either power or norms or both) exert a powerful constraining force on the scope for rational utility maximisation (expressed in such current buzz words as 'path dependency' and 'embeddedness').[2] Furthermore, Public Choice theorists are accused of being enamoured with theoretical models and ignoring, or not even caring about, empirical evidence, of ad hoc tinkering with their models to render them effectively unfalsifiable, of being ideologists rather than bona fide social scientists, and even of being immoral in that they appear to advocate selfishness in all realms of life (for example, Udehn, 1996; Petracca, 1991).

I have no intention of repeating these well-worn arguments here, nor of offering yet another 'impartial' assessment. Instead, I want to look at one particular variant of Public Choice which is especially concerned with (the proper role of) the public sector and which has had a highly controversial impact on public discourse about it. I refer to the so-called 'Virginia School' of Public Choice, represented most prominently by the work of Buchanan, Tullock and Niskanen. These authors and their collaborators and students have been concerned in particular with applying economic analysis to the behaviour of politicians, bureaucrats and interest groups, and the consequences for government and the public sector. Starting from the assumption that politicians and bureaucrats have the same motives of selfishness and utility maximising that economists attribute to economic actors, they argue that governments and the public sector are generally organised in such a way as to provide them with perverse incentives and opportunities to pursue those interests *at the expense* of the interests and preferences of the 'common man.' From this they tend to conclude that the best we can do is try and limit the role of government and the public sector as much as possible and leave as many of its allocative and distributive functions to the private sector and the market as possible. Thus, there is no question that 'the Virginia school is associated with [sic] distinct normative point-of-view, advocating markets as a better means of allocating resources than governments' (Fiorina, 2002).

Second, I will not level the usual criticism but instead I will try to do something different here. My argument will be that there is much in Public Choice theory that is useful but that it is not *consistent enough*. As may be clear already from my earlier quotes, consistency is a major consideration for Public Choice theorists, as it is for rational choice theorists more generally. Here is Becker again:

> The heart of my argument is that human behaviour is not compartmentalized, sometimes based on maximizing, sometimes not, sometimes motivated by stable preferences, sometimes by volatile ones, sometimes resulting in an optimal accumulation of information, sometimes not. Rather, all human behaviour can be viewed as involving participants who maximize their utility from a stable set of preferences and accumulate an optimal amount of information and other inputs in a variety of markets (Becker, 1976: 14).

Or, as Geoffrey Brennan, a frequent collaborator of Buchanan's, puts it

> [Let us] begin with the obvious fact that the agents who participate in politics are essentially the same agents who participate in markets. It

seems reasonable therefore to suppose that individuals will bring the same basic motivation to bear in the ballot-box as in the supermarket. To assume otherwise would be, as public choice economists have always insisted, to invoke a wildly implausible and analytically arbitrary schizophrenia. The rational choice tradition has stood firmly against any such institutional schizophrenia

   [...]

   Intellectual coherence is a feature prized above all others in the rational choice lexicon...[the aim being] to rescue political analysis from the kinds of ad hoc explanatory expediency that characterizes much conventional political science and that has been precisely the feature of alternative approaches that the rational choice approach has stood so firmly against' (Brennan, 2001: 215, 232).

Other Public Choice theorists could be quoted along similar lines at great length (see also Ekelund and Tollison, 1986: 440; Udehn, 1996: 35). But note that the assumption of behavioural consistency across social domains does not necessarily include the ultimate goals of that behaviour. Thus, Becker simply talks about utility maximising based on a stable set of preferences, *whatever* these preferences may be. This is consistent with Becker's general adherence to what is often referred to as the 'thin' theory of rational choice. 'Thin' rational choice theory only argues that people pursue their goals, *whatever they are*, in an instrumentally rational way. The *ultimate* goals can be anything, including pure altruism. The only thing people share is an inclination to economise on a limited set of generally valued scarce resources, which are usually the most fungible ones in the society in question, including time and material resources, power and prestige, in the course of pursuing those ultimate goals. This implies only a certain resource responsiveness.

Several of the famous contributions to Public Choice mentioned earlier, are 'thin' theories in this sense. Downs' famous theorem of convergence to the median voter, for instance, holds for parties whether they are run by pure idealists or political entrepreneurs, as does Riker's minimal necessary coalition rule, and some theories of bureaucracy as exchange systems (for example, Breton and Wintrobe, 1982). Note that such 'thin' theories also allow at least in principle for the possibility that actors in different social domains tend to pursue different goals, that is, that politicians *could* be more altruistically inclined than businessmen. But this, of course, opens the door dangerously wide to a return to the old orthodoxy.

The alternative is a so-called 'thick' theory which does not only assume instrumental rationality on the part of actors but also attributes specific goals to them, either on the basis of additional empirical evidence or axiomatically. In most cases, of course, the goals attributed to actors tend to be purely selfish ones like the maximisation of wealth, power and prestige, although this need not be the case in principle. My point here, though, is that the *differentia specifica* of the 'Virginia School' is precisely its 'thickness.' The authors working in this tradition ascribe quite specific goals to the actors in the political arena, and these tend to be purely selfish ones. Buchanan justifies this as follows:

> For a genuine predictive theory of politics, however, more is needed. If by 'theory' we mean the development of hypotheses about behaviour in the political process that can be conceptually refuted by observation of real-world events, some additional constraints must be placed on the manner in which separate interests differ. The most familiar of these constraints, again taken from economics, is the hypothesis that individuals act in politics as they are assumed to act in the predictive theory of markets, so as to maximize their expected utility, and that their behaviour in doing so is measurable in terms of some objectively identifiable magnitude such as personal income or wealth. In politics, this 'positive' theory implies that individuals, and groups, act so as to further their economic positions (Buchanan, 1966: 27–28).

Thus, '[t]he fundamental premise of public choice [of the Virginia variety] is that political decision-makers (voters, politicians, bureaucrats) and private decision-makers (consumers, brokers, producers) behave in a similar way: they all follow the dictates of rational self-interest' (Ekelund and Tollison, 1986: 440).

Voters are, according to this view, primarily interested in their immediate economic interests. As a result, they will be relatively well-informed about the politicians and policies affecting these interests but they will have little interest in anything else. This is the so-called 'rationally ignorant' voter (Downs, 1957) who is easily influenced by well-organised special interests on all matters other than his or her immediate economic interests. Similarly, politicians are entrepreneurs who are after the power, prestige and perks of office for themselves and who exchange public services with their constituents for votes in order to obtain and keep those offices. 'A politician is a person who makes a living by being elected by voters of the kind described above' (Tullock, 1987: 1041). Much the same goes for civil servants.

> Bureaucrats normally have several private motives. One is, of course, simply not to work too hard…Another is to expand the size of one's own department and in the process of so doing, being willing to go along with the expansion of all the rest. A third is to improve the 'perks' that accompany the particular position (Tullock, 1987: 1043).

In fact, Niskanen (1971) and Tullock (1965) attribute quite specific preferences to government bureaucrats: budget maximisation and size of bureau maximisation respectively, though these, in turn, are the means towards maximal perks, salary, power and prestige. Interest groups, finally, are viewed from the Virginia perspective as essentially rent-seeking organisations, pursuing various privileges and protections from the government for their constituents at the expense of efficiency and of the interests of the less well-organised (see Rowley, *et al.*, 1988; Tullock, 1993).

Starting from these basic motivational premises, the members of the Virginia School have set out to show in a variety of ways how governments, no matter how democratic and well-organised, tend to produce uncontrolled growth of the public sector, bloated bureaucracy, excessive taxation, and deficits, resulting in systematic distortion of democratic interest representation and enormous distortion of resource allocation and waste. The basic mechanisms that produce these deplorable results, given the assumed motivations on the part of voters, politicians, interest groups and bureaucrats, are relatively simple. Since their primary concern is the enhancement of their own perks, power and prestige, politicians and bureaucrats are only interested in serving the interests that matter for their ability to obtain these benefits for themselves, not those of their voters at large, much less any 'public' interest. Instead, they have a strong incentive to ally themselves with powerful interest groups who can provide them with the resources to win elections, deliver votes, and serve as ready clients and well-organised supporters for the services provided by their policies, bureaux and departments.

Thus, politics effectively becomes a market in which powerful actors exchange favours at the expense of the powerless majority. In exchange for interest-group support, the politicians and bureaucrats use the regulatory, allocative and (re-)distributive powers of government to provide rent-seeking interest groups with a variety of privileges and advantages which effectively divert resources and distort allocative efficiency at the expense of the tax payer and the consumer. Such special-interest privileges, most often amounting to protection against possible competition, include everything from non-competitive government contracts, subsidies, tax reductions, protective tariffs, and rate regulation, to occupational licensing, legal protection for unions and even zoning laws. Since the benefits of these practices accrue to small, well-organised minorities while the costs are spread over the large majority of passive and powerless consumers, voters and taxpayers, there is much to gain and little to lose from them for the politician and bureaucrat. The result is an indefinite proliferation of government programmes, an ever-growing public sector, rising taxes and budget deficits, massive inefficiency and waste. Instead of providing a check on government, democracy breeds and legitimates a system in which narrow interest groups are able to fill their constituents' pockets at the expense of everybody else.[3]

Thus, modern 'democratic' government has produced nothing less than an uncontrollable Leviathan serving the few at the expense of the many and doing so by destroying the economic efficiency of the private economy (Brennan and Buchanan, 1980; Mueller, 2003). What, then, can be done to stop or stem this 'cancerous growth of the public sector engineered by power seeking bureaucrats and politicians' (Samuelson, 1980: 666)?[4] The virtually unanimous conclusion that is drawn from the Public Choice literature is that there is only one thing that can be done: restrict the role and authority of government as much as possible. The reason for this stark recommendation is straightforward: since human nature obviously won't change, and since any attempts to turn mass democracy into a system more responsive to the varied interests of the ordinary citizen are doomed, the only alternative is to reduce the necessary evil to as limited a role as possible (Buchanan and Wagner, 1977).[5]

There is by now a vast literature arguing for the restriction of government functions, by means of a host of measures such as legal limitations on the right to tax, deregulation, privatisation, outsourcing, and so on, all more or less directly based on the arguments and findings of Public Choice theorists (see, for example, Shleifer and Vishny, 1999; Bruyn, 2000; Mitchell and Simmons, 1995; Clark, 1998). Invariably, the recommendations are buttressed by a kind of 'better safe than sorry' argument. Since we cannot hope to change basic human nature and we now know what it does to government, let us try and limit the possible damage as much as we can, so it is argued. Frequently, Lord Acton's famous dictum about power corrupting is invoked in this connection (see Udehn, 1996; Brennan and Buchanan, 1985).

Now, *prima facie*, such cautionary arguments would seem to have something to recommend them. In politics as elsewhere it is surely safer to assume the worst and guard against it, than the reverse. For all the sustained efforts to prove otherwise (see, for example, Lewin, 1991; Udehn, 1996), it would be rather surprising if politicians and bureaucrats – or, for that matter, voters and lobbyists – were entirely or mostly motivated by sheer idealism and altruism. While politicians and bureaucrats may not *only* be interested in their own aggrandisement and immediate material interests, such motives surely play a role. In the political system as elsewhere there surely is a tendency for inequality and inefficiency to beget more inequality and inefficiency and it is probably wisest, from a purely prudential point of view, to assume selfishness to start out with rather than the reverse.

In an article that ends by recommending as much private provision of government-financed goods and services as possible, Buchanan begins with the following apparently nuanced assessment:

> Without doubt, some considerable part of the observed growth in the public sector, at all levels, is directly traceable to the demands of the cit-

izenry, genuine demands for more services accompanied by an increasing willingness to shoulder the tax burdens required for financing. But, once this is acknowledged, there can also be little doubt but that a significant and remaining part of the observed growth in the public sector can be explained only by looking at the motivations of those who secure direct personal gains from government expansion, gains that are unrelated to the benefits filtered down to the ordinary citizen. (Buchanan, 1977: 6).

But this immediately raises an obvious question about the aforementioned remedies: if not through government, how shall we arrange for the citizenry's 'genuine demands' to be met? On this, as well, the literature just cited appears to be unanimous. It recommends transferring as many as feasible of the legitimate tasks of regulation and allocation now taken on by government to the private sector. As much as possible of these government goods and services should be provided instead by the private, competitive market, in which all consumers are free to choose according to their varied preferences and needs.

But this only raises a second obvious question: what assurances do we have that those selfish motives that have such deplorable effects in the public sector will be any less harmful in the private sector? Since private-sector entrepreneurs are at least as likely to be primarily interested in the greatest net returns for themselves as politicians and bureaucrats in the public sector are, what keeps them from gouging the unwitting consumer just as much as the politicians and bureaucrats gouge the unwitting voter?

From hard-nosed economists, always aware as they are of the implicit comparisons involved in optimising decisions, one might expect that such far-reaching recommendations to transfer many of the traditional functions of government to the private sector would be based on painstakingly rigorous comparisons of the relative performances of *really existing* systems of public and private provision of various goods and services. But this turns out not to be the case. Instead, those using the Public Choice literature to argue for privatisation of various kinds seem to be content to point to the demonstrable shortcomings of various government programs and policies and to *assume* that private markets will obviously do a far better job of it (cf. Sutter, 1997). In the words of the well-known, albeit somewhat unorthodox Public Choice theorist (see Mueller, 2001) Bruno Frey:

In much of (American) Public Choice a further conclusion has been reached: it is argued that markets are generally superior, and that politics is almost always inferior. However, this conclusion is based more on an ideological presupposition than on analysis, and it certainly does not follow from Political Economy (Frey, 1992: 130).

But however ideologically congenial the presupposition may be, it still remains rather an odd one. After all, at least since Adam Smith, economists have known and been much concerned about the fact that '[p]eople of the same trade seldom meet together, even for merriment and diversion, but the conversation ends in a conspiracy against the public, or in some contrivance to raise prices' (Smith 1981[1776]: 232). Now, it may well be that governments, in Adam Smith's day as much as in our own, have provided one major avenue for such tradespeople to conduct their conspiracies against the public, but, as any first-year economics student learns, this is *far* from the only such avenue. Yet the case for privatisation of governmental functions on the basis of Public Choice arguments seems to assume, *a priori*, that governments are the *only* possible source of resource misallocation and competitive distortions in otherwise fully competitive private markets. In fact a plausible case for the very opposite assumption can be made, namely that markets are almost *never* perfectly competitive and when they are that they are only very precariously so (see, for example, Fligstein, 2001).

One might be tempted to argue that those making Public Choice-based recommendations for curbing and privatisating the public sector are invoking *precisely* the kind of 'institutional schizophrenia' that Brennan ridicules in the passage quoted above. For is not the apparently unexamined assumption that the basic mechanisms of concentration of power and wealth are *entirely different* in the two institutional domains at least as 'wildly implausible and analytically arbitrary' as the assumption that people are greedy egoists in one and selfless idealists in the other? On the one hand, these hard-nosed advocates of economic rigour are unflinchingly exposing the myriad perverse incentives and outcomes in the public sector, yet on the other they appear to be touchingly naive in simply assuming that such things just *aren't done* in the private sector. The enormous problems that they claim are entirely irresolvable in the realm of politics have apparently been effortlessly resolved in the private economy.

Take, for example, the following quote from Gordon Tullock:

> In the case of a private company, whose motive is making money, the accounts do a reasonably good job (no more) of signalling what the various lower ranking officials are contributing to that goal. When we turn to government, however, we have the combination of a set of objectives that are either vague or not clearly specified, and a situation where there is no accurate way of measuring the contribution of each person to those objectives (Tullock, 1987: 1043).

It is as if he had never heard of monopolies, 'natural' or otherwise, and oligopolies, nor of incentive or agent-principal problems in private industry. I could cite many more instances of such off-hand remarks that betray a remarkably sanguine attitude towards what goes on in real markets (see van den Berg, forthcoming).

There is some justice, then, in the criticism that the Public Choice-inspired literature operates on a 'view of the state as hopelessly Machiavellian and the economy as perfectly Walrasian' (Epstein and Gintis, 1995: 386). But how can we account for this oddly lopsided treatment of the private and public sectors? No doubt, Public Choice theorists are quite right to be sceptical about the possibility of ever *fully* resolving the problem of perverse incentives in a public sector in which decisions and allocations require concentrations of decision-making power. But how can they then forget their scepticism and simply *assume* that all such incentive problems have been fully resolved in the market? The only possible answer that I can think of is that there is an implicit slippage here, inadvertent or otherwise, between 'really existing' private markets and the perfectly competitive variety that exists only as a textbook model. In other words, these advocates of privatisation do not compare really existing states with really existing markets but with the *textbook model* of a market. Put in terms of the people on whose behalf these theorists claim to make their arguments, the comparison is one between a model in which the consumer is sovereign *by definition* and a reality in which the voter is disenfranchised *in practice*. That is not the kind of comparison that lends itself readily to normative inferences about how the tasks of the two *real* sectors ought to be divided up.[6]

Let me return now to the political trauma attending the birth of economics referred to in the quote from Gabriel Almond at the beginning of this article. Given the main political division between left (pro-state, anti-market) and right (pro-market, anti-state) that we have come to take for granted, it is easy to lose sight of the originally profoundly subversive and indeed emancipatory aims that inspired Adam Smith and his followers to posit the legitimacy of the pursuit of self-interest as an alternative to the claims by office-holders or dignitaries of his time to represent the 'public interest.' They

> …were ardent debunkers and unmaskers…they were naturally fond of exposing self-interested motives wrapped in rhetoric about the common good … The idea of *universal* self-interest, as it was used at the time of Adam Smith, had a political rationale. It suggested that citizens should distrust every expression of disinterestedness on the part of authorities' (Holmes, 1990: 285–6).

This deep distrust of invocations of the 'common good' by self-serving politicians has remained an important element in the philosophical tradition running from Benthamite Utilitarianism all the way to the Austrian School of Von Mises, Hayek and Schumpeter and thence to today's Milton

Friedman and Public Choice.[7] It is this – no doubt often justified – distrust that seems to fuel much of the Public Choice animus against any form of collective decision-making, as opposed to the supposedly atomised decisions taken in the proverbial 'marketplace.' But the same sort of scepticism is surely also warranted with respect to the large corporations that now tend to dominate that 'marketplace' when they solemnly proclaim to have only the interests of the customer, or various other 'stakeholders,' or 'efficiency', or, for that matter, 'shareholder value' at heart. The only thing that should surprise us about the rash of corporate scandals from *Enron* to the *New York Stock Exchange* in recent years, really, is that we were so surprised by them. Putting it slightly differently, the perverse incentive problem is one that is permanently with us in all realms of social life and it will require continuous attention in markets just as much as in politics.

Let me conclude. I have not tried to level the usual criticisms 'from the left' against Public Choice. No doubt its behavioural assumptions are overly simplistic, informed, perhaps, by too cynical a view of human nature. No doubt the empirical support for at least its boldest predictions has not been impressive. In addition, adjustments and revisions in response to such findings may make latter-day versions of Public Choice hard to distinguish from other approaches.[8] Instead, I have taken as my starting point, plausibly I think, that the motivational assumptions of Public Choice carried at least a kernel of truth. I am also prepared to accept the many well-documented examples of government failure and the argument that among their most important causes are 'normal' human motives combined with perverse incentives. What I cannot accept, however, is any *a priori* assumption that private sector markets, as they are in reality rather than in the textbook, will inevitably produce better results. This depends, no less than in the public sector, on whether we can find ways to reliably eliminate perverse incentives and potentially debilitating information and market-power 'asymmetries' *there*. This cannot be *assumed* to be the case but must be *shown*, through research that is as deductively rigorous and as empirically sound as some of the best Public Choice research has been. Only then will we be able to make informed judgements about the best location for each of the regulatory, allocative, and (re-) distributive functions at issue today – given our (collective?) preferences, naturally.

Notes

1. Elsewhere, Mueller offers an even broader definition including the application of rational choice theory to political sociology as well (see Mueller, 2001: 343).
2. For some useful surveys of this 'new' institutionalism, see Hall and Taylor, 1996; Immergut, 1998; Ingram and Clay, 2000; and Thelen, 1999.
3. Besides the 'classical' sources already cited see, on budget deficits, Buchanan and Wagner (1977), Rowley *et al.* (1987); on bureaucracy, see Wildavsky (1984) and Niskanen (1994). See also Chapters 15–17 and 20–21 in Mueller (2003) and the many additional sources cited by Clark (1998: 127–9).

4. To be sure, Samuelson meant this as something of a caricature of the opinions of reactionary US businessmen.
5. It might be worth noting that the size of the US public sector – thought to be untenably bloated by Buchanan *et al.* – is actually considerably smaller than its counterparts in most other advanced capitalist countries. As Castles (1993) notes, the criticism of oversized public sectors is loudest in precisely the countries where they are the smallest!
6. In a related paper I try to show that 'sociological' critics of the economic approach often do the exact reverse: they compare the real world of cut-throat market competition and monopoly with an entirely idealised model of a 'one man-one vote' political system. See van den Berg (forthcoming).
7. Douglas Kinnear explains that 'public choice theory rests on an atomistic conception of society ... a democratic government becomes the equivalent of an economic market: both are merely devices through which individual desires are aggregated and reconciled. Generally, in this conception there is no "public interest," that is no values separate from the aggregation of individual values' (Kinnear 1999: 931).
8. Although Mueller rightly protests that such criticisms can easily degenerate into facile dismissal: 'To equate rational choice modeling with naive and simplistic behavioral assumptions, and then condemn any efforts to build more realistic and perhaps complicated models as post-hoc theorizing, as G&S [Green and Shapiro, 1994] seem to want to do, is to place rational choice scholars into a methodological straightjacket' (Mueller, 2001: 349).

3

New Public Management: Marketisation, Managerialism and Consumerism

Pauline Dibben and Paul Higgins

This chapter discusses the issue of New Public Management (NPM), and highlights, in particular, the implications for three areas. These are, firstly, how the marketisation involved in NPM affects the relationship between the public sector and other 'partners'; secondly, how NPM reforms impact on the public sector workforce; and thirdly, the way in which these reforms imply a redefinition of 'the public.' In each case, the changing dynamics of these relationships have far-reaching implications, and a particular concern of this chapter is to explore how these implications might impact upon the most vulnerable in society.

Much has been written about NPM over the years, and various definitions of NPM have emerged (see for example Dunleavy and Hood, 1994; Ferlie *et al.*, 1996; Dawson and Dargie, 2002; McLaughlin *et al.*, 2002). Probably the most widely cited definition is, however, that by Hood (1991) which is of a management approach that focuses on hands-on and entrepreneurial management; an emphasis on performance measurement, output controls, decentralisation and disaggregation; and the importation from commercial management of competition, private sector styles of management, and doing 'more with less'. This package encapsulates the way in which NPM reforms imply changes to both the internal working of the public sector and to external relationships. In themselves, however, these constituent parts do not necessarily appear to have negative connotations.

Although much has been written on NPM, there are good reasons to further debate this issue. NPM still appears to dominate the discourse of public administration, and has become the orthodox language of public administration. At the same time, there still seems to be some considerable dispute over whether NPM is a good or bad thing. Protagonists of NPM have viewed it as a positive, proactive move toward improved service provision, with prescriptions for how NPM should be introduced, and more recently, a positive spin has been put on NPM through reference to the term 'governance'. Thus, some have argued that over time, NPM has moved from being focussed on neo-liberal reforms, to a concern with ideas around 'governance' (see for example Osborne and McLaughlin, 2002) or 'good governance' (see for example, Wolmuth, 1998). Conversely, others have explicitly tried to take a 'neutral' stance to NPM (Hughes, 2003; McLaughlin *et al.*, 2002), dealing with NPM in a more descriptive way. However, this approach may be backing away from the big questions around the possible negative consequences of these reforms (Hope *et al.*, 2000).

The issues discussed in this chapter – marketisation, managerialism and consumerism – have each been tackled before. However, the intention of this chapter is to reinforce the idea that not only are they inextricably linked, but that they also require further exploration. This is necessary in order to ameliorate the worst excesses of NPM reforms for those already affected, to halt the downward slide where further NPM reforms are being considered, and to prevent similar weaknesses occurring in the re-thinking that needs to take place around a new reform agenda.

Drivers behind NPM reforms

Various arguments have been put forward for why NPM reforms have been introduced, since in common with the debate about what NPM entails, there have been similar debates about what has driven the reform of the public sector *per se* (see for example Flynn, 2002; Lynn, 1997). In particular, it has been suggested that drivers have varied for different countries, so that some countries have engaged in reform to maintain the status quo, some to modernise, and some to minimise the role of the state (Pollitt and Bouckaert, 2000; Hood, 1995). In turn, these differing agendas have been driven by political demands and socio-economic forces. For example, Hood (1995) suggests that,

> NPM may have been adopted by social democratic governments to give big government a new lease of life by making it more efficient, and by 'business democrats' and neo-liberal governments as a half-way-house to privatisation and a 'hollow state' (Hood, 1995: 16).

More specifically, this divergence can be seen in the evidence from both developed countries (see, for example, Schedler and Proeller, 2002) and developing countries (Polidano *et al.*, 1998). Polidano *et al.*, raise serious questions about imposing NPM on developing countries without taking proper account of local context, while Pollitt and Bouckaert (2000) examine a range of developed countries, and assess the results in terms of operational results, processes of management or decision-making, system improvement, and realisation of a vision. However, they also acknowledge that these are difficult to interpret since different 'results' are looked for by different people and there is a lack of comparable statistical data with which to make such comparisons. Another point they raise, which is particularly pertinent to this chapter, is that while some groups gain from NPM reforms, others lose from the introduction of certain reforms. This latter point raises important questions about the impact of reforms referred to positively under the term of NPM, and whether they might lead to the further marginalisation of those who are already disadvantaged.

Although it is recognised that drivers can vary between different countries, a central argument of this chapter is that the reforms and practices that can be described under the umbrella term of NPM generally arose out of neo-liberalism, and as such, involved in-built hostility to state monopoly provision of services. Thus, while utilities were once considered to be essential public services, they are now almost universally deemed to be commercial organisations through the process of privatisation in its various guises. This hostility, however, is against a background of some reluctance, in some cases, to privatising certain aspects of the public sector. For example, there seems to be some general agreement about the need to safeguard certain 'public goods', although there has been some debate about what these should entail (Dawson and Dargie, 2002). In the UK, there has been an enhanced public sensitivity toward areas such as health that have tended to make this a politically dangerous option. The lack of a 'true market' for, and the interdependency in, these types of services, have made the cost structures – and hence the potential attractiveness to investors – obscure. The answer to these problems has involved a range of 'solutions', foremost involving internal marketisation, managerialism and consumerism.

Marketisation: the relationship between the public sector and other 'partners'

In examining marketisation, three key questions emerge. Firstly, can the public sector be treated the same as the private sector? Secondly, if full privatisation is not undertaken, then what are the implications of public sector working with the private sector in some form of partnership? Thirdly, what are the implications of such 'partnership' working not just for the private sector, but also for the voluntary sector?

The term 'marketisation' can, at one extreme end of a spectrum, include the full transference of state assets into the private sector through privatisation, although more commonly it is regarded as involving the penetration of the administrative system within the public sector by the culture, values and practices of the market sector (Lane, 1997; Pollit and Bouckaert, 2000). However, moves toward marketisation underestimate the differences between the public and private sector. Savoie (1995), for example, argues that the new public management philosophy is incorrectly based on the notion of the superiority of the private sector, and ignores the distinctiveness of the public sector and its necessary attitudes toward risk taking, the need for accountability, and the difference between clients and citizens. The public sector operates in a very public environment where there is an extremely low tolerance for mistakes; mistakes made cannot be overriden by massive profits. Civil servants, moreover, are accountable both to the public and to ministers. There is also a large difference between clients and citizens. Clients can walk away from an unsatisfactory service provider, and turn to one of its competitors, while citizens usually do not have this option.

A third, middle road between full-scale privatisation on the one hand, and on the other, encouraging the public sector to use the working practices of the private, involves the public sector working jointly with the private sector in some form of partnership. Depending on the nature of this 'partnership', the public sector has more, or less control over how services are provided. However, the various ways in which this has been translated into practice have attendant problems.

One way in which the public sector works with the private is through contracting services out to the private sector, rather than providing services in-house. In the case of health, this has been through the creation of an internal or quasi-market (Robinson and Le Grand, 1994) whereby service providers are separated from the purchaser of services. In the case of municipal government this has been referred to as competitive tendering (Domberger and Jensen, 1997), and has been characterised by the client/contractor split. In these situations, services may be *provided* commercially, while the public sector maintains some discretion as to which services should be provided and the composition of such provision. A further distinguishing feature of quasi-markets, compared to, for example, outright utility privatisation, is that assets remain in the public sector with services continuing to be funded predominantly out of general taxation. One key paradox of quasi-markets is that in the attempt to bring them into being, *regulatory* legislation has been required, thus in effect increasing bureaucracy and as Deakin and Michie (1997: 124) rightly contend, this seems to be at odds with the Hayekian notion of the market as spontaneous. Effectively, therefore, quasi-markets replace public bureaucracy with contract bureaucracy. A further issue that should be noted is the implications that this new relationship has for those providing services. Where the voluntary sector is involved in providing the service, it can become dependent on public sector agencies, and ultimately lose its own identity. Questions may then arise around how it can avoid becoming just another public agent and a substitute for government, and how it can preserve its traditional role as an alternative, in supplementing and complementing public services (Kramer, 1994).

A second type of relationship is working together in partnership to provide services, for example through public / private partnerships (PPPs), PFI (Private Finance Initiative) or through some form of partnership such as the UK example of LSPs (Local Strategic Partnerships) that can also include other public sector agencies and the voluntary sector. Thus, while in the past the involvement of the voluntary sector has been seen as causing problems, they are now brought into service provision (Osborne, 2002). However, various criticisms have been made of such partnerships, and it has been suggested that in effect the private sector dominates, with little real influence for members of the public (Rhodes, 1996). Thus, political or business elites dominate decision-making, which can be to the detriment of those working in 'partnership', and also for those at the receiving end.

This existence of political and business elites has implications for the more recent discussions about an 'enabling' government, 'joined-up working', and local governance (Wilkinson and Applebee, 1999; Lowndes, 1997). 'Local governance' implies that public sector bodies, and in particular municipal bodies, are no longer the sole providers of services, but merely enablers. As such, they strategically utilise the services provided by other public agencies, and more specifically the private and voluntary sectors. Local governance thus implies a reduced role for municipal entities as direct providers and by implication assumes that new relationships will be based on co-ordination, reciprocity and trust. However, implementing local governance might be very difficult in practice in areas such as transport and land use planning, where there is a need for coordination and participation at a local level (Wilkinson and Applebee, 1999), or where there might be irreconcilable differences between interests (Booth and Richardson, 2001). Arguably, moreover, this perspective has failed to adequately take account of the different interests of those involved in service provision, or the need to incorporate 'power' into discussions of partnerships (Smith and Beazley, 2000; Goss, 2001). Lowndes (1998), for example, in her study of urban governance, suggests that a hierarchy of power can emerge resulting in the marginalisation of some parties such as the voluntary sector. Moreover, Geddes (2000), in examining local partnerships concerned with tackling problems of localised poverty, deprivation and social exclusion points to the tendency for excluded groups to be marginalised within partnership processes. Part of the reason for this is that their experiential knowledge of poverty and exclusion is often not valued by partners who recognise only the ' "expert" codified knowledge of formal organizations' (Geddes, 2000: 793). In summary, therefore, local governance can imply increased restraints on the public sector and unequal power relationships between partners.

Managerialism and the workforce

It is important to understand managerialism in the context of why it has emerged, since this has helped to determine how it has been put into practice, with tight controls for public sector workers. Managerialism has been linked to microeconomics, but has perhaps more importantly led to changes in working conditions, and an emphasis on performance management. The introduction of performance measures in the drive toward accountability, have however, arguably led to increased stress and the exploitation of public sector workers. At the same time, however, an interesting tension has emerged. This can be seen as a result of the emphasis within 'New managerialism' for entrepreneurialism, which logically conflicts with the controls put in place to ensure accountability.

The drive toward managerialism emerged out of public choice arguments, such as those advocated by Niskanen (1971; 1973) and Tulloch (1965), which emphasise bureau-maximising tendencies by those working within the public sector. More recently, agency theory has suggested that public servants (as agents) exploit their informational advantage over agents (politicians) (Borins, 2002), independently making decisions that are based on their technical expertise or knowledge (Woodman, 1998; Newman, 2002), or using information as a source of power (Kaye, 1995). However, the tendency remains to blame public servants for inadequacies or imbalances in service provision.

The 'solution' to the problem of public monopolies, and the abuse of power by public sector employees, has been based on the twin disciplines of microeconomics and management, or managerialism. On the microeconomic front, the dominant consideration has been the objective to break up public sector monopolies by ensuring the potential for alternative service providers (Robinson and Le Grand, 1995; Levacic 1995). The potential that alternative service providers may replace direct service providers is argued to create an efficiency incentive which is manifested in attempts by competing service providers to promise a given output with the minimum of inputs (Domberger and Jensen, 1997). In the microeconomic discourse, the way in which efficiency improvements are expected to derive from the possibility of alternative service providers is in effect a 'black box', however, because it depends on abstract economic models of competition (see, for example, Baumol *et al.* 1982). It is at this point, that the discipline of managerialism has intervened as a means by which the aspired microeconomic models can work in practice. In particular, by invoking a strategic / operational distinction it is assumed that improvements in efficiency can occur. In part, this is through overcoming overload at the strategic level and in part via greater motivation of management at the operational level. Thus, a 'principal-agent' relationship has been developed between central and local government in which local services are the agents mandated to deliver government policy (Newman, 2002).

Seen in this light, there is an apparent 'neutrality' to the twin use of microecomics and management, so that marketisation can be viewed as merely a disinterested process concerned with the introduction of competitive forces for monopolistic entities. Crucially, however, both the microeconomic and managerialist discourses are hostile to traditional notions of the public sector as a 'good employer.' This is true for the microeconomic discourse, because the monopoly position, which seemed to protect the workforce, is clearly seen as negative. Equally, in respect of the managerial discourse, being a good employer clearly involves 'interference' in the operational sphere. Consequently, when the economic models of competition have been used in practice via the role of management, public sector workers have tended to face the brunt of such competition (see, for example, Escott and Whitfield, 1995).

Thus, in explaining the 'principal-agent' relationship, Newman (2002) also points to the accompanying changes to working conditions, with tight monitoring of work, and 'neo-Taylorian' practices that lead to new forms of control (Sanderson, 2001; Brooks, 2000; Pollitt, 1993). This is evidenced through a growth in performance indicators in order to ensure accountability to the public (Boyne, 1999). Equally, by emphasising the need for accountability to the public, NPM reforms have often involved an assault on producer group interests, who have been faced with increasing user expectations whilst simultaneously being required to do more for less, thus implying the intensification of working practices (Cutler and Waine, 1997b; Ball, 1993). Thus public sector workers are faced with difficult, and oppressive, working conditions with supposed benefits for members of the public. However, doubts emerge around whether the tighter controls will result in more effective service provision and increased accountability, and questions have been raised around the way in which performance management, and performance measures have been used in practice (Sanderson, 2001; Bovaird *et al.*, 2002). In particular, debates have raged about the validity, reliability and consistency of performance measures (Cutler and Waine, 1997a; Bruijn, 2002). The measures introduced may not be the most appropriate, may not measure what they are supposed to measure, and are not necessarily applied in the same way in different situations or contexts.

In addition to the tighter working practices encouraged through the use of performance measures, Byrne (1994) meanwhile, points to disguised forms of discrimination or worker exploitation through, for example, flexible arrangements for pay and conditions. Taking the example of the EU, it can be argued that the introduction of features such as the Acquired Rights Directive protects workers from excessive variation of employment contracts. But at the same time audit and inspection forces through intensification and tougher working practices, and might not include costs that exist in terms of activities forgone, stress, reduced commitment, or loss of trust (Pollitt and Bouckaert, 2000).

At the same time as being subjected to managerial controls, an apparently contradictory emphasis has been placed on the need for public sector workers to become entrepreneurial and take forward the needs of the public. In taking an entrepreneurial role (Osborne and Gaebler, 1993), officers should place an emphasis on people, communication, culture and empowerment and play the role of champion and hero (Newman, 1994). In becoming 'civic entrepreneurs', they should combine varied resources and people to deliver better social outcomes, higher social value and more social capital (Leadbeater and Goss, 1998); in taking an 'enabling' role they bring groups together to clarify shared objectives (Cochrane, 1994). More recently, it has been argued under the banner of the 'New Public Service' that public sector workers should broker interests and build coalitions, but that their primary role should be to 'help citizens articulate and meet their shared interests' (Denhardt and Denhardt, 2000: 549). Worthy as these aspirations may be, they still fail to fully capture either the complex issue of public service ethics, tackled in a later chapter in this book (Wood, 2003), or the difficulty of reconciling stakeholders with divergent interests, as discussed below. Moreover, they conflict with the managerialist constraints indicated above. Thus, it has been suggested that officers experience a tension between entrepreneurialism and managerialism (Du Gay, 1996; Goss, 2001; Newman, 2002), which can lead to the undermining of public service values (Stewart and Walsh, 1992).

Consumerism: redefining the public

As part of the NPM reform agenda, and in particular the idea of good governance, a focus has been placed on the need to involve members of the public in decision-making. However, central to this is the way in which members of the public are perceived. Taking the analogy of the private sector, members of the public have tended to be viewed as consumers. However, this does not necessarily sit comfortably with their involvement in decision-making as citizens. Not only does the idea of consumerism not necessarily fit with that of citizenship, but in addition, it does not take proper account of the situation of the more vulnerable members of the public. However, although there seems to be a growing recognition of this tension, in practice governments still seem to be taking a consumerist approach, as explained below.

In addition to the role of the market and the involvement of other organisations (markets and networks), and managerialism, attention has also been paid more recently to the impact of reforms associated with NPM on the public and to the involvement of the public in decision-making (see for example Martin, 2002). The debate around how the public should be involved in decision-making is, of course, not in itself a new idea (Arnstein, 1969; Hoggett and Hambleton, 1987), and emphasis has been placed at different times on the idea of the public as customer (Brown, 1997) or as a citizen with rights (Van Huyssten, 2002). However, it should be noted that there is an increasing recognition of the tension between these two dimensions (see for example, Stewart and Walsh, 1992; Minogue *et al.*, 2002). A number of contentious issues relating to this discussion will be raised here, and then further developed in a later chapter in this volume by Jenny Harrow which focuses specifically on service provision.

The reference to the public as consumer has often been presented in a positive light. Sanderson (2001), for example, describes the new relationship with the public as 'consumerism', as one that implies providing users of services with more choice and more influence on decisions about policies and services as a spur to improved quality and value for money. However, an important problem with the idea of the public as consumer that has so far often been neglected, is that a market model cannot meet the needs of disadvantaged groups, especially since it implies an individualistic approach to service provision (Bolzan and Gale, 2002). This is since those who are disadvantaged are often not able to effectively voice their concerns, or make demands for services (Mackintosh, 1998). A further problem is that the customer analogy can effectively result in competition between those who are in need, which runs the risk for public sector producers of prioritising different groups of need as more or less worthy (Clarke *et al.*, 1994; Dibben, 2003). This is particularly important in areas such as public health, public safety or social work, where some people's 'wants' may displace other people's 'needs', but with very serious consequences. A further issue is the problem of when a 'customer' is not a 'customer', as in the example of where a social worker removes a child from a dangerous situation for their own protection.

In addition to the concerns raised above about the prioritising of 'consumers', another problem with the concept of members of the public as consumers, is that it seems to negate the possibility of the public as citizen, with the related notions of commitment and responsibility and collective rights (Stewart and Walsh, 1992). As citizens, the public should have a right to be involved in decision-making (Clarke and Stewart, 1992) and therefore a degree of power (Leach *et al.*, 1994). As noted above in the discussion on local governance, however, some partners in decision-making can have more power than others. This is, of course, not a new idea, as evidenced by Dahl's work in the 1960s, and the later work of Bachrach and Baratz (1970) and Lukes (1974). Moreover, in analysing the role of members of the public and the power relations that underpin participation, Arnstein (1969) drew up the much-cited 'ladder of citizen participation'. Each of the different rungs of the ladder relate to the different levels of power and knowledge held by different stakeholders, moving from 'nonparticipation' to 'tokenism' to 'citizen power'. However, for Arnstein, citizen participation should be based on much more than tokenism, and instead should be about:

> ...the redistribution of power that enables the have-not citizens, presently excluded from the political and economic processes, to be deliberately included in the future. (Arnstein, 1969: 216).

An important point to note here is the reference to 'redistribution'. This moves the discussion far beyond the mere invitation for members of the public to have some marginal involvement in decision-making. Furthermore, it interferes with the notion that market forces should be left to work out who has more and who has less. Perhaps not surprisingly, therefore, advocates of neo-liberal policies are explicitly opposed to redistribution, and for those such as Hayek (1984), such redistribution can be regarded as social engineering and therefore potentially evil.

In the context of the discussion about involving the public in decision-making as citizens with rights and power, a further issue that should be addressed is whether any fundamental change has occurred in the attitudes of those working within public sector organisations. While Newman (2002) points to the way in which public participation challenges established power bases, Benington (2000) points to the potential neglect of organisational and cultural change within organisations: cultural change is easier said than done. For example, mission statements indicate the need for public sector workers to be entrepreneurial, and the need to involve the public in decision-making, but this will not necessarily change what happens in practice. This can be seen in the example of the UK, where reforms have been introduced in recent years with the intention to increase the involvement of the public (DETR, 1999; DETR, 2000), and to more carefully take their views into account in decision-making. However, in contrast to rhetoric which casts the public as citizens, empirical research suggests that the reality is a continued tendency to treat the public as consumers (Martin and Boaz, 2001; Lowndes *et al.*, 2001a).

Conclusion

NPM has often been used as a positive term to encapsulate the introduction and establishment of neo-liberal reforms in the public sector. This chapter has sought to evaluate the effect of such reforms on three types of relationship that are central to the public sector: the relationship between the public sector and other bodies, that between public sector workers and their employers, and the relationship between service providers and members of the public. In doing this, a number of important issues have been drawn out. In particular, questions have been raised about the nature of the 'partnership' between the public sector and other bodies, and in particular, the potential for the dominance of private sector interests and the marginalisation of the voluntary sector in this partnership. This suggests that it is not enough simply to refer to 'marketisation', without exploring the dynamics between those involved.

The employment relationship has been characterised by managerialism, but more recently, issues have emerged around the drive toward performance, with increased work intensification, and the dubious use of performance indicators and inspection regimes. However, tighter controls on workers and on working practices may lead to increased stress in the workplace and a resulting fall-out in terms of high levels of sickness and turnover; centrally-defined performance indicators constrain the opportunity for entrepreneurialism and may also conflict with locally expressed needs and wants.

The relationship between the public sector and the public has also been impacted upon, with increased drives toward involving the public in decision-making, but relatively little attention to the underlying philosophy behind this. Attention was drawn here to the need to distinguish between consumerism and citizenship, and to explore the implications of this for different members of the public, at the same time, taking account of power relations, and the probable need for redistribution of resources. The way in which power could be redistributed could emerge through the devolving of power to communities. However, in the current context of a neo-liberal reform agenda it is questionable whether agencies will be willing to devolve power to the public when it comes to fundamental or strategic questions (Skelcher, 1993). Moreover, doubts can be cast on the actual ability of certain members of the public to participate in decision-making unless stronger attempts are first made to address structural inequalities (Taylor, 2002).

Each of the above factors should not be seen in isolation. Changes in the institutional make-up of the 'public sector' are inevitably linked to the nature of public sector employment. Moreover, the values held by those institutions delivering services, and the way in which work is constructed, will necessarily impact on the way in which decisions are made on service delivery. Since the various hats worn by the 'stakeholders' are numerous, then at any one time an individual may be a recipient of a service, a council taxpayer, a shareholder, an employer or an employee (Reimer, 1997).

More generally, it is arguably not possible, nor, in any case advisable to consider NPM reforms simply as administrative reforms (Hood, 1991) and divorced from the economic and political context. The nature of the broader context will impact upon the drivers for reform, the way in which the reforms are implemented locally, and the severity of their impact on those at the receiving end. Moreover, in interpreting the success, or otherwise of reforms, local environmental factors and the level of economic resources should be taken into account. Often, however, the use of performance indicators to build league tables and categories of public entities assumes that the problem is about management standards rather than structures and the socio-economic environment. The public is provided with a 'safety net' against presumably bad organisations, through 'name and shame' tactics, and the use of remedial actions, but context is largely ignored.

NPM has been regarded by some as a positive move toward increased accountability and efficiency in the public sector. However, in the light of the above discussion, it appears that more detailed analyses need to take place on the implications of the NPM reforms introduced thus far, before further reforms are rolled out to address their perceived weaknesses. In the aims of social justice, it is argued that in particular, attention needs to be paid to three main areas. Firstly, the implications of continued drives toward marketisation for both the 'partners' in service provision and those at the receiving end of service provision. Secondly, the resulting tensions within the public sector workplace that arise from attempts to instil performance management measures without properly taking account of the complex nature of public service provision and the local context. Thirdly, the extent to which 'consumerism' continues to pervade service provision, overriding notions of what should be meant by citizenship, and ignoring existing inequalities in social, economic and political resources.

4

Uneasy Partners: Democratisation and New Public Management in Developing Countries

Bruce Baker

The widespread assumption over the last 25 years has been that the best or only way to achieve better results from public sector organisations in developing countries is to adopt market-based mechanisms to replace the traditional bureaucracy. This view has persisted despite the fact that a five-year review of the role of government in transition economies in South Asia, Sub-Saharan Africa and South America found that, although NPM reforms have achieved some improvements in efficiency, there had been mixed effects on equality of service, whilst the transaction costs of autonomising service delivery agencies commonly outweighed the efficiency gains (Batley, 1999). This chapter, however, is concerned with its *political* impact, or more particularly, what effect it has had on democratic processes and institutions. This is particularly pertinent given that democratisation has often accompanied the introduction of NPM. Having clarified the distinction between the two, the chapter goes on to consider the extent to which NPM has been employed in the new democracies and evaluates how consistent with democracy are the NPM views of how policy is determined, who is accountable for that policy and to whom, what is the nature of political equality and what are the responsibilities of the democratic state.

The overlap in conception and timing of democratisation and NPM

NPM and democracy are often confused due to the fact that there is some overlap in the conceptualisation of the two. It is important, therefore, to clearly distinguish them, although this is problematic given that both are clusters of processes and institutions that are contested as to their content and usually only selectively implemented.

A number of the principles of entrepreneurial government have a democratic ring about them. Advocates speak of the empowerment of citizens as control is pushed out of the bureaucracy and into the community; of the redefinition of clients as customers who are offered choices; of decentralising authority so that decisions are more influenced and open to greater scrutiny by the recipients; and of bringing together public, private and voluntary organisations to solve community problems in a dynamic partnership (Osborne and Gaebler, 1992; Hood, 1991; Yeatman, 1994; Mayntz, 1993; Barzelay, 1992). Here are ideas that democratic theorists are familiar with – participation, consultation, accessibility, subsidiarity, accountability and transparency. But when transported from a political context to a management context do they mean the same thing?

Whatever the overlap in goals, NPM and democracy have quite different motivations. The motor of NPM is not political equality and popular control, but efficiency in a context of rising public demands that are outstripping public revenues. 'A significant component of new public management reforms is expenditure and cost reduction (often expressed in ways that disguise a reduction in output or services)' (Minogue, 1998: 19). Some would claim that improved efficiency and effectiveness has a democratic goal, namely: 'to strengthen the process of equity in the institutions that comprise the government, as well as increasing the professional quality, accountability and sense of commitment toward the community on the part of public servants' (Moctezuma, 2001, 5). But this is to confuse goal with outcome. NPM proponents do not see meeting the will of the citizenry as their first priority. The World Bank, for instance, identifies three key conditions for success in administration reform. The reform must be politically desirable to the leadership, that is the political benefits to them must outweigh the political costs; reform must be politically feasible, so that they do not lose ground to the opposition as a result; reforms must be politically credible to significant stakeholders such as employees and investors (World Bank, 1995). In these three conditions it is elite support that is important. Elsewhere it is the interests of international capital that are to the fore. It is significant, for instance, that alongside the promotion of the privatisation of health care by international financial institutions (IFIs) and the World Trade Organisation (WTO), there has been a substantial growth of exports of medical services from the developed world (Kim, Shakow and Bayona, 1999). As Farazmand notes, proposals for privatisation appear to be 'directed more towards serving the private market sector than towards serving the general public' (Farazmand, 1994: 76).

To what extent is NPM employed in the new democracies?

The marketisation of public administration constitutes a very large 'shopping basket' of policies that affect public management structures and processes. The developing world has certainly been influenced by elements of the NPM model, but Manning is convincing when he says that:

> Measured against its self-proclaimed universal relevance, NPM clearly has *not* become the predominant public management paradigm in

developing countries. Any review of public management developments in any less developed country demonstrates that hierarchical bureaucracies have not been replaced substantially by chains of inter-linked contracts. Certainly, there have been very significant reforms, particularly in the water and health sectors, that have drawn from the NPM menu. But most government functions are still performed by vertically integrated bureaucracies functioning pretty much as Weber imagined (Manning, 2000).

The principal areas that have been addressed are privatisation and civil service reform. However, even when privatisation is successfully undertaken (and there have been many failures), it is not always part of NPM rethinking. Rather, it is often no more than governments off-loading unprofitable commercial businesses and/or auctioning off the most saleable public assets for public or private gain. As far as most developing governments are concerned, privatisation has not been popular for political reasons of national pride, disturbing clientelist networks and fear of giving advantage to foreign or internal ethnic rivals. Under pressure, however, almost all developing countries have proceeded with privatisation transactions. The speed and scale of the change is recorded elsewhere (Shamsul Haque, 2000; for Africa, see Bennell, 1997; van de Walle, 2001; Saitoti, 2002).

In addition to the divestiture of commercial businesses, privatisation has also affected what have been regarded as traditional public services such as energy, water, transport and telecommunications. The most politically sensitive area of the public sector to reform is social welfare, where privatisation of control and of ownership has been tried in varying ratios. Some of the largest state owned enterprises are utilities and transport concerns, yet their sale has been strikingly absent in Africa, often owing to their large outstanding debts and years of under-investment and outmoded management structures.

Civil service reform has reviewed internal organisation, size, recruitment, remuneration, career development, expenditure and budget controls. The main apparent success has been in the area of reducing the size of the civil service, although this is not just from retrenchment, but includes attrition, the removal of ghost workers and divestment. During the 1980s and early 1990s central government workers in 11 African countries allegedly dropped by 9 per cent, though in most African countries there was considerable foot dragging and statistics are not reliable (on reductions in Africa, see Olowu, 1999; Goldsmith, 1999; van de Walle, 2001. For Latin America, see Moctezuma, 2001. For SE Asia, see Common, 2001).

Civil service reform programmes have frequently been found to be expensive, to be difficult to administer, to reduce lower grades that saved little expenditure, and to provoke the flight of skilled top management to commercial positions. They have also caused smaller bureaucracies that already have weak capacity, to face additional strain. To the critics, what was required was not so much concentrating on reducing numbers to improve efficiency, but the introduction of stronger systems of accountability, enhancing the capacity of parliament to scrutinise audit reports, better remuneration and a reassertion of meritocracy. According to Goldsmith, 'State bureaucracies are a problem in Africa mostly because they underperform, not because they are overexpanded' (Goldsmith, 1999: 521).

The complexity and political sensitivity of its agenda has ensured that the disaggregation of bureaucracies through contracting out has gone very slowly and internal quasi-markets and semi-autonomous agencies have not been popular. There has long been the conversion of government departments into parastatals, but it has primarily been about corporatising commercial functions. What has not been apparent has been the NPM approach of extending this to non-commercial functions, although Bolivia, Peru and Mozambique customs and Tanzania and Uganda revenue authorities are exceptions (Minogue, Polidano and Hume, 1998; James and Manning, 1996).

In summary, there has been in the developing world a selective introduction of managerialism that has brought some private sector management methods to the public sector. NPM's emphasis on professional management, explicit standards and measures of performance, value for money, and divestment of non-core activities or non-profitable enterprises has been broadly welcomed and implemented to a degree, especially in the newly industrialised countries (Commonwealth Secretariat, 1995). However, there has been much greater reticence concerning the more radical aspect of NPM, the so-called 'new institutional economics'. New institutional economics seeks *inter alia* to identify the obstacles, problems, imperfections, and failures, both in states that can or should be remedied by institutional means. The institutional solutions for public sector pathologies tend toward small, clean governments, strong property rights, and honest, efficient judicial systems (Doner and Schneider, 2000). The reality, however, is that assuming that universal principles of administration can be developed ignores the wide range of national environments that have arisen in markedly different cultural, economic, social, political, technological and historical contexts.

NPM and policy determination

The appeal of democracy is that decisions binding on the community are only made by that community. It rejects the idea that leaders or experts alone, however well intentioned, wise and considerate (an unlikely trinity) should determine social policy alone. Legitimate political decisions for democracy are those that involve full participation, representation and transparency. If there is true political equality and popular control, then citizens 'should be able to participate in a process of debate and deliberation, open to all on a free and equal basis about matters of pressing public concern' (Held, 1996: 302). No citizen in a democracy should be able to impose themselves on others using their social standing or economic power. Even more inconsistent with democratic autonomy is the possibility that anyone outside the community should participate in decisions that are binding on that community. However, the emergence of powerful international and regional institutions whose decisions and policies in effect preclude debate and self-determination have undermined the nature of state democracy. In looking at democratic policy making, this section will therefore consider, not only the degree to which national governments open debate to the whole citizenry, but the degree to which governments themselves are able to control important policy decisions.

There is no doubt that much of NPM is not only the policy of choice of the governments of most developed countries, but one they wish to see implemented elsewhere. There is an increasing consensus that a global model of efficiency has been found in NPM and a global model of accountability has been found in liberal democracy. The unquestioned assumption, therefore, is that the techniques (and values) of business administration from the context of multinational corporations (MNCs) and in the environment of the developed countries can be transplanted to (or worse, imposed on) the governments of the developing world. Being a product of Western liberal democratic states, NPM is orientated more towards the cost cutting, tax reducing concerns of the developed states, rather than the equally important concern of developing states for capacity building and development. It simply assumes 'the neutrality, anonymity and impartiality of the administrative apparatus and its accountability to elected politicians' (Shamsul Haque, 1996: 319), even though this is either absent or fragile in most developing countries. A breathtaking example of the underestimation of the problem of policy transfer is found in a recent book advocating NPM in Mexico:

> In order for the government to work according to the principles of effectiveness, efficiency, productivity, quality and honesty, it will be necessary to overcome behaviour patterns inherited from the past ... The introduction of principles of productivity and competitiveness from within the institutions, the modification of legal and institutional frameworks according to clear objectives of public policy, the introduction of adequate incentives for the work of public servants, the carrying out of periodic, objective evaluations of their performance and, basically, the professionalization of the public service, constitute strategies whose adequate implementation will surely create the context necessary for changing the government's image in the minds of the bureaucrats

and, even more importantly, in the minds of the citizens (Moctezuma Barragan and Roemer, 2001: 17).

Such staggering optimism in the face of such enormous obstacles can only arise from a total failure to understand why people act 'irrationally' and not according to NPM's logic, in developing countries. Interestingly the authors do recognise the necessity for popular support and yet it is not before implementation of policy change, but after. The change itself is beyond debate, it is only necessary in their view to get the public to see the value of the changes: 'administering the cultural change requires…getting [citizens] to participate in the change…[and] a serious communication strategy' (Moctezuma Barragan and Roemer, 2001: 17).

In this scenario there is no role for citizens collectively to articulate their interests, let alone set the agenda. At best, people as individuals must solve their own problems, but there is less and less relevance in them seeking collectively and after deliberation to offer solutions to complex social problems; those are to be left to the market. Politics is shrinking to the confines of issues of individual choice. The individualist model of the market is alien to the collectivist view of citizenship. Its focus on meeting customer needs exaggerates the ability of customers to articulate their needs or make choices, since they are often uninformed or do not have the resources to do so (Armstrong, 1998). As Borgmann notes,

> To extol the consumer is to deny the citizen. When consumers begin to act, the fundamental decisions have already been made. Consumers are in a politically and morally weak position. They are politically weak because the signals that they can send to the authorities about the common order are for the most part ambiguous. Does the purchase of an article signal approval, thoughtlessness, or lack of a better alternative? (1992: 115).

Though NPM lauds 'steering', the possibility remains that: 'In our rush to steer we are forgetting who owns the boat' (Denhardt *et al.*, 2000: 549).

The developing world is a very different context from the developed world for NPM. There are very different levels of tolerance and expectation of the state, and differing state capacity and resources. The stark reality is that many actors (especially the most powerful) have actually a lot to *gain* from administrative inefficiency and a lot to lose from reform. There is no substitute for the democratic principle that the people who will be affected by binding communal decisions should decide those matters themselves. Certainly there is no guarantee that in representative democracy representatives will genuinely put forward the views of their constituencies. There is even less chance of the popular will being met when the decision is made by others who know little of the political context, opportunities and characteristics in which the policy will be implemented. Further, if major policy choices do not have political and community support they will only be seen as externally driven and resented if not resisted (Kiggundu, 1998).

The design to propagate NPM worldwide does not necessarily mean that developed countries impose it in an un-democratic fashion. Policy transfer can lie anywhere on a continuum between voluntary and coerced. Typologies of policy transfer speak of copying, emulation and inspiration that all fall short of coercion (Dolowitz and Marsh, 1998). Determining which is predominant is less than straightforward. Financial and political organisations at both the international and regional level, as well as donor nations, do set the public administration agenda by example, inter-governmental fora, conferences, publications, consultancies and non-governmental organisations. Yet their promotion may well be to a willing political and or civil service elite or at least to an elite looking for external justification for policies already decided. It has not been uncommon for the technocratic elite to push through liberalisation programmes. Larbi (1998) claims this was so in the Ministry of Health in Ghana, although the bureaucratic elite was not unanimous and mistrust of officials in decentralised units and fear of abuse of public resources has created resistance in central agencies to releasing control over finance and personnel management.

When it comes to talk of coercion, it is normally the World Bank and International Monetary Fund (IMF) that are cited as prime examples. What the World Bank called 'good governance' was first introduced as a condition for loans in the late 1980s. By good governance it meant, in effect, the adoption of transparent, accountable and efficient administrations similar to those in the developed world. Yet though it spoke in terms of democracy, it was democracy conceived in terms of its economic and public administration components. These policies were invariably not welcomed by the leaders (though they were quick to expropriate the loans for personal accumulation) and, in as much as local publics were informed about or understood the consequences, were not welcomed by them either. As a matter of fact, large-scale popular resistance to IMF policies has been recorded in recent years in Argentina, Bolivia, Brazil, Columbia, Costa Rica, Ecuador, Honduras, Kenya, Malawi, Nigeria, Paraguay, South Africa and Zambia (Woodroffe and Ellis-Jones, 2000). What appears to concern institutions like the World Bank is not the process of policy choice by citizens and their representatives, but the construction of these policies by the administrations. In Hibou's view: 'The World Bank considers only the policy outputs of the state, not the internal politics that lead to a particular policy decision' (Hibou, 2002: 181). A striking example of their coercion was the 1998 debt relief offered to Mozambique under the Heavily Indebted Poor Countries Initiative. It insisted that before release of the debt Mozambique should first raise health service charges by five-fold.

As regards other forms of coercion, powerful economic organisations, whether donor controlled financial institutions or MNCs, have sought to use their leverage to pressurise governments to make national economic decisions subject to the consent of the international bodies, or even to try to veto public consultation. In this way they seek to circumvent anticipated popular dissent or parliamentary opposition. For all the talk of strengthening democracy it often appears that the economy is run with little reference to elected representatives. For instance, in 1995 the Mozambican government could not present its programme to the National Assembly because the bilateral donors and the World Bank had not yet met to approve the budget.

Even if the policy choice originates within the national government, it can suffer either from inadequate consultation with the public as to what they want or from inability to implement the policy. In the former case, government proposals to privatise public utilities commonly fail to publish the terms guiding the bidding process and the profiles of the bidding companies. When the time came to privatise the Ghana Water Company, even the World Bank project and evaluation reports and the Transaction Advisor's Report were not publicly available. It is hard to see how a national public debate on options for reforming the public sector can be conducted in such a climate of opacity. The gap between government policy and implementation arises partly from the way the new institutions function. For instance, autonomous agencies undermine policy objectives by creating constituencies that compel governments to maintain existing policies. Policy becomes what the agencies do, not what the government proposes. There can also arise an unhealthy institutional rivalry between the agency and the parent ministry which is legally responsible for a given policy domain. Agencies may circumvent the ineffectiveness of the traditional ministries and have the chief say in policy-making, but since they commonly lack formal authority for inter-agency policy coordination, the dominance of an agency in a particular policy domain can hinder intra-government policy coordination. It has also been reported that agencies in Africa have been created in an attempt to escape inevitable closure (Ives, 1998).

Policy determination in the NPM agenda, therefore, is primarily top-down, the product of elite thinking, not popular consensus.

NPM and accountability

Democratic government is not just about efficiency. It is about the accountability of rulers to citizens. The concept of representative democracy is that the government and its officials can be held accountable for action taken on behalf of the state, either politically or legally. Political accountability provides that directly elected officials are accountable to the voting public, whilst appointees are accountable to the voting public's parliamentary/ executive representatives. Legal accountability provides that government officials are accountable to the law/constitution, codes of conduct and judicial review for their actions. Through these means the government and its officials cannot breach citizens rights and abuse their power with impunity.

NPM, however, marks a shift away from political accountability to managerial accountability. In other words, from the public holding ministers accountable for the actions of their ministries, it has become agency heads holding managers accountable for their section. It is a shift that assumes that citizens only want efficient public services and low taxes and overlooks their equal concerns to have their rights protected, their voices heard, and their values and preferences respected. In other words, in a democracy, government accountability, responsiveness, and transparency together with popular control, participation and human rights, should be just as important as issues of economy and efficiency.

NPM argues that it enhances accountability by bringing government 'closer to the people', but the claim is based on an inadequate understanding of democracy. With NPM, citizens have been replaced by customers, or as Denhardt (1999) puts it: 'the integrative role of citizenship has been reduced to the narrow self-interest of customership – in government as in business.' When people act as citizens they assume personal responsibility for what happens in their communities. They focus on the common good and the long-term consequences to the community. However, when people act as customers they focus on their own limited desires and how they can be satisfied.

In fact it is often more difficult than imagined for governments to identify the appropriate customers of service as illustrated by prisons, customs and immigration and education (Peters and Pierre, 1998). Further, consumer choice and stakeholderism only gives voice to current consumers and stakeholders.

> Government serves more than just the immediate client. Government also serves those who may be waiting for service, those who may need the service even though they are not actively seeking it, future generations of service recipients, relatives and friends of the immediate recipient, and on and on. There may even be customers who don't want to be customers – such as those receiving a speeding ticket (Denhardt and Denhardt, 2000: 549).

If services are financed by collective resources then democratic government requires that instruments are available not just to present consumers or stakeholders of a particular public service, but to all. Few would defend democratic governments following the course of the private sector and providing the best services to the most wealthy or influential. They are expected to take into consideration other issues of fairness, equity and wider community matters beyond short-term individual need.

Jensen sees the prioritisation of consumer choice as representing 'a narrow, essentially economistic view of human behaviour' that fails to give 'any guidelines for how to establish priorities when there is a plurality of consumer needs and interests' (Jenssen, 2002: 298). Indeed, the discouragement of debate about questions concerning the quality and legitimacy of individual preferences and the conformity of those individual preferences with common interests only highlights the de-politicising tendency of NPM. Both politicians and citizens are increasingly absolved from responsibility to participate in public deliberation of public values. With public policy evaluated by *market* criteria, ethical and moral questions become pragmatic questions about functional efficiency and market regulation. It is a 'politics' that leaves out the normative dimension and is for many something less than democratic. Political decision-making should not be just about the aggregation of preferences (Jenssen, 2002).

Privatisation and decentralisation inevitably alters the degree of accountability. Once a publicly controlled service moves into or towards non-state control, the same constraints do not apply. Unlawful *private* behaviour can only be pursued under common and criminal law; there is no automatic accountability to the public. Market forces can never hold private service contractors, parastatals, quasi-public bodies or even executive agencies accountable in the same way for the public services formally provided by the government. There may be accountability to those with whom they have a service contract as regards quality of performance, or accountability to shareholders as regards profit, but concerns about equity or the constitutional and statutory rights of citizens are not a priority.

Accountability is also compromised by moves towards networks of autonomous and semi-autonomous agencies. These not only bypass local government, which *is* accountable, but quickly assume an independence of government. 'Deregulation, government withdrawal and steering at a distance...are all notions of less direct government regulation and control which lead to more autonomy and self-governance for social institutions' (Kickert, 1993: 275). Yet though agency self-governance may increase efficiency and effectiveness, it does not necessarily improve accountability to customers, let alone the public as a whole. In addition, the very fragmented nature of the interorganisational networks that are arising to deliver services obscures who is accountable to whom for what (Rhodes, 1996: 663). In particular, it is not clear where it leaves ministerial accountability. To manage both privatisation and fragmentation democratically there will have to be 'a reinvention of accountability to accompany the reinvention of government' (Gilmour and Jensen, 1998: 255).

Nowhere is the environment more difficult for establishing even the limited version of accountability than in developing countries. The legal, cultural, educational, technical and political contexts have all proved problematic. The legal context, for instance, is one in which there is little chance of judicial intervention to resolve disputes and many NPM 'public service contracts' are inevitably very fragile. Developing countries have large informal economies with relatively weak specification of property rights and only limited formal processes to regulate economic activity and enforce formal contracts.

The cultural context is important since the so called 'public service ethos' (that is, the sense of a vocation for service to the community and concern about achieving results and solving concrete problems) is a prerequisite for NPM (Moctezuma, 2001). Yet, as Schick (1998) notes, NPM discussions of performance contracts and decentralised authority all make important assumptions that are not necessarily valid in the developing world. First, it assumes that budgets function properly to constrain line departments, while committing central agencies to the provision of a certain level of funding. Second, that staff, despite natural self-interest are largely constrained by clear standards of behaviour. Third, that policy is authoritative and free of conflicting ministerial decrees. These assumptions of predictable resourcing, credible regulation of staff and credible policy are often absent. It is not uncommon that rules and regulations that control how public money should be spent and who should be hired are overlooked in the attempt to by-pass unresponsive bureaucracy, evade bad policy and to promote self-interest in a poorly paid service. Consider the recent events in Zambia. It was reported that one town mayor was accused of using council trucks for his own business and the agricultural coordinator in another district was accused of selling state fertiliser on the commercial market (IRIN, 20 May and 3 June 2003). In central government, the Director of Intelligence was accused of misappropriating very large sums of money from the intelligence account (IRIN, 12 September 2002). Meanwhile, the Vice-President apparently ignored a presidential decree to terminate a crude oil supply with a firm from whom he had received a large and undeclared donation for the ruling party. Instead, he gave orders to maintain the contract (IRIN, 2 June 2003).

The educational context in developing countries is one of a scarcity of professionally qualified personnel. As a result, structures for imposing accountability struggle to find suitable staff. Many African countries, for instance, simply lack the qualified accountants to produce audited accounts on time or sufficiently competent members of Public Accounts Committees in parliament to evaluate the financial reports (van de Walle, 2001). Overall, tracing the receipt of funds may have improved, but not the accounting of expenditure. The drive towards decentralisation in countries like Uganda has only exacerbated the problems, and not surprisingly the local government districts struggle to produce their audits on time. It should be noted that donor requirements have also put systems under additional stress, so that in Uganda, for instance, 40/50 additional accounts are required at the Ministry of Finance and 26 at district government level.

The difficulties in implementing NPM-style accountability reforms in the developing world are not, however, just legal, cultural and educational. The political realities are equally vital. Weak state capacity, regional-ethnic tensions, severe poverty and deep-rooted clientelism have to be taken into account. Yet often the new norms and condemnation of practices that have been introduced with democratic politics only 'incite power holders to displace their strategies of accumulation toward more hidden modalities' (Hibou, 2002: 185). The new reforms may mean that the distribution of public employment, the sale of import/export licences, and access to currency or procurement contracts may be more limited due to greater scrutiny. However, practices of accumulation have simply 'migrated to the fringes of legality, including protection of, or access to informal commerce; control of criminal activities; control of violence for economic ends; and the development of various kinds of fraud' (Hibou, 2002: 185). Unsurprisingly there has been a lack of transparency in privatisation sales. Often their main beneficiaries have been the political elite who, with insider information and sometimes closed bidding processes, have taken advantage of the illicit opportunities. There have been many instances where the sale process has been obfuscated, whether using pre-emptive divestitures to undervalue assets or direct sales in a self-regarding manner (Tangri and Mwenda, 2001). Attempts to institutionalise accountability without understanding and addressing the cause of its absence are unlikely to succeed.

NPM and equality

Democracy should spell the end of elite monopoly over decision-making and its benefits. With its insistence on political equality it rejects the use of gender, class, education, race and religion as a basis for enjoying citizenship rights. Many argue that democracy is about the processes of public decision making, rather than its economic and social outcome. Others insist on the inclusion of economic and social rights as an element of democratic equality. People, it is argued, cannot exercise civil and political rights without the capacities and resources to do so effectively. At the same time, people assess the quality of a democracy in terms of its ability to secure them the basic economic and social rights on which a minimally adequate human life depends (Beetham *et al.*, 2001).

If the latter position is followed, it becomes pertinent to examine how effectively the basic necessities of life, such as food, shelter and clean water are provided in a country professing democracy. Also relevant are the accessibility and reliability of the provision of social security, health protection and basic education. Such a democracy will be committed to making these fundamental services available to all without discrimination and to making adequate resources available for delivering them.

These are concerns on which NPM has a direct bearing, since it has been accused of increasing inequality in the accessibility of basic needs (Woodroffe and Ellis-Jones, 2000; Grusky, 2001). For instance, one of the problems of health and social welfare reforms that has never been resolved has been how to avoid the creation of a two-tiered system in which the wealthy have access to more and better care because they can afford user fees or higher insurance premiums. Take the example of Chile. In 1981 it created a market for private health providers, transferring primary health facilities to the municipalities, whilst also setting up a private insurance system with competitive private plans. In practice only 20 per cent can afford the private schemes, yet their members receive a third more funding than public insurance plan clients (Bossert, 2000).

The apparent failure of initial efforts at 'cost recovery' as a means of funding health care in poor nations has meant that this strategy has given way to more fully private provision, under the slogan 'financing demand but not supply'. Yet by imposing the criteria of choice on people who are in no position to exercise it, health care reformers have prioritised financial outcome over health outcome and further imperilled the health of the poor (Light, 2000; Stocker *et al.*, 1999).

The introduction of private insurance schemes has inherent problems for democratic equality. Insurers have an interest in avoiding having sick patients in their risk pool. At the same time, patients who know they are sick have an interest in being covered for their health care needs. These two phenomena combine in ways that shift the more costly patients to the plans least able to select – usually the publicly subsidised basic plans. These plans, however, will have higher costs per covered patient (Bossert, 2000). Such a situation clearly runs counter to the fundamental democratic principle of equality.

The debate over privatisation of health care, water and other basic services opens up a larger, more difficult question: should the burdens of human social life be considered public or private responsibilities? NPM's equality is one of opportunity, but it is not one of experience, because it ignores the barriers of poverty, whether they have a class, gender, racial or religious basis. In its pursuit of government efficiency it has undermined citizen equality. It has saved expense by transferring costs to a population, many of whom are not in a position to bear it.

Issues of equality also affect activities that are retained by the state, when NPM procedures are introduced. For instance, if remuneration is linked to simple measures of output, the civil servant will not want to undertake problem cases, because these lower the case rate over time. In other words, measures of quality as well as quantity need to be found if the most needy are not to be sidelined in the rush for efficiency (Sutch, 1999).

NPM and state responsibilities

NPM promotes a leaner state, but this in turn creates problems for democracy in developing countries. The first problem is a practical one concerning whether bureaucracies that are weak in funding and have limited trained personnel will be capable of steering the hollowed out state with its multiplicity of different governmental and non-governmental agencies. It is unlikely that they will be able to write complete performance contracts, manage them, control output and co-ordinate autonomous agencies before they have mastered an integrated centralised system (Schick, 1998: 127; Minogue, 1998). As Sutch notes, 'The capacity needed to define performance ex ante and measure it ex post, as well as to determine the value of rewards accordingly and in ways perceived to be fair' (Sutch, 1999) is one not available to developing countries. For new democracies grappling with establishing in their bureaucracies new levels of accountability, participation and transparency, these reforms look like attempts to run before one can walk and are likely to endanger the fragile first steps at introducing democratic procedures.

Second, if the government is to divest itself of many services previously regarded as inherently public, then the question arises as to who is to take on the responsibility for them. It is not clear that there are always appropriate non-government organisations or private businesses ready to take over.

Third, where government special-purpose agencies and/or the voluntary sector are employed to deliver services at the local level, these by-pass local government structures and leave central government with nothing but a financial control over these fragmented systems. Indeed, autonomous service deliverers may come to assume a monopoly of expertise in their policy area and become increasingly reluctant to accept central guidelines. A vision of the state as 'a collection of inter-organizational networks made up of governmental and societal actors with no sovereign actor able to steer or regulate' (Rhodes, 1996: 666) has lost sight of the principle that public services should be under the control of the public.

Fourth, the role of political leaders that is emerging in the leaner state is far from clear. NPM requires extensive relaxation of political control over public service and substantive discretion for managers at lower levels of the organisation (Peters and Pierre, 1998: 229). This leaves politicians with the responsibility for defining the long-term goals of the public sector. This 'hands off', indirect model of leadership separates political accountability from day to day management. Politicians are therefore encouraged to excuse blunders and deny responsibility whilst agency personnel who act autonomously can plead that they are not accountable. The state's capacity for direct control is weakened, to be replaced by merely a capacity for influence.

Simply reducing the state in the developing world is not, therefore, a cure all. Acknowledging this, the World Bank has abandoned the argument that a reduced government role is the priority. It now argues that:

> An effective state is vital for the provision of the goods and services and the rules and institutions that allow markets to flourish and people to lead healthier happier lives. Without it, sustainable development, both economic and social is impossible (World Bank, 1997: 1).

It sees that there are limits on what could be done through the non-state sector and that in developing countries the aim has to be to encourage the state 'to manage less, but manage better'.

If it is acknowledged that the state still has an important role in the developing world, then the core responsibilities of government and how to develop and maintain new systems of democratic governance to carry out those responsibilities have to be defined. Many argue that privatisation is inappropriate *in principle* when it concerns a commodity essential to human life: such commodities should be managed to ensure social equity. Thus if water is seen as a national natural resource to be used judiciously and preserved for the common good (particularly in water scarce regions and where there is a close link between access to water and health) then its ownership, control, delivery and management should be in the public sector which is designed to represent the public interest. The reality in Ghana, however, is very different. The government's water privatisation plans, part funded by the World Bank, split the provision of water between the profitable urban sector and an unprofitable rural sector without public discussion. The profitable sector was contracted to private sector companies, whilst a government agency took over the unprofitable section. In poorer areas of Accra it now costs a family half a day's minimum wage to use 10 buckets of water a day. It is now widely recognised that public ownership has often failed to provide efficient and effective services or to adequately maintain capital equipment. For example, the water authorities in Ghana prior to privatisation only provided safe water to 36 per cent of the rural population and adequate sanitation to 11 per cent, made inadequate provision of water to large urban areas and left debts of $400 million due to mismanagement and low cost recovery. If a democratic state's responsibility is to provide basic services it has to do better than this.

Drawing the line between what should and should not be a service provided by the state will always be contested. Denhardt (1999) suggests that the impasse can only be broken by talking about values of government and focusing on ethics, citizenship and public interest:

> Many of the contemporary efforts to 'reform' the management of government have gone well beyond adopting the practices or techniques of

business management. ... [and] have accepted a wide variety of business values, for example, the imperative of self-interest, the value of competition, the sanctity of the market, and respect for the entrepreneurial spirit. Under these circumstances, we should indeed ask about questions like participation, deliberation, leadership, expertise, responsibility, justice, equity, and so on (Denhardt, 1999).

If he is right, the threat of NPM to democracy is not over what the state does, but how it does it. Whether or not it keeps a particular function, it must promote democratic values. Having said that it must be acknowledged that experience so far shows that NPM has weakened those values.

Conclusion

Is NPM promoting, hindering or simply accompanying democracy? This review concludes that NPM has been applied only in a limited way in developing countries. Where it has been introduced, it is making only doubtful efficiency gains for governments at the cost of a loss of democratic values. It is a process that lacks the democratic legitimacy that comes from public debate prior to government implementation. Those elements of NPM that have been implemented in the developing world have frequently been resisted strongly (Woodroffe and Ellis-Jones, 2000). For example, when the sale in Bolivia of the city of Cochabamba's public water system was made without debate, pushing up the average water bill to more than 20 per cent of a monthly wage of a self-employed person, protesters shut down the city in a general strike for four days. The government claimed that its hands were tied by the IMF debt relief programme, which was conditional on continued 'progress in the implementation of structural reforms.' When further violent street protests took place, 13 days of martial law followed. Neither the policy formation, implementation or the outcome of NPM did anything to promote Bolivian democracy, which in the previous 15 years had failed to give direct access to water in the region for 60 per cent of the population.

What was missing in Bolivia and in many other developing countries when NPM policies were implemented was democracy. As a result of NPM, citizens are being still further squeezed out of the process of determining policy; accountability is becoming more and more managerial rather than political; under the rubric of 'equality of opportunity' structural inequalities are left unchallenged and equality of service provision abandoned; and those elected have less and less control of the services that benefit the whole community. When public administration comprehensively excludes the public, then whatever the gain in efficiency, it is no gain for democracy.

5

Taming the Market: Co-ordination of Economic Activity at Multiple Spatial Levels[1]

J. Rogers Hollingsworth

As great financial power is dispersed among several hundred multinational corporations and at least two dozen states, the trajectory of world capitalism seems to have become even more open and unpredictable than in the past several centuries. To most analysts who try to get some perspective on where the world is tending, there is even more confusion and myopia than usual. One hears utterances that history is coming to an end, that we are entering a period of unprecedented turbulence and chaos, and that a global fog is descending upon us as we blindly tap our way into the third millennium (Fukuyama, 1992; Arrighi, 1997; Wallerstein, 1995; Hobsbawm, 1994).

In many respects, the world is more complex than at any time in the past. For several centuries, economic coordination has been occurring, in varying degrees, at four different levels simultaneously: (1) regions within nation-states; (2) the nation-state; (3) transnational regions, such as the European Community; and (4) the global level. Even though some economic coordination has long occurred at each of these levels, most analysts have long been confident that one level was more dominant than the others, and they could know where most of the coordination of economic activity was centred. For much of the last century, most analysts were very confident that the dominant form of coordination took place at the level of the nation-state. But in the contemporary period the degree to which economic coordination is primarily at the level of the nation-state is a matter of some controversy.

For some observers, we have entered a new era of history called the Period of Globalisation. For these analysts, however, defining globalisation has proven to be very complex and controversial. Implicit in most of the literature on globalisation is the view that most economic activities have become internationalised and that the nation-state has lost its capacity as the locus of economic governance (Hirst and Thompson, 1997; 1994). It is true that there has been an increasing internationalisation of money and the capital markets during the past 25 years and that this represents a major change. Focusing on this phenomenon, many have concluded that national economies are no longer governable because international financial capital can penetrate national borders in an unprecedented manner. In response, Tomlinson (1988) and others (Hirst and Thompson, 1994, 1997) argue that the internationalisation of financial markets is not at all a new process and that at earlier moments of similarity, analysts did not rush to conclude that this marked the demise of the nation-state. For example, the penetration of financial capital in Britain and a number of other national economies was greater between 1905 and 1914 than has been the pattern in recent years. Moreover, foreign trade as a percentage of GDP was also greater in these same countries between 1905 and 1914 than in our own day (Tomlinson, 1988; Hirst and Thompson, 1997). Those who see globalisation as the dominant trend in our own day counter by arguing that other things are different in the contemporary world from in the early part of the century. Not only are the international financial markets increasingly penetrating the nation-state but this is happening at the very time of a paradigm shift in economic ideology: the change in the financial markets is occurring simultaneously with the deregulation of national economies. And it is this deregulation of national economies combined with the globalisation of the financial markets which is leading to a convergence in the governance of economic activity at all levels (for example, at the local and sub-national levels and at the level of the nation-state).

It is the contention of this chapter that the globalisation thesis is overstated. Such a view gains some credibility from the fact that another group of analysts sees the world moving in the opposite direction. Indeed, the disintegration of Yugoslavia and the Soviet Union, the threatened break-up of a number of African states, the intensification of ethnic regionalism (in Quebec, Scotland, Wales, northern versus southern Italy, among the Bretons, Corsicans, Catalans, Basques) suggest that the forces of localism and tradition are still very vibrant. And there are increased efforts to develop effective mechanisms of economic co-ordination at local levels of society. Moreover, there is a rich and vast complementary literature which has emphasised the extremely important role of regional economies and their co-ordinating mechanisms for the production of high-quality products in the contemporary world (Herrigel, 1995; Pyke and Sengenberger, 1992; Pyke *et al.*, 1990; Sabel and Zeitlin, 1985; Schmitter, 1997). In the meantime, within national states, there are social systems of production, parts of which also play an important role in co-ordinating economic activity at the level of total societies. Social systems of production are historically shaped, are not converging or adapting toward one best system, and are resistant to the forces of globalisation.

In sum, the contemporary world is far more complex than many observers recognise. Economic co-ordination is occurring at multiple levels, and no single level is decisive in shaping the world in which we live. Moreover, the levels are nested and linked with each other. One of the great challenges of our time is to comprehend the nature of this nestedness and the linkages which exist among the four levels mentioned above. Clearly, the idea that societies are converging toward one single set of practices brought about by the forces of globalisation is both *ahistorical* and overly simplistic.

While the world is changing rapidly, it changes in a very path-dependent way. Of course, path dependency does not imply historical determinism, but it does suggest that: (1) each society has its own past, present and future; (2) all roads do not lead to the same destination or end point; and (3) the historical paths taken by societies in their social development lead to enormous variability (David, 1988; Arthur, 1988a, 1988b; Håkansson and Lundgren, 1997). The directions of the future of particular societies are very much influenced by the directions set in their past. As Joseph Schumpeter observed (1983: 9), economic systems do not change capriciously or simply as a result of new technological forces but at all times in ways connected 'with the preceding state of affairs'. It is true that there are moments of great change, but even these are linked with previous paths. And diverse paths of social development of historical variation place enormous constraints on the capacity of mechanisms to be effective in co-ordinating all economic activity at the global level. The financial markets are only a small part of the global economy, and even if there is a globalisation of the financial markets, economic co-ordination of the rest of the global economy is much more complex. It is the historical diversity of path-dependent ways that helps account for the fact that despite the enormous activity taking place in the globalisation of the financial markets, systems and institutions which are societally specific are not withering away but instead continue to reflect much social diversity throughout the world (Whitley, 1992a, 1992b; Crouch and Streeck, 1996). One way of capturing this social diversity is to focus on societies' social systems of production.

Social systems of production

A social system of production is the way that the following institutions or structures of a country or a region are integrated into a social configuration: the industrial relations system; the system of training of workers and managers; the internal structure of corporate firms; the structured relationships among firms in the same industry on the one hand, and on the other, firms' relationships with their suppliers and customers; the financial markets of a society; the conceptions of fairness and justice held by capital and labour; the structure of the state and its policies; and a society's idiosyncratic customs and traditions as well as norms, moral principles, rules, laws and recipes for action. All these institutions, organisations and social values tend to cohere with each other, although they vary in the degree to which they are tightly coupled with each other into a full-fledged system. While each of these components has some autonomy and may have some goals that are contradictory to the goals of other institutions with which it is integrated, an institutional logic in each society leads institutions to coalesce into a complex social configuration (Hollingsworth, 1991a, 1991b). This occurs because the institutions are embedded in a culture in which their logics are symbolically grounded, organisationally structured, technically and materially constrained and politically defended. The institutional configuration usually exhibits some degree of adaptability to new challenges, but continues to evolve within an existing style. But under new circumstances or unprecedented disturbances, these institutional configurations are exposed to sharp historical limits as to what they may or may not do (Schumpeter, 1983; David, 1988; Arthur, 1988a, 1988b; Håkansson and Lundgren, 1997).

Why do all of these different institutions coalesce into a complex social configuration, which is labelled here as a social system of production? The literature suggests two contrasting interpretations. Part of the answer – indeed a controversial one – is that these institutions are functionally determined by the requirements of the practice of capitalism in each time and place (Habermas, 1975). Another explanation emphasises the genesis of the actual configuration, via a trial and error process, according to which the survival of firms, regions or countries is the outcome of complex evolutionary mechanisms (Maynard-Smith, 1982; Nelson and Winter, 1982). However, the problem is even more complex. Markets and other mechanisms for co-ordinating relationships among economic actors place constraints on the means and ends of economic activity to be achieved in any society. The other co-ordinating mechanisms include different kinds of hierarchies, various types of networks and associations (for example, trade unions, employers and business artisan associations; see Hollingsworth and Lindberg, 1985; Campbell *et al.*, 1991). These various co-ordinating mechanisms provide actors with vocabularies and logics for pursuing their goals, for defining what is valued, and for shaping the norms and rules by which they abide. In short, in contrast to the logic of the neoclassical paradigm, the argument here is that economic co-ordinating mechanisms place severe constraints on the definition of needs, preferences and choices of economic actors. Whereas the neoclassical paradigm assumes that individuals and firms are sovereign, this chapter is based on the assumption that firms are influenced by the hold that institutions have on individual decision making (Campbell *et al.*, 1991; Etzioni, 1988; Streeck and Schmitter, 1985; Hollingsworth *et al.*, 1994; Hollingsworth and Boyer, 1997; Magnusson and Ottosson, 1997; North, 1990).

Standard neoclassical economic theory has tended to downplay the role of production and consequently of firms. Even the transaction cost theorists who are concerned with analysing the firm as a co-ordinating mechanism have been relatively unconcerned with the various components of a social system of production. Indeed, as long as there was widespread optimism about the efficacy of Keynesian economics, there was relatively little concern among neoclassical economists with the supply side of the economy. Even in the opinion of most Keynesians, a group of experts should ideally be able to shape the size of aggregate demand while the supply side of the economy would be left to the two minimalist institutions of neoclassical economics – markets and managerial hierarchies. For more than two decades, however, it has become increasingly obvious that some of the most competitive and successful patterns of industrial output and industrial production in capitalist economies do not derive from the neoclassical prescription of unregulated markets and corporate hierarchies complemented by a neo-liberal democratic state. Indeed, empirical evidence has been growing for some years that certain highly successful production patterns require for their emergence and survival institutional arrangements and environments the very opposite of the prescriptions found in the neoclassical paradigm (see especially Streeck, 1991, but also Hollingsworth and Streeck, 1994). Thus if we are to understand the behaviour and performance of contemporary economies, social scientists have increasingly realised that concerns about social systems of production must be brought into the picture.

Production involves more than technology. It is for this reason that a number of social scientists have an increasing concern with social systems of production. The same equipment is frequently operated quite differently in the same sectors in different countries, even when firms are competing in the same market (Hollingsworth *et al.*, 1994; Maurice *et al.*, 1980; Sorge, 1989; Sorge and Streeck, 1988). Variations in production and process technologies are influenced, partly, by variations in the social environments in which they are embedded. In other words, firms are embedded into complex environments, which among other things place constraints on their behaviour. Thus, a social system of production is of major importance in understanding the behaviour and performance of an economy. How the state and other co-ordinating mechanisms (for example, markets, networks, private hierarchies, associations) coalesce and are related to particular social systems of production are important determinants of economic performance.

During the past 60 or 70 years there have been several broad types of social systems of production in the histories of Western Europe, North America and Japan. One system, labelled in the literature as a Fordist or a mass standardised social system of production, tended to produce highly standardised goods on a large scale with highly specialised equipment, operated by semiskilled workers. In contrast to Fordist production systems, there have been various types of flexible social systems of production, each tending to produce a wide array of products in response to different consumer demands, supported by a skilled workforce with the capability of shifting from one job to another within a firm.

Because both standardised and flexible social systems of production are ideal types, it is important to emphasise that, for analytical purposes, each is subject to the usual strengths and weaknesses of ideal types. They are not meant to be descriptive statements about specific firms, industrial sectors or individual firms at specific periods of time. Rather, they are heuristic devices to sensitise us to possible interrelationships that might exist among a broad set of variables or social categories. Neither type ever existed in a pure form in space or time. Even where a standardised mass social system of production was the dominant paradigm, there were always firms, or even entire industries, that were organised on opposite principles. The two organising principles were complementary: mass standardised production tended to respond to the stable component of demand, while batch or medium-size production systems tended to cope with the variable part of the same demand. So the coexisting forms of production broadly shared the same short-run flexibility and long-run performance. It is not uncommon for different components of varying social systems of production to exist simultaneously in a particular country (Herrigel, 1995). For example, standardised social systems of production have always required customised machines or some form of flexible production. And flexible social systems of production have required standardised equipment and therefore some standardised production processes. In other words, the customisation of products has long been based on the standardised production of component parts and equipment. A number of scholars (Hirst and Zeitlin, 1990; Pollert, 1991; Sabel, 1991; Zeitlin, 1997) have made the important point that firms frequently engage in hybrid forms of production, producing both long and short runs of particular products, sometimes engaging in both flexible and standardised production, but that these hybrid type firms are usually embedded in a dominant type of social system of production.

Of course, flexible systems of production predate Fordist systems of production. Sabel and Zeitlin (1985), as well as others (Hounshell, 1984; Zeitlin, 1992), have demonstrated that flexible social systems of production existed in a number of nineteenth-century industrial districts of Europe and Great Britain, from Lyon to Sheffield, as well as in parts of the United States. Though flexible systems of production both pre- and post-date Fordist, mass standardised systems of production, we must recognise that in recent years flexible social systems of production have become further differentiated into various subtypes. In the literature, one is labelled the flexible specialisation system of production (FSP) and another is labelled the diversified quality mass system of production (DQMP) (Aoki, 1988; Boyer and Coriat, 1986; Hirst and Zeitlin, 1990; Streeck, 1991). Originally, these models emerged from an analysis of local structural conditions; they were mainly concerned with co-ordination among actors and were less concerned with technology or innovation. For example, industrial districts with flexible systems of production existed long before the development of recent information technologies (Sabel and Zeitlin, 1985). On the other hand, the adoption of new, microelectronic production technology has increased the number of areas of the world that have social systems of flexible production (for example, either FSP or DQMP). Therefore, the existing institutions are filtering the emergence and diffusion of new technologies, and conversely, over the long run, some radical technological innovations seem to call for epochal changes in institutions. The success and ultimate outcome of these changes is quite uncertain.

In any case, the high flexibility of microelectronic equipment and the speed with which it can be shifted to a variety of products have permitted previous mass producers to engage in customised quality production and producers with only small batches of specific items to shift to larger batches of production. Thus, there has been a restructuring of two different trajectories of production: craft producers have been able to extend their production volume without sacrificing their high quality standards and customisation, and many mass producers have had the capacity to upgrade their product design and quality and thus to reduce the pressures of price competition and shrinking mass markets (Sorge and Streeck, 1988).

There was no single and unique pattern of industrialisation. Forms of flexible specialisation existed in the United States during the nineteenth century, for example in the textile industry (Scranton, 1984). As dominant forms of production, however, they were defeated by standardised mass production, at least in the United States but not everywhere, especially in Germany and Italy (Herrigel, 1995; Piore and Sabel, 1984; Sabel and Zeitlin, 1985). This was because the social environments in which production was embedded varied greatly from society to society.

Thus, in our own day, there are both similarities and differences between the social system of FSP and the social system of DQMP. Rather than viewing these two perspectives as competing or conflictual, it is best to see them as complementary (Elam, 1992; Sorge, 1989; Sorge and Streeck, 1988). In contrast with social systems of standardised mass production, both FSP and DQMP require workforces with broad levels of skills, that is to say employees who have 'learned to learn' about new technologies and who can work closely and co-operatively with other employees and management. Moreover, these systems tend to require that firms develop long-term stable relations with their suppliers and customers.

Social systems of mass production have performed best when firms serve large and stable product markets, and have products and process technologies that are relatively stable or have a low level of technological innovation (Chandler, 1962, 1977, 1990). However, technological complexity and the speed of technical change are not to be confused. For example, the car industry used to implement rather simple components but nevertheless exhibited complex co-ordination problems (Tolliday and Zeitlin, 1991). Markets, corporate hierarchies and inegalitarian and short-lived networks are the dominant forms of co-ordination in social systems of mass production. On the other hand, social systems of flexible specialisation and diversified quality mass production tend to function more effectively when firms are responding to small market niches with product markets that are unstable and volatile (the Italian garment industry) or whose product and process technologies change rapidly (microelectronics, biotechnologies) and are quite complex (aircraft industry, luxury cars). For firms to perform well under these circumstances, they require different forms of co-ordination from those that are most effective for social systems of mass standardised production.

Markets and hierarchies as co-ordinating mechanisms can work effectively in mass standardised systems of production even if the transacting actors are embedded in an impoverished institutional environment – one in which such collective forms of coordination as associations and promotional networks are poorly developed (Hollingsworth, 1991a, 1991b). But social systems of flexible specialisation and diversified quality mass production work best when transacting actors are embedded in an institutional environment in which collective forms of co-ordination are highly developed. Broadly speaking, both of these social systems of production are basically incompatible with neo-liberal regimes of unregulated economies (Pyke and Sengenberger, 1992; Streeck, 1991). Nevertheless, the relative success of the Japanese transplants in the United States and Britain does challenge the view that these alternatives to typical Fordism cannot be implemented in countries with weakly developed collective forms of co-ordination (Boyer, 1991; Florida and Kenney, 1991; Kenney and Florida, 1988, 1993; Oliver and Wilkinson, 1988). The long-term success of flexible specialisation and diversified quality mass social systems of production requires a high degree of trust and cooperation among economic actors – between workers and managers within firms and between firms on the one hand and their suppliers and customers on the other (Boyer and Orlean, 1991; Hollingsworth, 1991a, 1991b). This can be organised in some localities with a strong tradition of providing the collective goods of trust and co-operation (examples are the German co-operative partnership between labour and management and the Italian industrial districts). Firms operating in isolation from such collective goods may provide local examples of flexible production or diversified quality mass production, at least in the short run (for example, Japanese transplants in the United States and the Britain). But in the long run, successful firms that are involved in flexible social systems of production must engage in co-operative behaviour with suppliers, competitors and employees far in excess of what is needed for markets and hierarchies to function effectively and in excess of what single firms can develop for themselves (Streeck, 1991; Hollingsworth and Streeck, 1994). But in order to understand why these different types of production exist, it is important to understand the different social environments in which they are embedded and the different historical traditions from which they have evolved.

Multiple spatial levels of co-ordination

In previous work, Hollingsworth *et al.* (1994) were primarily concerned with economic co-ordination at the sectoral level, both within and across countries. Here, the concern is much more with variations in forms of co-ordination and social systems of production within particular spatial-territorial areas. More specifically, the concern is with understanding the interaction of spatially based forms of coordination with social systems of production. Economic coordination varies by territory, for social institutions are historically rooted in local, regional, national or even transnational political communities with their shared beliefs, experiences and traditions.

By sub-national region, is meant a territorial area with little or no state sovereignty over its borders. It is in particular regions within countries where the social systems of flexible specialisation have been located. Obviously, the development of regional economies does not necessarily lead to social systems of flexible specialisation. The concern here is with the existence of regional economies having a high concentration of small firms that are integrated into a social system of flexible production, a subject about which Sabel and Zeitlin have written both insightfully and extensively (Sabel and Zeitlin, 1985; Zeitlin, 1992). Historically, when the demand for products was differentiated and diverse, different forms of production have existed from those in use when demand has been more stable and homogeneous. In general, the more stable the demand and the less frequent the change in technology, the more firms have found it advantageous to organise production in large vertically integrated firms and to reap economies of scale by producing standardised products and extending the market. Historically, such a process tended to justify the large investment in single-purpose machines operated by relatively low-skilled workers (Chandler, 1962, 1977, 1990). But when demand has been differentiated, markets have been volatile, and/or technology has changed rapidly, then firms have chosen flexible strategies – flexible machines, labour and/or marketing. More specialised firms must constantly innovate. Being relatively small, however, they require a host of common services that individual firms lack the capacity to provide: sophisticated training facilities in order to develop a highly skilled labour force, a continuing supply of credit, and complex marketing capacity. In response to these needs, producers in some areas have engaged with other firms – sometimes competitors, sometimes firms in complementary industries – to produce collective goods. The collective activities have historically varied, but the most common have been co-operative training institutes and co-operative marketing facilities (for example, to forecast fashion trends, to monitor foreign technical standards, to establish co-operative sales facilities, local trademarks). Over time and across industries, the co-operative mechanisms for this kind of co-ordination have varied, but without artisan, employer and/or worker associations, this form of collaboration and co-operation has failed. In sum, for a social system of flexible production to survive, firms must be integrated into collective institutions which can balance co-operation and competition (Zeitlin, 1992).

Where social systems of flexible production are more developed, the boundaries between firms and their environment are extremely blurred, so much so that such firms are very reluctant to move from one region to another. Thus, local governments in Sardinia and Sicily have a limited capacity to attract firms from Prato even by offering free land, cheap labour and low taxes because the Prato firms are embedded in all kinds of collective institutions that provide a variety of world-class inputs. The underlying social conditions that facilitate the development of such social systems of production vary. Sometimes that development has emerged from a population viewing itself as a religious minority while elsewhere it has emerged from a common ethnic base, common craft pride, common forms of professionalisation or common political affiliation. Without some forms of common social bonds, it has historically been difficult to develop the collective institutions which are prerequisites for social systems of flexible production, though as Sabel (1992) has argued, common social bonds are not a necessary condition for an emergence of such a system (also see Zeitlin, 1992).

Examples in the contemporary world of regions with social systems of flexible production include Jutland in western Denmark, the Småland region in southern Sweden, and areas in the central and north-eastern parts of Italy. Each of these districts produces highly specialised products. For example, Bologna produces machine tools and small appliances, while Tuscan and Venetian towns manufacture textiles and footwear. Whether in the contemporary world or in the nineteenth century, social systems of flexibly specialised production involved an integration of petty entrepreneurship, family-based small-scale artisan firms and/or municipalism. While flexibly specialised systems of production are pursued in a variety of institutionalised forms, there are limits to their ranges of variation (Grabher, 1993; Pollert, 1991; Sabel, 1992). Clearly, unregulated markets do not provide adequate incentives for the survival of flexible social systems of production. Cooperation among competing producers, a minimum of conflict between employers and their employees, and long-term stable relations with suppliers and customers are prerequisites for the survival of flexible production systems.

Occasionally, the national state has been a modest actor in facilitating the emergence and persistence of flexible specialised production systems, but more frequently regional and local governmental authorities have promoted this form of social system, as with various German *Länder* or Italian local authorities. For example, the state has often facilitated the development of training institutes for labour, and provided low-cost loans as well as market and export information. However, the state alone has rarely been capable of promoting and developing the institutions necessary for the emergence of a flexible social production system.

Thus far, countries such as the United States and Britain have been deficient in the communitarian infrastructure necessary for the emergence of institutions with the capability of generating the high levels of trust among competing economic actors essential for successful social systems of production. Nevertheless, this is not absolutely fatal, since public authorities can use existing institutions to mimic or help in implementing flexible systems of production. Social systems of diversified quality mass production have certain similarities with those of flexible specialisation. Both social systems of production are embedded in distinctive environments and are not easily imitated by other societies. But whereas firms with a high degree of flexible specialisation tend to be small artisanal firms located in modest-sized regions – though there are exceptions – the key to understanding diversified quality mass production is the increased flexibility of large firms. New technology has enabled large firms to make their production functions more flexible and to reduce the batch size of specialised products inside large systems of production. Whereas social systems of flexible specialisation engage in diversified low-volume production and emphasise economies of scope, diversified quality mass social systems of production combine economies of both scope and scale and are thus able to emphasise quality differentiated mass production. In other words, scale is one of the major variables differentiating diversified quality mass production from flexible specialised production systems. Significantly, the territorial space in which firms are embedded also differs. In contrast to flexible specialisation social systems of production, diversified quality mass social production systems are generally either embedded in much larger regions or are more coterminous with an entire nation-state (Mueller and Loveridge, 1995). Nevertheless, wherever flexible social systems of production survive, whether they are systems with small firms engaged in flexible production or systems with larger firms engaged in diversified quality mass production, they are tightly integrated with the society's business associations and labour unions, the industrial relations system, the capital markets and the systems of training for both labour and management of an industrial district.

It is difficult to disentangle what differences between flexible specialisation systems of production and diversified quality mass production are related to their inner and theoretical properties and what parts of their systems derive from the fact that they have evolved in distinctive regions or nations with idiosyncratic institutional configurations. A priori, mass production presupposes institutions that transcend a region in a particular nation-state: a vast transportation system and other kinds of infrastructure, large quantities of capital, macroeconomic stabilisation in order to prevent large and unexpected economic fluctuations, and so on. These factors suggest the need for a host of *national* institutions. Historical analyses and international comparisons demonstrate that diversified quality mass production systems are *actually* embedded in national socio-political structures, while flexible specialisation systems can be embedded in sub-national socio-political structures.

Diversified quality mass social systems of production are unlikely to exist unless they are embedded in national socio-political structures that are democratic corporatist in nature. Examples of contemporary societies with relatively strong neo-corporatist institutional arrangements, and hence strong diversified quality mass forms of social production, were Germany and Sweden of the 1980s. Both had highly developed systems of trade unions and business associations that were embedded in an ideology of partnership, mitigating intense class conflict, and emphasising a careful balancing of conflict with co-operation among competing firms. For students of democratic corporatism, Japan poses a problematic case. Japan, like most democratic corporatist societies, has both peak associations of business and, at the level of the firm, a strong ideology of social partnership between labour and capital. But there is an absence of well-organised labour unions at the level of the nation-state. Nevertheless, the strong emphasis on social partnerships that exists in Japan leads many scholars to classify it as a democratic corporatist society. Therefore, it is understandable that Japan also has a social system of diversified quality mass production (Pempel and Tsunekawa, 1979; Schmitter and Lehmbruch, 1979).

How do we explain the absence of a diversified quality mass system of production in the United States? Indeed, why did its opposite, a system of mass standardised production, excel there and in many respects persist? In general, the larger the spatial-territorial area in which a social system of production exists, the larger the number of parties and interests that must be involved in efforts to develop national forms of collective co-ordination (for example, labour unions, business associations). Thus, a country as large as the United States, in contrast with smaller democracies, has a very complex economy (for example, large numbers of industrial sectors), as well as regions with uneven levels of development and racial, religious and ethnic diversity. With so much heterogeneity of interests, it has historically been more difficult to develop highly institutionalised collective forms of economic co-ordination. When these society-wide collective forms of co-ordination are either absent or weak, markets and corporate hierarchies are more prominent as forms of co-ordination, and as a result Fordist systems of production are more likely to occur (Hollingsworth, 1991a, 1991b). Nevertheless, a variety of co-operative ventures may exist among firms even in an environment that is weak in highly institutionalised forms of collective behaviour. Hence, in the United States there are among business firms numerous joint ventures, cross-licensing agreements, franchises and various forms of strategic alliances (Porter, 1986, 1990). Thus in the entertainment, biotechnology, publishing, microelectronics or software industries, there is a great deal of networking as a form of economic co-ordination (Powell, 1990).

To some observers, this kind of collaboration resembles the type of industrial districts in which flexible forms of social production flourish, but most of these forms of networking are not embedded in the same kind of rich institutional environment which Sabel, Zeitlin and others have discussed in their analyses of industrial districts. In most societies, geographical concentrations of related industries facilitate some degree of co-operation and trust, but these are generally developed quite modestly unless they are accompanied by an environment in which firms have membership in highly developed organisations of a collective nature.

Co-ordination at levels beyond the nation-state

At the level beyond the nation-state, whether at the global or at the multinational regional level such as the European Union, collective forms of co-ordination, such as associations and unions, are either weakly developed or non-existent (Coleman, 1997; Grant, 1997; Schneiberg and Hollingsworth, 1990). Moreover, the power of states as co-ordinating actors is weak at the transnational level. However, regardless of the spatial-territorial location, whether at the sub-national region, the nation-state or the transnational level, there is a need for some institutional arrangement to co-ordinate relations among economic actors. Indeed, irrespective of the territorial level at which economic co-ordination is to occur, economic actors confront many of the same problems: the issues of promoting efficiency among transacting partners, reducing macroeconomic instabilities, minimising distributional conflicts, reducing conflicts and resolving disputes, and monitoring compliance in regard to domestic and/or international norms and rules (Campbell *et al.*, 1991: ch. 1).

Just as economic co-ordination in domestic economies is carried out by different types of institutional arrangements, this is also true at the transnational level. At the lowest level of control, the market is the most prominent form of co-ordinating transactions among unrelated firms. At a higher level of control, there may be co-ordination through hierarchies such as transnational corporations or collective forms of co-ordination such as international trade associations or international cartels. Of course, co-ordination at the global level may also involve actions by nation-states, and their form of co-ordination may also vary from low control (for example, bilateral agreements) to high control structures (supranational government, colonial empires). International regimes are a form of middle-level control among states, somewhat analogous to international cartels or trade associations among unrelated firms (Eden and Hampson, 1997).

How do international regimes emerge and persist over decades? For some authors (Kennedy, 1987), the historical record suggests that a hegemonic power has been necessary for either the establishment or the persistence of international regimes. But when a hegemonic power is decaying without any evident successor, the stability of the international system is at stake. The 1920s provide an example of such a collapse (Kindleberger, 1978). Other authors argue that because international regimes provide public goods and lower transaction costs among their members, it is in the rational self-interest of states to abide by the rules and norms of regimes even if there is no hegemony to enforce them (Keohane, 1984; Snidal, 1985, 1991; Eden and Hampson, 1997). Of course, this argument assumes a 'pure' co-ordination problem and the absence of any conflict of interests. If, on the contrary, the configuration of the system is close to a Prisoners' Dilemma problem, the rational strategy of each nation will not lead to the emergence of co-operation. Conflict among international actors might then become severe, since a great deal of economic co-ordination takes place by markets and hierarchies at the global level.

Ultimately, it is the existence of international regimes that institutionalise the norms and rules that allows economic actors to carry out most effectively their transactions at a global level. Just as there are institutional arrangements that attempt to reduce transaction costs within nation-states, there are also international regimes, a major goal of whose is to reduce transaction costs. For example, the World International Patent Organisation registers domestic patents and copyrights internationally and attempts to protect these forms of property rights at the international level, an activity which greatly reduces transaction costs in international trading. Regimes that provide specialised trading privileges for members also have the effect of reducing transaction costs. Examples include GATT, the European Union structure and NAFTA.

Other regimes have been established to cushion and to control the effects of autonomous macroeconomic policies by individual states. Some of the institutional arrangements created to bring this about include the International Monetary Fund, the World Bank, the Bank of International Settlements, the Group of Seven and the European Monetary System (EMS). Finally, states attempt to minimise distributional conflicts with the following regimes: GATT with its preferences to less developed countries, the World Bank and the IMF.

Obviously the effectiveness of these regimes in lowering transaction costs, promoting macroeconomic stability and minimising distributional conflicts varies from time to time and from one institutional arrangement to another. However, as regimes acquire greater effectiveness in co-ordinating economic activity at the supranational level, there will be some alteration of co-ordinating mechanisms at the level of the nation-state. Hence, the emergence of a common European internal market is expected to lead to some kind of deregulation of various European economies, providing for 'regime shopping' by mobile capital and to a lesser extent by labour as national borders are weakened or abolished. Throughout the European Union there may well emerge political institutional arrangements with greater pluralism, institutional fragmentation, deregulation and voluntarism – in short, socio-economic-political forms of co-ordination that have many similarities to the neo-liberal type of institutions that characterise the political economy of the United States. There is increasing concern that, as the various European societies become integrated into the European Union, there will be an undermining of the essential institutional prerequisites of the type of bargained, co-operative political economy which has facilitated the development of such social systems of production as diversified quality mass production in Germany or flexible specialisation in Italy. Of course, it remains to be seen how much the emergence of a stable regime at the level of the European Union can erode local cultures, traditions and power structures on which flexible social systems of production are built. But even to pose the problem is to suggest that changes in co-ordination at one spatial-territorial location may alter the forms of co-ordination and social systems of production in place at other spatial-territorial locations.

Convergence or divergence among social systems of production

Discussions about convergence and divergence are still very much alive in the social science community. For example, some of the industrial organisational literature argues that firms competing in the same product markets tend to become similar in their structure and behaviour, or else they disappear. In other words, the convergence thesis assumes that there is one best solution for organising labour, raw materials and capital in order to manufacture and distribute goods. Producers, processors and distributors must at least emulate if not surpass their most efficient competitors in order to survive. Every time a group of innovators discovers a new but highly efficient method of increasing output, their competitors are likely to follow. Thus competition and survival involve discovering and implementing the best techniques and strategies (Chandler, 1962, 1977).

However, the argument for such a convergence is far from convincing (Whitley and Kristensen, 1997). The key to understanding the degree to which the economic performance of countries will converge is influenced very much by the extent to which they have similar social systems of production. Because the social systems of production of modern societies are complex configurations of numerous institutional sectors, however, it is problematic that they can diffuse across countries, except over an extraordinarily long period of time. In fact, given the strong complementarities and syncretic flavour of any national system of innovation (Nelson, 1993), it would be surprising to observe an easy catching up by followers: the structural advantage taken by a leading country or industry initially prevents an easy imitation. Followers, while trying to imitate, usually encounter unexpected problems, which trigger a series of induced adaptations or even innovations that may finally deliver a different model, building on their own national specificities. When France and Germany tried to follow the first British Industrial Revolution, both countries moved toward quite different new models (Gerschenkron, 1962). Similarly, after World War II, many Japanese manufacturers wanted to follow American mass production practices, but got, quite unintentionally, diversified quality mass production (Ohno, 1989).

Not only are different co-ordinating mechanisms associated with different social systems of production, but also different co-ordinating mechanisms and different social systems of production result in different types of economic performance. Hence, as long as countries vary in the type of co-ordinating mechanisms and social systems of production that are dominant in their economies, there are serious constraints on the degree to which they can converge in their economic performance. Different social systems of production tend to maximise in a more or less explicit manner different performance criteria, usually mixed considerations about static and dynamic efficiency, profit, security, social peace and economic and/or political power. In short, in contrast to the implications of neoclassical economic theory, in real world economies there are no universal standards all economically rational actors attempt to maximise. Economic history provides numerous examples of how a variety of principles of rationality are implemented in different societies.

Whether or not a social system of production can sustain its particular performance standards depends not only on its intrinsic economic 'rationality', but also on where it fits into a larger system. If a particular social system of production is immune from the competition of an alternative system, survival can be long-lasting. But if different social systems of production, with diverging criteria of good economic performance, meet in the world arena, the arbitrariness of nationally imposed constructed performance standards may be superseded by alternative performance criteria as a result of international competitiveness.

As Wallerstein (1995) and others (Chase-Dunn, 1989) have demonstrated, the world economy is also socially constructed, just as are national economies. Even if different social systems of production are competing in the international arena, it is not always possible to determine which is more competitively effective at any moment in time. Hegemonic nation-states can shape, *within the short run*, the rules of trade that favour their industrial sectors and firms. But the history of hegemonic powers suggests that in the longer run, social systems of production, sustained largely by military and political power, eventually give way to more dynamic and competitive social systems of production (Gilpin, 1987; Kennedy, 1987; Keohane, 1984). In our own day, as nation-states are increasingly integrated into a world economy, economic competition is likely to turn into competition over social systems of production. As a country's social system of production loses its international competitive advantage, its share of world output decreases, even if it is a hegemonic power. Such a country will slowly experience deindustrialisation and/or will attempt to restructure its institutional arrangements and to readjust its performance preferences. But such a restructuring generally calls for a major redistribution of power within a society. Largely for this reason, societies have historically had limited capacity to construct a social system of production in the image of their major competitors.

But firms in lagging economies do attempt to mimic some of the management styles and work practices of their more successful competitors. We observed this in both the UK and the United States during the 1980s, where there emerged the concept of 'the internationalisation of Japanese business' (Trevor, 1987). However, this phenomenon was grossly exaggerated. Many who contended that there was an emerging Japanisation of the world economy had not confronted the problem of what is distinctively Japanese. True, some Japanese practices were exported elsewhere. But much of our scholarship on Japanese firms in foreign settings demonstrates that they pragmatically adapt to foreign conditions rather than duplicate Japanese practices. As Levine and Ohtsu (1991) observe, Japanese companies in foreign settings generally find that they must contend with the foreign culture as well as the laws and rules of alien governments, foreign unions and employers, all of which are at great variance with Japanese institutions. Of course, one may point to the joint venture which developed between Toyota and General Motors in Fremont, California, as well as the cases of Honda and Nissan in the United States, as examples in which a number of Japanese management practices appear to have diffused to the American setting. But close examination of even these more extreme cases demonstrates a hybridisation of Japanese and American practices. Nevertheless, this kind of hybridisation did result in much more flexible patterns of production than were previously observed in the American automobile industry.

This, of course, raises the larger issue of joint ventures and strategic alliances taking place in advanced capitalist societies. In an era when the rate of technological change was relatively low and there were homogeneous demands for a particular product, production processes in an industry were relatively standardised, and production runs were quite long, vertical integration was an appropriate strategy for firms that faced high uncertainties and small numbers in their interdependent relationships with other firms. However, when technology changes very rapidly and the costs of technology are very high, firms are less inclined to engage in vertical integration, and joint ventures and strategic alliances become more frequent, particularly among firms in different societies. Of course, the motives for this form of co-ordination are varied: the search for economies of scale, the need for market access, the sharing of risks, the need to have access to technology, and the need to pool know-how if no one firm has the capability to achieve its goals. Such projects have occurred in a variety of sectors, but especially in the pharmaceutical, computer, aerospace, nuclear energy, electronics and automobile industries. Is the increasing frequency of this form of coordination leading to the convergence of national economies?

Undoubtedly, the increased frequency of joint ventures and strategic alliances does lead to some convergence in certain management styles and work practices among co-operating partners. However, the diffusion of these practices does not bring about convergence in social systems of production. Before World War II, foreign firms attempted to borrow certain principles of scientific management that had become widespread in the United States, but in general the American practices were greatly modified when implemented. Moreover, in making these modifications, foreign actors did so within the developmental trajectory of their own social systems of production. Similarly in our own day, selected principles of Japanese management styles and work practices are diffused to other countries, but they are selectively integrated into local institutional arrangements.

Each country's social system of production is a configuration of a host of institutional arrangements. Each system is constantly changing and is open to influence from other systems. And indeed many technologies and practices diffuse from one society to another, but the direction of change is constrained by the existing social system of production. Thus, the same technology may exist in numerous countries, but how it is employed varies from one institutional configuration to another.

One recent comparative study (Hollingsworth *et al.*, 1994) has demonstrated that, across countries, clusters of industries develop along particular trajectories, each having its distinct microeconomic dynamics within which markets, corporate hierarchies, networks, associations and governments operate. Because skills, management techniques and modes of governance are embedded in distinctive social systems of production, they do not easily diffuse from one nation to another. As a result, variation across countries in social systems of production remains substantial, even if there is convergence at the global level in how selected industries (for example, chemicals, oil, large-scale aircraft, and so on) are co-ordinated.

This variation remains substantial for there have been great differences in the path dependencies of countries. For more than a century, the German economy had an emerging diversified quality system of production (Herrigel, 1995), whereas since the 1950s, the Japanese have hybridised mass production along with diversified quality production. In both countries, specific institutional arrangements allowed for the distinctiveness of their particular social system of production. In contrast, the United States has been very much constrained by its earlier Fordist mass production system and its 'short-termism' under the influence of its distinctive financial markets, weak unions and business associations, norms, rules and recipes for action.

A double shift in modes of coordination

Economic co-ordination within societies takes place within social systems of production which evolve in directions which are quite path dependent. Because of the path dependency of societal evolution, variation remains quite distinctive among social systems of production throughout the globe. Even so there are common changes that are taking place within most social systems of production, trends which are in response to changes in the global economy. The intensification of foreign competition, the increasing sophistication of financial markets, the diffusion of a market ideology across the globe, and the decline of autonomy of state structures are bringing about marked changes in particular social systems of production. On the one hand, there is some movement toward an internationalisation of the economy with the emergence of transnational rules of the game (for example, the Maastricht Treaty, NAFTA, GATT), thus narrowing the opportunity for manoeuvre by nation-states. At the same time, there are shifts to more localised or regional arrangements, particularly in regard to some manufacturing sectors. These two movements suggest a double shift in terms of co-ordination from the nation-state to the transnational regional and/or global level on the one hand, and on the other to sub-national regional levels.

While the management of money continues to be an important function of the nation-state, national states have nevertheless experienced a considerably diminished capacity to conduct this activity. For example, the stabilisation of exchange rates within the European Monetary System has reduced the ability of members of the European Union to use interest rates to solve problems. In the meantime, some activities are easier to carry out at the regional than at the national level. Training and education programmes, research and development policies, strategies involving international marketing tend to be more efficient when conducted at the regional or local level. As a result, nation-states are subjected to a double weakening by sub-national regionalisation on the one hand and on the other by a kind of supranationalisation. Increasingly, major institutions of co-ordination are intertwined at all levels of the world – at the sub-national region, the nation-state, the transnational region and the global level. As a result, no single authority has the power to monitor and to regulate all economic activity in such a complex system and, as a result, coherence in economic co-ordination is becoming increasingly difficult.

More and more, the various functions of society do not occur at the same level. Co-ordination of money and finance are increasingly regulated at levels beyond the nation-state, whereas taxation, welfare functions and training take place within national boundaries. The rhetoric of business firms expresses preferences for market freedom, while the rhetoric of other groups targets the nation-state for protection against the effects of the logic of markets. Thus, the complexity of nestedness makes coherent economic policy and institutional planning more difficult than ever. Market-type forces tend to regulate exchange and interest rates at the global level, while nation-states struggle to address the welfare, health and training of their citizens.

As societies experience a shift from a national embeddedness of economic institutions to institutions nested within a multilevel global system, it has become increasingly difficult for societies to adjust their industrial relations systems, levels of skills and system of innovation to external forms of competition.

The institutional arrangements that at one time were somewhat congruent at the level of the nation-state are now diffused at multiple spatial levels. This means that impressive economic performance requires that economic actors be co-ordinated at all spatial areas simultaneously. A well-co-ordinated system must have actors intricately linked with other actors at all levels.

Even so, co-ordination of economic actors at the level of the nation-state has not completely disappeared. However, the future of social systems of production remains uncertain. So many contradictory forces are operating that it is quite difficult to gauge the direction of the global economy and its constituent parts. The future is very much open, but a long-term historical perspective suggests that taming the market has always been a more rewarding path for societies to take rather than myopically following it. Only short-term and marginal choices can be left to the market, whereas collective forms of co-ordination must be addressed by other forms of co-ordination. But as our institutions are increasingly nested in a world of sub-national regions, nation-states, transnational regions and global regimes, we are faced with the perplexing problem of how to govern ourselves. Clearly, one of the great challenges of our time is to create a new theory of governance for co-ordinating institutions nested in a world of unprecedented complexity, one in which sub-national regions, nation-states and continental and global regimes are all intricately linked.

Notes

Research for this chapter was supported by a generous grant from the Council for European Studies in New York City. The author also wishes to acknowledge the moral support and co-operation of Dr Ioannis Sinanoglou of the Council for European Studies. A number of colleagues have been involved with the author in a team project on the study of the social systems of production of individual countries, and the author wishes to acknowledge their intellectual stimulation for some of the ideas developed herein. They are Robert Boyer, Tom Burns, Jerald Hage, Hal Hansen, Christel Lane, Yoshitaka Okada, Wolfgang Streeck, Carlo Trigilia, Frans van Waarden, Richard Whitley and Jonathan Zeitlin. A number of the other themes developed in this chapter are the products of numerous conversations with Robert Boyer and Wolfgang Streeck. For elaboration of these, see Hollingsworth and Boyer (1997) and Hollingsworth and Streeck (1994). The author is also grateful to Steve Casper, Gerhard Lehmbruch, Philippe Schmitter, David Soskice, Bo Stråth, Sig Vitols and Erik Wright for their intellectual input to the agenda explored in this chapter. Finally, Ellen Jane Hollingsworth has contributed to all the ideas developed here.

1. This chapter was previously published as the following: J Rogers Hollingsworth. 1998. New perspectives on the spatial dimensions of economic co-ordination: tensions between globalisation and social systems of production. Review of International Political Economy. (5) 3:482–507.

Part Two

Public Sector Reform: Issues and Practices

6
Ethics and the New Public Management: Challenges and Alternatives

Geoffrey Wood

Since the 1960s, there has been a proliferation in the literature dealing with public sector ethics. This represents both a response to periodic corruption scandals in the advanced societies – such as Watergate – and the outright failure or near-failure of a significant number of newly independent states in the developing world. As Bowman *et al.* note, 'the tenets of public service ethics include value awareness, reasoning skills, law, and implementation strategies' (Bowman *et al.*, 2001). More contentious would be the relative value assigned to each of these variables, and the manner and extent to which the rights of the individual citizen can be reconciled with the need to promote equity and general social progress. Furthermore, public sector ethics encompass both internal (the manner in which the public sector is internally organised and managed) and external issues (the relationship between the public sector and wider society); the upholding of ethical conduct is about both the culture and values shared by public sector employees and the law. Public sector ethics are both about *what* the state should be doing to promote a 'good' society, and *how* the best standards of conduct may be promoted and upheld amongst employees.

Ethics and morals

As Singer (1995) emphasises, there is a central difference between ethics and morality. Ethics are universal; central to the human condition are notions of good and evil, and social taboos that are found in all societies. Morals are rules governing conduct specific to individual or sets of societies. This distinction is one of great importance in assessing the role and operations of the public sector; an over-emphasis on moral strictures is often deployed as a mask for great social injustice. For example, the former apartheid regime of South Africa combined institutionalised racism – and associated systemic brutality – with claims to be an upholder of 'Christian and Civilised Standards'. In order to buttress its (undeniably false) claims of moral superiority, all manner of erotic (but not, of course, violent) literature and goods were banned, along with sexual congress between races.

Again, in post-Thatcherist Britain, the gutter press tirelessly recycles tirades against the 'undeserving poor' (the 'benefit cheating' asylum seeker, the 'promiscuous' single mother, the 'feckless' homeless), which it is alleged, persistently engage in immoral conduct, which should be 'corrected' by the state, whilst consciously neglecting the great ethical outrages of the age. The latter would include the general worsening of the material conditions of the poor, wholesale environmental degradation, and unrestrained corporate greed. Ironically, such sweeping moral judgements are often themselves founded on appeals to the reader's own selfishness (asylum seekers are likely to 'steal your jobs' and 'spread disease', and single mothers 'clog up your social housing') exposing the ethical bankruptcy of such claims. Upholding genuinely 'good' conduct within, and ensuring positive outcome from the operations of the public sector is above all about ethics and, as such, of rather greater importance than tired contestations on the role and potential of the state as guardian of the morality of the day.

The state and the dilemma of the free-rider

Shared ethical values may be upheld by cross-societal rules and norms. Rules may be formal and embedded in law or informal and unwritten. The latter allow for greater flexibility and, enforced by social pressures, are relatively resource-effective. On the other hand, voluntary restraints face constant erosion through free-riding. As Tarantelli argues: '… in order to be induced to free-ride the actor must expect his or her behaviour not to influence the aggregate outcome (Tarantelli, 1986: 2). In other words, individuals are more likely to pursue their short-term interests to the detriment of society if they believe that the overall condition of society will not be adversely affected. However, free-riding enables the unprincipled to gain short-term advantages over those exercising greater restraint. In the long term, this may make it extremely difficult to uphold ethical conduct in specific areas. Thus, for example, a number of leading designer clothing brands – despite periodic protestations that the sector is committed to good practice – have been able to seize short term cost advantages by sub-contracting to factories in labour repressive third world states making widespread use of child labour. Again, firms tendering for outsourced public sector functions often base their competitiveness on the use of labour repressive policies (Moody, 1997). Whilst the bad publicity that might flow from such practices may have adverse consequences, this may easily be offset by the ability to cut prices; in the absence of any legal restraints, this may make the position of more principled firms untenable.

In addition to curbing free-rider behaviour, the state may uphold specific sets of rules founded on shared ethical values in order to minimise transaction costs. Exchange relationships are contingent on a basic degree of shared trust; should levels of trust fall, the costs of doing business (or of any other form of social exchange for that matter) are likely to be higher.

Finally, the state may institute measures to uphold ethical conduct in the overall interests of humanity, and indeed, the biosphere. Most states would claim to be in the business of upholding social progress; laws governing behaviour have done much to improve the human condition. Examples of such laws would include both prohibitions on child labour and restrictions on the production and use of CFCs, the latter representing a significant advance in undoing human damage to the atmosphere (Mellahi and Wood, 2003).

Ethical traditions and the public sphere

Utilitarianism

Utilitarianism holds that what is 'right' is invariably what is best for the bulk of society; utilitarians believe that intrinsic good – or the maximisation of 'utility' – is the maximisation of pleasure, of the quality of life of the majority (Lamsa, 1999). A number of contemporary utilitarian thinkers have broadened the latter to encompass the entire biosphere (Singer, 1995). The major limitation with utilitarianism is that 'maximising utility does not require judging people's values, only aggregating them' (Sandel, 1984: 2). Whilst this might suggest a democratic tolerance, the utilitarian calculus may allow an intolerant majority to impose their wishes on the rest of society, even if the outcome may be extremely repressive for a few. An aggregation of individual wishes, may for example, result in the state enforcing particular modes of moral conduct that may be extremely detrimental to vulnerable minorities. The pursuit of the general welfare defined in objectivist rather than ideal terms tends to discount the happiness of other individuals as an end in itself worth pursuing (Sandel, 1984).

Again, resting on the assumption that the practice of free market, rational-choice economics is likely to maximise the material wealth of the bulk of society, 'vulgar utilitarians' have argued that the untrammelled pursuit of the profit motive is likely to be to the general social good, and therefore commendable (see Evensky, 2001). This perspective holds that the state has little role in supporting, promoting or being associated with ethical conduct other than in terms of securing personal safety and protecting private property; rather, the operations of a free market will naturally lead to the best possible outcome for the bulk of society. Whilst such individuals claim to be in the intellectual tradition of Adam Smith, they demonstrate an ignorance of his works that can only be termed remarkable; Smith repeatedly stressed that:

> ... society cannot exist unless the laws of justice are tolerably observed, no social intercourse can take place among men who do not generally abstain from injury of another ... Man, it has to be said, has a natural love of society, and desires that the union of mankind be preserved for its own sake, and though he himself was to derive no benefit of it' (Smith, quoted in Bowie, 1991).

Rights and the overloaded state

The roots of the managerial revolution in the public sector lie in contestations over what the state should actually be doing; to many more conservative commentators, democratic pressures from below pose the threat that government might be overloaded by excess demands by vested interest groupings (Crouch, 1979). For example, Wagner suggested that a 'political trade' cycle had emerged; governments increasingly are forced to offer 'bribes' to gain popular support from key constituencies. This would result in a bloated and over-stretched public sector, with public expenditure increasing to unsustainable levels (Crouch, 1979). Similarly, Huntington argued that the relationships between interest groups and governments often become strained; excessive demands can over-stress the authorities (Huntington, 1968). A number of writers in the rights-based tradition, most notably Nozick (1984) and Hayek (1984), have suggested that the simplest solution to this, and associated dilemmas, would be to do away with the state as a site of patronage: the state's role should be simply confined to that of a night-watchman upholding the most basic of rights.

The concept that in the end ethical conduct rests with the individual and is best secured through the development of individual rights reflects:

> ... the American tradition, perhaps best exemplified by Emerson, has generally held that no genuine, lasting, meaningful social improvements can be realized without first reforming the individual human being. This view was often vilified by the 'realistic' materialist left as hopelessly naive and therefore ultimately dangerous to workers' true interests. While the New Socialist Man utterly failed, an old-fashioned American movement to reform the individual is re-emerging, stronger than ever, and in many forms ...' (Smith, 2000).

This intellectual tradition can be divided into two distinct strands. The first holds that:

> ... certain kinds of policy can nonetheless assist and reinforce this moral evolution, and that first and foremost among these would be a strategy

which gives people an ownership stake – a real stake, not a 'sense' of ownership – in the companies that employ them and the institutions that most shape their lives (Smith 2000).

It is argued that, *inter alia*, through the distribution of share ownership across society on as wide a basis as possible, individuals may best be able to express their wishes, and to reach compromises for the common good. The role of the state should be minimised. The citizen-shareholder possesses the means to pursue his/her best interests, and, hence, ultimately the good of the economy as a whole, through horizontal linkages based around minimalistic rules of economic decision-making and exchange. As with utilitarianism, this approach can also be used to justify the relentless pursuit of profit by managers (c.f. Friedman 1997). However, from a rights-based perspective, the ethical foundations for such behaviour would be founded on a respect for the autonomy of the shareholder as an individual (c.f. Nozick, 1984). As the agents of shareholders, managers must respect their wishes at all times. However, if shareholders demanded that managers be bound by a particular set of values or code of conduct, the latter would be bound to respect their wishes.

This viewpoint ignores information imbalances – individual shareholders may possess insufficient knowledge to make informed decisions on corporate governance. Moreover, despite rhetoric to the contrary, the notion of the citizen-shareholder remains elusive; a large proportion of the individuals who possess shares do so via financial institutions (Blackburn, 2002; c.f. Lazonick and O'Sullivan, 2000).

A second strand draws heavily on the Victorian notion of the undeserving poor. This strand is particularly influential in the contemporary popular conservative discourse, and has heavily informed decision making within the Bush II administration. This viewpoint holds that a large proportion of the poor find themselves in that position owing to personal moral failures. State assistance to the disadvantaged is unlikely to alleviate this situation; rather social security benefits should best be channelled via conservative religious and philanthropic associations who can combine handouts with moral teachings (see Gibelman and Gelman, 2002). In practice, the track record of such initiatives has been mediocre. Moreover, an extensive analysis of the activities of (mostly conservative) faith-based providers in the United States from 1995 to 2001 revealed that such groupings were just as susceptible to managerial and accountability inadequacies, and outright wrongdoing as their secular counterparts (Gibelman and Gelman, 2002).

Whilst the response of neo-liberals to the mixed results from outsourcing core state functions has generally been one of outright and angry denial, a few have grudgingly acknowledged something of the scale of the problem. For example, reverting to classical virtue theory (c.f. Aristotle, 1952), Kobrak suggests that the inevitable ethical failings can be resolved if:

> High-echelon line executives from every agency involved in public/private enterprises sponsor, and themselves participate in, training sessions to increase the likelihood that … institutional ethical concerns will become part of the administrative agency's culture' (quoted in Williams 2000).

However, internal conduct is inherently bound up with overall organisational culture and objectives; the personal conduct of public sector employees is closely bound up with conceptions of the role of the state and the relative importance assigned to the public sphere.

Durable inequality and rights

In the bulk of his works, Rawls stressed the importance of the right over the good (Sandel, 1984), that is that in most cases the liberties of the individual are of greater value than the promotion of a common good. However, unlike the social Darwinism of writers such as Hayek and Nozick – and indeed, Benthamite utilitarianism – Rawls (1984) argues that inequalities are only justifiable if they can be demonstrated to benefit the position of the worst off in society. In other words, poverty is not necessarily the just deserts of the less competent, but is a condition that needs to be examined rather than ignored (Parekh, 1982). Welfare represents a basic right (Sandel 1984).

In a persistently unequal society, certain individuals may be in a stronger position to exercise their basic rights than others; such rights are worthless without the right to equality of opportunity. The solution Rawls recommended was a set of measures designed to promote greater equity that might be broadly termed 'welfare statist'. This reflected a recognition that 'the endowments and opportunities that lead to good character are arbitrary from a moral point of view' (Sandel, 1984). In his final work, *Justice as Fairness*, Rawls suggests that justice is only possible through widespread property ownership or a kind of market socialism (Rawls, 2001; c.f. Rogers, 2002).

There is little doubt that this approach is probably closer to the Kantian roots of the rights-based tradition than the minimalist alternative; if freedom is seen in purely instrumental terms, then rights are vulnerable, and, hence, the inherent dignity of the individual. Actions are only morally right if you are happy that everybody in a similar situation could act in a similar way. People should be treated not only as a means, but also an end (Lamsa, 1999).

Communitarian perspectives

To communitarians, political arrangements – and structures of governance – cannot be justified without reference to shared purposes and ends; we are not just individuals, but also citizens, participating in a common life (Sandel, 1984). Politics – and economic activity – are not just about individual expression, but also the effects on the promotion of a common good. It is about not just participation but also commitment; the citizen is concerned about the well-being of the world, and the well-being of the whole (Parekh, 1982). Whilst communitarians would be suspicious of excessive corporate power, they would also be critical of a remote and bureaucratic public sector. The latter should be closely linked to, and supportive of the community (Sandel, 1984). The sustainable welfare state is founded on notions of sharing and membership, not on individual rights (Walzer, 1984). Behaviour is not just driven by the profit motive, but also by interlocking moral commitments (Etzioni, 2003). The role of the state in society should reflect this.

More conservative communitarians such as Michael Oakeshott (1983) point to the fragility of the community in the face of the relentless rationalisation of social life. The 'ship of state' should be concerned simply with refining the mechanisms of 'staying afloat', with tried and trusted procedures and operations, rather than trying to reach a more egalitarian future. To Oakeshott, it is intolerable that individuals comprising the community should be forced 'to dream the dreams of others'; a focus on rationality and progress has led unprecedented human misery, as the means becomes subordinated to the end. Along with more radical writers such as Lipietz (c.f. Jessop, 2001), Oakeshott correctly points to an authoritarian strand within both mainstream leftist and rightwing politics. However, Oakeshott underplays the relative importance of the economic, and the fact that social progress represents not only evolution, but also the bold adoption of alternatives at times when the status quo has demonstrably failed.

Postmodern ethics

Baumann (1993) echoes Oakeshott's concern that the great wrongs committed by many twentieth century states – including innumerable social engineering projects – and unprecedented environmental degradation, reflect inherent problems within the modernist project. To postmodernists, administrative evil represents the outcome of modernity and technical rationality. This represents an inversion of the correlation Weber drew between rationalisation and socio-economic progress.

For postmodernists, this has 'created a profession of public administration that is blind to the existence and importance of administrative evil' (Menzel, 2001). Rather, there is a need to take account of the diversity of society, and of the specific and the local; the modern state is a repressive 'apparatus of capture', that 'overcodes' individual desires to creativity and self-expression (Deleuze and Guattari, 1988: 380). The solution is not so much a reform of public administration, but the fracturing of the modern state into smaller units more closely rooted in communities. This glorification of the local, does, however, ignore the possibility that grass-roots political movements may be focussed on highly exclusivist notions of identity, that might engender particularly nasty brands of micro-politics (Wood, 1997).

Practical concerns: politicians, public servants and whistle-blowing

The relationship between elected politicians and public servants is necessarily a contentious one, even prior to the market reforms of the 1980s. For example, how ethical is it for public servants to expose activities they uncover or are asked to participate in, that they deem inimical to the public interest? Conservative accounts would suggest that any whistle blowing is simply rank disloyalty, designed to derail either legitimate commercial enterprises, or the elected government in its battle against the country's enemies. For example, conservative radio talk show hosts in the United States regularly claim that any attempt to expose the Bush II administration's repeated violation of the Geneva Convention or question the use of 'dirty war' tactics in Iraq amounts to no less than treason. However, as Williams (1985: 19) notes, whistle blowing is really about making things public. An elected government that acts in an ethical manner has little to fear from public exposure; conversely, the need for whistle blowing rises in direct proportion to the amount of secrecy a government generates. If adequate mechanisms exist for the free flow of information – that is that the public are adequately informed as to what the government they elected actually does – then the need for whistle blowing becomes very much less.

Again, it is generally accepted that, within the public sector, work should be divided between those performing administrative functions, and those who support, develop and have genuine rather than simulated agreement with the government of the day (Ridley, 1985). However, where the line is drawn varies greatly from national context to context. Political appointments are only likely to prove functional where career interests are safeguarded – in other words, reasonable alternative prospects for those temporarily excluded when the party they support is in opposition. Nonetheless, with the increasing polarisation of politics that has taken place in the Anglo-American world, it is increasingly difficult for senior civil servants to preserve neutrality and abstract notions of public service (Ridley, 1985). More contentious is whether greater politicisation should be allowed, and under what conditions this takes place. On the one hand, it can be argued that certain national problems require radical solutions. On the other hand, a civil service that preserves some vestiges of neutrality can act as a check on the worst excesses of an extremist government.

Ethics and the managerial revolution

> Ethics may be only a means to an end, but it is a necessary means to an end. Government ethics provides the preconditions for the making of good public policy. In this sense, it is more important than any single policy because all policies depend on it (Thomson, quoted in Williams, 2000).

However, whilst the state has a central role to play in underpinning a good society, much of the contemporary debate on public sector ethics has shifted away from what the state should be doing, to ethical issues related to internal organisational functions (Bowman *et al.*, 2001). The increasing hegemony of neo-liberalism in the United States and Britain in the 1980s and 1990s has fuelled 'pervasive beliefs that government policies and public officials are corrupt, inept, or out to take advantage of citizens' (Berman, quoted in Williams, 2000). Moreover, neo-liberals alleged that excessive emphasis on the importance of the public sphere has led to an 'accumulation of excessive power, lack of accountability and representation, indifference towards public needs and demands, official secrecy and inaccessibility, and role in depoliticising the public sphere' (Haque, 2001; Schultz, 2002).

It has therefore been argued that public administrators not only should be more effective – and trustworthy – but also demonstrate these attributes to the public at large (Williams, 2000). However, research evidence would suggest that declining public confidence in the ethical conduct of public sector employees can be directly ascribed to the introduction of new public management techniques (Haque, 2001). Moreover, neo-conservative suggestions that ethical failures in the public sphere can be simply ascribed to individual lapses of trust and to poor communication draw an artificially sharp distinction between the political and the economic spheres. Many ethical failures are the result of the pursuit of wealth by inappropriate means; a large proportion of ethical lapses by public servants are the result of interchanges between private firms and the public sphere. More generally speaking, there is a close correlation between the scale and nature of individual instances of misconduct and overall organisational culture. As Adams and Balfour note:

> ...strong democratic communities, and public servants do not so easily wear the mask of administrative evil when their role entails a critically reflexive sense of the context of public affairs along with a mission to educate and build an inclusive and active citizenry' (quoted in Menzel, 2001).

Nonetheless, the adoption of neo-liberal policies in many advanced and developing societies has led to the relentless marketisation of the public sphere, and the decline of the notion of 'publicness' (Haque, 2001), to be replaced by the concept of new public management (NPM). The latter has encompassed the erosion of the distinction between the public and private realms, the reduced coverage of social services, and lower levels of accountability (Haque, 2001).

The rise of NPM has meant that the market and business models have replaced notions of service as the central currency of the public sphere. As Riccuci argues, NPM 'fails to account for critical differences between the government and private sectors, and, in particular, ignores the constitutional premise that government is based on a rule of law and not market driven mechanisms' (Riccuci, 2001). Other writers, such as Rosenbloom have argued that better government is in the end about better politics – and policies – rather than about the lock-stock-and-barrel adoption of the private sector management model (Riccuci, 2001).

The managerial revolution not only encompassed the adoption of the rhetoric and some of the form of private sector business techniques into the public sphere, but, in most national instances, the outsourcing of state functions as well. To its proponents, privatisation is held to result in greater administrative efficiency through the reduction of inefficient – and expensive – layers of bureaucracy and processes, and in addition, the introduction of the profit motive. In the public sector, there is not always a direct relationship between profits and expenditure, reducing incentives to cut costs (Cohen, 2001). Finally, state owned enterprises that do not perform traditional government functions may be unprofitable, imposing a heavy drain on the exchequer.

However, there are serious limitations to privatisation. The first is directly economic: outsourcing areas that are automatic monopolies – such as the management of core physical infrastructures, railway networks, water provision, and so on – removes the competition incentive. Attempts to infuse some competitive motive through regulatory measures designed to emulate the market through comparative competition (Jones, 2001), short term contracts and incentives for greater efficiency have had a rather mixed track record.

Private firms operating in these areas will naturally desire to extract the maximum returns from the citizen consumer as possible. If prices are capped, returns have to be maximised by cost-cutting in other areas, which may have adverse consequences for users. Again, the introduction of market mechanisms creates serious equity concerns that are, at best only partially redressed through redesigned social security measures. Moreover, the inevitable desire to maximise short term returns has, time and again, resulted in the reduction of basic maintenance, and the decay of national assets that took generations to construct.

Secondly, there are a number of practical ethical concerns that spring from the outsourcing of core state functions. The outsourcing of law enforcement functions may, for example, result in private security firms executing suspects, rather than incurring the expense, inconvenience and lengthy delays associated with having to participate in legal proceedings. Nor is this a hypothetical case; such practices are widespread in countries where security has been largely privatised, such as Columbia and South Africa (see Steinberg, 2002). Again, the outsourcing of health care to the private sector should, hypothetically speaking, allow the consumer to choose between the most efficient and effective service provider for any particular procedure. However, in practice, consumers (other than in the case of the very rich) are inevitably bound to an individual private health care insurance or medical aid plan; firms administering the latter have a strong interest in minimising payouts. This may be achieved by channelling claimants to 'approved' providers, which have established a reputation for high turnover rates and for encouraging consumers to opt for the cheapest possible procedure. In cases such as South Africa, they are often owned by the medical aid – private health insurance operator outright. Finally, the cost gains made by private sector operatives may not so much represent the outcome of any greater efficiency, but rather the result of labour repressive policies. Some illustration of the extent of reliance on the latter was provided by the outraged reaction by private sector subcontractors in Britain to proposed measures (introduced in early 2003) to force them to grant their employees comparable terms and conditions of service to their public sector counterparts. Conversely, research conducted in the United States would suggest that private sector operatives are not necessarily better or more efficiently managed than the areas of the public sector they replaced (Schultz, 2002). Moreover, a nation-wide survey of accountability at local authority level in the United States revealed that financial pressures were ineffective in instilling a greater sense of accountability within service providers (Wang, 2002).

Contrary to predictions that marketisation would result in more efficient service provision and better governance, it has, *inter alia*, been associated not so much with the overall reduction, but rather a shifting of the composition of wage bills (in the favour of senior managers), increases in unemployment (and a reduction in the number of 'good' jobs) and increased economic volatility (Haque, 2001). Marketisation has resulted in a focus on managerialist targets rather than the overall quality of provision; rights and entitlements have been replaced by economic efficiency.

Haque argues that marketisation has had even more serious consequences in terms of undermining the notion of public service, and the quality of the public sector as an institution (Haque, 2001). Publicness is of critical importance for ethics: it is about the common good of society, realising shared concerns, and in securing equality and openness, representation and impartiality. The broadness and scope of service provision recipients represents a measure of the scale of publicness; marketisation of even the provision of basic social services to the poor represents not just poor practice but a serious ethical breach, forcing the most vulnerable to 'pay for the privilege of living' (Desai, 2002). As Gregory notes:

> ...a central measure of publicness remains to be the public trust in the credibility, leadership, and responsiveness of public service to serve the people. If a public service begins to act like a business enterprise, its credibility as a public domain is undermined; if it plays an indirect and limited role, its public leadership comes under question; and if it fails to respond to the needs of all citizens (not just the affluent class), its overall public responsiveness is compromised' (quoted in Haque, 2001).

The failings of marketisation underscore the close relationship between internal organisational cultures and overall organisational goals; the extent of ethical conduct amongst public sector employees is inherently bound up with the relative importance assigned to, and aims of, the public sphere as a whole. Again, NPM's casting of the citizen as a consumer trivialises the complex web of rights and obligations between citizen and state that characterises a democracy (c.f. Riccuci, 2001).

Towards a new public ethics

It is commonly suggested in the literature that the neo-liberal style NPM represents an unstoppable juggernaut. However, there is considerable evidence to suggest that 'alternative drivers of reform are not obliterated but remain influential' (Schultz, 2002); this is particularly the case in countries with established neo-corporatist traditions, such as much of Scandinavia. In such cases, there remains a widespread commitment to 'egalitarian social and economic outcomes through public policies and employment practices' (Schultz, 2002). Whilst reflecting the cyclical nature of capitalism, periodically such alternative models come under stress, and sets of policies tend to be only temporarily suspended, rather than completely abandoned (Harcourt and Wood, 2003). Pressures to marketisation often face countervailing pressures toward democratisation and equity (Wise, 2002).

This might suggest that the NPM should be contested through the revitalisation of the traditional communitarian ethical project. Underpinning this would be the need to separate economic and political power; barriers against concentration represent a vital mechanism for reconstituting communities, and the needs and values of the whole, rather than the individual or the supposedly efficient private sector firm (Etzioni, 2003).

However, critics have suggested that contemporary communitarianism fails to take account of the more fluid nature of contemporary institutional forms; paradigms constructed on the premises of a dichotomy of the economic and social are unsustainable (Piore, 2003). An alternative would be centring a new public sector ethics within the broad political ecology advanced by writers such as Lipietz (2001). Whilst sharing the emphasis on the social and the vitality of social relations, it argues that the ecological is the most inclusive of all social relationships. People's relationships with each other and the ecosystem are inherently contradictory, and in need of new forms of mediation (Jessop, 2001). The public sector, with its capacity for socio-economic mediation and intervention, represents only one of a range of necessary sites of negotiation and compromise toward new ways of working and the promotion of a more sustainable developmental trajectory (Jessop 2001).

Finally, whilst the scale and consequences of globalisation are widely debated, there is little doubt that nations are interconnected through the operations of contemporary capitalism (Meiksins Wood, 1997). This raises the question as to the demarcations of societies: who should the state serve (Schultz, 2002)? It should be recognised that the operation of the public sector inevitably raises a range of ethical challenges, issues and concerns that affect not only citizens of a specific state, but also individuals living beyond its bounds, and, indeed, the entire biosphere. Again, this would underscore the need for the development and active promotion of a broader ecological ethic (c.f. Singer, 1995).

Conclusion

Above all, the new public management is about a shift from administrative bureaucracy to entrepreneurship; a shift that, critics have charged, is contrary to both the democratic tradition and notions of public service. Nonetheless, much of the literature on public sector ethics remains focussed on promoting moral conduct amongst individual public servants, rather than on what the state should be doing to promote equity, uphold 'goodness' and/or secure social progress (c.f. Streib *et al.*, 2001). Yet, it can be argued that the two are inherently bound together; moreover, unbridled marketisation has led to a proliferation of internal ethical concerns. This would underscore the need to locate public sector ethics both within a broad political economy framework, and in the context not only of the needs of the community, but the sustainability of a biosphere.

Note

The author would like to thank Nick Nye for very helpful comments on an earlier draft.

7

Mechanisms and Values in the Delivery of a Patchwork of Public Services

Jenny Harrow

A prominent feature of public management reform has been the breaking of the once-vital symbiotic chain between policymaking on public services and the direct delivery of those services by recognisably governmental organisations. Historic ways of working in conventionally bureaucratic organisations, where government-employed professional groups allocated resources, have given way to a range of organisations as service delivery agents. Now, in various combinations, public, quasi-public, private and voluntary organisations all have provider roles as delivery agents in the cast of the long running play that is 'public services'.

Expanding or making more opaque the notion of 'a public service' is central to this development. A service is 'public' when it attracts a significant element of public funding in support of public policy purposes, whether its providers are direct government employees, contractors, grant recipients or combinations of these groups. Public services represent a variety of forms, their content dependent on factors such as geography, technical and managerial capacity, the services users' profiles, services' history and modes of regulation, inspection and review. As some services move further away from their public parents, for example through formal transfer of activities to voluntary bodies, new areas hitherto outside the public sphere seek credence, via funding, as public services. An example is the transformation of the private family member-helper role to that of quasi–public worker, 'the carer'. The core questions – 'who delivers "public" services and for whom?', 'how and why do public services develop and change?' and 'who judges public services' successful delivery and outcomes?' are subject to multiple answers and to a variety of interpretations within nations adopting NPM strategies, systems and operating frameworks.

Such a loose and ambiguous understanding of what constitutes 'public services' makes for a fragmentary services picture across countries. In the mixed economy of welfare, the mixture is capable of wide cross-national variations. There are also contested views on whether services' movement across economic sector boundaries represents service reform (in the sense of improvement) or a scene-shifting arrangement, giving the all-important impression (or reality) of government 'moving out'. Ironically, a focus on services *delivery* appears to be a relatively neglected part of, or latecomer to, the New Public Management debate. This may be on the possible (and erroneous) assumption that once core NPM reforms had taken place, services deficiencies and problems would be self-righting. By the end of the 1990s, when NPM solutions or panaceas were anything but 'new', emphasis on the *delivery* (process, outputs and outcomes) of public services, as well as on their provision (inputs) had become a renewed interest of politicians, managers of these services, users and would-be users.

Pressure on funding bases and scrutiny of services' performance has fuelled drives for evidence-based policy making and service provision, notwithstanding that whose evidence is accepted may itself be challenged, or that the evidence may be simply unclear. Programme evaluation, albeit patchy and often from problematic baseline data, is becoming a gradual NPM hallmark; although the outcomes of such evaluations are highly uncertain. In the case of NPM financial reforms, Olsen, Humphrey and Guthrie (2001) contend that public services and their providers are caught in an 'evaluatory trap', where reform programmes continue to be promoted, despite being based on questionable accounting techniques. Taken together, these combinations of elements have led virtually to 'no-win' situations for whichever body provides the 'public' service, given that it is being required to show that it is *'doing more with less, but doing it nicer'* (McGuire, 2001, quoting O'Conor and Showchuck).

This chapter examines the 'how' of public services delivery, in the context of increasingly complex interpretations of NPM tenets and practices. Three interlocking elements are important. These are: the institutional and technological *mechanisms* for service delivery, the *values* underpinning, illustrated or sought from that service, and the type of *product* which the service exemplifies. Figure 7.1 below, sets these elements out, in summary form.

Mechanisms for delivering public services

The institutional mix

The expectations from some early NPM advocates that the direct governmental hand would be progressively withdrawn from *all* service provision have not been fulfilled. The phrase 'market testing', for assessing the appropriateness of retaining a directly delivered public product instead of a publicly funded but market delivered product, has, at least in Britain, fallen out of use. Interest in private suppliers to act as service contractors has

Mechanisms

Direct public agencies
    • central
    • regional
    • local governments

Direct public agencies working jointly
Arms' length government agencies

Contracts with other sectors
    • private
    • non profit
    • charity

Partnerships between and across sectors
    • public/private;
    • public/voluntary;
    • private/voluntary

Values
Modernisation Competition Improvement Quality / benchmarking / 'best practice'
Innovation
Consumerism
Evidence based provision and practice Accountability and openness

Products

Supporting products
    • social work
    • income support
    • health
    • housing

Enabling /empowering products
    • education
    • transport
    • employment
    • economic development
    • culture
    • recreation

Protecting and restraining products
    • emergency, disaster and defence services
    • environmental services
    • criminal justice

Figure 7.1   The triangular basis of a 'public service' in NPM contexts

not been so buoyant in western governmental societies as to exclude completely the appearance of directly delivered public services. At the same time, public organisations remaining have been expected to behave with some of the characteristics of private organisations, and on occasion to compete with would-be private suppliers. Joldersma and Winter (2002: 84) draw the distinction between 'task organisations', closely linked to and funded by governments and constrained by them in decision-making terms; and 'market organisations', delivering to the users capable of paying for services and independent in strategic decision-making, such as contraction and expansion.

The NPM dual imperative, of improving services' efficiency whilst reducing spending on those services, has led to efforts to privatise public services, defined by Joldersma and Winter as 'all initiatives for marketisation of task organisations' (2002: 85). Yet privatisation is not – yet – wholescale; leaving remaining public bodies as hybrids, with characteristics of both task and market oriented bodies.

Identifying the necessary pre-requisites for changing institutional systems for services delivery has thus been problematic, with growing debates about the travelling capacity of NPM core drivers and practices. A parallel theme with the prominence given to the market as service supplier has been that of services devolution to lower levels of government. Yet Polidano and Hulme (1999) emphasise how many developing countries, choosing selectively from NPM approaches, have retained centralised governmental systems as a response to public corruption and other problems. Even where services devolution is extensive (and not necessarily always wanted), central governments' control over those services is mostly retained, and mostly through the setting and monitoring of the services' 'performance targets'.

Nor does service devolution to localities in developed countries follow a set pattern. It seems a truism that for every recognised trend of new public service management, the reverse can also be found, yet with the same core rationale and NPM flavour. In Norway, for example, from January 2002, responsibility for all public hospitals was transferred to the central government away from the range of locality providers. However, their relative independence remains unclear. Although these hospitals are now wholly owned by central government, which will determine the principal health policy objectives, they are nevertheless also 'organised as enterprises...separate legal subjects and thus not an integral part of central government administration' (OECD, 2002: 5). Having it both ways could also be said to be an NPM hallmark, where services 'ownership' is considered.

In institutional terms, the boundaries between service providers in public and private sectors are in a state of flux, encouraged by a variety of interpretations as to what constitutes service failure and the need/opportunity for private sector involvement as service provider. Private firms now have a range of entrees in public services provision. They may offer services to be purchased through public funds, with a resulting mix of private and 'public clients' (for example, residential care services for elderly people). They may compete for pre-defined contract work (the earliest NPM developments such as refuse disposal and public cleansing) or co-exist alongside public provision. They may also participate in close encounters with existing public services suppliers to provide public infrastructures in what are now universally known as 'public private partnerships' (providing, for example, hospitals, bridges, and student accommodation).

To bring this range of working arrangements together under a blanket descriptor of 'privatisation' is problematic, although it is tempting to do so as an explanatory slogan of governments' signal of intent to withdraw from hitherto stable service sectors. (See for example, Moist's assertions concerning the Canadian Federal Government's abandonment of public services and its consequences for provincial and local government services (Moist, 2001). Torres and Pina (2002) distinguish between 'privatisation of public utilities' and 'externalisation of public services' in their survey of changing public services delivery in 20 EU cities with populations over 500 000. In the former, disinvestment in and deregulation of public utilities governments is involved, while in the latter '...only the management of public services is transferred' (Torres and Pina, 2002: 41). Among the exceptions to productivity and quality improvements in post-privatised EU industries are '...the privatisation of railways in Britain (causing more problems than it solved) and electricity privatisation in Spain, where investment deficiencies have led to supply failures' (Torres and Pina, 2002: 46).

Public/private partnerships

The explosion of academic and practitioner literature on this aspect of services delivery emphasises the prominence of this service provision 'model' (both as type, and as exemplar). Pongsiri (2002) presents the nature of this activity in terms of the 'mutual benefit' which public and private co-operators will gain, characterised by '...a perception of equity and mutual accountability' (Pongsin, 2002: 487) among them – the 'win-win' situation beloved of organisation strategists. A polarity of views provides a contrasting picture of what this development means for the future shape of public services. Whitfield (2002: 2) assesses the total cost of public-private partnership (PPP) projects in Britain, whereby private firms fund, supply and maintain assets which act as part of the public service infrastructure, as over £150 billion in total cost terms, either already committed or in the planning and procurement stage. Fields include health, education, transport, defence and criminal justice, making both a piecemeal yet widespread appearance on the public stage.

Central to the argument for PPP is the claim that the government and the public do not need to own public buildings to provide public services. Whitfield (2002) questions, however, whether the ownership and operation of buildings can be separated from the services provided in those buildings. In Britain, he foresees a future scenario of dominance by a few multi-national firms, a yet more shrunken state, and a mass exodus of senior managers and skilled staff into the private sector unless a long-term evaluation of PPP initiatives occurs.

Elsewhere, PPP developments are not quite the juggernaut that they appear to be in Britain. In Australia, for example, Arndt and Jelinek (2001) identify a 'trailing off' in the number of signed PPPs over the last two years, emphasising industry scepticism at state levels, and issues of public servants' capability to manage such complex projects. The 'in house' 'commercialisation' model also continues to exist, arguably reducing problems of dissipation of expertise and disruption of service delivery (Brown *et al.*, 2000).

'Partnership' as a service delivery mechanism and service structure

The recruitment of private sector firms into the public sector sphere which PPP typifies falls also within the scope of the wider case that governments are making for services to flow from both a structure and a service value, that is 'partnership working'. Partnerships are formalised structures that bring together institutions and organisations to address an identified problem or to work towards a specific organisational goal. Key characteristics include a focus on organisational rather than individual relationships, evident working boundaries, relatively stable composition, and membership defined by formal agreement (Painter & Clarence 2001). Reid's typology of partnership in social housing (Reid, 2001) distinguishes between ideological partnerships (creating new policy rhetoric), structural partnerships (to implement new areas of policy change), and mechanistic partnerships (to increase sectoral capacity and introduce cross cutting activities).

Public service provision areas where partnerships are prominent include urban regeneration, housing, health, social services and criminal justice. The uniqueness of partnership working is also often seen as resting on the principle of synergy, more than an exchange of resources, and part of a process of creating something new, and fostering comprehensive and 'transformative' thinking (Hastings, 1996). Yet, partnership of itself does not create the conditions for the synergy characterising effective collaborative working, so that managerial and partner skills become critical in the achievement of partner targets. Painter and Clarence (2001), studying British education and health action zones (HAZs), identify issues concerning competitiveness *within* partnerships; the micro-political realities that lie behind the formalities of partnership structures; and the length of time it takes to establish collaborative working arrangements. Difficulties in balancing different or competing priorities, slowness of decision-making, loss of autonomy and the management of individual 'egos' have also been identified as problems within partnerships (Hutchinson 1995; Maddock 2000, 2002).

This makes not only for complexity in partnership working, but uncertainty and possible variation as to what partnerships are able to deliver to end users and over what time scales. 'Talking up' partnership working as a service panacea runs particular risks when reviewing the outcome of partnership work. Newman (2002), in discussing partnership discourses developing in Britain, draws attention to expectations that partnerships 'drive up performance'. Clarke (2001) emphasises the multiple stakeholders that must accompany partnership work. He sees such devices and structures as reflecting 'the reality of contemporary society where single organisations no longer "own" issues and problems' (Clarke 2001: 6). However, it is also useful to note that the expected beneficiaries of partnership work – community members, tenants, health users for example – may have to wait some time for the formal partners to embed their relationships and work out their respective partnership contributions. Partnership 'solutions' to social problems may have intellectual integrity and common sense appeal but they are unlikely, it now seems, to be fast-acting.

This issue of speed, timing and timeliness is itself a growing and uncertain theme in NPM reform. Examples of governments moving quickly from pilot to full programme implementation are widespread; but the need to embed NPM ways of working may have been insufficiently recognised in such cases. A contrasting scenario is Pollitt *et al.*'s (1997) report for the Finnish government, comparing NPM reform in Finland with Britain, the Netherlands, Denmark and New Zealand, in which Finnish developments are characterised as deliberate and consensual.

The voluntary sector as service provider and public services partner

In pre-NPM service delivery eras, voluntary organisations' activities were essentially complementary to those of public welfare bodies, in Taylor's terms, 'playing to their strengths', including flexibility, and user closeness. Taylor examines the results of 'the ambivalent response of non statutory providers...to the new opportunities created by the transfer of services delivery away from the state' in Britain (Taylor, 2002: 113). Some, mostly larger, organisations acting as suppliers in a public purchasing environment appear to have gained from participation (in income and power terms). Others have been adversely affected, especially where moves from grants to contracts removed or diminished core funding.

The 'partnership' word has now appeared so extensively, in the context of statutory-voluntary sector relations, that the sector as a contributor *within* the public service sphere now appears virtually a foregone conclusion across a range of NPM nations. In Ireland, with the voluntary sector seen as 'essential partners in economic and social development' (Government of Ireland, 2000:3), new levels of interaction are promised, with 'voluntary activity support units' in relevant government departments and 'broadly representative development boards' for each city and county local authority (Hayes, 2000: 260). In Canada, restructuring and reduction of the federal budget to provinces in the early 1990s challenged non-profits' survival, with governments simultaneously and increasingly looking to non-profits to fulfil its service providing role (Miller, 1998). In Australia, a doctrine of 'constructive compassion' to justify human services delivery through private firms and voluntary organisations has developed (Wallis, 2001).

Even so, grasping the implications of such partnerships at the most local level is not to be gained from top-level policy documents. One small scale study of 'stage setting' for partnership between area based non-profits and Sedgwick County, Kansas provides the authentic local voice and exemplifies the critical operational as well as strategic frameworks within which such partnerships could flourish. For example, working challenges include the county's lack of appreciation of non-profits' need to be accountable to diverse and multiple funding sources; and county managers identifying difficulties in determining 'exactly what the county's dollars are buying when there are multiple streams of funding to one non-profit...' (Self-Help Society of Kansas, 2000: 37). This emphasises the need for trust between partners that something of value is being purchased; not, it must be said an early pillar of NPM thinking, in which transparency and tangibility in costings to produce value-for-money was given primacy.

Some kinds of voluntary organisations appear more in public policy vogue than others. In the United States, heightened focus on public welfare contributions of organisations reflecting and vouching for religious commitment has produced the White House 'Office of Faith-Based and Community Initiatives'. This is linked to seven federal agencies, in response to the argument that hitherto such groups' '...compassionate efforts to improve their communities have been needlessly and improperly inhibited by bureaucratic red tape and restrictions placed on funding' (www.whitehouse.gov, 2002). Controversially, this development begs questions as to which, if any, faiths are most prominent, whether the initiative is 'new' at all, and how guidelines to distance service provision and faith promotion can be managed, in the context of US legal frameworks. At the same time, the Initiative's client populations – the homeless, prisoners, at risk youth, addicts, elders in need and families moving from welfare to work – represent those traditionally supported by voluntary organisations, when mainstream public services marginalise or simply fail to provide for these groups. This approach continues to endorse the voluntary sector's fallback or safety net role as 'the last social service' but in a more publicly recognised and compensated for fashion.

More pragmatically, such organisations' cash reserves, rather than their compassion, may be the policy target. This is prompted by Twombly's study of the organisational and financial characteristics of over 2,000 large religious and secular human services provider organisations in the United States, showing near identical spending patterns but contrasting revenue sources (Twombly, 2002). The former are dependent on donor contributions, and the latter substantially more inclined to rely on government grants and contracts. Twombly provides a critical caveat to government policy: '...despite the strong fiscal health of faith related providers, their heavy dependence on donor contributions raises important questions regarding faith–based policy initiatives' (Twombly, 2002: 947). These might include service stability, and sustainability. Moreover, this sector's ability to work with whom they choose is also limited by partnership terms. In the case of the British probation service, Gibbs (2001) for example, reports voluntary sector partners 'aggrieved' by the public service partner's role in agenda setting. Here, the service

> ...allocated most of its money to the organisations which could show best value for money and were more likely to view service users in terms of their offending behaviour rather than more holistically, as many of the voluntary organisations preferred to view them (Gibbs, 2001: 18).

Gibbs' work illustrates how such organisations are being grafted into statutory processes. For example, partner voluntary organisations are obliged to inform users' probation officers where non-take up of their service by that user had occurred, '...actions...leading to the client being in breach of their probation order and at risk of being returned to court' (Gibbs, 2001: 19).

Even where voluntary and statutory services' working principles do align, the enrolment of the voluntary sector as a central element in public services provision begs another question, that of the capacity as well as the willingness of such organisations so to act. The strongest sectoral contributions seem most likely when the services contexts are at their most demanding. A key example exists in Northern Ireland. Here, Williamson, Scott and Halfpenny (2000) assess that the sector has played a significant role in civil society rebuilding, through the District Partnership programme of the EU's 'Peace and Reconciliation Support'. A number of individual governments are also accelerating funding for what is loosely known as 'capacity building' for the sector, to increase and enhance sectoral involvement (Harrow, 2001). In Britain, for example, the Treasury cross-cutting review in September 2002 announced major funding increases for sectoral support, where central government was seeking '...a voluntary and community sector that is strong, independent and has the capacity and skills where it wishes to be a partner in delivering world class services' (HM Treasury, 2002). This is notwithstanding the fact that such organisations might wish to develop their capacity to work in different directions from, and with different priorities to public services.

Major debates continue concerning these developments' impact on the public services landscape, given the patchy geographical locations of voluntary organisation activity, and the extent to which the voluntary sector becomes divided between the 'independents' from and the 'handmaidens' of public services. The linkage between NPM thinking and voluntary sector-state relations points to the latter, with voluntary organisations receiving support as a function of their performance, not their intrinsic nature. Johansson's exploration of Scandinavian voluntary organisations, for example, identifies the extent of diffusion of NPM discourse as a prime factor in such development, and a consequent shift from the voluntary sector's role from that of 'voice' to that of 'service' (Johansson, 2003).

Values in public services delivery

The values range

Beck *et al.* (2002) provide the crucial case for considering the value base of services:

> ...producing goods and services rarely is just a question of what is produced to the immediate in-contact users, and how efficiently it is done... it involves considerations of side effects on the public at large, and whether some basic values should be taken into account when producing...services and when deciding to do so (Beck, Jorgensen and Bozeman, 2002: 64).

They explore the existence of 'modern reform values' (user orientations, a business like approach, efficiency) and 'classic public sector values', including political accountability, professional standards of working and a balancing of interests, in the context of contracted-out service cases in the United States and Denmark. From three contrasting cases, they emphasise how the role of values in decision-making varied. In those concerned with water and sewage, whilst the paramount concern was 'efficiency,' '...in sharp contrast to the USA, there is no firm belief in Denmark that contracting out will ultimately achieve efficiency' (Beck *et al.*, 2002: 63). Even 'efficiency' as a value, therefore, is at times having to make its own case, rather than being heralded as an inevitable outcome of NPM style change.

Equity and business values

Equity as a service-value has either appeared highly absent from much pro-NPM debate, or has made a rather belated appearance as an add-on benefit in some public services (Harrow, 2002). At the same time, in the ongoing efficiency / equity debates in public services, it has been argued that the *personal* values of the range of public services managers are among the (unresearched) keys to the shaping of service delivery for equitable outcomes for citizens (Harrow, 2002), especially where business penetration into, or 'business like' methods in public services are occurring. In the case of British public housing, Sprigings (2002) cites a case of tenant eviction recommendation to a housing association board where

> ...the misguided interpretation of the NPM business drivers...led the manager to believe that it was better to write off £4000 than to invest in six hours work in supporting the tenant (Spriging, 2002:14).

Moreover, in a study of 50 providers of residential care for elderly people in England, Kendall explores provider motivations under three groupings – empathisers, professionals and income prioritisers (Kendall, 2002). This leads Kendall to develop Le Grand's initial 'knights and knaves' categorisation, to a threefold grouping of providers as 'knights, knaves and merchants'; and to emphasise that public policy decisions in this area need to take cognisance of the range of motivations of private suppliers of such public services.

Modernisation

Of all the much cited NPM services values, that of 'modernisation' seems all encompassing. Maddock's authoritative analysis of its nature demonstrates how political desires for instant results, and media focus on ' "the good", "the bad" and "the failures" keep the debate about change and modernisation in the closet' (Maddock, 2002: 15). The tendency exists to equate modernisation and magic – failing schools given super-heads, action zones set up in disadvantaged neighbourhoods, individuals blamed for 'age old' practices. 'Modernisation' stands out as a value that is well nigh impossible to contradict, and one from which other values flow and interlink. In turn, 'innovation' (as a basis for gaining better if not cheaper services) may be seen as an expression of modernising activities or the activities of 'modern' people and managers. In service terms, innovation is then markedly associated with technological investment and change, with implied but expected major gains for service users. Ironically, it seems possible that the emphasis on public services' contracting may itself act to constrain innovation, insofar that contracts give little space and no reward for such developments.

It may then be easier, and certainly more recognisably 'modern', to cast important discussions around public services innovation firmly in the new technologies camp. The phrase E-government is the increasingly familiar shortcut phrase for all the ways in which 'modern' governments interact with and serve 'modern' citizens; but therein lies a key service dilemma. How 'modern' is the citizenry, as active, passive and would-be services users? To what extent are public preferences for services contact aligned with changing technologies; and what are the implications for even further exclusion of potentially already vulnerable clients by such developments? Smith and Webster (2002), examining the challenges for digital television to act successfully in delivering public services, and noting 'the high failure rate typically associated with public sector ICT projects', are to the point. They argue that, '...the key social challenge will be whether users will adapt to the new and unfamiliar ways of using their TV' (Smith and Webster, 2002: 31). This leads directly on to a further key value in NPM contexts, variously described as an attempt at neutrality in the user orientation or focus, or more clearly as the ideologically rooted value of consumerism, where primacy is given to product responses by 'purchasers', whether direct or indirect.

Consumerism and social inclusion

Consumer challenges to services provision – whether concerning effectiveness, efficiency or equity – require the input of the articulate user (in the case of health services, Neuberger's 'educated patient', 2001). Advocacy groups may not capture the nuances of users' needs; and user sophistication may be a critical prerequisite in engaging in dialogue with providers (see Mechanic's 2002 critique of health care consumers' responses to new preventative and treatment technologies). This suggests a high degree of uncertainty, where public services deliverers claim that user involvement challenges and breaks down the experience of social exclusion which western governments seek to abate, if not reverse.

Taylor (2002) presents social exclusion as a relational concept. This focuses not on the individual and their relationship with society '...(such as "poor") but on the relationship between individuals and the rest of society, and the ways in which lack of income has acted as a barrier to participation in normal life' (Taylor, 2002: 108). Where 'normal life' involves use of – and entitlement to – public services, then it can be argued that the goal of social inclusion can be attained. This may, however, be reached in roundabout fashions. Thus, Bolzan and Gale (2002) illustrate, in an Australian context, how two marginalised groups – older people and people with mental illness – have used traditional consumerist avenues (such as local government public meetings, user support groups) and 'created solidarities and resisted consumer processes in their moves towards increased exercises in social citizenship' (Gale, 2002: 374). An alternative perception, that a consumerist 'smart shopping' service model excludes those people with minimal access to up to date information and network ties, (mostly elderly people), is also present – see for example Klinenberg's (2001) analysis of the 1975 heatwave deaths of over 700 Chicago residents, who were likely to be elderly and impoverished.

Getting a services as well as policy handle on the notion of social inclusion is proving difficult. In Scotland, for example, there are 48 'Social Exclusion Partnerships' (SIPs) of which 34 are area-based. However, case study research on work in SIPs has demonstrated a focus on a more recognisable phenomenon than that of 'social exclusion' – that of 'child poverty' (Kemp *et al.*, 2002). In Greater Govan SIP, for example, initiatives included a credit union, and projects on children's rights and key skills work for parents. Kemp *et al.* (2002) note that the SIPs' role in the alleviation of child poverty was more a positive by-product of their work than an explicit goal (Kemp *et al.*, 2002). This, in turn, suggested that the Scots Executive might consider explicit goals for SIPs in targeting child poverty. However, parallel dangers were then identified – 'goal overload for SIPs [yet] the danger that without such a goal, their contribution to defeating child poverty may be unfocussed' (Kemp *et al.*, 2002: 4). Such uncertainty suggests that the overall impact of such partnerships will remain very unclear, and that there, thus, will continue to be a paucity in the evidence base of such – apparently – 'joined up' programme approaches to social problems.

Further doubts about the user / citizen / sectoral provider nexus are provided where private providers' activities are identified as amounting to 'bad practice' in the guise of public provision. Thus, Dawson's (2002) British research uses this term in relation to private providers' intimidation of, and generally sub-standard provision toward, asylum seekers, to the point where the only distinction between contracted and non-contracted provision, is that it treats asylum seekers as either second-class or third class citizens.

Accountability and new pressures in 'patchwork' public services

The services patchwork is therefore a confirmed feature of public services' life, given that governments consistently identify the importance of cross-sectoral working, or 'joined up' working by inter-related services. This is justified as both a means of achieving more efficient and effective provision and, it is presumed, more likely to be welcomed by service users. The extent to which this recognises the complexities of many users' needs, acts as reproach to hitherto 'silo'd' organisations, or acts to change the ways in which services are delivered continues to be debatable. 'Joining up' services when they have differing funding sources, roles for professionals and a variety of service objectives remains more problematic than simply organising some liaison meetings and coming up with shared initiatives. The rationale for 'joined up' services working is one which also challenges a central tenet of NPM practice, that of measuring performance outcome, since disentangling who takes responsibility for what becomes highly problematic. Equally, where cross-sectoral boundary provision and user involvement are added together, the elements of success to enhance future service learning need close scrutiny, and often deep understanding of the communities in which these developments occur.[1]

The expectation that there will continue to be 'public services' will not, however, go away. Where human actions make for a lethal urban environment, public services responses are required to 'be there', to be targeted but widely accessible, compassionate yet cost-aware, comprehensive, fast in response and there for the long term. Whether the 'services patchwork' model can do this best is already under test, with analyses of New York public services' responses during and post September 11. Boscarino *et al.* (2002) explore community mental health and medication utilisation following the attacks. They conclude that while mental health services were extensive in the City, post the disaster, males between 18 and 24 and those without insurance may not have received adequate post-disaster care.

Future disaster planning scenarios may therefore increasingly challenge the multi-provision and partnership models of services responses, as may future service planning in the light of predictable demographic change.[2]

The very existence of the patchwork creations that are now public services have led in turn to an extensive growth in a particular facet of public service work: that of service inspection and regulation by or on behalf of the state. This is critical where poor performance is highlighted. As Dawson and Dargie (2002: 53), write, in a British health context, 'extensive failure invites state intervention'. Although 'inspection', 'regulation' and 'audit' are often used interchangeably, Boyne *et al.* (2002: 1198) identify 'inspection as one element of a system of regulation', with its focus on visits to services sites and focus on services standards and outcome. In Britain, with long traditions of inspectorates for police, future services, education probation and social services, Boyne *et al.* outline the impending 'massive expansion of inspection in local government and the health service' (Boyne *et al.*, 2002: 1197). They highlight what could be described as a further NPM 'trailing wire'. This is that in a managerial climate where service evaluation and 'what works' are central to governmental decision-making, 'there is no systematic body of evidence on the benefits and costs of inspection regimes or on the characteristics of such regimes that are likely to lead to a favourable cost-benefit ratio' (2002: 1198). It is especially ironic that the *managerial* aspects of organising and delivering high quality inspections appear to have been neglected, as Pike has shown, in relation to the contracted-out work of schools' inspections in Britain (Pike, 2002). Further, of all the areas of public service, it appears that it is in service delivery regulation and monitoring that users have the least influence; a case strongly made by Cope and Goodship (2002) in relation to Britain's Audit Commission and its claim to act in the public interest.

Conclusions

In this review of service development, both the expected and unexpected consequences of NPM reforms have been highlighted. The strong marketisation theme has produced uncertainty as well as limited boosts to public funds, especially where public/private joint work has 'enabled' public infrastructures, for service delivery in the longer term. Assumptions about the necessary links between service quality and the private supplier continue to be challenged. Individual users are faced with public service and cross-sectoral delivery strategies, with a plethora of impressively named programmes. Many of these programmes offer apparently new ways of working with users, against demanding targets, but the majority lack the important characteristic of stability.

This lack of stability is an outcome of the rush to involve multi-partners and especially private sector partners in delivery systems. Issues of the need for speed in changing services delivery styles, structures (and by implication, costs) have been highlighted, pointing toward correspondingly uncertain results. A degree of NPM slowdown might be able to produce less innovation disappointments, as well as supporting and managing user expectations more successfully. Cross-sectoral partnerships in service delivery may be timely where they deliver new insights into effective working. They are also time-consuming for the working partnerships, and in turn will take time to deliver benefits. Where NPM advocates continue to promote partnerships as the optimum paradigm for services delivery, the time costs of partnerships must be acknowledged openly as the 'slow fix' for public services.

Given NPM strictures concerning the focus on services outcome, it is not surprising that when attention focuses on joint working failure, for example, in the case of child protection tragedies, criticism emphasises what are believed to be 'pre NPM' habits. These include professionals' narrow views and refusal to work across service boundaries. Yet the core challenges for NPM service systems – to achieve and to demonstrate services *effectiveness* – is a challenge shared and still accepted by those professionals, upon whom service delivery continues to depend. Thus far, it appears that the NPM elevation of consumer perspectives as a gauge of service impact and outcome, and an implied critique of professional dominance, is injecting ambiguity and disappointment into the reform arena. This may be inevitable, given the realisation by some politicians and managers that service 'effectiveness' for many users (and voters) is a subjective issue, reliant on anecdote and individual experience, rather than on target achievement, rising in service league tables and offering transparent accounting methods.

Shifting services provision, delivered by a variety of cross-sectoral actors, may be variously experimental, developmental, transitional or virtually permanent. An implied NPM value, running throughout the chapter, has been the value of 'reform' itself. From this perspective, reform as a demonstrator of power, or a token of authority, rather than as a means of effecting service change *per se* may have become the more important in key NPM areas, such as provision in health and education. The hybridisation of organisations responsible for services at the point of use continues to make the case for pragmatism – that the best of all three sectors of the economy should be drawn upon. Yet this hybridisation raises long term issues of accountability that are not resolved easily, and is likely to create continuing problems as to what is recognised as a 'public service', even among the most sophisticated clienteles.

Impending demographic changes, regionally, nationally and globally, changing family structures and unexpected national and international events, however, are also factors that have the power to challenge or divert NPM-style service organisation and provision. Together, these are capable of creating situations where the by-now-familiar NPM 'services as patch-work' approach may be seen as a deficient model, or in turn as a model requiring further reform.

Notes

The author's grateful thanks are expressed to Laura Karhela, Centre for Government and Charity Management, London South Bank University Business School, for her work in support of this chapter.

1. See, for example, the Finnmark study, a six year community health intervention programme in an Arctic fishing community, where the nature of the community itself provides a test for the suitability of such work (Lupton, *et al.*, 2002).
2. See, for example, Knickman and Snell's (2002) work on 'The 2030 Problem: caring for ageing baby boomers.'

8

Industrial Relations in the Public Sector: Collective Bargaining Reform and the Issue of Convergence

Philip James

Other chapters in this volume draw attention to a set of common pressures that have been serving to prompt governments to introduce reforms to the composition and management of public sector activities. These pressures include the perceived need to cut public expenditure as a proportion of GDP, usually in order to reduce budgetary deficits – pressures that in the case of European Union (EU) member states have stemmed, in part, from the convergence criteria laid down in the pact on European Monetary Union. Pressures have also encompassed changing views about the appropriate role of the public sector. Such views have been driven by concerns about levels of taxation and the quality of public services; by the desire to improve the cost-effectiveness and client focus of service provision; and by the adoption of private sector notions of what constitute effective management structures and processes.

These pressures for reform have generated considerable debate about whether a two-fold process of convergence is occurring with regard to the management of public sector activities. Thus, on the one hand, it is argued by some commentators that a common feature of the reforms being introduced across countries is the adoption of a set of prescriptions that are frequently associated with the notion of new public management (NPM): this being the greater empowerment and financial accountability of managers; the establishment of more devolved and fragmented management structures; and the privatisation and, more general 'marketisation' or 'contractualisation' of public services. On the other hand, and relatedly, it has been further suggested that a growing similarity is arising between the management practices and processes utilised in the public and private sectors (Treu, 1987; Ferner, 1994). Indeed and more generally, the Public Sector Management Service of the OECD has argued that, in order to improve performance, personnel practices should be reformed to bring them more into line with those in the private sector. For example, it is suggested that greater responsibilities should be devolved to line managers, and more flexible pay and grading systems should be introduced (OECD, 1995).

In many countries collective bargaining has provided the main forum through which changes in working practices, terms and conditions of employment, and the mechanisms used to determine such terms and conditions have been introduced. Consequently, it might be expected that, in order to facilitate the more general process of public sector reform, the role of such bargaining and the nature of the agreements that arise from it would also be undergoing a process of change that embodies the above two-fold process of convergence. The present chapter consequently sets out to review the changes that have been occurring in the area of public sector collective bargaining in order to identify how far this is true. The chapter proceeds as follows. Initially, the reforms that have taken place in Britain over the last two decades are reviewed: this initial focus on Britain being adopted on the grounds that it has been widely acknowledged that this is the western European country where the process of public sector reform has been most dramatic (Ferner, 1994; Bach and Della Rocca, 2000). Subsequently, attention is paid to the 'two limbs' of the convergence debate by considering how far a growing similarity has developed between (a) the collective bargaining arrangements in the British public and private sectors and (b) between those that exist within the public sectors of a number of other EU member states.

This focus on EU countries has been adopted on the grounds that trade union organisation and collective bargaining arrangements are invariably well established in them. As a result, they provide a good basis for the comparison of trends. It should, nevertheless, be remembered that the objectives and assumptions that have informed the trends identified below are also informing public sector reforms in both developing and other developed economies. Consequently, where collective bargaining arrangements exist, it can be expected that similar agendas of change might also exist.

Reform of British public sector industrial relations

In order to draw out the key reforms that have occurred in industrial relations in the British public sector, attention is paid below to four main, but related, areas of change. The first of these is the relative role that the public sector, and hence public sector industrial relations, plays in the economy as a whole. The second is the trends that have taken place with regard to the coverage of collective bargaining in the public sector. The third is the way in which the structure of such bargaining has been revised, and the final one is the degree to which these structural changes have acted to increase the autonomy of local trade unions and employers through the disaggregation of collective bargaining structures.

The relative role of public sector industrial relations

In the post-1945 period, public sector employment in Britain grew substantially and continuously over a period of more than 30 years as a result of two factors: the nationalisation of private sector undertakings in a number of industries, including the railways, coal mining, health care and steel; and the creation of an extensive welfare state. This period of growth subsequently came to an end following the election of a Conservative government in 1979 which was committed to 'rolling back the frontiers' of the state while simultaneously increasing the relative importance of the private sector. This objective of 'public sector withdrawal' was pursued by the Conservative governments that ruled continuously between 1979 and 1997, first under the leadership of Margaret Thatcher and latterly John Major, through the privatisation of public sector undertakings and the 'marketisation' of public sector services.

In the case of privatisation, this initially occurred via the selling of shares in publicly owned companies, most of which, such as British Petroleum and Cable and Wireless, already operated as private enterprises (Colling and Ferner, 1995). Later, it came to encompass the sale of more traditionally publicly owned enterprises and utilities, including British Telecom, the electricity generating and supply industry (excluding British Nuclear Fuels), British Airways, British Gas, British Telecom, British Rail, and the nationalised water and shipbuilding industries and ports. The end result of these developments was a dramatic decline in employment in public sector corporations (outside of the National Health Service) from nearly 1.9 million people in 1981 to 400 000 in 1997 (Safford and McGregor, 1998).

As regards 'marketisation', successive Conservative governments introduced a range of measures to increase the exposure of public sector services to market forces. This was done most directly in the National Health Service and Local Government by the imposition of increasingly wide-ranging requirements to expose certain activities to a process of competitive tendering (Colling, 1993, 1999). Elsewhere, other mechanisms were introduced to enhance the role of market forces. For example, in the Civil Service requirements were introduced under which services had to be 'market tested'. Meanwhile, in the NHS, and to a lesser extent in schools, purchaser-provider splits were established whereby semi-autonomous providers were separated from funding authorities.

These market-led reforms resulted in significant workforce reductions. For example, it was estimated that the introduction of competitive tendering in 1983 led to the loss of 111 000 jobs in the health service by the early 1990s (Labour Research Department, 1991; Colling, 2000). However, such cuts did not mean that employment dropped significantly throughout the public services (Morgan and Allington, 2002). Indeed, in some areas, such as the police, social services and education, some limited growth was seen in the numbers employed over the period 1981–97, albeit that some of these increases could be an artefact of the substantial rise that has occurred in the use of part-time workers in the sector (Winchester and Bach, 1999). Nevertheless, overall, when considered alongside the impact of privatisation, the period saw the public sector workforce fall from 7.2 million to 5.1 million (Safford and McGregor, 1998).

Since the election of a Labour Government in 1997, this picture of employment decline has been somewhat reversed as part of 'New Labour's' programme of public sector investment, notably in the NHS and school education (McGregor, 2001). At the same time, New Labour has partially privatised air traffic control and continued to seek the greater involvement of the private sector in the delivery of public services. In local government, for example, while compulsory competitive tendering has been abolished, a new 'Best Value' regulatory regime has been introduced that also places a strong emphasis on market considerations through what are referred to as the '4 Cs': compare, compete, challenge, and consult (Higgins and Roper, 2002). In addition, the present government has continued to utilise the Private Finance Initiative (PFI) that it inherited from its Conservative predecessor under which private firms bid to finance, design and operate public facilities, such as new hospitals, roads, prisons and schools. It has also expanded its underlying rationale to encompass a wider range of public-private partnerships (PPPs) (Bach and Winchester, 2003).

Coverage of collective bargaining

From the early decades of this century, state policy towards those that it employed, either directly or indirectly, was informed by the notion of being a 'good' or 'model' employer (Beaumont, 1987; Fredman and Morris, 1989). Encompassed, among other things, in this notion was support for trade union recognition, the encouragement of union membership, a commitment to the process of collective bargaining, and an acceptance that public sector terms and conditions should be 'fair' in relation to those in the private sector. Against this background, trade union membership became extensive, today standing at more than double that in the private sector (Sneade, 2001), and collective bargaining machinery was established across the whole of the sector.

Under the post-1979 Conservative governments, this objective of being a 'good employer', and the support for trade union organisation and collective bargaining arrangements associated with it, was now seen as an impediment to the development of both cost-effectiveness and efficiency, and was explicitly challenged.[1] Instead, the approach adopted was to encourage public sector employers to emulate the 'best practice' of their private sector counterparts (Farnham and Horton, 1992). This loss of commitment to union organisation and collective bargaining exhibited itself most clearly in the adoption of a much more hostile and aggressive approach towards industrial relations, a shift perhaps most clearly illustrated by a willingness to withstand a series of large-scale public sector disputes in the early to mid-1980s, most notably in the coal industry.

Nevertheless, successive Conservative governments did not engage in a full frontal assault on trade union recognition rights or directly attempt to secure the widespread abolition of collective bargaining. They did, however, through the process of marketisation, act to reduce the bargaining power of unions and remove groups of workers from the reach of existing bargaining machinery via the outsourcing or externalisation that it stimulated (Colling, 1999). In addition, steps were taken to remove certain groups of public sector workers, at least partially, from the coverage of collective bargaining.

In 1984, the decision was taken to withdraw trade union and collective bargaining rights from workers at the Government Communication Headquarters (GCHQ) at Cheltenham on the grounds of national security; a decision that, ultimately, led to the dismissal of a number of workers who refused to relinquish their union membership. A year earlier, against a background of industrial relations difficulties, it was decided to remove collective bargaining over pay from nurses and midwives, and 'professions allied to medicine' and henceforth have their terms and conditions determined by pay review boards that were empowered to make recommendations to government on the basis of their own research and evidence submitted by interested parties, including the government itself, trade unions and employers.[2] Eight years later, similar action was taken in respect of schoolteachers (White, 2000).

These pay review arrangements continue to remain in operation. However, the more pro-union approach of the post-1997 Labour governments did result in the re-establishment of union recognition and collective bargaining at GCHQ, as well as the making of offers of reinstatement to those workers who had been dismissed.

At the present time, collective bargaining therefore continues to cover a large proportion of public sector workers employed in the three main areas of public sector employment – the civil service, the National Health Service and Local Authorities. Consequently, against a background of a substantial decline in the coverage of such bargaining in the private sector, a far greater proportion of public than private sector workers continue to have their terms and conditions determined by such bargaining and, because of the role of pay review bodies, an even higher proportion do not have them determined unilaterally by management. This can be seen clearly from Table 8.1, where it is shown that while 92 per cent of public sector employees had their pay fixed in 1998 by one of these two methods, the corresponding percentage for their private sector counterparts was just 29 per cent.

Levels of collective bargaining

Collective bargaining in Britain can take place at one of three main levels: the multi-employer 'sectoral', the level of the single employer, and in the

Table 8.1   Employees covered by different pay-fixing arrangements in 1998 (per cent)

Category of employees	Collective bargaining	Set by management	Negotiated with individual employees	Other (for example pay review bodies)
All employees	35	50	3	10
Public sector	61	15	0	31
Private sector	24	66	4	5

Data weighted, based on population of Great Britain, workplaces with 10 or more employees
Source: Adapted from Brown *et al.* (2000).

case of multi-site undertakings, at a decentralised level below that of the corporate body as a whole. Prior to 1979, negotiations in the NHS and local government took place primarily through the first of these levels and those in the civil service via the second. What then has happened to these negotiating arrangements over the last two decades?

A key theme of the public sector reforms introduced by the successive Conservative governments over the period 1979-97 were attempts to create more devolved and performance-orientated systems of management. In the case of the civil service, this desire led to the vast majority of staff being transferred to more than 100 new executive agencies (Corby, 1998). Similarly, as part of the already mentioned purchaser-provided split, the majority of health service staff were transferred to NHS Trusts that were responsible for providing hospital and community health services and negotiating contracts with those purchasing these services on behalf of the public.

The creation of these more devolved management structures was, in turn, accompanied by related reforms aimed at the establishment of more decentralised collective bargaining structures. Within the civil service, this aim was accomplished in 1992 by making the new executive agencies responsible for negotiating terms and conditions for their staff. However, the government was less successful in the NHS, where although, on several occasions during the mid-1990s, pay review boards made provision for centrally laid down pay increases to be supplemented by local Trust-based bargaining, the take-up of this opportunity was very limited (Duncan, 2001).[3] As a result, since then, only national pay increases have been recommended.

As regards local authorities, the government also publicly voiced its support for a shift away from central national negotiations. However, such a negotiating framework has remained in place, albeit that in 1989 a small number of authorities, mainly in the south of the country, where serious recruitment and retention difficulties existed, chose to opt out of it and conclude local agreements.

As with the marketisation of public services, the post-1997 Labour governments have similarly sought to encourage the greater decentralisation of public sector management. At the same time, they have not, as yet, aggressively pursued the greater decentralisation of collective bargaining. That said, it does seem that greater decentralisation is on the agenda. Thus, in the NHS, the government has brought forward legislative proposals to create Foundation Hospitals which would be accorded greater freedom of local action, including some flexibility as to the terms and conditions on which they employ staff. Meanwhile, and more generally, the Chancellor of the Exchequer has made clear that he favours a greater emphasis on the establishment of pay arrangements in the public sector that take into account differences in regional labour market conditions.[4]

In summary then, the last two decades have seen some changes in public sector collective bargaining arrangements, although not always as a result of direct government action, and it seems possible that further ones are on the horizon. Thus, in the civil service highly centralised national negotiations were abolished and replaced by 'single employer' arrangements operating through new executive agencies. Some decentralisation also occurred in local government, where a number of authorities broke away from national, multi-employer bargaining. However, notwithstanding government attempts, bargaining arrangements in the NHS remained highly centralised, although Trusts were given the right to employ new staff on locally determined terms and conditions and a minority are now employed on them.

The growth of local autonomy

There is, nevertheless, one important qualification to this picture of relative stability in the levels at which bargaining takes place in local government and the NHS. This is that the agreements concluded have tended to become 'less tight', or to put it another way, have provided for greater local discretion concerning the implementation of some of their provisions. Recent developments illustrate this clearly.

In local government, for example, a 'single status' agreement was signed in 1997 which brought together the two agreements which had previously covered manual and non-manual workers and established a single pay spine covering both groups. Key features of this agreement include a new job evaluation scheme, which individual local authorities can choose whether they use, provision for authorities to move away from national grades and the possibility for them to modify some conditions of service through local negotiations (Industrial Relations Services, 1997).[5] In a similar vein, in the NHS lengthy negotiations have taken place over a government initiated *Agenda for Change*, which will herald major changes in existing pay systems. Such changes will, among other things, reduce the number of different pay spines to just three, enable service-based incremental progression to be modified by progression based on new responsibilities and competencies, and allow variations in some conditions of service to be negotiated locally (Bach and Winchester, 2003).

Such changes in the NHS and local government therefore embody a substantial increase in local autonomy, albeit within a framework of centrally negotiated agreements. In doing so, they raise a more general point, namely that the last two decades have seen public sector employers seeking to develop local human resource strategies and related policies that are both more 'enterprise' focussed and embody a range of initiatives concerned with improving organisational performance and reforming individual employment relations. These initiatives have encompassed the establishment of new channels of communication with employees, the introduction of new work practices, the adoption of appraisal schemes, and the creation of individual forms of performance-related pay (Heery, 1998; Cully *et al.*, 2000; Millward *et al.*, 2000). Indeed, in relation to this last issue, it should be noted that such pay arrangements exist across the civil service following a government decision to abolish the system of incremental progression through pay grades on the basis of service (Marsden and Richardson, 1994).

The issue of convergence

In the introduction, it was noted that two forms of convergence have been alleged to be occurring internationally as a result of managerial reforms introduced into the public sector. First, a move towards the adoption of private sector models of behaviour by public sector employers. Secondly, a trend towards an increasing degree of similarity between countries in the public sector management strategies and practices utilised. In this section, these two alleged forms of convergence are explored by considering, in turn, two issues. First, the issue of how far recent changes in public sector collective bargaining arrangements in Britain, a country that has been seen as at the leading edge of 'managerialist' reforms in the sector, echo those found in private undertakings. Secondly, the question of to what extent these British changes are echoed in those that have been taking place in other western European countries.

Public-private sector convergence in Britain

In exploring the issue of whether there is an increasing convergence between industrial relations in the British public and private sectors, an important difficulty immediately arises. This is that no clear model of private sector industrial relations can easily be identified. For example, in reviewing the findings of the four workplace industrial/employee relations surveys conducted over the period 1980-98, Millward *et al.* note that it is hard to interpret the changes identified as providing a firm indication of the adoption of a new model of employee relations and go on to argue that 'more plausible is the notion that a number of alternative approaches… are being adopted in different types of workplaces and in different parts of the economy' (Millward *et al.*, 2000: 246–247). Nevertheless, it can be stated that, in broad terms, the degree of convergence which has occurred in the area of collective bargaining, to date, is limited.

Trade union membership in the public sector, for example, remains considerably higher than in the private sector, as noted earlier. Furthermore, the difference in membership between the two sectors has been growing, rather than declining. In a similar vein, in contrast to the private sector, the unilateral determination of pay by management remains rare in the public sector (see further below).

At the same time, some similarity of trends between the public and private sectors can be identified. One such trend resides in the way in which the attempts made to decentralise collective bargaining arrangements in the public sector, either by the breaking-up of centralised single employer bargaining in the civil service or the 'loosening' of multi-employer agreements in the NHS and local government, echo the move towards individual, enterprise-based bargaining arrangements in parts of the private sector where multi-employer negotiations previously existed (Millward *et al.*, 2000; Brown *et al.*, 2003). Another, similarly concerns the degree to which both sectors have seen a growth in the subcontracting of work to other providers and hence a corresponding rise in the reliance placed on inputs from staff who do not have their terms and conditions determined in-house (Colling, 2000).

Other related developments in the public sector similarly echo those that have occurred in the private sector. For example, while union membership does remain considerably higher than in the private sector, it is also true that the proportion of workers belonging to unions has declined significantly since 1989, although not across all parts of the public sector (Cully and Woodland, 1997; Mathieson and Corby, 1990; Millward *et al.*, 2000). Ironically, however, since this decline has been lower than that in the private sector, the differences in the density of union membership in the two sectors have increased rather than reduced. For example, Millward *et al.* report that while union membership density in workplaces with 25 or more employees fell by 2.6 per cent during the period 1990–98, the corresponding decline in the private sector was 3.6 per cent (Millward *et al.*, 2000: 88). In addition, there is some evidence that the proportion of employers who 'strongly recommended' union membership declined somewhat over the period 1984–98, although, as with the fall in union density, the extent of this decline was considerably less than in the private sector (Millward *et al.*, 2000). Furthermore, some limited derecognition of unions for collective bargaining purposes has taken place, notably in respect of senior management grades (Corby and White, 1999). Once again, however, such derecognition has been much less common than in the private sector (Claydon, 1996; Millward *et al.*, 2000).

Developments with regard to the role and influence of workplace union representatives in workplaces where unions are recognised similarly do not clearly portray a picture of convergence (Millward *et al.*, 2000; Terry, 2003). For example, while the period 1980–98 saw some reduction in the presence of such representatives in the public sector, this trend would seem to have only been mirrored among private service workplaces and not private manufacturing ones. In a somewhat similar vein, the scope of workplace bargaining over non-pay issues changed little in the public sector over the period 1984–98, while, on average, it reduced in private manufacturing and rose slightly in private services.[6] Indeed, in the public sector, in contrast to private manufacturing and services, the period 1990–98 saw a marked growth in the proportion of employers reporting union constraints on their ability to organise work.[7]

Overall, then, a number of developments in public sector collective bargaining have, in 'directional terms', accorded with those that have taken place within private sector organisations. At the same time, they have been generally much less marked. As a result, and somewhat ironically, the differences between public and private sector arrangements have tended to grow, rather than reduce: a picture that could be described as the public sector 'heading towards convergence, but succeeding in becoming more different'. Indeed, strikingly, such a description is also applicable if attention is paid more widely to trends in the use of such methods of employee involvement and communication as problem-solving groups and team briefing systems. For example, in their analysis of the findings obtained from the 1984–98 workplace industrial / employee relations surveys, Millward *et al.* note that the growth in the use of briefing groups was 'entirely confined to private sector workplaces' Millward *et al* (2000: 120). It would therefore seem that, insofar as developments of this type have been occurring in public sector organisations, they have been much less marked than in private sector.

International convergence: the case of Western Europe

Across much of Western Europe, attempts have been made to reform the composition, structure and management of public sector activities.[8] In a number of countries, including Spain and Denmark, the division of public service responsibilities between central, regional and local levels of government have been reformed in order to both clarify them and introduce a greater degree of local autonomy and managerial accountability. In the case of Sweden, central government managerial responsibilities have, in a similar fashion to what has occurred in the British civil service, also been devolved to a large number of state agencies (Wise, 1993). In addition, state enterprises, in countries such as Denmark, France, Italy and Spain, have been 'corporatised' and sometimes privatised in sectors like air transport, banking, telecommunications, railways and postal services, and a greater use has been made of outsourcing. However, developments in these last areas have generally been on a smaller scale than has been the case in Britain.

In relation to collective bargaining, the overall trend has been towards it playing a greater role in the determination of the terms and conditions of public sector staff. Somewhat ironically, given the antipathy exhibited towards collective bargaining by British Conservative governments over the period 1979–97, this trend has, broadly, occurred in order to *increase* the flexibility of internal labour markets.

In many Western European countries, a significant proportion of civil servants have traditionally not been employed on standard employment contracts. Instead, in order to guarantee their commitment to, and neutrality towards, government policies, they were accorded a special legal status and, relatedly, worked in internal labour markets marked by highly detailed job classification systems and rules governing recruitment and promotion, and had their terms and conditions unilaterally determined by the state. Increasingly, the desirability of this status both from the point of view of unions and government has come to be questioned. In a range of states, including France, Italy, the Netherlands and Spain, it was therefore decided to bring the determination of many aspects of such workers terms and conditions within the ambit of collective bargaining:[9] decisions that have had the effect of bringing public sector industrial relations more into line with those of the private sector. As a result, there has, as in Britain, been a similar trend to reduce the distinctiveness of pay determination arrangements in the public sector. However, this trend has acted to expand, rather than challenge, the role of collective bargaining.

The collective bargaining structures across the public services of western Europe have traditionally been highly centralised. This is now also true of those which apply to the civil servants that have recently been brought within their coverage. That said, attempts have been made in recent years to introduce a greater degree of flexibility and local autonomy into the bargaining arrangements. In Denmark, for example, following an earlier initiative in 1987 to establish 'wage pools' whereby one per cent of the pay award was reserved for distribution locally, a new pay system was introduced in 1997 under which a substantially higher percentage of centrally determined aggregate pay would be distributed via three components. First, a supplementary amount based on job characteristics, such as degree of responsibility; secondly, a qualifications allowance; and thirdly, a component based on performance, paid either on an individual or group basis. A key objective of this reform, which has, in practice, been implemented variably across the public sector as a whole, was the replacement of automatic, seniority-based pay increments with a system in which pay more accurately reflected the qualifications and performance of each employee, or group of employees (Andersen *et al.*, 1999).

Denmark has also, more generally, seen the delegation of some bargaining to the local level with regard to such matters as the re-classification of jobs and the content of personnel policies. In a similar vein, in Germany and Italy centrally negotiated provisions on working time have provided for them to be implemented through local negotiations (Keller, 1999), and in France, provision has similarly been made for such negotiations to play a role with regard to some matters, including occupational training (Mossé, *et al.*, 1999). Similarly, in Italy, national agreements have set aside a maximum amount of money that can be used locally to pay overtime, performance-related increases and other allowances (Bordogna *et al.*, 1999) and, in Spain, provision has been made for the payment of 'productivity supplements' (Jodar *et al.*, 1999). More generally, these processes of decentralisation have often been accompanied by a range of locally driven initiatives to reform human resource management policies and practices, often with the aim of improving communications and securing higher levels of workforce involvement.

Overall, then, with the exception of the extension of collective bargaining arrangements to civil servants – a development that reflects the differing legal status that they have often held in countries other than Britain – many of the industrial relations reforms introduced across western Europe are not only similar, but echo the nature and thrust of those that have taken place in Britain. At the same time, the scale and the pace of national level changes have varied significantly and have, for the most part, been considerably smaller and slower than those in Britain, notably with regard to the degree that decentralisation has occurred and the extent to which there has been an individualisation of employment relationships. Thus, as Bach (1999) has observed, while developments in Britain come closest to representing the transformation of public sector employment relations, those in Germany embody a substantial degree of inertia. Meanwhile, developments in other countries can be seen as falling somewhere between these two extremes.

Conclusion

Governments, internationally, are seeking to improve the cost-effectiveness and efficiency of public sector activities, and to dispose of ones that are viewed as being more appropriately operated on a private basis. The reforms that have been introduced to achieve these objectives of cost-effectiveness and efficiency include, at a general level, the re-structuring of public services in order to devolve managerial responsibilities and make managers more accountable. In the area of industrial relations, they have also included attempts to revise collective bargaining structures and in doing so decentralise them and thereby provide a greater degree of local flexibility, including the greater ability to reward workers on the basis of their qualifications, work responsibilities and performance.

It has been argued that this reform process is giving rise to two forms of convergence. First, a trend towards the adoption by public sector organisations of policies and practices that are utilised by private sector employers. Secondly, a tendency for a growing similarity between the policies and practices being used by public sector employers internationally.

This chapter has sought to explore how far these two types of convergence are occurring. It has done so by, initially, reviewing the industrial relations reforms that have occurred over the last two decades in Britain, the country that is seen to have introduced the most radical public sector reforms. It has then used this review to explore (a) how far, in the case of Britain, there appears to have been a convergence between collective bargaining arrangements in the private and public sectors and (b) the degree of similarity that exists between the reforms that have been made to such arrangements in Britain and those introduced in a number of Western European economies.

With regard to the convergence between collective bargaining in the British public and private sectors, a rather mixed picture emerges. Thus, on the one hand, collective bargaining continues to occupy a much more important role in the public sector than the private sector. The growth that has occurred in the unilateral determination of pay, terms and conditions in the latter has only very partially been mirrored in the former. Yet, on the other hand, a number of developments in the public sector, such as the decentralisation of collective bargaining, the growth in subcontracting, the decline in union membership density and the extent to which employers encourage workers to join unions, echo those found in the private sector. These developments, however, have generally occurred on a much smaller scale than has been the case outside of the public sector. As a result, it seems reasonable to argue that, at the aggregate level, public sector industrial relations have become more, rather than less, distinctive.

Turning to the issue of public sector convergence in Western Europe, there are clear signs of a similarity in the developments that have occurred, particularly if the expanded role accorded to collective bargaining apparent in a number of states is discounted when comparisons are made with Britain. The nature and scale of the changes introduced have, however, varied considerably, with the result that marked differences continue to exist between countries with regard to the degree of decentralisation that has occurred. Moreover, it cannot be straightforwardly assumed that these differences will significantly decline in the future, given the complex networks of economic, political and social factors that act to shape national processes of public sector reform. This last point, in turn, serves to raise a more general point. This is that while, on the basis of the preceding analysis, it can be expected that similar pressures for collective bargaining reform can be found in a range of other countries across the world, the precise changes that they engender are likely to embody a number of country specific features. Insofar as convergence between countries occurs, it is likely to be of a partial nature.

Notes

1. One important indication of this change of philosophy was the government's decision to remove a number of mechanisms, notably the Standing Committee on Pay Comparability Chaired by Professor Hugh Clegg, which supported the establishment of comparability in pay. See Winchester and Bach (1999) and Duncan (2001).
2. It should be noted that pay review boards already existed prior to this in relation to doctors and dentists, senior civil servants and the armed forces.
3. Since their foundation, however, NHS Trusts have been empowered to appoint new staff on local terms and conditions.
4. The introduction of such regional variations in pay raises the issue of how far they would act, against a background of recruitment difficulties in parts of the public sector, to encourage competitive and potentially damaging, bargaining between differing regional negotiating bodies. For a discussion of how this occurred in respect of train drivers, see Ewing 2003.
5. It should also be noted that in order to prevent the externalisation of work under competitive tendering exercises many workers experienced the introduction of terms and conditions that were below those specified at national level. See Foster and Scott (1998).
6. These aggregate findings should not be taken to mean that the influence of unions has not declined in some public sector workplaces. See, for example, Corby (1998), Bryson *et al.*, (1995) and Carter and Poynter (1998).
7. Some authors see decentralisation as providing a platform for the *renewal* of workplace union organisation. See, for example, Fairbrother (2000).
8. This section draws heavily on Ferner (1994) and the various contributions in the edited volume by Bach *et al.* (1999).
9. Such a trend has, however, not been universal. See Keller (1999) concerning the position in Germany.

9

Managing Quality in Public Services: Some Distinct Implications for the Re-organisation of Work

Ian Roper

This chapter seeks to identify issues relating to the 'public service labour process', with special reference to the role of quality management as employed within the discourse of 'new public management' (NPM). The issue of quality has received relatively little attention in the discussion of NPM in recent years. However, as will be seen, this is as a result of the underlying assumptions within quality management being now so fully entrenched within NPM that it is no longer deemed necessary to explicitly link these two issues. Nevertheless, quality management does warrant specific attention to its application in public service provision, not least because of its stated objective for reorganising work.

It tends to be assumed that, because 'quality' is an inherently good thing, 'quality management' must necessarily be a rational extension of this. However, 'quality', under the definition set by 'quality management', is a highly specific attribute closely tied to utilitarian, market-based assumptions of what constitutes 'goodness'. Within this context, 'quality', within quality management, is a much more contestable concept than would first seem apparent: quality becomes explicitly tied to the issue of productivity and managers become the arbiters of those customer desires that constitute quality. Managers and workers do not, then, have a shared interest in quality. In the context of public services, this issue is further exacerbated by a range of factors. First, quality management presents a challenge in its attempt to redefine 'quality' away from 'traditional' means that are reliant on the knowledge, expertise and values of the provider. Secondly, however, this challenge to the professional autonomy of the public service worker is countered by the need to harness the commitment of the self-same workers to the goals of management in its drive for improving quality. In this sense there appears to be an ambiguous relationship between quality management and the 'public service ethos' that is said to motivate public servants.

Using examples drawn from research conducted in British local government, the aim of this chapter is to reappraise what quality management actually aims to 'manage' in these circumstances. In the context of public service delivery, it is proposed that quality management manifests itself in a number of competing tendencies. First, the abstract notion of 'the customer' creates tensions when mixed with the 'public service ethos'; second, quality management is identified as intensifying work through the conflation of quality with value-for-money; and third, quality management is identified as challenging professional autonomy through the managerial concern for demonstrating equity and probity in service outcomes. However, these agendas are sometimes mutually inconsistent and are uneven in their effects.

The chapter proceeds in the following way. First, a justification for applying a 'labour process' approach to the seemingly difficult area of public service work is made. From this, the context of applying commercial quality management initiatives in local government is described, indicating that a managerial definition of 'quality', in such an environment, is an inherently ambiguous concept. After a brief description of the research methodology, evidence is then presented which indicates that quality management affects the organisation of work in a number of different, and sometimes contradictory, ways in the delivery of public services. Finally, these issues are reflected on, in terms of their wider implications for work in public services, at the end of the chapter.

A public service labour process?

A number of underlying factors make the notion of a 'public service labour process' possible, despite some seemingly inherent problems in such a claim. The labour process debate, from Braverman through to recent disputes about Foucaldian subjectivism, has primarily been concerned with the management of work in a commercial environment, because it is the market imperative that provides the driving mechanism for the managerial regulation of work within labour process analysis. Yet little has been said of how these issues are manifested, if at all, in public services where such commercial imperatives do not constitute the central organising principle for the managerial organisation of work.

In the initial debate, following Braverman (1974), the labour process – being the process of transforming labour power into surplus value – is defined as being systematically degraded through the deployment of technology informed by Taylorist management practice to deskill workers (Thompson, 1989). Here, deskilling permanently transfers worker discretion into the hands of management, affecting the effort bargain through increasing management's ability to dictate the rate of work while simultaneously undermining workers' bargaining power in the labour market. Management, then, is identified explicitly with the furtherance of the process of capital accumulation. In the Foucauldian reconstitution of labour process theory, while any driving logic of capital accumulation is rejected *per se*, managerial attempts to harness worker subjectivity are still based upon coherent strategies (or narratives) based upon the interests of the organisation as perceived by managers (Knights, 1990). In all definitions, then, the labour process is initiated by management and is driven by the motive of profit; be this commercial success or commercial survival.

The notion that labour process analysis may be of relevance in the public sector is not new. Braverman's attentions, in the latter stages of his work, concerned the effects of deskilling in administrative and clerical work. This theme not only brings in important issues relating to how the deskilling debate crosses into gender and labour market re-segmentation (Crompton and Jones, 1984), but also, how these trends might be felt acutely in the employment growth area of public sector administration. Indeed, the growth of the state in the twentieth century – and the subsequent growth of workers therein – is identified by Braverman as being of prime import-ance to the increasing degradation of clerical work in the twentieth century. A more specific reason for applying the logic of labour process analysis to public service work, however, is the rise of NPM. A more general discussion of NPM is provided in chapters 2 and 6 and will not be re-attempted, here. However, to summarise, NPM could be said to incorporate the following guiding principles and assumptions (Hood 1991):

- An enhanced managerial prerogative to drive change
- Explicit standards, goals and targets to drive change
- Greater emphasis on output controls
- Disaggregation of units in the public sector
- Increased competition in the public sector
- Greater use of private sector management styles
- Greater discipline and parsimony in resource use

The introduction of the discourse of NPM has, for obvious reasons, enhanced the applicability of labour process analysis in the public sector, whose relevance may previously have been more tenuous. However, there remain significant differences between a marketised public sector and the private sector. The 'public' nature of public services means that marketisa-tion can only ever be partial. Additionally, there remain some significant areas of work that are not readily reducible through a process of systematic deskilling: professional discretion remains at the core of much public service work. Nevertheless, the coexistence of two counterpoising imperat-ives create some common underpinnings in all public service work. Firstly, 'the market' does not ultimately determine the quantity and quality of work for public services. The market allocates resources by 'wants', not 'needs' and in public services, 'wants' and 'needs' are not the same thing.

Following from this, success in fulfilling 'needs' does not automatically trigger market-based incentives and rewards – measured in terms of increased revenue, market share and / or profit. In this context then, any attempt at operating a 'market' in public services can only ever be partial and artificial; it is never 'natural'. Secondly, however, the organisation of public services cannot be isolated from wider economic imperatives. So, not only is *all* work in public services affected by the broader mechanisms of the labour market, but it is also affected by the very objective of attempting – however inappropriately – to artificially impose some form of market.

It is this tension, then, that underlies the labour process in public services. NPM prescribes that public servants be 'entrepreneurial' and act more like their private sector counterparts. Accordingly, managers should operate on the assumption that their 'customers' have a choice and will not return if they feel they can get a better service elsewhere. Leaving aside the fact that such a rational definition of manager behaviour in the private sector is hugely simplistic, this model clearly cannot be applied to managers working in public services. Firstly, many of the services in question are regulatory, which means that the service being offered is intended to restrict some aspect of their 'customers' behaviour. Secondly, in the absence of a 'real' market, aspects of public service provision have always been about rationing on an equitable basis. Finally, as a consequence of the above, aspects of public service work are inevitably about dealing with conflicting interests. All in all, attempting to force 'the customer' metaphor into complex situations such as this could only be done if the concept is stretched so far as to make it meaningless; meanwhile, the demand for public goods remains inherently 'political' and discretionary. Yet governments from the 1980s onwards have been geared to reigning-in what was seen as over-employment in public services by transforming it into a pseudo-private sector. Driven by a mixture of new right populism and public choice theory, government policy aimed to impose the discipline of the market onto a wide range of public services, while simultaneously cutting expenditure. Where privatisation was seen as inappropriate – that is in public services – the emphasis shifted to introducing various forms of 'quasi-markets' (LeGrand, 1990).

In Britain, as elsewhere, these changes were met with anticipated resistance from public service trade unions and büro-professionals in centralised public services. This process was further complicated in local government, however, by the obstruction of 'politics'. During the most intense period of reform, the majority of local authorities in Britain were controlled by Labour, who at this time were pursuing, at the local level, a very different agenda to that of NPM – where quality of service was being equated with favourable employment conditions for public service employees. In some high profile cases, obstruction extended to organised political resistance by the 'new urban left' (Lansley *et al.*, 1989). Therefore, the vehicle for imposing markets in local authorities was through compulsory competitive tendering (CCT) (Flynn, 1994; Walsh, 1995a). Through CCT, services were sub-divided into being either 'purchasers' or 'providers'; with providers then being required to 'compete' for contracts with external contractors under strict rules to prevent 'anticompetitive behaviour' – rules which sought explicitly to prevent the inclusion of employment protection measures as part of contract specification.[1]

The combined effect of introducing quasi-markets with the ever-increasing financial constraints centrally imposed onto local authorities created lasting effects on the organisation of work in local authorities. Work organisation is no longer determined by political decision-making normally associated with public sector management. Neither, however, is it determined by any 'natural' consumer demand for public services. Instead, workers are expected to adapt their behaviour according to arbitrarily determined indicators of success, laid down by central government, but monitored and administered by local managers. While such mechanisms may provide some form of negative incentive for workers – that is the need to be seen as *not* failing to meet minimum targets – the positive incentive associated with market definitions of success – financial reward – is not present.

The adoption of NPM in Britain during the 1980s and 1990s was tied explicitly to the Thatcherite assumptions of the Conservative administrations of the time. However, it would seem that NPM has had a much wider resonance than through this narrowly Conservative agenda. It could be plausibly argued that similar reforms were being introduced by Labour administrations in Australia and New Zealand during the same period of time as the Thatcher reforms in Britain (Alford, 1993; Gregory, this volume). In addition, NPM in Britain has latterly become fully entrenched under 'New Labour': the vigorous pursuit of performance-based regulation, competition and public-private partnership as the basis of 'modernisation' is proof of this (Martin, 2002). However, the ever-narrowing partisan divide between Conservative and centre-left parties on these issues does not mean that the content of NPM has become a value-neutral issue: NPM remains rooted in neo-liberal assumptions. Because the origins and underlying assumptions behind NPM, such as consumerist individualism, Public Choice theory, and Monetarism among others, *are* New Right assumptions, this suggests that it is the values of those administrations (Labour administrations in Australia and New Zealand; 'New Labour' in Britain) that have changed, rather than the content of NPM. This points to a further influence that has increased pressure to 'reform' public services in European countries along the lines recommended in NPM, as is noted in Bach *et al.*, (1999).

Quality management in a public service context

Quality management can been seen as being particularly influential in the drive to reform public service provision, for a number of inter-related structural and ideological reasons linked to the growth of managerialism (Clarke and Newman, 1997; Pollitt, 1993). The expansion of CCT in the late 1980s was more closely tied to arguments of 'quality' than the initial wave in the early 1980s. Indeed, the White Paper introducing this expansion was entitled 'Competing for Quality' (HMSO, 1988) thereby making the explicit link between competitive tendering and a specific definition of quality – the one built into commercial quality management initiatives. Structurally, quality management matched well with the more 'cost centre' oriented organisational structures being introduced during this time. It also offered a means of dealing with the ever increasing demands for meeting performance targets. Ideologically, quality management embraces the rhetoric of the market and customers. In addition, it is likely to appeal to managers as it raises the profile of managerial decision-making during a period where local political decision-making has been eroded by central government. Finally, quality plays a prominent role in the NPM discourse in academic, training and consultancy advice offered to local authorities (Pollitt, 1993).

The essence of the quality management boom in the 1980s and 1990s was the result of the influence of the so-called 'quality gurus', with Deming (1986), Juran (1988) and Crosby (1979) being the most prominent. The quality gurus' message was initially appealing because of their purported contribution to the 'Japanese economic miracle' of the 1970s and 1980s. Combined with this was the, perhaps even more powerful, message that quality could be demystified from an abstract honorific concept, into a manageable process aligned to the needs of business (Juran, 1988).

Despite these assertions, quality itself remains elusive. This is particularly the case in the area of public services because of their inherently political nature (Kirkpatrick and Martinez-Lucio, 1995; Pfeffer and Coote, 1991; Walsh, 1995b). Indeed, all parties involved in public services can legitimately make claims to be promoting 'quality': from 'defending jobs and services'; to promoting equal opportunities; to empowering user groups; to maximising taxpayer value-for-money. The definition in quality management, however, is hampered by being an exclusively utilitarian, consumerist 'value-for-money' one. Broadening the quite specific 'guru' conceptions of quality into wider 'stakeholding' definitions – so that the quality management package can be made to suit public service scenarios (Gaster, 1995) – therefore implies an encroachment into more general areas of work organisation not immediately associated with quality, with associated implications for the labour process.

The growth of quality initiatives in the public sector has grown rapidly from the 1980s. Yet the initiatives introduced often contained widely varying assumptions about what was, essentially, being managed. Table 9.1 shows the incidence of quality management initiatives being operated in 1996, ranging from holistic practices such as total quality management (TQM), through to more systems-oriented accredited schemes like ISO 9001, to simple complaints procedures made almost mandatory by central government regulatory initiatives.

Interestingly, the evidence for the continuing trend is not available in this format more recently. It is likely that this is a result of a rationalisation of management practices in the area of quality. When Labour replaced CCT with their policy of Best Value (BV) in 1999, rather than it being a retreat from the demands of competition and regulatory prescription, BV strengthened these aspects (Higgins *et al.*, forthcoming). In relation to quality, BV requires this issue to be dealt with in a more strategic and more holistic way, to the extent that Boyne *et al.* (2002) suggest that BV may go so far as constituting the formal transfusion of TQM into local government.

How, then, do quality management methods change the nature of work in public services? This is a contentious issue even in private sector services, where quality management has been variously identified with the increased encroachment of managerial regulation into the 'emotional' aspects of work (Taylor, 1998), through to the notion that worker responses to discourses of 'excellence' may have been used by workers to turn back on management (Rosenthal *et al.*, 1997). Some suggest that TQM tends to be viewed as either enriching work or intensifying work but that the perceptions of workers may vary according to how such policies are implemented (Edwards *et al.*, 1998; Wilkinson; Redman *et al.*, 1995).

Table 9.1   Use of quality methods in local government 1996

Quality management method	Per cent usage
Complaints procedure	89
Investors in people	69
ISO 9001	67
Service charter	67
Customer involvement	66
QCs (teams)	52
TQM	40
Charter mark	31

Source Data: LGMB Quality Survey 1996 (England and Wales only)

The research case studies

The evidence reported here is taken from research in two English local authorities in a wider four-authority study conducted between 1995 and 1997. The research involved documentary analysis; the interviewing of managers, trade union officials and staff; and a questionnaire survey of union membership.[2] The first case was a London borough – '*LonBoro*' – a politically marginal borough, recently under control of a 'new suburban right' (NSR) (Holiday, 1991) Conservative administration. The second was an urban city council in the north of England – '*NorBoro*' – under long term control of a 'paternalist' Labour administration.

LonBoro's quality management policy was at the forefront of a large-scale transformation of the authority. Consciously tied to a politicised manager- ial transformation of the Council structure and culture, quality manage- ment was part of a holistic strategy involving the creation of internal markets, contract relationships and the selective outsourcing of services. As a result, direct employment was reduced from 7500 to 4000 over a three year period.

NorBoro was a strongly entrenched Labour administration. It had not been influenced by the 'new urban left' agenda of the 1980s but neither was it identifiably 'New Labour'. *NorBoro* had a track record of successful retention of direct services up until the 1990s – when the financial squeeze from central government began to bite. Quality management at *NorBoro* was piecemeal, due to the weakness of the corporate centre, and the strength and entrenchment of the union within the authority. While all departments officially had a quality policy, only one fully pursued the agenda pro-actively. In this department – a multi-functional department – quality was being approached in a procedural, systemic manner through the ISO 9001 quality system standard.

Quality management and the labour process in two authorities

The first observation to make is that, on the whole, workers at both author- ities 'approved' of the quality policies being pursued in each case (Table 9.2). What is *also* apparent, however, is that there are clear distinctions between these two authorities: at *LonBoro*, approval of the quality policy was gener- ally high, while at *NorBoro* opinion was more indifferent.

Beneath these general trends, there were significant differences of worker perceptions of quality management. These differences were due to the dif- fering nature of quality management policy and the difference that this had on different areas of work. These differences will now be described in terms of customer orientation, work intensification and work standardisation.

Table 9.2   Approval rating of quality management policy (per cent)

	Happy	*Indifferent*	*Unhappy*
LonBoro	52.8	33.6	13.6
NorBoro	43.2	45.9	10.8

'Customer orientation' and the 'public service ethos'

One of the most notable aspects of introducing quality management into public services is its role of redefining work activity around the 'cult(ure) of the customer' (DuGay and Salaman, 1992) – this being part of a general attempt to re-imagine large bureaucratic organisations into becoming 'entrepreneurial', 'anti-bureaucratic' organisations that are constantly striving to improve (DuGay, 1994; 1996). It is, therefore, not surprising that the language of the 'customer' was widespread by managers throughout the wider four-authority study. Managers at *NorBoro*, however, were more reluctant to use this terminology, for 'political reasons' and for fear of provoking hostility from some workers who may have seen such a re-emphasis as a challenge to their autonomy and 'public service' values. Overall, opinions on how the customer metaphor affected work was divided. Table 9.3, based on responses to a statement proposed on the staff questionnaire, indicates some cynicism among staff at *LonBoro* – where opinion seems sharply polarised; and ambivalence by staff at *NorBoro*.

The 'customer oriented' aspect of quality management is the means by which professional autonomy is challenged. This challenge is based upon a mistrust of the professional's motives being based variously upon self-interest, büro-maximisation, task demarcation, and abuse of knowledge-power. Quality management potentially enables professionals to be reigned-in and the use of the customer metaphor could be seen as a useful device by which roles could be redefined around what Broadbent and Laughlin (2002) term an 'accounting logic'. At *LonBoro*, 'customer orientation' was official policy and managers at *LonBoro* were less concerned about such constraints:

> ...people can also hide behind [the notion of public service ethos] because it means they can develop life routines that make their life easier for a reasonable return and convince themselves that they are still motivated entirely by public altruistic leanings...(Senior Manager: *LonBoro*)

Subverting the public service ethos, however, can pose problems for managers. On the one hand, an inherent tendency in quality management is of

Table 9.3 Opinions on customers

	(agree)				(disagree)
	1	2	3	4	5
LonBoro	37.5	23.5	18.4	8.8	11.8
NorBoro	26.8	17.1	26.8	14.6	14.6

('Concern for Council customers is all very well, but it's Council staff who seem to be bearing the brunt of it all')

reigning-in the professional's discretion – and the public service ethos provides legitimacy for this discretionary power. On the other hand, managers are increasingly dependent on the intrinsic motivational rewards that could be said to be embodied within the pubic service ethos – especially in areas where similarly qualified professionals in the private sector are on significantly higher levels of pay. This dilemma is manifested in the link between quality and performance, particularly at *LonBoro*. If an 'entrepreneurial' motivation is to be successful, employees may nominally expect rewards for their involvement in the increased success of the organisation – in terms of remuneration or a widening of roles or status. Such rewards would be unlikely, however. This is because, firstly, 'success' in delivering services would be unlikely to deliver increased income and, secondly, because rewarding success through expanding the remit of büro-professionals is anathema to entrepreneurial governance. In practice, such problems have been identified in attempts to introduce performance related pay *equitably* into public services (Heery, 1998). In *LonBoro* the attempt to allow 'forward thinking' individuals to leap-frog established staff was undermined by budget cutting from above. This forced one local manager – responsible for redundancy payments from his budget – to contemplate losing his newly promoted staff ahead of the longer standing members of staff, now resentful of being bypassed by newer staff.

Inducing worker commitment to management-defined goals is often legitimised through the rhetoric of 'empowerment' – encouraging workers to show increased initiative through increased delegation of decision-making. Nominally, such delegation avoids significant loss of managerial control because the decision-making *process* is defined and strictly ring-fenced by management. In both authorities, however, this became more difficult where operational decisions become blurred with 'political' issues – primarily resources.

At *LonBoro* devolved decision-making was restricted to service managers being given increased autonomy within pre-determined budgets, and this varied from service to service. Libraries were a case in point. Here, the marketisation of the council structure combined with the discretionary nature of the service as a whole, created a high level of fear within the workplace, which was implicitly used by one manager to mandate outward signs of 'commitment' by workers. One manifestation of this was a reluctance of staff to take sick leave:

> Unfortunately there is an element of fear in it. I sometimes have to really work on people to persuade them, when they've been ill, that they shouldn't take it as annual leave...Fundamentally it is to do with changing work culture...It's to do with work culture change; it's to do with the idea of Quality Management – that people are no longer going to be allowed to get away with this sort of thing. I think commitment is part

> of it as well – getting people to actually work together as a team and to understand the impact of absenteeism for the rest of the team (Library Manager: *LonBoro*).

The effect of empowered local managers, with increased insecurity among staff – the result of working in a 'low priority' service, with budgetary decisions being isolated from local managers and the recent record of job losses – combined to create an atmosphere where local staffing arrangements could be made with limited resistance:

> …those people who aren't up to it, either they're gone, or they're on less money and there's always a problem with that – I'd prefer it if they were gone, but usually there's a choice…and, yeah, there's a few people who aren't going to be happy about it, because they're being paid what they're worth' (Library Manager: *LonBoro*).

Far from devolving authority and downplaying hierarchy, as is the orthodox claim of introducing decentralisation and cost centres, at *LonBoro*, devolution *increased* the hierarchical authority of the devolved manager over staff. Promoting employee 'commitment', in such an environment, belies the adage that 'you cannot mandate enthusiasm'.

The effects that 'customers' had on worker behaviour were greater in those areas where services were discretionary. Such services included libraries and leisure. In both cases, attention was paid to aesthetic issues – dress codes and the appearance of buildings. Here the impact on the 'emotional labour' of workers was restricted to the outward displays of commitment and, while displaying an increased capacity on the part of managers to dictate attitudes to workers, this did not seriously affect worker autonomy.

In the case of *NorBoro*, the situation was different. Decision-making was not delegated, but work processes were codified through ISO 9001. Because commitment to managerial objectives was not enforced through the contract mechanisms utilised at *LonBoro*, workers still felt able to express concerns about quality in a wider context – unconstrained by the managerial definitions of quality-as-effectiveness. This is not to say that workers at *LonBoro* could not – and did not – do so; or that workers at *NorBoro* were fully able to realise their concerns. Rather, it is that greater scope existed at *NorBoro* to address issues relating to quality that were outside a managerial agenda:

> The problem that the Council has got…is that people forget about the internal customer – that's us. They are totally pre-occupied with how the service is perceived by the external customer – except that in our case that means their customer, which are adults and councillors; it really

should be young people...We, the deliverers of the service, have been more or less forgotten. We're required to be mechanistic operators, just to ensure that we've got part-time workers in place in which ever section they're supposed to be in; that the building is safe and we make sure that we fill in all their forms – that's about the level of our operation... (Youth worker: *NorBoro*).

Quality management and work intensification

Because of the implicit difficulty of defining 'quality' in terms of 'customers' where *paying* customers are not present, the measures used to approximate 'customer need' are likely to vary from service to service. Moreover, definitions of quality are often definitions equally definable as indicators of performance efficiency; indicators identifying attributes such as speed of service, responsiveness, efficiency, economy (Gaster, 1995) as well as effectiveness and 'value for money'. In this form, improving quality equates directly with improving productivity by increasing the exposure of workers to the scrutiny of 'internal customers'. While the emphasis is on creating 'internal customer chains', then, in practice the 'internal customer' is a euphemism for increased exposure to managerial scrutiny through making all work routines transparent. As such, this process could legitimately be defined as work intensification (Delbridge and Turnbull, 1992).

While *LonBoro* had pursued a policy of voluntary outsourcing and *NorBoro* had strenuously resisted outsourcing, managers in both cases acknowledged that the CCT process had been a positive catalyst for increasing managerial control over the labour process. The importation of quality management methods into the devolved 'cost-centres' proved to be mutually supportive. The sub-dividing of services into more identifiable cost-centres made it easier to identify individual workers' performance. Customer 'needs' could now be channelled through streamlined management systems and 'customer feedback' on staff performance could be more accurately monitored. The deployment of team-based working in conjunction with performance targets for throughput resulted in tangible increases in workloads. Nevertheless there were differences between the two authorities, as to the impact of this (see Table 9.4).

Quality through work intensification was central to the quality programme being operated throughout *LonBoro*. *LonBoro*'s policy went beyond the organisational requirements of CCT and pursued quality vigorously

Table 9.4 Perceived effect of quality management policy on workloads (per cent)

	inc a lot	*inc a bit*	*Unchanged*	*dec a bit*	*dec a lot*
LonBoro	49.2	28.5	20	2.3	0
NorBoro	27.8	50	22.2	0	0

through its devolved internal market structure. While there were notable differences between how this affected work in different services, all services at *LonBoro* were affected. In contrast to the combined effects that contracts, performance monitoring and insecurity had on work, the conflation of quality with efficiency, here, meant job losses and the resultant 'productivity gains' became the end, rather than the means, of quality management. Such benefits were not universally appreciated by local managers, however:

> ...the degree, now, of the reduction of the work-force and the extra work we're expected to do – the demand that's placed on us – is such that there comes a point where actual quality of service, now, will reduce. We've soaked-up lots of work – lots of extra demands being placed on us. We managed to take on extra work ... but they don't seem to accept there is a limit to how far you can go with that. (Senior Manager, regulatory service business unit: *LonBoro*)

Quality and work standardisation

Contrary to the rhetoric of a move towards a more 'entrepreneurial' approach to public service management, some 'new' aspects of quality management in the case studies were inextricably based on apparently 'old fashioned' work standardisation. This was most evident in services where equity of service provision was deemed important (for example, regulatory services), where health and safety issues were considered important (for example, sport centres and day centres) and where staffing was based upon low paid, relatively unskilled work in quasi-commercial environments (for example, sports centres). Amidst the rhetorical pre-occupation with entrepreneurial approaches to public service, then, some of the quality management methods being introduced were distinctly 'Taylorian' in character. To look at this in reverse, staff at *LonBoro* and *NorBoro* did *not* equate quality management practices with empowerment – as the responses to the statement shown in Table 9.5 indicate. In this case, however, staff at *NorBoro* seemed to be more hostile.

While quality through work standardisation was applied in both authorities, the emphasis varied. At *NorBoro*, *ISO 9001* was initially deemed appro-

Table 9.5   Opinions on increased worker autonomy (per cent)

	(agree)				(disagree)
	1	2	3	4	5
LonBoro	16.8	17.5	20.4	19.0	26.3
NorBoro	4.8	23.8	21.4	33.3	16.7

('Quality Management offers employees more say over their own work than was the case before')

priate for leisure centres – for reasons articulated above – but was then pursued in the operation of Youth Day Centres. While this was justified as providing greater service equity and ensuring health and safety procedures, it is likely that the pursuit of this strategy – rather than the use of a more 'cultural' approach – was a desire to apply some universal methods of control in the vastly different workplace scenarios covered by the corporate department involved:

> To some extent work routines are possibly more regimented in that we now have to state what it is we do in terms of a daily operation and we have to, sort of, say this will be done on a four week cycle or a five week cycle, or whatever. Whereas before, if it got missed nobody noticed… now staff, individually – doesn't matter what their job – need to be accountable for the work that they do… (Quality Officer: *NorBoro*).

Standardising work routines for youth workers was restricted to peripheral areas of their main work activity – administrative, health and safety and maintenance procedures – rather than the intangible and wide ranging nature of the experience and skills involved in youth work itself.

While the base logic of work standardisation as a means of controlling output quality is one of deskilling, at *NorBoro* this method of control simultaneously increased exposure of managerial responsibilities to the scrutiny of workers. Rather than this being within the managerialist framework of quality – providing information that could be used to improve efficiency or value – it was often on broader issues – the lack of facilities/funding, bad working conditions, lack of political / managerial will, among others.

The effects of work standardisation were not uniform over services. In regulatory services, the increase in managerial control was through the standardisation of administrative procedures for reasons of service equity and improved administrative efficiency. While this was partly tied-up with an emphasis on 'customer care' – through a determination to improve communications with clients – the main outcome was the standardisation of administrative accountability. Among a broad range of regulatory functions this was pushed through via increased scrutiny required for customer feedback, the introduction of quality systems (*IiP, ISO 9001, Charter Mark*) and the use of technology to monitor administrative throughput. While this entailed a loss of individual work autonomy, quality management *in itself* did not seriously impede the professional worker's decision-making capacity in their core work activity.

Work standardisation was most noticeable in quasi-commercial operations – particularly leisure in *NorBoro*. Much of the work involved in leisure tends to be mundane, focusing on labour intensive safety functions (pool watching). Quality management, in this context, involved high levels of work standardisation.

Conclusions

One of the indisputable imperatives of New Public Management has been the importing of commercial management practices into public service administration. Perhaps the most high profile of this plethora of management initiatives have been those associated with quality (in one guise or another). Given that such initiatives were explicitly intended to change the way work is conducted in public services, it should not be surprising to find that work organisation has been changed by the introduction of quality management regimes. The evidence presented here suggests that managerial initiatives aimed at improving quality in public services, under the direct influence of NPM, have had definite effects on the work routines of those involved. These effects, however, are not the same as would be experienced in private sector organisations. Nor do they simply reproduce the 'empowerment' rhetoric found within much of the prescriptive TQM literature.

Because of this, quality management's impact on the labour process is more complex than may previously have been conceived. This is because, first, local government organisations – like many institutions operating public services – are inherently complex and not readily reducible to a 'core business activity'; and second, because 'quality', in this environment, is equally complex and irreducible to the logic of the 'customer'. Indeed, much of the unique character of these outcomes relates to the tension created by management attempting to impose work regimes built upon foundations reliant upon consumerist metaphors that are unable to be translated in the 'real world' of public service delivery.

In the case of the two local authorities described here, quality management operated at different levels of control and regulation (see Figure 9.1). Different approaches were applied, in some cases, according to the nature of the service and, in other cases, according to managerial preference determined at the authority. These choices, themselves, were affected by political issues surrounding the policy orientation of the respective ruling administrations and the perceived strength of trade union opposition in each case. In their own way, however, quality was seen as an issue that could legitimately be delegated to management. In one authority, a systemic approach was used, whereby managers hoped to ensure minimum levels of service consistency. At the other, a more holistic approach was adopted, incorporating the use of internal contracts. As such, the former was relying on an approach to quality based upon work standardisation while the latter, although using work standardisation, also included the more consistent use of work intensification and the mobilisation of worker commitment – to the extent to which it could be consistent with 'management by stress' (Parker and Slaughter, 1988). There was, however, no evident contradiction between these various approaches and no indication

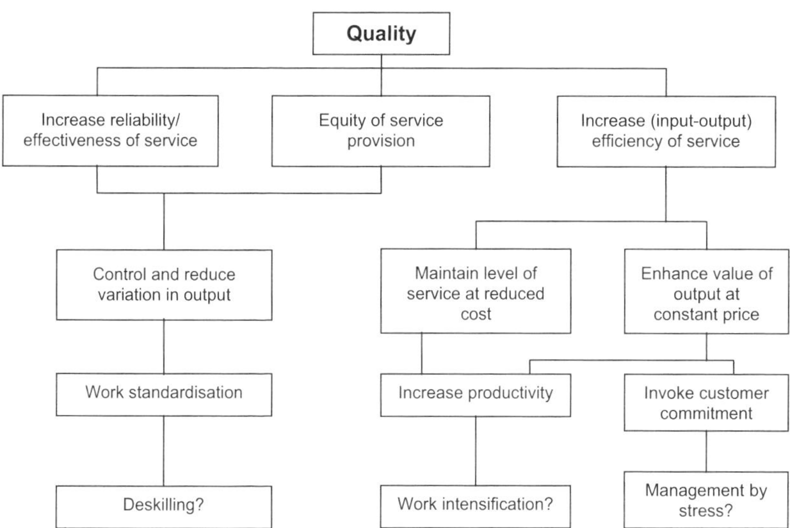

Figure 9.1   Managing quality in public services: implications for the labour process

that (for example) managing quality through mobilising commitment, was a more developed form of managerial control.

While these findings are applicable to the specific issues raised in the organisation of work in British local government, there are wider implications. First, the complex nature of public services means that quality management cannot appropriately be understood as having unified meanings or implications. Quality means more, in public services, than 'what the customer wants at the price they want to pay'. Rather, quality management operates on different rationales of control, depending on the particular attributes of 'quality' that may be applicable to the services involved. An implication, here, is that quality management is not appropriately conceptualised within some Taylorian/Post-Fordist dichotomy; or on some Bravermanian/Foucauldian continuum – as is increasingly implied in critical, as well as prescriptive texts – because the various methods described as supplanting 'traditional' methods may, in reality, be working *in addition* to such 'traditional' methods. It seems, for example, that the use of 'the customer' has had some effect on reorganising work, but not through undermining hierarchies. Managers may see themselves more as 'entrepreneurs' than as 'public administrators' now, *but they still see themselves as managers,* and the effects of internal markets, if anything, seems to have increased hierarchical authority through the increase of managerial scrutiny of employee performance.

Another important implication is that none of the above mentioned descriptions of quality management practice precludes 'resistance' from workers. Here, findings tend to support critiques of certain trends in contemporary labour process theory (Ackroyd and Thomson, 1999; Martinez-Lucio and Stewart, 1997; Thompson and Ackroyd, 1995). The awareness of workers of their relative bargaining power within the workplace – which is variable over time – affects the limits of managerial authority. Work-based knowledge and tacit skills are important factors here. First, quality management affects, say, professionals differently to semi-skilled workers. Second, the viability of the 'customer relationship' to a particular workplace scenario affects some workers more than others. Finally, the perception of employment security in any workplace is important – so workers in a 'discretionary' service with declining morale are more likely to be affected than workers who are *relatively* unmotivated by career prospects, or by workers in mandatory services.

Notes

1. It should be noted that the full impact of this was dulled as unions found they were able to deploy the EU Acquired Rights Directive in the form of 'TUPE' which prevented transferred employees from having their terms and conditions undermined by their 'new' employer.
2. For *LonBoro*, respondents totalled 144 (18% response rate); in *NorBoro*, respondents were taken from one corporate department only and totalled 50 (21%).

Part Three

Public Sector Reform: Regional and National Studies

10

Canadian Public Management Developments

Zsuzsanna Lonti and Anil Verma

It is not difficult to make the argument that public management in Canada in 2003, at the time of this writing, was substantially transformed from its post-World War II growth phase that lasted until the early 1980s. The twists and turns in public management in the last two decades of the twentieth century have followed the larger shifts in the macro-economic and the macro-political shifts in Canada in particular and, to a lesser extent, in North America and the rest of the world. For example, the drive towards leaner government, the shift from service delivery to policy and the growing use of technology within public management, are trends that can be linked to the growth in competition from free trade and deregulation, the growing pressure from business for smaller and more efficient government and the public pressure to cap and cut taxes while delivering quality services.

Many of the changes in public management have resulted in leaner, more efficient practices. Yet, these changes have not come about without controversy. Government employment, after falling for a number of years in the 1980s and the early 1990s, began to creep up gradually in the early 2000s. Labour-management relations went through new lows as conservative, market-oriented governments pushed through reforms often without union consultation or acquiescence. At the workplace level, public employers strove to introduce innovations from the private sector such as employee involvement, incentive pay, more training to create functional flexibility, and work teams. At the same time, these workforce reductions coupled with the introduction of various workplace innovations led to significant work intensification for most public employees.

Our objective in this chapter is to describe developments in public management in Canada and to set it within the context of changes occurring in public management internationally. Our primary focus is on public management developments at the federal and, to a lesser extent, the provincial levels of government subject to limitations of available information. We start by describing the structure of the Canadian public sector followed by a discussion of the major drivers of public sector reform in Canada. This is followed by a critical account of these developments from several vantage points. First, we provide a detailed chronology of the major public management initiatives since the early 1980s. Second, we look at the impact of these management reforms on labour-management relations. Thirdly, we augment this macro-level information with more micro-level data focusing on how these changes are experienced at the workplace level by presenting the results of a survey of workplace middle managers and two employee surveys. We conclude by putting Canadian public management developments into an international perspective.

Structure of the Canadian public sector

Canada is a highly decentralised federal state with 10 provinces and three territories. The Canadian public sector includes public administration at three levels of government: federal, provincial, and municipal; almost all of the education and health sectors, and a dwindling number of public enterprises. In 2002 the public sector employed 2 885 000 people, 22.8 per cent of all employed (Statistics Canada, 2002). From those, 760 000 were employed in public administration.

The British North America Act of 1867, later to be repatriated as the Constitution Act of 1982, dictates the separation of powers between the federal and provincial governments in Canada. The federal government has a relatively modest role in the economic and social spheres of the country. The Constitution gives the provinces great independence from the central government and wide-ranging powers, including substantial taxation capabilities. The federal government and the provincial governments have their own distinctive political cultures. The provinces also vary substantially in geographic size, population, economic base, and social composition.

The federal government has exclusive jurisdiction over defence, monetary and fiscal policy, and primary responsibility for external affairs. The provinces have primary responsibility for health, education, social welfare, labour issues, local government, non-criminal law, and natural resources. The provinces share power with the federal government for transportation, agriculture, economic development, the environment and other policy areas. Both levels of government derive most of their revenues from personal and corporate income taxes and from sales taxes. The federal government also provides large financial transfers to the provinces, mainly in the form of unconditional block grants (White, 2001). Most police, fire services, local transit, garbage collection and urban infrastructure are under municipal jurisdiction or are run by locally controlled agencies. Municipalities are created by provincial governments and are funded by a combination of provincial grants and local property taxes (Thompson, 2001).

Canada operates a Westminster-style parliamentary government. At the federal level Parliament consists of two chambers: the House of Commons, whose members are elected by popular vote, and the non-elected Senate. Senators are appointed by the Prime Minister. At the provincial level only one-chamber legislatures exist. Executive authority is vested in the Crown but exercised by the Prime Minister (and the Premiers at the provincial levels) and the ministers of his/her Cabinet that constitute the government. Cabinet members are elected representatives of the governing party, and, as a result, cabinet government is 'party government'. However, at the federal level Cabinet often includes one or two senators, even though they are not elected. Ministers are accountable to the House of Commons for their exercise of executive authority. Consequently, through the dynamics of party politics government is subject to democratic control ensuring representative and responsible government. Legislative authority resides in Parliament that also includes the government. In addition, good government is secured by a professional, non-partisan state bureaucracy, staffed on the basis of merit. With some very limited exemptions, state officials are subordinate to the executive authority of ministers (Auction, 1995).

After two unsuccessful attempts at constitutional reform[1] and due to the strong separatist sentiments of the French Canadian population of Quebec,[2] the new evolving federalism involves a more modern relationship between the two levels of government based on the principles of partnership (Treasury Board of Canada, 2002; Simeon, 2002).

Major drivers of public sector management initiatives

Increasing global competition, pressures to control mounting government deficits and debts, the impact of technological advances, changing public expectations of the government's role and the quality of public services, and an ideological shift advocating a diminished role for governments compelled Canadian governments since the 1980s to change their *modus operandi*. In this section we briefly discuss the continuing impact of these pressures on Canadian governments.

Trade liberalisation and deregulation, which intensified in the 1980s, led to increased international competition, and raised competitive standards for efficiency, productivity, and quality for Canada, a country that has always relied heavily on international trade. As national economic efficiency is dependent on the efficiency of both the private and the public sectors, Canadian governments realised that improving public management is an integral part of the structural adjustment needed for better economic performance in a changing global environment.

The economic boom years following World War II resulted in a broadened scope of Canadian government activities and major increases in government expenditures, as well as increased public sector employment. But economic growth in the 1970s slowed down while government spending kept increasing gradually. Continuing recessions and economic uncertainties first related to the oil-shocks and then to globalisation, produced high unemployment, lower government incomes, and higher public expenditures leading to mounting public debts (Purchase and Hirshhorn, 1994). Large deficits and debts became a serious problem for both the Canadian federal government and the provincial governments by the early 1990s. Most provinces' deficit more than doubled between 1991 and 1993, and on average reached 3.3 per cent of provincial GDP (Swimmer, 2001). By 1995 the accumulated debt of the federal and provincial governments combined reached Canada's total GDP (OECD, 1995). As a result, increased pressures were felt from global financial institutions and domestic public opinion to control Canadian government spending and to balance budgets. Many governments felt that they had little choice but to restrict the scope and nature of their activities in order to bring spending under control and balance budgets. However, as deficits and debts were successfully reduced by some governments by early 2000s these fiscal pressures have eased. In the latter half of the 1990s Canada enjoyed stronger economic growth that helped reduce government debts, deficits and budgetary surpluses in some jurisdictions. The current Liberal government of Jean Chretien is intent on using half of the surplus to reduce the debt and cut taxes and the other half to increase spending on social programs. Other provincial governments, most notably Alberta and Ontario have introduced substantial tax cuts that have been very popular (Borins, 2002).

New information and communication technologies also continually change the way Canadian governments operate. By making capital cheaper and information readily available, new technologies undermine the traditional 'economies of scale' arguments supporting large bureaucratic organisations and practices. They enable the disaggregation of bureaucratic structures and the decentralisation of management systems without loss of central control (Borins, 1995). They also facilitate the introduction of new forms of service delivery, leading to the proliferation of alternative service delivery mechanisms in Canada. New information technologies also allow changes in the policy making process by creating new mediums and forums for public participation in the design and delivery of public services (Charih and Daniels, 1997). Finally, they require new skills from workers and managers, while making others obsolete, calling for new management approaches and allowing the introduction of more flexible workplace arrangements (Verma and Lonti, 2000).

Demographic changes in the Canadian population also contributed to changes in government operations. The ageing population poses several challenges for governments in their roles as employers, service providers, and policy makers. For example in 1997 it was projected that 70 per cent of the executive cadre in the Canadian federal public service would be due to retire in the next 10 years. The federal government responded by formulating a new vision for the future of the public service and identifying recruitment, retention and learning as their corporate-wide human resource priorities (OECD, 2001). An older population also increases the demand for, and changes the mix of, required government services and might warrant special service delivery considerations. The policy impact of an ageing population is reflected in the policy priorities of governments, such as the increasing importance of health care and pension issues.

The increasing educational attainment of the workforce, its growing racial and ethnic diversity, and the rising labour force participation of women also poses challenges to Canadian governments. More flexible work arrangements are needed to accommodate family and other personal responsibilities. Better-educated workers also demand more autonomy in their work and might resist the 'command' style of bureaucratic organisation. It is argued that these changes are reflected in the workplace policies that governments pursue and the standards they enshrine for the private sector as well (Borins, 1995; Osborne and Gaebler, 1992).

Changes in public management practices are also strongly influenced by changing public expectations regarding the role of governments, their efficiency and the role of citizens in the formation of those policies. There also have been ideological and intellectual challenges to the Canadian welfare state, although to a far lesser extent than in the United States, Britain or New Zealand. However, neo-conservative and neo-liberal ideas were reflected strongly in public management reforms in some of the provinces, most notably in Alberta and Ontario (Rose, 2001; Reshef, 2001).

In a citizens' survey conducted at the height of government restructuring, Graves (1995) found signs of a government legitimacy crisis in Canada. While Canadian citizens have never rejected the need for government intervention in the economic and social spheres of society, they felt that governments failed to deliver real progress in those areas. The Canadian public is very cynical about the effectiveness and efficiency of public investments and demands more transparency, a higher level of ethical standards, better results, value for money, and a new level of inclusion in the design and delivery of public services. At the same time, by 1999 the public expressed a declining concern about the level of taxes and increasing support for an active government (Graves, 1999).

Recent Canadian public management initiatives

The first major attempt at government reform in the 1980s was the formation of the Nielsen Task Force of Program Review (1984). It was charged with reviewing federal programmes for their efficiency and accessibility. It recommended programme cuts, privatisation, and devolution of activities. However, the Progressive Conservative (PC) government of Brian Mulroney

(1984–1993) did not act on those recommendations. Public sector reforms under Mulroney encompassed privatisation of Crown corporations – two good examples are Air Canada and Petro-Canada – the Increased Ministerial Authority and Accountability (IMAA) initiative, the creation of a few Special Operating Agencies (SOA), the Public Sector 2000 initiative, and the Public Service Reform Act (PSRA) of 1992.

The IMAA allowed departments to increase their autonomy by special agreements with the Treasury Board, but fewer than half of the departments took advantage of it. The SOAs were modelled on Britain's *Next Step* agencies, and were created from organisations that charged for their services and were likely to be privatised. SOAs are located within a particular department and report to the Minister of the department. SOAs have more management flexibilities than traditional departments in exchange for a negotiated level of performance and accountability. They have the right to opt out of common services and to adopt innovative financing approaches. Between 1990 and 1997 18 SOAs were created and since 1997 no new SOAs have been created (Zussman, 2002).

The Public Service 2000 project was a public sector renewal initiative examining issues of staffing, staff relations, classification, compensation, benefits, and staff training. It was designed to empower managers and front-line employees and remove red tape (PSC, 2000). The Public Service Reform Act of 1992 introduced a less complicated and burdensome performance management regime, reduced central administrative controls and granted greater autonomy to Deputies to manage their departments. Decentralisation and devolution were pursued to improve the working environment and to encourage innovative ways to increase efficiency and improve programme delivery. Optionality in the common service policy was introduced, which gave the opportunity to line managers to purchase more goods and services from the private sector. The 'running costs' budgeting model allowed departmental budgets not to be divided and limited further, and a five per cent carry-over was allowed. The federal government also encouraged the extensive use of contract workers (Aucoin, 1995).

The (Liberal) federal government of Jean Chretien initiated another *Program Review* in 1994, which aimed primarily at restoring fiscal balance. The objectives of the review were to clarify federal roles and responsibilities; to reduce costly overlap and duplication; to ensure that resources were devoted to highest priorities; to respond to public demand for better, more accessible government; and to achieve more affordable government. Under this *Program Review* departments were forced to evaluate the usefulness of their programmes, to decide whether they should be funded by government or not, and to examine if delivery of services was best carried out in the federal government, in other governments, or in the private sector. The *Program Review* led to the abolition of many subsidies, privatisation of some programmes, and substantial cost cuts, primarily by the application of new information technology. As a result of the *Program Review* the federal government reduced its staff by about 25 per cent, leading to significant workplace and work restructuring. Federal government deficits were reduced through significant cuts to grants to the provinces, which in turn reduced its grants to municipalities, the health and education sectors. These initiatives achieved their major objective of first reducing and later eliminating the deficit at the federal level. Similar deficit cutting initiatives had been carried out by most of the provinces, leading to significant employment reductions in all governments in the 1990s. For example, between 1993 and 1997 civil service employment was cut between 18 per cent (Manitoba) and 24 per cent (Alberta) (Swimmer, 2001).

In Canada, rising public demand for services combined with declining resources led to the search for innovative public delivery mechanisms, called Alternative Service Delivery (ASD). According to Ford and Zussman 'Alternative Service Delivery is a creative and dynamic process of public sector restructuring that improves the delivery of services to clients by sharing governance function with individuals, community groups and other government entities' (Ford and Zussman, 1997: 6). These governance structures could take many forms, including the set-up of electronic kiosks, single-window service delivery mechanisms, common service providers, SOAs, service agencies, employee take-overs, privatisation, and devolution. ASD entails partnerships among several government departments, among federal and provincial governments, as well as between the private and public sectors. ASD has three major objectives, which are (1) service efficiency, (2) management flexibility, and (3) collaboration. Advancements in information technology act as a major enabler of these new service delivery initiatives.

The major new organisational forms created by the Chretien government are the service agencies, such as the Canadian Food Inspection Agency, the Canadian Customs and Revenue Agency, and Parks Canada. Service agencies are created by legislation that sets out their mandates, governance regimes, powers and accountabilities. Special flexibilities are granted by legislation and could include increased human resource management authority, more freedom to opt out of common services, and various financial flexibilities. Service agencies are run by chief executive officers and report directly to the minister (Zussman, 2002).

The federal government is committed to the development and publishing of service standards and reporting performance. The main source of information on results is the annual departmental performance reports. A common measurement tool has also been developed to improve the measurement of client satisfaction. In order to link cost information to actual results accrual accounting practices are being adopted. Program evaluation is also gaining increased significance. Social indicators are also developed to provide an overview of Canada's performance regarding the quality of life of its citizens. Service quality initiatives are also introduced, called 'citizen-centered service' (Treasury Board, 2000).

As the *Program Review* has successfully tackled the deficit issue and the federal government is achieving budget surpluses a new priority has arisen: to rebuild the career civil service after the downsizing in the 1990s. This is reflected in the last major federal renewal initiative, 'La Releve' (1997), aimed at building a modern institution that is able to utilise fully the talents of its people. This entails commitments to strengthen the policy capability of the federal government as well as improve its people management (Aucoin, 2002). Currently the federal government is recruiting aggressively, mainly at the entry level, and is committed to internal training and development of staff through its management training programme (Borins, 2000). However, the provinces do not necessarily follow the example of the federal government.

Public sector industrial relations climate

The Canadian public sector is highly unionised, and 72.5 per cent of employees in the public sector were union members in 2002, while 75.9 per cent were covered by collective agreements. This compares very favourably to unionisation rates in the Canadian private sector, where 18 per cent of the employees were union members and 19.7 per cent of the employees were covered by collective agreements (Statistics Canada, 2002). Public sector unionisation is also higher in Canada than in other Anglo-Saxon countries: the United States being 37.5 per cent in 2002 (US Department of Labour, 2003); in Britain being 59 per cent in 2001 (Brook, 2002); in New Zealand being 62 per cent in 2002 (May *et al.*, 2003) and Australia being 47.9 per cent in 2001 (Australian Bureau of Statistics, 2001).

However, as Swimmer points out '[union] membership growth did not occur as a result of militant activity. Rather, the new unions were ushered in by favourable legislation and benevolent employers' (Swimmer, 1989: 401). Nationally union representation in the public sector is quite fragmented. There are separate unions for each of the three major levels of government, and many unions represent different occupational groups in the health and education sectors. The existence and membership of public sector unions are determined by special legislation in the federal and each provincial jurisdiction, while municipalities are covered by the private sector labour legislation in every province. Public sector labour laws confer both special privileges and constraints on unions representing government employees. Bargaining units are defined by legislation, in most provinces often at a highly centralised level, leading to large, comprehensive bargaining units. In this regard the exception is the federal jurisdiction, where unions are organised along occupational lines. However, in the 1990s, both the federal government and the Canada Industrial Relations Board imposed more centralised bargaining structures at the enterprise level by combining bargaining units.

By legislative fiat, public sector unions also enjoy various forms of union security that either require employees who perform bargaining unit work to join the union or pay the equivalent of union dues. The exclusive bargaining rights granted to public sector unions coupled with union security provisions ensures that public sector unions have high membership and coverage. However, these provisions also lead to many 'reluctant' union members and a relatively weak union presence at the workplace level.

In many provinces and at the federal level the range of bargainable issues is also restricted. For example, in the federal jurisdiction collective bargaining is not permitted with respect to the criteria that govern appointment, promotions or layoffs, the content of job classifications, or the impact of technological and organisational change (Swimmer, 1995).

In seven out of the ten provinces and in the federal jurisdiction government employees are allowed to strike with some restrictions. At the same time, Canadian policy makers have developed various mechanisms for avoiding or settling work stoppages in the public sector. These include interest arbitration, back to work legislation, and the designation of essential service workers leading to 'controlled strikes' (Thompson, 2001). Governments used various approaches to labour relations to achieve their restructuring objectives in the 1990s. Some governments, such as the Alberta and Ontario PC governments bargained 'hard' by demanding concessions at the bargaining table. Other governments, taking advantage of their dual roles as employer and legislator, have resorted to unilateral changes by ratifying legislation that overrides collective agreements, and imposes wage freezes and wage cuts, as in Manitoba. At the most extreme, the federal government suspended collective bargaining by legislative action for six years from 1991–1996. Governments also carried out other legislated changes that altered the balance of power between the workplace parties, such as the Ontario PC government's removal of 'successor rights' provisions in case of the privatisation of public sector operations. As a result, workers whose jobs were privatised lost union representation. Finally, some left-leaning governments have tried co-operative approaches by 'opening their books,' but still asking for concessions (for example, the NDP governments in Ontario and Saskatchewan).

Unions' reaction to these changes varied from being largely ineffectual in influencing the restructuring process in any significant way – Alberta and Manitoba – (Reshef, 2001; Phillips and Stecher, 2001) to increased militancy by using both political tools and traditional collective bargaining weapons to fight government restructuring, with only modest success in the case of Ontario (Rose, 2001), the federal jurisdiction and most other provinces. At the federal scene the first ever government employee strike took place in 1991 and ended in 'back-to-work' legislation. The ensuing protracted suspension of collective bargaining diminished the negotiating power of the federal unions and undermined their credibility and legitimacy. However, while collective bargaining for federal employees was suspended, the federal unions participated in joint union-management initiatives with considerable success in representing their members' interests. As a result, the federal unions were successful in minimising lay-offs, ensuring that their members received relatively generous incentive packages, and avoided wage reductions. While organised federal employees lost the ironclad job security provisions, various measures ensured their relative employment security (Swimmer and Bach, 2001).

Given the pressures of the 1990s that led to poor labour-management relations, the federal government set up in 1999 an Advisory Committee on Labour-Management Relations in the Federal Public Service – the *Fryer Committee* – to investigate ways in which labour-management relations can be improved in the federal jurisdiction. The Committee described employment relations in the federal public service represented by low morale, mistrust, increased workloads, and blocked career development opportunities leading to retention problems of younger employees (Identifying Issues, 2000). The Committee's major recommendations include broadening of the scope of bargaining by permitting consultation and co-development of staffing, job classifications and pension issues; changing the basis for determining bargaining unit structure from occupational groups to community of interest; the establishment of a dispute resolution commission vested with wide-ranging powers to assist in collective bargaining; and establishing a degree of individual department and workplace-level bargaining (Swimmer, 2002; Lonti *et al.*, 2002). The federal government had not responded to these recommendations at the time of this writing in early 2003.

Overall, labour-management relations in the 1990s in the Canadian public sector were rather adversarial, although there were some isolated but promising examples of successful union-management co-operation as well. However, those joint initiatives often focussed on 'downside' labour adjustment, that is, softening the blow on affected employees, and engaged less on the 'upside' issues of proactive engagement on skill development, work organisation, and so on. Significant innovations across the public sector industrial relations system have yet to occur.

Middle manager and employee views of public management developments

Our discussion so far has focussed on general trends observable at an aggregate level in public management. To supplement this overview, this section provides an assessment of these changes from the perspective of managers and workers. We draw on evidence from a representative survey of Canadian federal and provincial government middle managers, and two surveys of federal public service employees. It provides a unique, micro-level view of public management developments in Canada.

The Survey of Workplace Issues in Government (SWIG) was conducted in 1998/99 in the federal government and the governments of Nova Scotia, Ontario, Manitoba and Alberta, covering all departments and agencies (Verma and Lonti, 2001). The main respondents were workplace managers. The results of the survey provide systematic empirical evidence, for the first time, on Canadian government workplace practices and the extent of change in those practices since the early 1990s. The results of the survey suggest a significant shift in the way Canadian governments are organising their work and the workplaces.

Workplace managers felt that changes in the work of their units in the 1990s were driven primarily by pressures to produce results and budget constraints. Service and citizen involvement issues ranked last in importance among the pressures units faced. The most widely used methods for restructuring work were downsizing (62 per cent of units reporting) and scaling back of operations (54 per cent). Contracting out and devolution to other levels of government were not nearly as common.[3] Change in the nature of government work was pervasive. Only a small minority of workplaces (16 per cent) had no change in either the content of work or in work methods. Work intensification was extensive as well, with nearly 57 per cent of the work units experiencing an increase in work volume relative to the size of the workforce.

In order to adjust to the outside environmental pressures and to changes in the nature and volume of work, work units most often turned to various flexible staffing practices, most notably flexible working hours, functional flexibility, and increased overtime. All of these practices build on the existing workforce, responding both to possible increases and contractions in the volume of work. They also provide more flexibility, choice and variety of work and working hours both for management and workers. In contrast, different methods of employment reduction were utilised significantly less. The differences in the constraints various functional units contended with were instrumental in the units' use of various staffing practices. Compensating time-off was highly popular as well – 71 per cent of units used it for non-managers and 57 per cent for managers – providing some flexibility without the use of extra budgetary resources.

In terms of functional flexibility, government workplaces used various flexible job design mechanisms – multi-skilling, job enrichment, and job enlargement – extensively. Leading practices were job enrichment and job enlargement, applied at 70 per cent of the units. Almost 60 per cent of the units utilised multi-skilling/job rotation. The incidence of flexible job designs in the government sector is triple that reported for the private sector in Canada (Lonti and Verma, forthcoming). Employee participation in these practices also increased in the last three years. Flexible job design practices were found in work units with a higher volume of work, measurable output and outcome, a high level of local managerial autonomy, and in tandem with self-directed work teams. Self-directed work teams were utilised at 47.9 per cent of the units. Autonomous work teams were most likely to be found at workplaces with greater budgetary constraints and public accountability pressures, at service delivery units, and in workplaces with a high percentage of scientific and professional employees.

More than 80 per cent of managers reported that they shared information directly with their employees. Quality issues were most likely to be discussed with employees early on, while budgets, workforce reduction, and changes in organisational structure were discussed at later stages. Direct information sharing with employees has been linked positively to the severity of budget constraints experienced by the work unit, the amount of managerial and supervisory training provided, and the use of quality circles and self-directed work teams. Forty per cent of the units utilised quality circles. Units with intense public pressures resorted more to quality circles, which were also more often used among scientific and professional workers.

Major skill requirements were problem-solving and team skills and more generally 'ability to learn new skills'. Training of employees increased slightly compared to three years before. On average two thirds of the employees received training. Computer and other office equipment training was provided almost universally, while more than 90 per cent of the units reported professional and technical training. Training activities at the workplace were positively related to the extent of union involvement in training decisions, to being in 'core' government, and to the use of various flexible job design mechanisms at the workplace.

Workplace managers reported a high level of autonomy in quality of services and client consultation issues, in performance management, training and development, and staffing decisions. These are areas, except for staffing decisions, where their autonomy has also increased the most from 1995. Managers have the least autonomy regarding remuneration, as it is still highly centralised in Canadian governments.

Merit increases for managers and non-managers were adopted at around half of the workplaces. Bonuses for managers were used in 39 per cent of the units, for non-managers only at 11 per cent of the units. Knowledge/skill-based pay was applied only sparsely, although it might logically accompany the use of job enrichment and multi-skilling. Performance pay for managers – including merit increases and bonuses – was associated with policy units, work units with high level of managerial autonomy, and lower unionisation rates.

The survey results confirm that measuring performance of various government functions is extremely difficult. Despite heavy pressure for measuring results, only half of the government workplaces used performance measures in 1998/1999. In addition, approximately 60 per cent of units measured the costs of their services, while only 34 per cent measured the benefits of services. A mere 30 per cent of the units measured both costs and benefits. Policy units were the least able to measure their performance, while units providing services to the public used formal performance measures the most. Overall, the use of performance measures at the work unit level was positively associated with the amount of outside pressure for measuring results and the ease with which those results could be measured. In terms of work unit performance, managers reported the largest increase in efficiency/productivity, and somewhat less in terms of quality and on-time delivery.

According to workplace managers, union involvement at the work unit level was minimal. Meetings with management were ad hoc, and there were no joint union-management initiatives operating at the workplace level. While managers reported that they had an excellent relationship with their union counterparts at the workplace level, they also felt that it was determined by union-management relations at a centralised level. Service delivery units had the most union involvement of all government units. The extent of union involvement was positively associated with the severity of budget constraints.

Managers appeared to be in control in terms of using various policies described above. However, they did recognise the problems that had arisen often as a result of the significant restructuring. These problems included employee burnout and fatigue, loss of experience and corporate memory, low employee morale, and problems in hiring and staffing.

The information gained from the manager survey can be augmented by evidence from two surveys of federal employees carried out in 1999 and 2002 in the federal government (Hammar, 2001; Treasury Board of Canada, 2002). These survey findings show the effect of changing public management practices on workers. Federal employees viewed their work as important and were relatively positive about their employer. In 2002 most employees agreed that their department was a good place to work and they were strongly committed to making their organisation a success. These findings are significant given the negative impact of restructuring on workers in general. Just over half of the employees felt that they were encouraged to be innovative or take initiative in their work. At the same time employees also suggested that the quality of their work often suffered because of constantly changing priorities, lack of stability in the organisation, too many approval stages, unreasonable deadlines and/or having to do the same or more work with fewer resources. Almost half of the employees suggested that during the past three years staff turnover had been a problem in their work unit. Twenty nine per cent of employees indicated that they were planning to leave in the next five years with the three main reasons for departure being retirement, to pursue other employment opportunities, and health.

Most employees indicated that their work unit had clearly defined client service standards and that their work unit regularly applied those standards. Most employees also agreed that they received the training they needed to carry out their jobs and most of them were satisfied with their career progress. However, only half of all employees agreed that they had opportunities for promotion. Approximately three-quarters of employees were satisfied with the support and recognition they received from their immediate supervisor.

Conclusions and discussion

The major impetus for public management reforms in Canada in the 1990s came from a variety of factors, but the need to reduce government deficits was the most prominent among them. While methods varied by jurisdictions, government expenditures were reduced primarily by cutting payroll costs through wage freezes and wage reductions, as well as substantial staff cutbacks, related to work reorganisation. Significant government restructuring leading to diminishing the scope of government activities happened to a lesser extent in Canada than in other countries, such as Britain or New Zealand. Public management reforms were also less driven by neo-conservative and neo-liberal ideas, except in some of the provinces, such as Alberta and Ontario under PC governments. Neither were they as coherent or systematic as reforms in Britain and New Zealand. Nonetheless, changes in public management in Canada were shaped by similar ideas of a shift from service delivery to policy, setting of performance standards, and extensive application of new technology to cut costs.

Pollitt and Boukaert (2000) characterise Canada as a 'moderniser', where a relatively large role for the state was never fundamentally questioned. However, Canadian governments acknowledged that far-reaching changes to their administrative systems were necessary. They pursued both managerial and participatory modernisation with varying degrees in the different jurisdictions. Even as they cut spending and restructured operations, governments in Canada put increased emphasis on the development of new partnerships across departments, across different levels of governments, and with the private sector, introducing alternative service delivery mechanisms using leading edge information technology. As a result of the reforms a more decentralised, results and service-oriented public service emerged and the Canadian government has become a leader in providing integrated and seamless services to citizens and business (Bent *et al.*, 1999).

Government restructuring was more radical in jurisdictions with strong, ideologically driven, market-oriented governments, such as the Progressive Conservative (PC) governments of Alberta and Ontario. Union-management relations in the public sector deteriorated during this period as governments used their unique powers to change legislation governing public sector labour relations and override collective agreements or to by-pass collective bargaining processes.

Survey data from managers and employees also show that these new public management initiatives filtered down to the workplace level to change the nature of work. They report that substantial workforce reductions led to the adoption of flexible staffing practices that, in turn, often resulted in work intensification. While these practices increased the efficiency of government operations, less improvement was experienced regarding the quality of public services and their on-time delivery. Waves of government restructuring have also led to increased employee burnout, fatigue, and low morale. Incentives to leave the public service often backfired, leading to a loss of experience and corporate memory and difficulties in hiring and staffing.

Recently, Canada has been making the transition from a deficit reduction environment to one of greater choice, while pursuing the goals of being a responsive, well-managed, citizen-oriented public service that works in collaboration with other levels of government and with the private/non-profit sectors (Treasury Board, 1999). After the turmoil of the 1990s, the agenda at the federal level is to rebuild the public service, putting special emphasis on strengthening its policy capacity.

Notes

1. The two attempts were the Meech Lake Accord of 1987 and the Charlottetown Accord of 1992.
2. Two referenda on separation from Canada have taken place in Quebec. The first referendum ended with a 60 per cent victory for the federalists and the majority of francophones voted federalist. The second referendum ended in a (51%) victory for the federalists.
3. The SWIG sample might under-report the incidence of contracting out and devolution, as it surveys work units that survived the restructurings.

11

Hollowing and Hardening New Zealand's Homely State

Robert Gregory

The changes to the New Zealand state sector during the past two decades were radical and far-reaching. They have been the subject of considerable comment among academics and practitioners, in New Zealand and beyond (see, for example, Gregory, 2000; Halligan, 1997; Norman, 2001; Schick, 1996, 1998, 2001; Scott, 2001). However, according to Schick (2001: 2) they have 'generated more fascination than emulation', in the international community. Most of the commentary has addressed issues such as accountability, institutional capability, financial accounting, contractualism, corporatisation and privatisation, and political-bureaucratic relationships. This chapter will first discuss some general issues of New Zealand public administration, before focusing on one aspect that has received little direct attention – the changing nature of the relationship between the state and its citizens, in the provision of social services. The new managerialist emphasis has created a more fraught and contentious relationship between citizens and core social service departments, contributing to the transformation of the egalitarian tradition of New Zealand statism.

Political and social background

Pragmatic expediency characterised New Zealand's political culture during the four decades after World War II. A welfare state was developed and sustained by the two main political parties, National and Labour, which contested three-yearly elections through appeals to the political middle-ground. But the election in 1984 of David Lange's fourth Labour Government brought with it an unexpected political *volte face*, in the form of 'Rogernomics', the eponymous neo-liberal economic strategy of Minister of Finance, Roger Douglas (Nagel, 1998). It deregulated financial markets, floated the New Zealand dollar, abolished agricultural subsidies, and generally followed neo-classical, or 'monetarist', economic policies aimed at correcting a legacy of neo-Keynesian 'government failures' (Bollard and Buckle, 1987; Rudd and Roper, 1997).

The government adopted a 'crashing through' strategy, implementing its policy changes before political opposition could coalesce to impede them (Douglas, 1993; Mulgan, 1992). Especially in the crucial years 1984–87, the strategy was controlled by a highly cohesive political executive which dominated Parliament, and was informed by policy prescriptions devised by a small group of like-minded advocates within the Treasury, the Reserve Bank, and the influential Business Roundtable, an interest group comprising many of the country's top business leaders (Goldfinch, 1998, 2000). This policy elite was largely committed to the ideas embodied in the so-called 'Washington Consensus' of the early 1990s, which advocated a range of steps for the structural adjustment of ailing capitalist economies, in sympathy with 'Chicago School' theoretical paradigms (Bollard, 1988).

After the demise in 1990 of the Lange government, in the face of widespread public unease over its policy directions, the National government nevertheless extended neo-liberal policies to social welfare, health, and industrial relations (Boston and Dalziel, 1992; Kelsey, 1995). It cut back and targeted welfare benefits (Boston and Dalziel, 1992; Boston *et al.*, 1999), introduced a market model of public health reform (Gauld, 2001), and abolished the system of state regulated industrial relations arbitration (Walsh, 1997).

Reconfiguring the state

Along with Britain and Australia, New Zealand was at the leading edge of the international state sector reform movement of the 1980s and 1990s, which became known as New Public Management (NPM). The Lange Government believed that New Zealand's economic problems could not be adequately addressed without major improvements to the efficiency of the state sector. Government expenditure, including transfers, accounted for about 39 per cent of Gross Domestic Product (Scott *et al.*, 1990). The state sector, particularly the Public Service, was seen to be inefficient, inflexible, too centralised, and preoccupied with administrative process rather than programmatic results.[1]

The components of the New Zealand reorganisation have been well detailed elsewhere (Boston *et al.*, 1996; Scott, 2001). Those who designed the new structures, mainly analysts in the Treasury, drew heavily on public choice theory and agency theory. In their view, 'self-interested utility maximisation' had enabled public officials to 'capture' policy processes, which therefore had to be separated from service delivery. Their perception of widespread 'government failure' impelled them to prescribe much greater 'outsourcing' of public goods and services, and the creation of quasi-markets in the delivery of such services. The greatly increased use of competitive tendering and contracting out of goods and services have seen New Zealand's state become more 'hollowed out' (Rhodes, 1994).[2]

In the terms of a new managerialist lexicon the government became both an 'owner' and 'purchaser' – an owner of institutional capacity in all its forms, and a purchaser of the vast range of 'output' produced by executive agencies. The output was in turn distinguished from 'outcome', the consequences for the community of public policy interventions and initiatives. And the government became simultaneously both a 'provider' and 'funder', especially of public health services.

These dualities, all of them central to the design and operation of the new state sector, reflected an essentially *mechanistic*, as opposed to an *organic*, interpretation of governmental institutions (Burns and Stalker, 1994). Mechanistic approaches talk of such things as 'the machinery of government' and 'policy settings'; organic ones may talk of 'the spirit of public administration', and 'the public service ethos'. What Goethe wrote of the new modern man typified the theoretical architects of New Zealand's state sector: 'in the palm of his hand he holds all of the sections; lacks nothing except the spirit's connections' (quoted in Heclo, 2002).

The state and the citizen: 'the coldest of all cold monsters'?[3]

A new zeitgeist

As a British colonial society, New Zealand has been characterised by a pragmatic rather than ideological spirit of governance. Its incipient late nineteenth century welfare state was consolidated and expanded greatly by the first Labour government, in office from 1935 to 1949. During this period and until the latter years of the last century, the Parliamentary process was dominated by two main political parties, Labour and National, both of which were committed to maintaining the country's welfare state and modern 'mixed economy' (Rudd, 1997).

Within this tradition, the state in New Zealand has been perceived by citizens to be a manifestation of their collective aspirations, rather than as a dominating, external, force as is more common in the European tradition. This perception was eloquently expressed more than 50 years ago by New Zealand's first professor of political science, the American Leslie Lipson:

> ...no one could reasonably say that New Zealand places a gulf between the state and the public, that it is run by an exclusive governing class, or that its government is a remote and inaccessible *Ding an sich*...The people, or at any rate most of them, look upon the state quite healthily as being themselves under another form. When it acts, they feel that they are acting. What it owns, they own...To them it is simply a utilitarian instrument for effecting their will (Lipson, 1948: 481–2).

A similar view of the state was well put by Janet Fraser, wife of the 1940s Labour Prime Minister, Peter Fraser. To her mind New Zealand's state was 'the home enlarged' (Stace, 1998: 64).

This *zeitgeist* has changed markedly in New Zealand since the 1980s. The governmental reorganisation transformed a spirit of public administration into an ideology of generic management. The latter acknowledges few if any differences between running private or corporate businesses and running governmental agencies, nor among differing public sector tasks. The architects of the New Zealand changes held more strongly to these views than advocates of NPM-styled innovations in just about any other OECD country. To borrow Peters' (1986) metaphor, more so in New Zealand than elsewhere did the 'reformers' feel that in order to save the country's public sector 'village' it was first necessary to burn it, and then rebuild it according to an apparently coherent and 'rigorous' theoretical blueprint.

Other aspects of the changes have had a major impact – intentionally or otherwise – on the structural contours of the New Zealand state, and on state-citizen relations. Foremost among these have been the ideologically-driven privatisation of many state assets built up over more than a century as an expression of the utilitarian ethos alluded to by Lipson, and the neo-liberal revamping of social welfare policies. One of the most significant effects of the centrality of Public Choice theory in the design of New Zealand's public organisations has been the valorisation of the virtues of the individual as consumer rather than as citizen. The latter's rights, duties, and obligations in his or her relationship with the state have been super-seded by the former's *choices* in a marketised exchange relationship. While the idea of an exchange relationship between the state and its citizens is not without validity (Alford, 2002), to the extent that the consumerist par-adigm displaces the idea of citizenship then it is likely to affect relations between public officials and citizens in ways that are not necessarily beneficial to the latter's interests. The value of 'efficiency' (narrowly defined) becomes pre-eminent over others like democracy, equity, fairness, and compassion.

The positivist-inspired theories underpinning the state sector changes reinvented the policy/administration (or rather, management) dichotomy and made it foundational for a new structure of policy ministries separated from their relevant operational agencies. They reconfigured the holistic trusteeship role of the government into the conflicting roles of owner and purchaser of state resources. They gave rise to a uniquely explicit statutory prescription for 'goal displacement' (the Public Finance Act, 1989), in the form of an artificial separation of agency outputs and policy outcomes, and to the provider/funder duality, which formed the basis of the quasi-markets that would supposedly enhance the efficient delivery of public goods and services.

The new neo-liberal state

Just as the state sector changes were a component of a much wider neo-liberal programme of economic and social reform, so too has that broader ideological context changed the relationship between state agencies and the citizens they supposedly serve. Under a neo-liberal policy regime the proper role of the state is redefined as security not welfare, risk management becomes central to the residual duties of government, and accountability comes to matter far more than responsibility (Culpitt, 1999: 9). The irony is that the managerial preoccupation with accountability is effectively a preoccupation with control, which becomes the very antithesis of the managerial autonomy that the supposedly 'anti-bureaucratic' changes were intended to produce.[4]

The 'results-orientation' of managerialist regimes is manifest in a concern to 'produce' specified rates, meet preordained 'targets', and elevate the value of efficiency (narrowly defined) over and above all else. Consequently, the Inland Revenue Department was the subject in 1999 of a Parliamentary inquiry, which found strong evidence of an 'inhumane' organisational culture, which had resulted in unacceptably high levels of stress and trauma (possibly including some cases of suicide) among some taxpaying 'customers'.[5] The Accident Compensation Corporation (ACC) is confronting persistent allegations that its case management of claimants (referred to in its corporate language as 'stock') is geared primarily to getting them out of the system, often before their injuries are appropriately treated. Early in 2003, a new 'claimants' code of rights was drawn up by the Corporation, reminding its managers that claimants should be treated 'fairly, with dignity and respect, and have their culture, values, beliefs and privacy respected' (The Dominion Post, Wellington, 30 January 2003: 5). The Corporation in the late 1990s also conducted a radio and print media campaign encouraging the public to call a toll-free number to report suspected ACC fraud. Similarly, and at about the same time, the former Income Support Service (now subsumed within the Ministry of Social Development) ran a television campaign encouraging the public to 'dob in' persons suspected of being welfare cheats.

The health reorganisation institutionalised the anti-democratic 'crashing through' spirit akin to that which had characterised the wider policy changes in the 1980s (Easton, 1994). Elective policymaking bodies (area health boards) were abolished. Moreover, the 'arms length' contractual relationship between funding authorities and service providers (hospitals were renamed 'crown health enterprises') was technocratically-orientated and distanced ordinary citizens from decisions that affected their communities (Gauld, 2001). It allowed for very little meaningful participation by citizens in regard to decisions to close hospitals; and time frames for public submissions were usually unrealistic.

The public choice-inspired governmental reorganisation, embracing the contractualised 'out-sourcing' of public goods and services, has undermined the egalitarian and communal sense of collective citizenship that formerly characterised the welfare state in New Zealand. In its place are autonomous, self-interested individuals, *qua* consumers, customers, and clients, who are felt to be separately and solely responsible for their own choices and life circumstances. Under this new ideological regime the proper subject of government is 'no longer "the social" but the complex networks of interaction, bargaining and compromise which interpose and counterpoise interlocking, but separate, networks of individual obligation' (Culpitt, 1999: 81). Welfare dependency comes to be reframed politically as a serious threat to a 'healthy economy' (Culpitt, 1999: 148).

All modern bureaucracy, in whatever form, is essentially impersonal, but is more or less humane according to the policy purposes that guide its operations. Central government agencies in New Zealand before the 1980s and early 1990s were not paragons of public service virtue. They were susceptible to the worst deficiencies of the Weberian model, and were overdue for appropriate reform. But because the managerialist waves that swept over them were a part of a larger neo-liberal tide the service ethos that was still deeply embedded in their welfarist culture was displaced by attitudes and commitments which are less caring of citizens' needs than they are bent on controlling their entitlements.

The separation of policy ministries from their relevant operational agencies tended to disconnect policy analysis from practical experience. Formal policy analysis, theoretically-driven, and often conducted by those with little 'street-level' experience, usually prevailed over the knowledge that could be gained by public officials' everyday relationships with their fellow citizens. Abstract 'expertise' locked in bureaucratic ivory towers became immune to practical reflection. In areas like social work, formal qualifications became privileged over practical work experience, resulting in a more detached and 'clinical' relationship between public servants and citizens.

The state in New Zealand, at least its central government component, is now smaller but more coercive, at once more immediate but more hard-edged, acting more upon, over, or against rather than *with* its citizens. In Le Grand's (1997) terms, it has become more knavish than knightly. The influence of public choice and agency theories, and the assumptions about self-interested individual behaviour on which they are based, seem to have become self-fulfilling. The dominant economistic language of commodification has helped facilitate the management of citizens as objects rather than as people.

Public trust

Neo-liberal theory, as well as 'third way' thinking, promotes the transfer of resources and capacity from state institutions to both the market and 'civil society', the latter comprising the myriad not-for-profit groups that provide goods and services mainly to local communities. In New Zealand in the early 1990s the National Government explicitly promoted the idea that greater reliance on civil society capacity would enhance levels of 'social capital', or the bonding forces of collective public trust, as highlighted by American political scientist Robert Putnam (Putnam *et al.*, 1993; Putnam, 1996; Robinson, 1999).

This is too complex an issue to try to explore in any depth here. On the face of it at least, there seems to be little evidence of any enhancement of 'social capital' in New Zealand. On the contrary, as in most other western democracies, there has been in New Zealand a marked decline in levels of public trust towards political and governmental institutions during the past 20 years or so. It can plausibly be suggested that the restructuring of state sector organisations has done little if anything to reverse this trend, despite arguments that governmental processes have been rendered far more 'transparent' than ever before (or possibly because of them). In 1985, 8.6 per cent of New Zealanders had 'a great deal' of confidence in the government, but by 1998 that figure had fallen to 2.5 per cent. The figure for those who were 'not at all' confident of the good intentions of the government doubled from 11 per cent to 22 per cent during the same period (Perry and Webster, 1999). Also, 'relatively few people' believed that central government was responsive to the public. A survey conducted in 1997 showed that 44 per cent of respondents disagreed or strongly disagreed that, 'most public servants can be trusted to do what is best for the country', while 24 per cent agreed or strongly agreed (Massey University, 1997). Between 1975 and 1994 public confidence in the Public Service declined from about 27 per cent to 10 per cent (State Services Commission, 2000).

Late in 1998, 70 per cent of respondents to a national survey agreed with the proposition that '...this country is run by a few big interests looking out for themselves...' (rather than being run 'for the benefit of all the people'). This result was 16 per cent higher than that produced by a similar survey conducted nine years earlier (Massey University, 1997).

Trust is not only a crucial component of state-citizen relations, and for more participatory forms of governance, but is also essential for effective working relationships within governmental institutions. This is especially important at the political-executive nexus, where the reorganisation of the 1980s and 1990s was intended, through the introduction of fixed-term contractual appointments, to enhance the 'responsiveness' of the bureaucracy to ministerial direction. Politico-bureaucratic relations have become more fraught, and less trusting (see James, 2002). As Bryson and Anderson (2002) observe:

> Although formally chief executives are accountable to ministers, who
> are in turn accountable and answerable to Parliament, the new struc-

tures have had the result, in practice, of shifting responsibility down-
wards and the focus on accountabilities has often personalised particular
issues. It is, for example, not uncommon for individual line managers,
rather than their chief executive, to front the media over contentious
issues in their units. Nor is it unusual now for Members of Parliament
and Ministers to publicly point the finger at individual public servants
...Ironically, it seems that a lack of trust in government by its citizens
has fuelled governments' lack of trust in its agencies...resulting in a
number of recent high profile cases of a complete breakdown in the relationship ... (Bryson and Anderson, 2002: 18).

The outsourcing of service delivery to local communities, under contract to
governmental funding agencies, appears to have done little to overcome
the problems commonly associated with top-down, centralised bureaucracy. A social services working party set up by the new Labour-led coalition government in 2000 reported, *inter alia*, that

> ...there was a sense that narrowly defined contracts for services had
> turned many aspects of social service and other community activity into
> 'commodities' or commercial transactions, losing sight of the whole
> service provided – or the whole organisation which had previously
> been the focus of central government's funding to community organisa-
> tions (Report of the Community and Voluntary Sector Working Party,
> 2001: 91).

The working party also reported adversely on the micro-management of
provider contracts by government agencies; on 'young, inexperienced or
unknowledgeable (sic) officials [who] often deal inappropriately with voluntary sector people who are long on experience and have records of skill
and success' *ibid.*: 80); 'a climate of mistrust' between government agencies
and the community sector, resulting from the policy/operations and
funder/provider separation, and from the social and economic reforms of
the previous two decades (*ibid.*: 61, 76); and a 'culture of contempt' towards
community groups on the part of government organisations, which treated
them 'arrogantly' and did not understand or respect community organisations' values, objectives and operating constraints *ibid.*: 110).

There was, in short, a large gap between official rhetoric and governmen
tal reality, which only enhanced citizens' disillusionment. New 'customer-
driven' public services, supposedly run along the lines of corporate
business, may have given bureaucracy a more human face, but that face
often turned out to be a cosmetic mask for policies and decisions that were
not genuinely sensitive to citizens' needs. For example, the income support
agency could claim that it was a world leader in turn-around time for pro-
cessing welfare applications, but in 2001 the High Court scathingly rejected

its policy of not paying out unless applicants sought an exact benefit (The Dominion, Wellington, 6 August 2001). The department's argument ran counter to a directive from its own minister that it should tell all beneficiaries about their full entitlements.

Moreover, contracting-out along commercial lines is problematic for 'core' public services, where the 'bottom line' is really about inducing change in citizens' behaviour, rather than producing tangible goods or providing readily quantifiable services (Gregory, 1995; Lane, 2000).

All in all, life within government social service organisations has probably never been more stressful than it has become during the 1990s. Required to meet growing demands with diminishing resources, caught between conflicting corporate and public service management imperatives, sometimes in no-win situations where political and public opprobrium always follows when things go wrong but little credit is given when they go right, executives, managers and street-level workers are all working, often conflictingly, under severe pressures. Staff turn-over rates in the central social work agency, where employees are very much at risk of physical assault by angry 'customers', are high, and the image of friendly, customer-driven service is more illusory than real.

New privilege

Roberts (1977, 1987, 1996) well depicts the formerly egalitarian character of New Zealand government:

> It is probably true to say that in New Zealand neither politicians nor administrators feel themselves to be members of an elite distinct from their fellow citizens...If one were to seek an average group socialised by standard values, much of the administrative elite in New Zealand would be included...What we have is a picture of dedicated long service employees with ordinary social backgrounds...it is...unlikely that they would form a remote and superior power-seeking cabal. If there is a case for ending the career service in New Zealand, it must rest upon attacking inertia and the preference for the status quo rather than reducing the power of an elite mandarin class (Roberts).

Today, however, there is evidence of a cultural shift towards a more elitist managerialist ethos, with the emergence of a new class of top-level managers, both public and corporate. The financial rewards paid to members of this newly privileged elite are not unambiguously related to actual performance, despite the rhetoric of accountability and performance appraisal (Elayan *et al.*, 2000). The top state sector salary packages today cannot match those paid in corporate business, but when they are compared with the average New Zealand wage, it is clear that current state executives are now far better off in real terms than they were before the reorganisation.

Notably, there has emerged a dramatic shift in the relativity of pay between top public servants and members of the political executive. Between 1982 and 2000 the remuneration paid to New Zealand's top departmental chief executive, the Secretary to the Treasury, rose by 463 per cent, as compared with an increase of 169 per cent for the Prime Minister, and 165 per cent for cabinet ministers and members of parliament. In 1982 the Prime Minister was receiving 24 per cent more than the Secretary, but by 2000 the Secretary was receiving 59 per cent more than the country's top politician. By then all cabinet ministers were paid less than the most highly paid public service chief executives, and several heads of government agencies earned considerably more than the Prime Minister (Gregory, 2002a).

A national survey found in 1999 that 75 per cent of respondents thought that income differences in New Zealand were too large; only 30 per cent believed that large differences in income were necessary for the country's prosperity; and 60 per cent saw New Zealand in the image of a social pyramid. Most respondents preferred 'a more egalitarian society' (Massey University, 2000).

The introduction of contractual fixed-term appointments has undoubtedly produced some problematical unintended consequences. Several prominent public controversies in New Zealand during the past few years have involved governmental appointees who could be removed from their jobs only by paying them large 'golden handshakes'. In the biggest controversy, it appeared that a departmental chief executive had been kept on mainly because it would have been too politically costly to have paid her out of her contract (Wallis, 2001).

These controversies may not have been so significant had the neo-liberal policy transformations of the 1980s and 1990s clearly produced the economic benefits promised of them. But this has not been the case. New Zealand was ranked fourth on the OECD's GDP per capita index in 1960 but by the late 1990s it was ranked at around 20th place. After an economic contraction from 1985 to 1992 there was a strong cyclical recovery in the mid-1990s, but this has not been sustained (see Roper, 1997; Dalziel and Lattimore, 1999). During the 1990s New Zealand's egalitarian tradition took a big hit, with one of the largest increases in income inequality in the western world (Hills, 1995; O'Dea, 2000). The uneven effects of New Zealand's neo-liberal economic transformation were noted by the social services working party referred to above:

> …while some New Zealanders have benefited financially and welcomed the consequent modernisation of business and expansion of consumer choice, others found themselves marginalised and relegated to an ongoing cycle of state dependency and economic hardship. In particular, the negative impacts were keenly felt in communities where state

services previously had a significant presence, and amongst Maori, many of whom had been employed in the services and industries that were restructured (Report of the Community and Voluntary Sector Working Party, 2001: 76–77).

Conclusion: a new way forward, or more of the same?

The relationship between the state and citizen in New Zealand has been transformed during the past two decades. For more than a century it was characterised by pragmatism, egalitarianism, and pluralism, and for a period during the post World War II decades, corporatism. At no stage did New Zealand's political culture embody a sense of the state as being (in Lipson's words) a *'Ding an sich'*, any sort of dominating, deeply impersonal, coercive force, whether serving and/or constituting an elite class.

It cannot be said that such a perception of the state in New Zealand is now dominant. But the state sector changes of the 1980s and 1990s have been instrumental in shifting the collective perception in that direction, away from the 'spirit of public administration as an agent of "public trust"', towards a new conception of a business-like state as a 'subservient agent of corporate elites' committed to globalisation imperatives (Farazmand, 2002: 146–7). The state today, especially in its delivery of social services, is decidedly more 'hollow' than before, measured not only by the scope of 'out-sourcing' but also by its increasingly apparent want of genuinely public-spirited soul.

The centre-left coalition government that came to power late in 1999 appeared determined to reassert a more traditional public *service* ethos within government departments, and more broadly across the state sector. Following more of a 'third way' approach it took some steps in this direction, including the establishment of a State Sector Standards Board to advise it on such an ethos. The government reintroduced elective policy-making bodies in public health governance, and it has conducted a 'Review of the Centre', which it intends will reconnect political purpose with managerial accountability (policy outcomes and organisational outputs) and, *inter alia*, address problems relating to the organisational fragmentation that became institutionalised after the original restructuring (Report of the Advisory Group on the Review of the Centre, 2001). Allen Schick has become 'more critical and less ambivalent' with regard to the New Zealand model, and 'less convinced that it is the right way to go'. He has observed 'the plain fact that few countries, and none of the developed ones, have modelled their public sector along the lines of the New Zealand version' (Schick, 2001: 2).

Yet the theoretical coherence which reshaped New Zealand's state sector seems to be stubbornly self-sustaining. The Review of the Centre proposals espouse an incremental approach to change, as if the problems identified are not themselves manifestations of major flaws in the original theoretical design (Gregory, 2002b). No major changes are so far heralded to the two statutory pillars of the New Zealand central governmental system – the State Sector Act and the Public Finance Act. Schick observes that, 'In contrast to other countries in which reform meant adding peripheral elements to the pre-existing managerial system, in New Zealand, the reforms are the system...Unlike most countries which assemble reforms as if they were putting together lego blocks, in New Zealand, taking away a critical element, such as an output orientation, would strip the system of its magnificent conceptual architecture' (Schick 2001: 3).

In other words, the New Zealand reforms are designed in such a way that radical revision of them is extremely difficult, both politically and technically. In themselves they can be seen as an example of Horn's (1995) 'political economy of public administration', designed to withstand any radical amendment by subsequent legislatures. Such an interpretation is supported by Newberry's (2002) analysis. She argues that the Review of the Centre's belief that the current public management system in New Zealand is 'a reasonable platform to work from' is 'demonstrably wrong if the current government's objective really is to "maintain and strengthen the State Sector"' (Newberry, 2002: 326). More critically, she concludes that departmental 'resource eroding processes' were deliberately built into the government's financial management system and 'function in a manner highly consistent with a privatisation strategy' (Newberry, 2002: 327).

This conceptual coherence has now become institutionalised in a way that reinforces its own 'path dependency'. The challenge remains to strike a new balance between the spirit of public administration on the one hand, and effective managerial practice on the other. This will not be easy, but those who continue to advocate a further 'rolling back' of the state through more privatisation and marketisation of public utilities and services now have only minority political support. There is an opportunity to re-establish a public sector that better reflects the image of government as an expression of the public interest rather than as a dehumanised instrument of privileged elites.

Acknowledgements

The author thanks Ann Walker of the PhD programme of Victoria University of Wellington's School of Government for her valuable comments on a first draft of this chapter. The usual disclaimer applies.

Notes

1. The 'state sector' in New Zealand embodies all organisations of central government (the 'Public Service', offices of Parliament, the Reserve Bank of New Zealand, crown entities, other departments, and state-owned enterprises). The state sector, together with the organisations of local government, are known as

the 'public sector'. The Public Service as such comprises ministries and departments under the direct control of the political executive. In 2002 there were 36 such organisations.

2. The number of employees officially classified as public servants dropped from about 90 000 in 1987 to 30 000 in 2002. However, many former public service employees are now working in the large number of crown entities, which operate beyond direct ministerial control, and which have taken over functions formerly carried out within large, multi-purpose departments. The level of government expenditure has remained relatively stable, declining from 39 per cent in the mid-1980s to around 35 per cent over the past few years.

3. Foucault, 1988.

4. As Lucas (1976: 84) puts it, 'Accountability is a form of quality control. We avoid the really bad, but have to forego the really good'.

5. See the Report on the House Finance and Expenditure Committee's Inquiry into the Powers and Operations of the Inland Revenue Department, House of Representatives, Wellington, October, 1999.

12

New Public Management and Europeanisation: Convergence or 'Nestedness'?

Geoffrey Wood

New public management (NPM) has been depicted as a policy response to the economic crises of the 1970s and the increasing influence of neo-liberalism in the 1980s; it represents the marketisation of public sphere, at the expense of democratic accountability (Wise, 2002; c.f. Anon 1997). Alternatively, it can be argued that there are a variety of agents of change; the predominance of one does not obviate the others, whilst no one set of policy prescriptions is likely to remain hegemonic indefinitely. This has led numerous scholars working in the field to argue that NPM is neither new nor very coherent (Wise, 2002). However, whilst the exact definition of the term may be disputed, at the core of neo-liberal reforms to the public sector in the 1980s and 1990s, lies a commitment to marketisation, and to paring back the public sphere in the interests of cost-effectiveness and, ostensibly, greater accountability. However, alternative pressures – towards maintaining the role of the West European state both as a model of good employment practices and as a mechanism to actively promote greater social equity – persist. In this chapter, we explore the interrelationship between European integration and NPM, and evaluate the extent to which integration represents the pioneer of marketisation, or the broadening of an existing functional social model.

Europe and the NPM context

The term 'New Public Management' was first coined in New Zealand (Schedler and Proeller, 2002: 163). NPM principles were rapidly adopted in Thatcher's Britain, but with substantial ideological borrowings from the then Reagan administration in the United States (Thiers, 2000). NPM is characterised by an attempt to infuse private sector business practices in the public sector in the interests of greater efficiency. The NPM has been associated with the adoption of 'managerialist' rhetoric and practices associated with:

> ...change, decentralisation, responsiveness to consumers, performance, and the need to 'earn' rather than to 'spend'. Borrowing from the world

"

of private-sector management, the vocabulary of the new public management has so far shown a remarkable degree of consensus among the political leadership and opinion makers of various countries about the desired nature of change. Change is to be primarily organisational: its goal is to strengthen management capacity in government operations (Maor, 1999).

In the 1990s, a large number of European countries adopted NPM techniques to restructure their public sectors. Pressures for reform included cyclical budgetary pressures, the increasing amount of public spending as a proportion of GDP in many Western European states, and demands for improvements in service quality given productivity improvements in other areas of the economy (Flynn and Strehl, 1996b). In addition, rapidly ageing populations have placed increasing pressures on established European welfare states. However, as Pierson (1991) notes, the core requirement of supporting a growing dependent population is unlikely to be resolved simply through privatisation; in whatever way, the costs will still have to be met from current economic output.

> *Inter alia*, reforms have included the disaggregation, decentralisation and 'externalisation' (using the private sector, either totally or in part) of public services (Torres and Pina, 2002). Nor does this represent a brief, passing managerial fad, such as Total Quality Management (TQM) or 'Zero-Based Budgeting', but rather, a far-reaching historical development, significantly recasting the role of the public sphere (Kearney and Hays, 1998; c.f. Anon 1997).

Drawing on the evident failures of governments in a range of areas despite the allocation of substantial resources, critics in the public choice school of thought argued that 'budget maximising bureaucrats' diverted resources away from more productive areas of the economy. More populist neo-liberals mounted a particularly sustained attack on the provision of social services, which, they alleged, was largely wasted on an unruly, unproductive, and increasingly disorderly undeserving poor. Much of government power is, in the advanced societies, invested in a career civil service. The latter represents an 'essential ingredient in the maturation of a nation's social and political systems', but, like any other collective human enterprise, is periodically prone to shortcomings, above all in areas such as accountability, providing some ground for neo-liberal attacks (Kearney and Hays, 1998; c.f. Anon 1997).

Undoubtedly, the diffusion of NPM has been an uneven process, and with certain universal problems in areas such as the development of techniques for conducting value-for-money audits for outsourced or privatised public sector functions. Despite this, most Western European governments

have introduced measures attempting to instil some measures of performance management (Halachmi, 2001). Invariably, this has entailed a loosening of the bonds binding together the bureaucracy, with, in many cases a
decentralisation – and fragmentation – of functions taking place (Kearney
and Hays, 1998). Nonetheless, Wallace (2000) argues that pressures
towards greater marketisation meet with specific responses in the European
case; national and regional institutional ties are likely to result in a particularly European outcome. However, to more pessimistic commentators,
such as Streeck, the implication is that traditional national systems and
practices remain vulnerable; inevitably, the role of transnational institutions such as the EU will be to further erode individual national particularities, in the direction of 'Delaware' standards (O'Hagan, 2002: 40).
Similarly, Masters (1998) suggests that one of the major effects of the EU in
terms of national public administrative practice has been in the direction
of governmental cutbacks, albeit that these have been 'pursued with
varying degrees of enthusiasm' (Masters, 1998). Poorer regions of Europe
simply cannot afford the burden of a comprehensive north-European style
welfare state, leading to inevitable pressures towards ongoing 'social
dumping'.

The public sector, economy and society: European archetypes

Certain forms of productive organisation will be characterised by particular
structures of authority. Specific organisational forms cannot be understood
outside of specific organisational and environmental contexts (Hirst and
Zeitlin, 1997); there is a close correlation between dominant economic
models and the nature and structure of the public sector. As Stillman
(1997) notes, a variety of state forms and public administrative traditions
within Europe persist, ranging from the corporatist-style state of
Scandinavia, to the predatory state found in the European periphery.
Pressures towards greater marketisation may be exacerbated or alleviated
owing to differences in constitutional arrangements, national political cultures, and the receptivity of different governing parties towards neo-liberal
ideologies (Flynn and Strehl, 1996b). In some states, a long democratic tradition is counterbalanced by the relatively late development of a professional public sector, whilst in others, the converse is true (Stillman, 1997).
Indeed, a number of national archetypes are readily identifiable.

Firstly, there is the *Rhineland* model, associated with countries that have
a long tradition of neo-corporatist accommodation. Within such contexts,
the state plays a central role in mediating the interests of business and
labour, and, in doing so assumes part of the costs of making concessions
when one or other party is in no position to do so. For example, if a
country faces adverse external economic pressures, business may be dependent on the goodwill of organised labour, but cannot afford to grant

meaningful concessions (c.f. Teague, 1995). In such cases, the state will step in, and offer either improvements in social expenditure, and/or an associated expansion in public service provision (Wood and Harcourt, 2001). Neo-corporatist governments are likely to spend more on active labour market policies, which train workers for shortage occupations, subsidise labour demand in high-unemployment regions and industries, and match existing labour supplies to labour demands by providing a recruitment agency function (Kraft, 1998). Again, this is likely to make the state a relatively large employer (Harcourt and Wood, 2003). As Pracher (1996) notes, the power of unions and other associations may also result in certain reforms – such as the large-scale outsourcing of state functions – being indefinitely deferred. Marketisation continues to be considerably less popular than in the Anglo-Saxon world (Schelder and Proeller, 2002: 178). For similar reasons, the rhetoric of change may greatly surpass the reality (Kuitenbrouwer, 1996). Reforms have tended to be most pronounced at local government level, where specific regional dynamics may allow greater room for manoeuvre (see Schedler and Proeller, 2002).

Secondly, there is the *semi-peripheral Fordism* model, common to Greece, Spain, and Portugal. Here, a long period of relative isolation from the global economy has been followed by directed modernisation and austerity (Holman, 2001). Although some writers, such as Perez Diaz, have argued that these countries are gradually evolving towards the *Rhineland* model of capitalism, others, such as Roca, have pointed out that, to date, corporatist deals seem rather more strategic than accommodations, and long term institutional reform (Martinez-Lucio and Blyton, 2001). The outcome has been the attainment of the 'core position of the previous stage of development of the world economy', when most of the advanced societies have already moved on to later variations. This has resulted in a somewhat painful period of adjustment, especially for small factories and retailers, which were placed under pressure to centralise and concentrate their activities (Holman 2001). In turn, this has resulted in the emergence and/or increased penetration of competitive corporations, displacing former parastatals, followed by the development of a professional managerial class (Holman, 2001). This results in the direct role of the state in economic activity diminishing; the role of the public realm shrinks from the management of enterprises to more narrowly defined administrative, security, and social service provision functions. However, the implementation of public administrative reform measures has been an uneven and contradictory process. In some cases, such as Portugal, 'virtually everything of significance remained the same...despite the reform legislation' (Rocha, 1999). This reflected judicial checks and balances, which precluded the implementation of unrestrained marketisation, and the contradictory agenda of conservative politicians. The latter sought both to increase their own direct control over the bureaucracy, and infuse managerial responsibility into differing functional areas; invariably this proved self-negating (Rocha, 1998). In the areas of public service provision that were privatised, quality decreased and costs rose. In Spain, public sector reforms reflected a desire to build decentralised democratic structures at regional and local level, while the main reforms at local level continue to be generated by central government (Schedler and Proeller, 2002).

Thirdly, there is a *transitional model*, found in Eastern Europe since the collapse of Stalinist rule in 1989. After a period of rapid marketisation, many firms have coped through recourse back 'to parastatal organisations and old systems of barter and exchange' or 'involution' (Smith and Swain, 2001: 453). However, above all, strategic thinking centres on the need to cut costs; in many cases, this has been achieved by cutting back on production and administrative costs (Voskamp and Wittke, 2001). Again, this model is characterised by the shrinking of the public realm, but rather more radically than in the previous instances. A similar 'contradiction of managerialism' results in a desire both to place the bureaucracy clearly under the control of politicians and vest public managers with real managerial responsibility (Guess, 1997). The outcome may be either that of gradual convergence to more Western models, or a new form of specificality. The latter would be characterised by a chronically weak state, the lack of a fully supportive banking network, an erosion of the social coverage of the state, and the permeation of the public sector by informal networks of support linked to emerging capitalist 'robber barons' (c.f. Boyer, 2001).

Fourthly, there is the *Anglo-American model*, characterised by a wider institutional context and individualised fragmentation. On the one hand, this has led to endemic failures of more advanced areas of social provision, and the lack of a fully functional technical and vocational training national infrastructure. On the other hand, a modest welfare state was constructed in the early twentieth century, partially in response to fears of systemic instability. In Britan, radical reforms were characterised by a long period of Conservative Party rule, facilitated by highly centralised use of political power (Flynn and Strehl, 1996b; Flynn, 1996). This allowed central government to impose policy, not only on central state institutions, but also on locally accountable local authorities, including the restructuring of functions and the (compulsory) introduction of competition. Whilst this led to certain functions of management being decentralised, this was into the hands of a small coterie of 'professional managers', rather than genuinely to community or local council level (Flynn, 1996).

Fifthly, there is the *regional or industrial districts model*, characteristic of Italy (Whitley, 1999). This represents the product of a specific pattern of state development, resulting in considerable regional differences in the manner in which economic networks and firms operate, and the role of government in shaping social and economic life (Whitley, 1999). Indeed, government power in Italy is dispersed among over 40 000 autonomous and semiautonomous public agencies (Kearney and Hays, 1998). An extremely wide-ranging national privatisation programme was implemented in the 1990s, aimed at cutting back a relatively large parastatal sector, and promoting a specific national developmental trajectory (Segreto, 1998). However, this had limited impact on wider Italian economy and society. Indeed, the process served to strengthen both larger enterprises and family networks, with small and medium sized enterprises (SMEs) gaining very little (Segreto, 1998).

Finally, there is the *French model*. Here, a well-developed public administration sector played an active role in shaping the role of business in society (Whitley, 1999). A highly independent – and intransigent – civil service has actively resisted 'repeated reform efforts by a succession of political leaders' (Whitley, 1999: 71). This has led to the French bureaucracy facing regular attacks both from French politicians and EU reform initiatives (Thiers, 2000). As in the case of Britain, there is a tradition of centralisation of power. However, in France, functions have not been progressively delegated to an emerging class of 'professional managers'. Rather, senior officials from sub-national government – such as regional inspectors, and local arms of ministries – retain a strong vested interest in preserving the traditional powers of the centre (Flynn and Strehl, 1996a).

Convergence – the low road

In an essay and follow-up volume that were both as overrated as they were influential, Francis Fukuyama (1992) argues that 'a remarkable consensus' has emerged around liberal democracy and associated market economics which constitutes the 'end of history' as we know it. Taken to their logical conclusion, this would make for an emerging homogeneity in the public realm world-wide. Responsible to the broader electorate, and in the context of increasing prosperity, the public sector's role would primarily be a regulatory one, transcending the traditional administrative state.

Since then, the failure of the promises of 1980s-style neo-liberalism have become increasingly clear; examples would include increasing social inequality (matched by declining welfare provision) and the decay of public infrastructures in the face of repetitive rounds of cost cutting. It can be argued that increasing numbers of Western European countries have adopted NPM techniques in the 1990s; neo-liberalism's gains reflect not only the collapse of state socialist alternatives and the apparent failure of the Keynesian model, but also the lack of viable new alternatives. At best the outcome has been mixed, as countries have battled to effectively monitor the relative benefits of the privatisation and outsourcing of state functions (Torres and Pina, 2002; Halachmi, 2002). Nonetheless, as Thiers (2000) suggests:

> ...it would seem that the universalisation of problems on our planet is leading to a kind of standardisation of solutions. In this sense, all of the States are in transition today (Thiers, 2000).

It can thus be argued that the advance of neo-liberal practices in Western Europe remains unchecked: even centre-left governments have engaged in further privatisation and reforms to company law (Blackburn, 2002; Budgen, 2002). Whilst paying lip service to the 'social model', such governments have, again, actively contributed to its erosion (Budgen, 2002). The adoption of market-driven policies in the public sector has been particularly pronounced in Eastern Europe, with the gutting of social provision and the relentless outsourcing of functions.

Again, the EU's internal structures and external policies have not been immune to pressures towards restructuring. The European Commission launched two successive programmes for internal reform, the 'Sound and Efficient Management 2000' initiative, followed by the 'Modernising Administration and Personnel'. Both initiatives incorporated an emphasis on decentralisation and deregulation; for example, the latter sought to decentralise personnel management (Pollitt and Bouckaert, 2000). Externally speaking, the *Maastricht* convergence criteria for currency unification in the late 1990s placed downward pressure on the expenditure of aspirant governments. The introduction of the European single currency has placed further restrictions on deficit spending by member governments, albeit that there are growing demands for these strictures to be eased.

More broadly-speaking, a further implication of NPM is that, as political executives gradually find themselves losing control of large areas of what used to be the public sphere, they attempt to counter-balance this balance by the exertion of more direct control over residual bureaucratic functions. As Moar (1999) notes:

> ...this outcome is best formulated as a paradox: investing in the public administration's managerial capacity is most likely to result in political executives' disinvesting in the public administration's political capital so as to resolve the problems of loss of control over policy implementation raised by the managerial reforms put in place under the new public management (Moar, 1999).

Based on an international study, Moar finds that similar processes have been at work in Austria, Britain and Malta, despite the very different historical traditions, and very mixed results. These developments have led writers such as Torres and Pina (2002) to question whether currently fashionable methods of delivery, and auditing the performance of private sector concessionaires are at all 'appropriate for twenty-first-century public services', or whether alternative models have to be developed (Torres and Pina, 2002).

Convergence – the high road

Wallace (2000) notes that 'the creation and the development of the EU are in themselves responses to Europeanisation and reflect a set of choices about ways of channelling or influencing the patterns of Europeanisation' (Wallace, 2000). It can be argued that whilst there are undoubted pressures towards a convergence in philosophies and practices of public administration, this is not necessarily in the direction of marketisation and cost cutting. Rather, through the operation of transnational institutions, such as the EU, a broad social model is gradually diffusing across Europe with beneficial consequences for public administration functions. Europe would evolve into a region of highly competitive firms, a generous welfare system and policy making embedded in social dialogue (O'Hagan, 2002). This will take place as European member states gradually cede power to an emerging 'supranational powerhouse' (O'Hagan, 2002: 43) in Brussels. This viewpoint assumes that states remain 'airtight compartments' retaining absolute power over traditional areas of decision-making and that there is a natural evolutionary tendency towards stronger unity (O'Hagan, 2002: 44).

A variation on these arguments is provided by 'new governance' theories (c.f. Hix, 1998), which suggest that a new model is gradually developing in Europe, which results in the EU governing previously unanticipated policy domains (O'Hagan, 2002). This reflects 'the development and sustaining of systematic European arrangements to manage cross-border connections, such that a European dimension becomes an embedded feature which frames politics and policy within the European states' (Wallace, 2000), with corresponding transnational institutional supports. As Wallace further notes, a number of distinct modes of interaction can be identified within the EU and associate fora. These include an established method of supranational governance, associated with early moves towards common policies in areas such as agriculture; a regulatory mode associated with a range of market-making or supervising activities; distributional interventions at both national and sub-national levels; and increasing 'soft policy co-operation', *inter alia*, through the operation of Directives (Wallace, 2000). The Treaty of Rome, the 1985 Single European Act and the 1991 Maastricht Treaty all paved the way for a unification of practices, both in underpinning the way for subsequent monetary union and political co-operation. They also mapped out rules of the game for an emerging neo-polity, potentially allowing for mutually supportive public administrative functions operating at a range of levels (Schmitter, 1997).

Both the 'Sound and Efficient Management 2000' and 'Modernising Administration and Personnel 2000' for the internal reform of European Commission administrative structures, placed stronger emphasis on cost-cutting and efficiency than marketisation: a commitment to key public service values persists (Pollitt and Bouckaert, 2000). The internal culture and practices of the Commission continue to reflect the strong French influence during its formative years, whilst the fragmentation of functions, and a tradition of collegiality at Commission level make it difficult to drive through managerial reforms.

Despite external pressures, the West European public sphere remains very much stronger than, for example, the United States. This is sustained by the provision of public space, state sponsorship of cultural activities, and public ownership of significant components of the media and physical infrastructure (Blackburn, 2002). Nonetheless, as poorer regions enter the EU, it becomes very much harder to marry the development of a 'social model' with pressures towards greater marketisation (O'Hagan, 2002).

However, it can be argued that the greatest threat the European social model faces is not so much its sustainability, but rather a crisis of confidence. A supportive institutional environment continues to underpin superior manufacturing performance to the United States; European modes of economic organisation and associated governmental structures continue to perform relatively well when compared to more deregulated models. Freed from the pressures of US style financial engineering – which prioritises short term shareholder value – firms located within European social democracies are in a position to spend far more on research and development than their US counterparts (Blackburn, 2002). In part, the superior performance of European manufacturing firms when compared to their US counterparts, represents the product of a particular regulatory environment, that 'drives them towards business building rather than financial engineering' (Hutton, in Blackburn, 2002: 136).

Again, it can be argued that current pressures faced by European social democracies represent the product of shocks, such as the expense of German unification, and austerity prompted by the need to establish the credibility of the Euro, rather than genuine systemic failure (Blackburn, 2002). The EU has the capacity to ride out these shocks and continue with the European social model project. However, collective European positions depend on a complex of interlocking understandings, rather than on 'crisply defined and clearly authorised hierarchies of authority'; consent for common European positions 'generally depends on a series of interlocking understandings' (Wallace, 2000).

Diversity and institutional 'nestedness'

Alternatively, it can be argued that national level institutions (within and without the realm of the state) remain remarkably resilient against the homogenising pressures of both global capitalism and transnational bodies such as the EU.

Whitley (1999) argues that the limited significance of pan-European agencies and European systems of economic organisation, despite 40 years of the existence of the EEC and it successors, underscores the tenacity of national institutional arrangements and practices. The diffusion of specific modes of governmental or economic practice depends on both the cohesion and strength of host institutions and the willingness of state authorities to accept supra-national organisations. As Wallace (2000) argues:

> Europeanisation and resilient domesticity are necessarily at odds with each other, in so far as there is a 'good fit' between the two. On the other hand, some western European countries have been outliers less at ease with Europeanisation, but nonetheless permeated by its impacts – Norway and Switzerland are the key current examples. In central and eastern Europe the disruptions to connections across borders have produced a contrasting long history, in which options for managing transnational relationships have been more constrained. Thus Europeanisation is not an even process across the continent...Europeanisation can coexist with protected domestic political spaces (Wallace, 2000).

In short, to Wallace, Europeanisation remains an uneven and contested process. Salinas (2002) notes that whilst the EU requires national governments to adhere to certain guidelines and fulfil mutually agreed goals, national authorities frequently retain the choice of means, as if the latter was neutral or irrelevant, when, in practice, the two are closely interlinked. This has led Wallace (2000) to argue that, contrary to what some commentators have suggested, this process is less one of 'multi-level governance', which implies some type of hierarchy, and more an uneven and changing division of labour between levels of government, that are contested in such a manner as to have uneven outcomes. Indeed, even relatively small and vulnerable states such as Ireland and Finland, have used Europeanisation to buttress domestic transformation, whilst preserving distinct national characteristics (Wallace, 2000). Thus, the EU is unlikely to play a uniform, overcoding role, in forcing the implementation either of a broad social model, or alternatively, the marketisation associated with NPM. Rather, its influence will reflect the specific configurations of national institutional structures and particularistic developmental trajectories.

As is the case with transnational institutions, it can be argued that global economic pressures are unlikely to result in uniform responses. Some nations will choose the path of deregulation, seeking competition purely on cost grounds, whilst others will aim to develop national economic competitiveness around the production of high quality, innovative and niche market goods, made possible through a comprehensive supportive infrastructure, underpinned by a vibrant and robust public sphere.

Institutional configurations are both adaptable and subject to evolutionary pressures for change. Whilst it is unlikely that 'globalisation' will uniformly erode national boundaries, institutions may exist – and co-exist – at different levels: sub-national regions; nationally; transnationally (such as in the case of the EU); and globally (Boyer and Hollingsworth, 1997). Institutional arrangements may operate horizontally (such as in the case of a common market or community) or vertically (including both hierarchical arrangements of authority and, ultimately, the state). Again, different mechanisms of governance – such as the market, communities, associations, and state – are characterised by differing organisational structures, rules of exchange, and mechanisms for ensuring compliance. Whilst the state has seen its role eroded in some areas, national institutions remain important. There has been no convergence in institutional configurations; rather national institutions can be said to be 'nested' between transnational and regional ones.

Whilst the ability of national governments to implement wide ranging social policies in the face of transnational economic pressures is limited, certain countervailing forces reconstitute themselves. Whilst institutions are not purely nationally embedded, overlapping tiers of institutions can be said to be nested (Boyer and Hollingsworth, 1997: 470). Whilst the nestedness of institutions in multi-level systems may in some respects diminish national differences, it can also create differing tiers of restraint; whilst the nature and form of national forms of mediation may be subject to change, they continue to mould conduct.

Schmitter (1997) argues that a major barrier to the convergence of policies and practices in Europe – in both the public sector and macroeconomic management – is the persistence of mechanisms that are neither governmental nor market; these would include strong informal and formal associations, inter-firm and inter-sectoral alliances, and 'private interest governments'. Nor are these mechanisms dysfunctional; they underpin the competitiveness of much of European industry, allowing for flexibility, the sharing of research and development costs, effective training and greater long-termism.

As Thiers (2000) notes, at best NPM constitutes 'a rather incoherent reform wave, consisting of a combination of ideological and instrumental elements that are partly inconsistent and contradictory' (Thiers, 2000). The development of public administration is moulded by specific state traditions; this ensures that public administration in Europe will remain distinct from that of the United States (Stillman, 1997). Across Europe, the role of the state remains relatively more important; even in recently democratised central Europe, a strong emphasis continues to be placed on 'policy planning, judicial oversight, economic control, and effective program implementation' (Stillman, 1997). Meanwhile, the Eurozone remains large and strong enough to defend the social gains of its peoples, albeit that there is a need for 'new measures and institutions' (Blackburn, 2002: 139); the real challenge is in the realm of ideas, in developing viable and sustainable alternatives to NPM.

Conclusion

Both to many proponents and critics of neo-liberalism, marketisation represents a process that national institutions are powerless to mediate; countries face the stark alternative of deregulating and fitting into an emerging neo-liberal world order, or face economic marginalisation. NPM represents part and parcel of this process; the state trims back its role to allow more room for private enterprise, and adopts within its remaining areas of activity 'efficient' public sector methods, centring on targets and monitoring, rather than delivery, and promoting equity and progress. Alternatively, it has been suggested that NPM has been recast in Europe to a different, specifically European, set of practices. Through the role of national and transnational institutions, an emerging social model is gradually being diffused across the continent, mediating the worst excesses of marketisation, whilst allowing for the expansion of the public sphere in vital areas.

However, it can be argued that both these visions underplay the importance of national governmental and residual (that is, neither governmental nor market) institutions. The preservation of the increasingly threatened public domain, and its development, depends not only on the vitality of these institutions, but also on the development of policy alternatives, that preserve and develop the social gains of the past in a manner relevant to the needs of the early twenty-first century.

13

Recruiting and Training the New Cadre: Reform of the Civil Service in the People's Republic of China

Jonathan Liu and Jane Wang

Public sector management reform in China offers an interesting comparison to other national case studies in that it does not fit comfortably with the usual reference points for such reform elsewhere. On one hand, the logic for reform is remarkably similar to Western examples: the desire to reduce the size and enhance the efficiency of the state bureaucracy, combined with familiar external influences on the reform agenda, including the influence of complying with World Trade Organisation (WTO) membership and of the desire to use received 'best practice' reforms from other countries' public sector reform agendas. On the other hand, however, the drive for reform in China is routed deeply in the Chinese national context: the legacy of the world's first civil service, dating back over 2300 years, combined with the tumultuous events of the twentieth century, culminating in Deng Xiaoping's reform package aimed at creating the 'socialist market economy'. The system in China, then, is defined by this mixture of long traditions and of the embracing of modernising reforms.

For centuries, the Chinese government operated a personnel management system based on strict examinations in selecting and recruiting civil servants. This system lasted some 1299 years before being abolished in 1905 in the late Qing Dynasty. However, no effective replacement of the old system was introduced during the years between 1905 and 1949, due to frequent changes of government and general social instability in China. Nevertheless, after the founding of the People's Republic in 1949, the new government introduced a personnel management system reflecting its own ideology. Since the government was placed in office by military forces, naturally many of the positions were filled with army veterans and other party affiliates, rather than by meritocracy. However, as China strives for economic modernisation and accession into the WTO, the appropriateness of the selection and appointment process has been questioned, and its ability to meet the demands of its new environment challenged. China has recognised that administrative support needs to be carried out by trained professionals, and consequently, meritocratic progression has become the centre of debate once again.

The chapter aims to comment on the steps taken by the Chinese government to (a) restructure the government and reduce the size of the bureaucracy, (b) recruit civil servants with the appropriate qualifications for key positions, and (c) reform the civil service training regime to ensure that candidates are provided with the relevant and necessary training for them to be able to play an important role in China's economic modernisation. It also reflects on how lessons have been learnt from other countries in China's pursuit of developing sustainable and stable systems.

Researching the public sector in China

Conducting any study on the state of public administration, management and public policy in Asia is both difficult and challenging, particularly because of the diversity of culture and political systems that exist in the region. In addition, there are traditions going back over a very long period of time, and some of the earliest records of public administration have been found in the region. It is also challenging, however, because these ancient civilisations have, in recent years, experienced high levels of economic development and have needed to transform their public sector systems rapidly to keep pace. More importantly, whilst the transformation has been assumed to follow the path that Western style modernisation has occurred, it has not necessarily been the case.

Transformation in the modern world has, by and large, been driven by both economic and political change. In a comparable example to China, reform in the former Soviet Union and countries in Eastern and Central Europe was based upon a change to the political system combined with the marketisation of the economy. The mixed results of this approach did not appeal to China, whose reform package, in any case, predated 'Glasnost' and 'Perestroika'. The Asian model has, in contrast, been based on economic drivers with little change to political systems, and with a clear focus on maintaining political and social stability (Cheung, 2002). Furthermore, changes in the public sector in Asia have been based on the need to modernise but not necessarily Westernise. In many respects, the transformation has been via adaptation strategies rather than completely new theories and concepts. Asian public sector principles have therefore changed little, because of the ability of the political systems to adapt to the demands of their countries' economic needs. However, we could argue that these political systems themselves have changed and adapted to new ideas such as privatisation. Through adaptation, we have seen new concepts such as 'Two Systems – One Country' emerge as drivers for radical change to economic systems but not political destabilisation.

Reform of the public sector in Asia has been through a series of reforms that can be characterised into four categories (Cheung, 2002). They include reforms that promote accountability and transparency in government and public administration; reforms that transform workplace practices and customs; reforms that assist in developing organisational and managerial productivity; and reforms that promote customer and service orientation. These reforms are, in many respects, radical, and reflect the changes occurring in the West such as moves toward deregulation and privatisation. The way in which these reforms have been introduced, however – through a phased or staged process – has arguably allowed them to be more socially and politically acceptable.

The reform agenda in the People's Republic of China

The reform agenda in China should be seen against the background of the long traditions of public administration, and more specifically the way in which civil servants have been recruited for government over the years. For some 40 years until 1993, the Chinese government adopted a highly centralised and single-mode personnel system for the recruitment of staff to cover vacancies in public sector and governmental positions. This system covered governmental offices, universities, schools, and state-owned enterprises as well as government-sponsored institutions. Staff were recruited annually according to the plans of the central government, through a planned-job allocation system, and one could apply for the job simply through recommendation, without going through a formal selection process. University graduates were assigned directly to posts in the government offices or public administration institutions upon graduation and such jobs were for life.

The allocation system was a very generous one for the young university graduates, but there were shortcomings in the system as far as running the government and the public sector was concerned. There was no clear definition of what was meant by 'government officials', and thus whoever worked in the governmental offices, educational institutions, hospitals, enterprises and other civil organisations were all ranked as 'cadres'. In addition, all appointees received salaries and pensions in accordance with a common hierarchical system. There was no benchmark to measure the performance of each and every cadre, and the assessment of cadre 'efficiency' was almost unheard of. Seniority was primarily the only criterion of promotion. The *Iron rice bowl* (job for life) and *lun zi pai bei* (promotion according to seniority) systems were the norms of the day. Complex procedures abounded in the system. Foreign entrepreneurs entering China in the late 1970s commented that this was a primary reason why 'the Chinese machine runs slowly' (Harvie, 1999). The lack of a fair and transparent process made it impossible to promote or fit the right person to the right post. As a result, there was no motivation to improve the state of the government, nor was there any desire to attribute, or shoulder, task responsibility.

In 1978, China adopted an open-door policy toward foreign investors and began introducing economic reforms. As the plans for reform unfolded, the government announced that the civil service personnel system needed to be overhauled to keep abreast with economic modernisation. In August 1980, Deng Xiaoping highlighted the problematic issues as being an oversized bureaucracy, an excessive concentration of power in the hands of cadres, and lifelong tenure in official posts leading to an abuse of privileges – all of which were hampering China's development and progress. These problems derived from faults in China's organisational and personnel management systems (Saich, 1999).

An overview of the Chinese civil service system

The *ke ju zhi du* (traditional qualification examination) came into being in the *Sui* Dynasty, which was subsequently used by the emperors of *Tang, Song, Yuan, Ming* and *Qing* Dynasties to select officials for their imperial courts and local governments. This system was in operation for over a thousand years until its abolition in 1905, and was open to all, but had very strict rules. The examination was mainly based on the examinees' knowledge of the Confucian, which would in many respects imply that there would be some kind of 'job' or 'person' specification, but there is little evidence that such specifications existed.

It could be argued, however, that the *ke ju zhi du* nonetheless did provide a fair and impartial means for recruitment since the profession was (in theory at least) laid open for all those who were sufficiently talented regardless of their social background. It also had other advantages, such as securing the basic qualifications for office work and determining the type and grade of office, which a candidate was fit to hold. The examinations were almost exclusively of a literary nature. Candidates had to show a profound mastery of literature and familiarise themselves with the codes of ethics associated with the great Confucius and his doctrine, so much so that they could tell a short quotation on sight, and were able to complete the remainder of the passage from which it was derived. They should also show their ability to compose prose and poetry in a variety of styles.

In the *Ming* Dynasty (1368–1644), the government paid greater attention to education and training. No fewer than 1200 local schools were established in the prefectures and counties, with financial support from the central government and with officially appointed teachers. This original number had gradually risen to 1810 by 1886. At the same time, a new system was provided for examinations at the three levels, locality, province and the Capital, on a regular basis. The examinations were held in three-year cycles. The first degree was taken in a local city. Those who passed held the degree of *Xiu Cai* (Flowering talent). It did not mean employment, but it did qualify the *Xiu Cai* to sit for second degrees. Examinations for these second degrees were held at provincial capitals. Only a handful passed – about one in a hundred. They were called *Ju Ren* (Recommended Men) and could expect, at some future date, to be given a position such as that of district magistrate. They were also entitled to sit for the third degree in Beijing. About a quarter of the candidates for this would pass out successfully as *Gong Shi* (Presented Scholars), who were finally examined in the presence of the emperor himself. The candidates who passed this examination obtained the degree of *Jin Shi* (Advanced Learning), were sent to Hanlin Academy in Beijing for further study and had future prospects as provincial governors, or ministers of state.

These examinations remained the normal route to government employment until their abolition in 1905 in the late *Qing* Dynasty. From the *Sui* Dynasty to the *Qing* Dynasty, about 100 000 *Jin Shi* and over a million of *Ju Ren* were selected (Yui, 1998). China's scholarly elite were proud to be one of the world's most enduring ruling classes. Having passed through a gruelling series of examinations, mandarins were given powers to decide the life and death of the emperor's subjects.

There were, however, problems with this system. The examinations – the gateway to both official employment and family honour – were theoretically open to almost every male. In practice, the competition was intense and success did not come cheaply. The majority of the scholars were from those wealthy or high-ranking officials' families that could afford private education, since such private education was beyond the reach of the poor. Preparation for the examinations demanded arduous training, and not every family of the land, particularly in the more remote provinces, could find suitable teachers for a potential candidate or the necessary resources to exempt him from his share of work in the fields. The training, syllabus and tests provided a general education of a strictly limited type, without reference to contemporary realities. Moreover, the excessive concentration on the precepts and practices of an obsolete past engendered a false respect for the golden ages of long ago, irrespective of their faults and errors, and resulted in the stifling of intellectual initiative and restricted development of technical expertise.

When, under the *Qing* Dynasty, there was a growing awareness that Western countries' science and technology surpassed theirs, it was decided that the old examination system could not meet the needs of the national development that was deemed necessary. In order to sustain the dynasty's flagging fortunes, Cixi, the Empress Dowager decided to reform, although previously she had opposed the reforms put forward by the emperor Guang Xu. Constitutional and administrative changes were introduced, and among the most striking was the ending of the traditional Confucian examination for civil service entrants in 1905.

After *Ke Ju Zhi Du* was abolished, there was no new system to replace the old one, because in 1908, the plight of the *Qing* Dynasty deepened suddenly and dramatically with the death within 24 hours of both Emperor Guangxu and Empress Dowager Cixi. This left the dynasty in the hands of the two-year-old Emperor Puyi, with the deceased Emperor's brother, Prince Chun, acting as Regent. It was the lack of support for the *Qing* Government that meant that the last years of its life between 1908 and 1911 were described as a revolution waiting to happen. Subsequently, in 1911, the expected revolt against the *Qing* Dynasty began, resulting in its overthrow by revolutionaries led by Sun Yat-Sen.

From 1912 to 1926, the Republic of China was established, of which Sun Yat-Sen was President, and from 1912 to 1949, the Guomindang (Nationalists) more or less ruled China. During this period, the Guomindang government experienced the Warlord Era (1916–1927), the Northern Expedition (1923–1927), the Sino-Japanese War (1937–1945) and the Chinese Civil war (1945–1949). China was hence, basically ruled by a military government. The political and social instability at the time was a primary reason behind the lack of development of a proper civil service system.

In 1949, the Communist Party came to power and founded the People's Republic of China. Party officials were quickly assigned to posts at different levels in the public sector, and the majority of these officials were veteran army officials who had neither a professional education in governance nor experience in managing government affairs. There was no proper system to manage these officials and no clear definition for the role of the civil servant. China had more than 1.3 million state-run institutions with over 29 million employees. Forty-eight per cent of them, some 17 million, could be classed as skilled workers. Nepotism, although not prevalent (notwithstanding a brief period after Mao's death), had stained the reputation of the civil service. A more serious flaw was that civil service positions were tenured. Once a person became a civil servant, they would be privileged to stay in that position for the foreseeable future, unless they committed a crime or were promoted. Thus, low efficiency and poor service was increasingly being linked to the nature of job tenure in the civil service.

The Chinese government began economic modernisation in 1978 while maintaining its political structure, with the aim of improving the efficiency and effectiveness of the civil service. By 1984, the Chinese government had asserted that a new civil service system had to be established, to cater for the needs of a socialist market economy and modernisation. China had been fostering a market-driven economic system, whereas the old personnel mechanism was not conducive to achieving this goal.

Reform of the recruitment system for government officials in China

Reform of government institutions was thus directed towards improving efficiency and competence. This led to constant calls for the streamlining of executive organs of government and for a reduction in the number of ministries and other bodies, as well as their levels of staffing. Deng Xiaoping was prominent in the condemnation of 'bureaucracy', under which he included a formidable list of faults – divorcing oneself from reality and the masses, spending considerable time and effort in putting up an impressive façade, indulging in empty talk, sticking to a rigid way of thinking, being hidebound by convention, circulating documents endlessly without solutions being offered, and shifting responsibility on to others (White, 1993).

In August 1980, Deng Xiaoping advocated his ideas on reform, one of which was the abolition of lifelong tenure of office and the related issue of old age. He believed that there was too great a concentration of power, with too many senior leaders holding too many posts both in the Party and the government. He called for tighter rules on the retirement of old cadres, and a major infusion of young blood into the Party and government at all levels. In September 1985, 64 full or alternate members of the Central Committee resigned. Amongst them were very senior figures including 10 Politburo members. Younger and better-educated members were in turn elected to the Politburo, with the purpose of setting an example for the others and also to take a lead in deepening the reform. Deng Xiaoping's talk laid the foundation for the forming of the modern Chinese Civil Service System, a process that did not reach completion until 1993, by which time open examinations for the recruitment into governmental departments had been introduced. The new examinations included a written element, which assessed the participant's general and professional knowledge, and was followed by an aural examination in the form of an interview. As such, it was very different to the former Confucian exam. Any person who intended to take the examination had to meet the following entry requirements:

- to be a citizen of the People's Republic of China, entitled to enjoy political rights.
- to hold a university diploma or higher degree and have at least two years' work experience when applying for a job at or above the provincial government level – education level for jobs below the prefecture government level being decided by the provincial department of personnel.
- to be under 35 years of age.

Life tenure of office was condemned as contributing to the ossification of the bureaucratic structure and blocking the appointment of more competent officials. Consequently, an intention to strengthen institutions was demonstrated by the introduction of a de facto 'civil service system', involving matters such as recruitment, training, performance appraisal and wages.

In order to implement the new system, the first step of the reform was to extricate the government from day-to-day business management and to redefine what was meant by 'civil servant'. The reform was first piloted in institutions of scientific and technological research, higher education and medical services. Only those who worked in governmental departments, with the exception of general staff, were henceforth defined as civil servants. The institutions also now had the final say in employment practices, so that institutions could, for example, reward top performers with high wages. Since then, in 1998, departments of the central government also underwent restructuring with almost half of the former civil servants leaving their posts (China Daily, 2 May 1999).

By 2000, about 1.5 million people had taken these examinations (Xie Chuanjiao, 2000), and between the years 1996 and 2000 nearly 4400 Chinese citizens were recruited as civil servants in their own right. Most of those who succeeded in the examinations were under 35 and held a university degree or higher. By 1999, the civil service system had been introduced in 31 provinces and autonomous regions, and within six years, a total of 2636 farmers and 10 631 workers had taken up positions in local governments of provinces, prefectures, counties and townships through similar open examinations. This was part of the total of about 150 000 people from all over the country who had become civil servants in this way.

The reforms ended the 'iron rice bowl era' in the civil service, where employees were given jobs for life irrespective of their abilities, and it also opened up careers for other people regardless of their social background. The 'iron rice bowl' – a name people dubbed civil service employment for its permanence – was thus no longer unbreakable. One positive outcome from this was that the new recruitment system apparently had an impact on the type of people working within the civil service. Follow-up surveys carried out by the National Environmental Bureau and National Tax Bureau suggest that 98 per cent of the new recruits were 'competent', 91 per cent were 'working on their own initiative', and 95 per cent had 'great potential'. Some recruits had been promoted at an age much younger than had been the case in the past (Xu Songtao, 1997). A further positive outcome is that the new practice of choosing civil servants by examinations helped to create a cleaner image among the public, and may also have helped to improve the general quality of services provided by governmental departments.

In order to ensure that the reforms were successful, the Chinese government also put into place systems to ensure that the reforms were being carefully implemented. Reforms included the disciplining of civil servants that abused their positions. In addition, more than 11 000 civil servants at or above division level were removed between 1996 and 2000 as qualification examinations indicated their incompetence (China Daily 8 August 2000). Governments at various levels removed 2680 civil servants in 1996, 2898 in 1997, 2937 in 1998 and 2881 in 1999 (Xinhua, 31 July 2000).

The reform of the Chinese civil service was, however, not without its problems. No one wanted to leave the prestigious governmental departments. Furthermore, the organisations or institutions that people were re-assigned to, were themselves deemed to be overstaffed. For many civil servants on the receiving end, to 'deepen the reform' was merely rhetoric, and they were not willing to conform to the arrangements when their own interests were impaired. In order to maintain stability, the Chinese government therefore undertook the following three measures to ease the transition:

- Those who were selected to leave their posts were encouraged to work in the enterprises or grass-roots level governments;
- Those who had worked for 30 years were persuaded to take early retirement with a full pension, paid by the government; and
- Those who had worked in government offices for less than 30 years were able to go to university to take another degree, again paid for by the government.

Training of government civil servants

During the same period, in order to provide civil servants with the new skills that were deemed necessary for the socialist market economy, and also to promote the new culture, further training was provided. This included training for civil servants both within China and abroad. The latter was due to the Chinese Government's wish to integrate itself with the developed countries, and to help in its preparation for joining the WTO. The training was implemented with the following objectives:

- To train new recruits, and to help them to understand the nature, characteristics, and practices of the governmental offices, in addition to mastering the rules and regulations laid out for civil servants;
- To train potential candidates who are going to be promoted, and help them to develop appropriate leadership skills;
- To provide specialised professional training for officials according to their job requirements; and
- To provide ongoing training for all civil servants, in order to help them to update on new information, knowledge and skills.

Approximately two million civil servants attend training courses every year (Xu Songtao, 1997: 94). The training in China has been carried out by 3009

Party Schools, 3217 Cadre Training Schools, 368 Management Colleges for Government Officials and 20 Administrative Colleges. In addition, a large proportion of training is carried out overseas. Between 1995 and 2001, approximately 4500 people were trained using government funding in short-term training programmes. Table 13.1 shows the breakdown of approved trainers.

The highest concentration of training, then, has been focussed on the Americas, with the United States taking the largest single slice. There are several reasons why the groups have targeted the United States, the primary reason being the geographical size of the United States and the number of organisations that delegates could visit to gain first hand experience. However, the focus in China has moved from breadth to depth of understanding, and therefore the larger number of industries available is not seen as significant.

The Chinese Government uses a three stage bidding process and a fixed upper limit fee scheme in an open tender process for the selection of training courses offered by preferred training providers. In the first stage, the training needs of individuals, associations or organisations, are identified by the Chinese Government or via its own State Bureaux and agencies. Quite often, experts who either represent, or are themselves training providers, advise the government. In the second stage, using a closed network, the government then seeks tenders from training providers. During this second stage, the training providers prepare training schedules and training fee estimates. These are usually prepared in English and Chinese. The third stage is when the training schedule and fee has been approved, and both exit visas from China, and entry visas to the target

Table 13.1   Breakdown of training providers, by country

Country	Number of providers	Total providers	Number of trainees	%
USA, Canada, Brazil	57, 10, 2	69	21300	71
Australia, New Zealand	22, 2	24	1500	5
Germany, UK, France, Belgium, Netherlands, Austria, Switzerland, Sweden, Spain, Denmark, Italy, Russia	23, 10, 10, 3, 2, 1, 1, 4, 2, 1, 4, 3	64	3900	13
Japan, Singapore, Hong Kong, Korea, Thailand	9, 10, 10, 4, 1	34	2700	9
Israel, India, South Africa	4, 1, 2	7	600	2
Total	26 Countries	198	30000	100

country are obtained. Once the third stage is completed, the training group will arrive at a mutually agreed timetable. Quite often, the arrival time is agreed with very short notice because of funding issues, so training providers have to be prepared to provide some flexibility in the system to accommodate this.

In terms of the nature of the training involved, the Chinese Government has focussed on six key areas of managerial development: education reform; transformation of industry; public sector management; health management; knowledge updating, and skills training. The common element that binds the training areas is in the generic 'management' component and, in particular, current developments in Western management practice. It has been estimated that over the next decade the Chinese will focus more on 'management' than on any other single issue because 'having the right systems in place' has been identified as being at least as important as having the right infrastructure (Liu and Mackinnon, 2001).

Developing the systems that are needed in China is, however, not straightforward. Firstly, the size of China demands that any system must take into account 'volume', which Western management practice at times pays little attention to. Second, the spread of development in China is considerably uneven. Much of the East Coast is well developed, but further inland, the stark differences become evident. There is much debate about the next few years of development in China and how the inland regions of China will develop, however what is certain is that the developments inland will be at a much faster pace than the Coast has experienced. Third, developments in China over the last few years have been focussed on developing the underpinning technology infrastructure. Much of that is now complete and there is now a focus on using the technology to accelerate the development in China.

Involvement in the running of such training has led to a number of observations by the authors. Firstly, the average age of the senior official is now much younger than in the previous decade. Secondly, the senior officials have travelled more extensively than previous generations of leaders. Their exposure to Western methods and culture is much more extensive than was the case for older generation civil servants. Thirdly, there is a genuine commitment from senior officials to transform China at grassroots level. The adoption of new policies in China has been fast, but uneven. This has, in turn, highlighted a need to more carefully evaluate the impact of training. There are already signs that this is happening, as measures to survey the quality of training are now used to indicate the success of such schemes, with a more systematic approach being used to gain feedback on the training. For example, individual reports and questionnaires are now used to gain trainees' opinions on the training that they have completed. More importantly, the criteria for promotion into senior management positions in the government now requires the candidate to have spent a period abroad or have evidence to show that they have participated in training schemes or been exposed to new skills development methods.

Trainees are now under some pressure to demonstrate what they have gained from training abroad and in some cases they are required to show how changes can be implemented in their organisations. This is seen as justification for the investment made by the Chinese Government in allowing training to be conducted abroad, which is more expensive than conducting training within China. However, this has been difficult in many cases due to the lack of support from senior managers who have not been given the opportunity to travel, and are not supportive of changes to the current system. Nevertheless, it does appear that trainees are often promoted to more senior positions on their return to China. This might be due to their new sources of expertise, but could also be due to pre-selection taking place before the trainees are selected for overseas training. In itself, this might not be a negative occurrence because overseas training is very costly, and the sponsor will need to feel that they receive value for money.

Conclusion

The Chinese Government began economic modernisation in 1978 while maintaining its existing political structure. Unlike the former Soviet Union, which attempted both economic restructuring along with political reform, China has emphasised economic reform over political reform. The reform of the Chinese civil servant system and its public sector from 1984 was driven by the realisation that the civil servant system needed to be transformed in order to meet the requirement of building up the 'socialist market economy' and to achieve the modernisation of China. In particular, the reform package was seen as being vital to increase the quality of the civil servants both politically and professionally, and to run the government and public sector more efficiently. The Provisional Regulations for Government Civil Servants and other relevant regulations and practices have been stipulated for these purposes.

The main drivers of change have come centrally and from the higher levels of the Chinese Government. However, it is interesting to observe that whilst there have been significant changes to the country's economic base, the socialist structure and political decision-making base has changed very little. This has provided a stable transition for a country that is not only vast in terms of geographic spread, but also the most populous country in the world. Whilst observers may indicate that the Chinese Government decision-making process tends to be top-down, there is evidence to suggest that there is an appreciation, within the government, of the need for consultation at lower levels in the early stages of policy implementation; hence the measures used to 'soften the blow' when removing under-qualified civil servants.

The reform of the Chinese Economy has also meant that the old system of recruitment has come under pressure, with the introduction of senior personnel from industry and commerce rather than from the armed forces. Whilst this may cause observers to be concerned for the stability of government, there is very strong evidence to indicate that as long as the Chinese economy is growing, dissent will be kept at bay. This concern is of course a very real one because in three decades, the Chinese economy has not faulted in growth. Entry into the WTO has enabled further development to take hold, but should the economy come under pressure from a decline in growth, there is some doubt as to whether the political reform process would remain stable.

The Chinese reforms have in many respects been influenced by the West, however a key factor behind this is that the Chinese appreciate that the West is more developed and technologically advanced than China. Therefore, as more and more managers are given the opportunity to travel, observe and learn from the West, their ideas for change in China will have Western foundations and principles. However, the Chinese are past masters of harmonisation, and the hybrid system that is likely to emerge in China is unlikely to be a mere cloning of Western types.

So what is the future for the civil service in China? One can take a glimpse of what it might become from the speech made by Hou Jianling, department chief in China's Ministry of Personnel in 1998 during the 3rd International Administrative Conference held in China. It was a bold vision, since in his speech he described how by 2008 China would have an almost perfect system, but one that was not dissimilar to a Western civil service and public administration system. This would be made possible by the setting up of an entirely new administrative system with interlocking regulations to ensure that *renzhi* – arbitrary rule by man, will be replaced by *fazhi* – the rule by law. A key factor was the recruitment of the civil service, but in addition, other changes were suggested such as regular performance reviews. As indicated, this is not the first time that the old cadre system has come under attack. However, this time Hou wants to replace the system totally: 'By the time the socialist market economy is fully established, it will be possible to create a permanent government structure' (Zhu, 2001). This is no easy task in such a large bureaucracy with long traditions. Nevertheless, it now seems possible that China, the country that can lay claim to having invented the first state administration system in the third century BC, might be in a position to learn from both the successes and failures of the West, in order to effectively combine new practices with existing traditions.

14

Contradictions Confronting New Public Management in Johannesburg: the Rise and Fall of Municipal Water Commercialisation

Patrick Bond

South Africa is an excellent laboratory to assess a brave experiment in public management. Johannesburg is one of Africa's few integrated financial-commercial-industrial-mining megalopolises, and is the world's largest city without a natural water supply. Fiscal constraints are the primary rationale for the move to neo-liberal principles of cost-recovery and differential service standards. However, the inability of New Public Management ideology to factor in eco-social considerations and public goods is part of the reason that popular opposition has emerged, particularly from women who are the most adversely affected.

In considering this case, we stand to learn a great deal from the past decade of institutional restructuring aimed at providing municipal services to a vast population ill served by prior apartheid administrations, using cutting-edge tools of institutional efficiency imported from a Paris-based water company (Beall *et al.*, 2002; Bond, 2002a; Harrison *et al.*, 2003; Murray, forthcoming; Tomlinson *et al.*, 2003). The New Partnership for Africa's Development has advocated such 'public private partnerships' as the main basis for future infrastructural investments across the continent (Bond, 2002b).

An important recurrent theme is the role of aid agencies (especially US AID and British DFID) and the World Bank.[1] 'The World Bank has worked with the city [of Johannesburg] in recent years to support its efforts in local economic development and improving service delivery', according to Bank (2002) staff and consultants:

> In 1993, the World Bank with financial support from US AID, undertook research in the metropolitan centers to quantify the backlogs and estimate the cost of overcoming the backlogs. In 1994, after the African National Congress (ANC) came to power, the World Bank, together with a counterpart South African team and assistance from US AID, funded a municipal finance study and prepared the Municipal Infrastructure

Investment Framework (MIIF). The Bank's empirical work provided the 'first cut' database for the MIIF, which in addition to backlog and cost estimates, provided recommendations as to how services might be delivered and financed... The [Johannesburg] 2030 strategy (popularly called Vision 2030) draws largely on the empirical findings of a series of World Bank reports on local economic development produced in partnership with the City of Johannesburg (CoJ) during 1999–2002, and places greater emphasis on economic development. It calls for Johannesburg to become 'a world-class business location'.

The Bank stresses that Johannesburg 'does not consider service delivery to be its greatest challenge to becoming a better city as nearly 96 per cent of the households have access to basic water, 84 per cent to sanitation, 85 per cent to electricity and 85 per cent to waste removal; and, only about 16 per cent of the households receive less than basic service levels'. The Bank's strategy to help Johannesburg 'alleviate poverty' is through 'job creation by creating an enabling business environment for private sector investment' (World Bank, 2002).

The Bank here takes a strong stand on one side of South Africa's political spectrum, namely neo-liberalism. Based upon its privileged policy advisory location in both national and municipal government, the Bank advocates a minimalist approach to urban infrastructure and services. This entails, firstly, decentralisation and corporatisation, as discussed below; secondly, a lack of urgency in dealing with those Johannesburg residents who lack services; and thirdly, the promotion of 'competitiveness', which often translates into business self-interest.

The first point codifies Johannesburg's so-called 'Igoli 2002' restructuring of most public utilities (and the outright privatisation of several other major assets, such as an airport and fresh produce market). The second point reflects the Bank's – and some in Johannesburg municipal government's – own satisfaction with 'basic' levels of services that are, as we will observe, deemed unsatisfactory by many residents. The third point is that for private investors to become internationally competitive, they will require inexpensive infrastructure and services (such as cheap water and electricity tariffs). This traditional short-termist technique of urban entrepreneurialism logically overrides the needs of poor people for higher municipal services' cross-subsidies from business.

South Africa's municipal water commercialisation policy

The commercialisation of water is typically introduced so as to address classical problems associated with state control: inefficiencies, excessive administrative centralisation, lack of competition, unaccounted-for-consumption, weak billing and political interference. The desired forms will vary, but the options include private outsourcing, and management or partial/full ownership of the service. In the field of water, there are at least seven institutional steps that can be taken towards privatisation: short-term service contracts, short/medium-term management contracts, medium/long-term lease/affermages, long-term concessions, long-term Build (Own) Operate Transfer contracts, full permanent divestiture, and an additional category of community provision which also exists in some settings (Bond *et al.*, 2001).

In South Africa, as the New Public Management philosophy and more general neo-liberal approaches to development policy solidified in the immediate wake of the 1994 election, lead bureaucrats within the Department of Constitutional Development (DCD – subsequently renamed the Department of Provincial and Local Government) and the Department of Water Affairs and Forestry (Dwaf) began pushing a 'partnership' programme. From 1995, municipalities were encouraged to contract out infrastructure-related services to the private sector using what were initially called public-private partnerships (PPPs). In 1997, the DCD issued guidelines and helped establish a Municipal Infrastructure Investment Unit based at the Development Bank of Southern Africa. This was followed by DCD's draft regulatory framework in August 1998, in which PPPs were rebaptised as Municipal Service Partnerships (MSPs) and characterised as 'a variety of risk-sharing structures within public-public, public-private and public-NGO/CBO partnerships' (Republic of South Africa Department of Constitutional Development, 1998, p. v). By December 1998, the SA Local Government Association (Salga) and DCD had negotiated a Municipal Framework Agreement with unions to regulate such partnerships. The MSP programme was run from DPLG, involving a task team with participation from Finance, Trade and Industry, Public Works, Dwaf, Public Enterprises and the Municipal Infrastructure Investment Unit. Trade unions were also invited to help shape the national programme, partly on the basis of the Municipal Framework Agreement of 1998.

Amongst key pilot projects with several years of experience were late-apartheid water supply projects established by the Suez-controlled company Water and Sanitation South Africa (WSSA) in three Eastern Cape towns: Queenstown (1992), Stutterheim (1994) and Fort Beaufort (later named Nkonkobe) (1995). Similar supply deals with foreign firms in Nelspruit and the Dolphin Coast were temporarily stalled in 1998 by trade union-led resistance, but were resuscitated in 1999. Johannesburg followed in 2001. These early MSPs suggest a penchant for long-term management contracts, entailing delegation of defined municipal functions for a ten, 25 or 30 year period. They include the operation, rehabilitation, maintenance, customer services and expansion of assets, which are, however, still owned by the municipalities. Contracts are flexible, allowing for the company to extend or upgrade facilities but with municipal or non-company finances. Unlike concession contracts, they involve less greenfield investment (such as extension of services to townships) and hence far lower risks for the successful bidder.

Criticisms of the MSP approach include its alleged unsustainability, lack of consumer affordability given cost-recovery pricing policy, poor technical design, poor community control functions, mismatched NGO/private-sector roles and expectations, systematic inconsistencies with neighbouring government-subsidised water schemes, and lack of training and transfer prospects, as well as traditional trade union concerns about job loss. Moreover, there exists a classical problem associated with a municipality's 'natural monopoly,' namely whether a state can pass along implementation responsibilities to a delivery agent while still holding control over basic services policy (for example, on coverage, quality, access, cost, labour conditions, and so on, all of which the private sector would ordinarily skimp on to the public's detriment). The propensity of a private firm to, for example, provide cross-subsidies and lifeline tariffs, is extremely low. The extent to which a public monopoly is simply replaced by a private one gives rise to yet more concern.

In any event, only 100 of the 284 new metropolitan, district and municipal entities were anticipated to offer sufficient profits to attract private sector partners, according to the head of the Demarcation Board (Business Day, 11 February 2000). Nevertheless, pressure intensified on South African cities, especially Johannesburg, to outsource a variety of functions. The primary advocates of privatisation were the World Bank and its private sector investment arm, the International Finance Corporation, as well as local and international firms. For example, Banque Paribas, Rand Merchant Bank, Colechurch International, the Development Bank of Southern Africa, Generale des Eaux, Metsi a Sechaba Holdings, Sauer International and Suez had all met with officials of Port Elizabeth municipality by 1997, in the wake of a week-long 1996 World Bank study of the council's waterworks which suggested just one policy option: full privatisation (Bond, 2000; Port Elizabeth Municipality, 1997).

One important point emphasised by both the World Bank and neo-liberal aid agencies, we will see below, is the way water is priced under conditions of commercialisation. In the course of outsourcing to private (or even NGO) suppliers, the environmental, public health, gender equity and economic multiplier features of access to water are often lost. The aspect of commodification that is both most dangerous from the standpoint of low-income people, and most tempting from the side of management, is to reduce cross-subsidisation within the pricing system. This temptation allows the supplier to avoid distorting the end-user price (the 'tariff') away from its 'natural' market level (that is, marginal cost, or full cost-recovery of operating and maintenance costs). As shown in Figure 14.1, this tendency away from a cross-subsidised 'rising block tariff' (Line C) under conditions

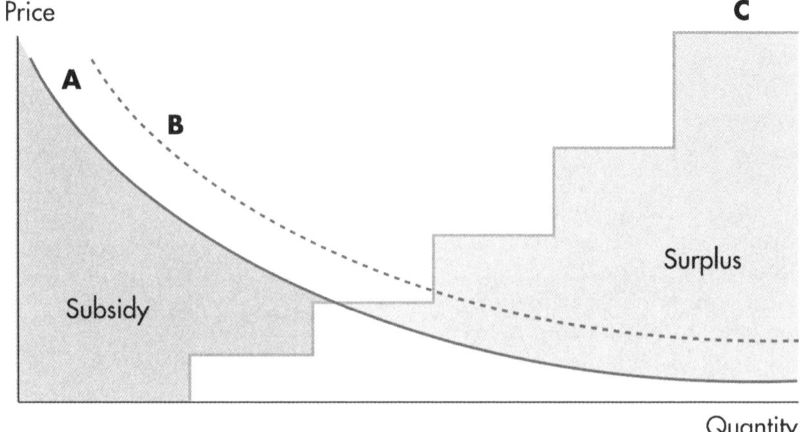

Figure 14.1   Services commodification and decommodification tariff curves

of commercialisation would initially seek to match the tariff with the short-run marginal cost (Line A), and then add a price mark-up to incentivise profitability (Line B), which in turn would attract a private-sector investor.

In sum, the main dangers of municipal partnerships are associated with excessive corporate control of essential infrastructure and services, and the pricing decisions that logically follow. Such control mitigates against both adequate service levels and cross-subsidisation. To what extent did these become problems in Johannesburg?

Johannesburg's thirst

The post-apartheid managers of Johannesburg faced awesome pressures in the wake of the city's first-ever democratic election in 1995: social justice demands from below (and a 1996 constitution which guarantees access to water as a human right), against growing export-competitiveness requirements imposed from above, notwithstanding Johannesburg's poor geographical location far from the major harbours. The 1996 national macro-economic policy (misnamed 'Growth, Employment and Redistribution'), with its orientation to export-led growth and foreign direct investment, gave municipal authorities visions of joining the rank of 'world cities' (Rakodi, 1997; Robinson, 2002; Sassen, 2001). From 1997, a dramatic fiscal crisis compelled Johannesburg authorities to outsource the vast waterworks to Suez, notwithstanding a record of aggressive water privatisation across the Third World that has been the subject of extensive criticism.[2]

Simultaneously, however, low-income townships in the Johannesburg region began to reawaken to worsening socio-economic conditions, with periodic riots beginning in 1997 and spreading quickly through the lowest-income neighbourhoods (Bond, 2000). Racial apartheid had been replaced by a democracy characterised by one-party-dominated centralised rule, under conditions of widespread economic liberalisation, resulting in intensified class/gender polarisation and segregation. In virtually every area of business and government, jobs were shed, wages were kept relatively low, and the price consumers paid for state services rose dramatically as subsidies were withdrawn. A government agency, Statistics South Africa, released a report in October 2002 confirming that in real terms, average black 'African' household income had declined 19 per cent from 1995–2000, while white household income was up 15 per cent (Statistics South Africa, 2002a; Business Day, 22 November 2002). Suffering from worsening poverty and from rising water and electricity prices (which together accounted for 30 per cent of the income of those earning less than R500 per month, where in mid 2003, US\$1 = R7.5), ten million people reported having had their water cut off in one national government survey, and ten million were also victims of electricity disconnections (Statistics South Africa, 2002b; http://www.queens.uca/msp).[3]

Disappointments with the ANC government are perhaps greatest in the largest site of anti-apartheid militancy, working-class-consciousness and democratic community organisation, Johannesburg. The metropolitan area has a population of 3.2 million people. Racially, Johannesburg is comprised of 72 per cent black 'African' people, 17 per cent 'white' people, 6.5 per cent 'coloured' people and 3.7 per cent 'Asians' of mainly Indian origin (Johannesburg, 2001a).[4] With a 26 per cent adult HIV-positive rate, life expectancy has fallen rapidly (Tomlinson, 2003). The municipality counts 791 367 households within the expanded city limits, of which 53 per cent reside in the southern region's black townships of Soweto, Diepkloof and Orange Farm (Johannesburg Star, 28 February 2003). Across the city, an estimated 120 000 households live below the poverty line. Although the city's Gross Geographic Product represents 16 per cent of South Africa's national output, during the 1990s it rose only two per cent per annum (less than the city's population growth). One quarter of adults in Johannesburg are technically illiterate, 39 per cent have less than Grade 12 education and only four per cent have degrees. The formal unemployment rate rose from 27 per cent to 30 per cent from 1998–2001 (Johannesburg, 2001a).

There is only one recent (2000) official survey that systematically measures citizen satisfaction with municipal services, and it is not flattering: 'There is a strong indication that residents from all areas are beginning to feel a heightened sense of frustration and decreased sense of control that they have over their communities and the city generally due to perceptions of the council's decreasing ability to manage the services under their jurisdiction'. Amongst their top five complaints with the council, pluralities of residents chose electricity (48%), water (42%) and toilets (33%) as three of the five worst problems (the other two were the city's failure to create jobs and maintain health clinics). For black ('African') Johannesburg residents, the figures were, respectively, 58 per cent, 53 per cent and 45 per cent, ranking as the first, second and fourth worst problems. In contrast, Johannesburg's white households ranked as their main grievances job creation, community litter, emergency services, pollution and parks/public transport (Johannesburg, 2001b: 8–9; 14–17).

Most of the dissatisfied residents live in the low-income townships, especially the 83 informal settlements which house an estimated 189 000 dwellings (mostly shacks) (Johannesburg Water, 2001: 26). Most lack piped water/sanitation, electricity and other municipal services such as solid waste removal, stormwater drains, street lights, fire and emergency services, libraries, recreation. Water is a crucial resource for the urban poor, given the enormous public health problems that have resulted from overcrowding, communal taps and inadequate sanitation. Cholera killed four residents of Alexandra township in early 2001, catalysing the municipality's brutal forced removal of thousands from a riverbank to faraway locations reminiscent of apartheid's worst days. Diarrhoea kills hundreds of Johannesburg children each year. The transition from HIV+ status to full-blown AIDS often is made via a minor water-borne disease.

It is in this context that Johannesburg Water (JW), an arms-length 'private company with limited liability', was formed as the operating vehicle for both the City of Johannesburg and Suez. Johannesburg Water has a performance contract with the City and the primary owner, Jowam, a joint venture made up of Northumbrian Water Group plc (51%), Water and Sanitation Services SA (Pty) Ltd (29%) and Suez Lyonnaise des Eaux (20%). In turn, however, Suez controls 100 per cent of Northumbrian and 49 per cent of Water and Sanitation Services South Africa. For Suez, this appeared a potentially lucrative proposition in the medium-term, even though the bid for the initial 'loss-leader' contract called for very low returns. The business plan for Johannesburg called for (after-tax) profits to increase from R3.5 million in 2000–2001 to R419 million in 2008–2009. The City's mandate to JW is 'to provide an efficient and cost effective service in order for the city to attract economic growth and development. JW must provide sufficient lifeline and subsidised tariffs at the lower level of consumption to maintain social stability amongst the populace'. JW has 550 000 domestic, commercial and industrial customers, but only takes billing responsibility for 15 000, leaving the rest to the municipality (although this will change progressively over time).

The deal with Suez lasts until 2006, when it could be renewed for more decades. However, this is only the latest manifestation of water sector restructuring, and it is by no means certain that the institutional arrangement will remain the same, given the turbulence in both the form and content of water supply since the early 1990s. Three crucial political-economic processes shaped the way Johannesburg has come to provide water to its citizenry since 1990: popular protest and advocacy; the administrative restructuring associated with Igoli 2002; and price increases caused by new bulk infrastructure.

Firstly, the flow and ebb and subsequent flow of social activism affected the price, quantity and quality of water provided in Johannesburg's townships – and the health, environmental and economic implications which tariff-setters have traditionally failed to factor into their pricing calculations. The most important social struggles of the early 2000s were over water disconnections, the installation of pre-paid water meters and experiments with shallow-sanitation and pit latrines. Secondly, dramatic period changes in the city's administrative and political structure (including its very boundaries) disrupted the process of establishing a metropolitan-wide authority to handle retail delivery of water, until new boundaries were finally demarcated in late 2000. Thirdly, the city's 1997 fiscal crisis set the stage for the major players to turn to the private sector. Since the corporatisation of JW is central to the way that administrative processes then evolved, it is useful to consider the financing crisis and investment drought that provoked the most recent round of restructuring.

Corporatising Johannesburg

Lack of capital was the ubiquitous reason that Johannesburg's pro-corporatisation bloc – namely, the City Manager, a 'Transformation Lekgotla' of 15 councillors, and a team of World Bank advisers – gave for embarking on an asset-stripping spree during the late 1990s. 'Mismanagement' was another rationale, and indeed the city's officials were having major difficulties in simply maintaining the inherited systems, in part because they refused to enter into constructive relationships with workers who could have pointed out areas for improvement. Indeed, as an example, as the main report for the short-term Igoli 2002 rescue operation noted, 'No one is responsible for R176 million of unaccounted for water [annually], substantial non-collection, inaccurate or non-reading of meters'.

To the extent that capital-drought was genuine, the fundamental financial problem Johannesburg faced was a triple-squeeze by powerful funders. The first group was in the national Department of Finance, which reduced central-local grants by 85 per cent (after inflation) from 1991–99, leaving Johannesburg with a measly R24 million in 1999 (Financial and Fiscal Commission, 1997). Johannesburg was not particularly creative in attracting other national funds such as housing subsidies, infrastructure grants, poverty relief funds, and so on, for its vast impoverished population. Finally, when the Department of Finance granted Johannesburg R500 million in 2000, it came with extremely tight strings attached, insisting on the rapid implementation of Igoli 2002's privatisation and commercialisation components.

The second group of financiers was the banks and insurance companies. Before 1992, they financed *white* Johannesburg's capital expansion programmes. As Johannesburg desegregated, the capital market institutions turned off their loan funds for municipal capital bonds, preferring to send financial resources into the stock market, suburban shopping centres and office buildings (Bond, 1992). Johannesburg officials failed to pass by-laws against geographical discrimination ('redlining') as a first step towards compelling financial institutions to fund city bonds. The financiers' sabotage of transformation went unchallenged.

The third group who denied the city money was the wealthy households and corporations who did not pay their fare share of the city rates bill. For decades, wealthy ratepayers received an enormous subsidy from township residents. Township workers laboured in factories and offices, and township consumers bought goods in shops, that were all located in white-controlled municipalities. Those factories, offices and shops paid rates to Johannesburg, while township administrations relied mainly on beerhall revenues and, during the 1980s, some central government funding. During the mid-1990s, the Sandton Ratepayers Federation and Liberty Life insurance company, a major Sandton property investor, challenged redistributive rates that would subsidise Sowetans. Although the wealthy white residents lost their case in the highest courts in 1997, the effect was to intimidate Johannesburg politicians at a crucial moment, and reflecting the hidden victory of the Sandton property owners, the rise in rates revenues from approximately R500 million in 1995 to nearly R1.5 billion in 1997 then slowed to a halt.

In short, rather than decisively address the historical legacy, the politicians largely accepted the squeeze put on them by the Department of Finance, the private sector financiers and the ratepayers. Other government actors – Pretoria's Department of Provincial and Local Government and the Midrand-based Development Bank of Southern Africa – offered no comfort. Johannesburg's elected officials and bureaucrats then shifted the costs of the 'redlining' of the bureaucracy onto those who could least afford them: low-income residents.

To take one characteristic example, the installation of Ventilated Improved Pitlatrines was agreed upon by Johannesburg's Transformation Lekgotla in June 1999, without public debate, participation and announcement. But in budgeting R15 million worth of pit latrines (from privatisation revenues) instead of water-borne sewage, which would obviously save money for the soon-to-be corporatised Johannesburg Water, the city officials – guided by the World Bank, as noted above – failed to factor in the environmental or public health implications.

Johannesburg has highly dolomitic (porous) soils. In February 2001, the result was an outbreak of high-density E. coli which led to panic even in Sandton (Sandton Chronicle, 2 February 2001). Rather than treat the issue as a sustained threat to the region's water table, Sandton's wealthy house-holds and institutions invested in their own additional borehole water purification systems, consistent with the tendency to *insulating* the upper classes from socio-environmental problems, rather than *solving* those problems.

Why did the city not budget for higher standards of sanitation, that would have provided better health and environmental benefits? Johannesburg's fiscal stress at the time of Igoli 2002 included vast budget deficits that forced a dramatic decline in capital spending (from R1.2 billion in 1997 to R302 million in 1999). The rationale for the outsourcing to JW followed logically from the artificial credit squeeze, whereas were capital markets better regulated and provisions made for central government guar-antees, there would have been no problem in raising sufficient capital for infrastructure investment. According to the Council, 'If the utility is inde-pendent it can then utilise its own balance sheet and its revenue stream against which it will be able to mobilise the capital resources... If the utility functions remain within the Council the money would need to be raised by the Council which means that the credit risk would be spread across all Council activity and therefore get a much lower credit rating than the utility would be able to' (Greater Johannesburg Metropolitan Council, 1999).

Yet this pessimism was belied by Johannesburg's enormous tax base and good opportunities to cross-subsidise between wealthy, large-volume consumers/corporations and low-income, modest-consumption house-holds. Even prior to the incorporation of Midrand following the December 2000 municipal demarcation, the Johannesburg Metro area could claim a rated tax base of R33.5 billion, and annual revenues arising of more than R4 billion. In addition, by 2000, Johannesburg raised service revenues of approximately R2 billion from sales of electricity, and R1.5 billion from water, wastewater, solid waste disposal and gas.

On the expenditure side, there were large and growing debts by people who could not pay their water, electricity and municipal service bills. Moreover, in the budget of 2001, the city began implementation of an African National Congress promise of free six kilolitres of water per house-hold per month, and in July 2002 households with incomes of R1000 were eligible (upon application) to receive all sanitation and refuse removal ser-vices free. In the 2002/03 budget, R355 million was set aside to cover the subsidy, which would allegedly benefit about 250 000 households in the city.

Was it possible for the city to cover these bills, including the growing arrears? On one hand, the annual central-local grant allocation for Johannesburg finally began increasing dramatically, from R35.7 million in 2000 to R238.8 million in 2003. But in addition, there were much greater sources of internal resources within the metropolitan area that could be tapped. The three most logical means of doing so from the vantage-point of the municipality were through redistribution of wealth, income and the responsibility to pay for municipal services consumption:

- wealth redistribution could have been achieved through rerating property, both through revaluation to reflect updated values and through higher rates on property, including buildings and other improvements to the land which were not assessed due to an outmoded taxation philosophy strongly influenced by the real estate industry;
- income redistribution could have been expanded through the Regional Services Council levy on economic activity and payrolls, a small tax that had not been increased in many years; and
- services redistribution could have occurred through repricing consumption on municipal utilities in a more progressive manner, using a steeper rise in services tariffs for high levels of consumption than was attempted.

The first two strategies for redistribution could easily have been justified based upon the illegitimate wealth and income enjoyed by many Johannesburg residents – predominantly white, upper-income and male – because black, lower-income, and women residents were, throughout the city's history, systematically oppressed. The moral case for a wealth tax on Johannesburg's rich to pay for better municipal services for the poor hardly needs restating.

In addition, however, there was a central problem in Johannesburg's management of infrastructure-related services: pricing. The cost and price of water, sanitation, electricity and other municipal services are central to three other debates, namely,

- whether such services should be corporatised and privatised (and priced accordingly);
- whether conservation of natural resources can be increased through more sensitive use of electricity and water, taking into account their merit good and public-good characteristics; and
- whether all citizens of the city can claim that their constitutional rights to live in dignity are being realised through municipal services.

In each case, a firm neo-liberal position emerged in the Johannesburg Council, consistent with the New Urban Management approach promoted by the World Bank. As reflected in the water price, by the time Igoli 2002 was established in 1999, Johannesburg's tariff structure had become more regressive than during apartheid (that is, with a flatter slope in the block tariff). One fifth of metropolitan residents did not receive water directly at their yard or house (many thus resorting to purchasing water from extremely expensive vendors), while municipal services subsidies were often redirected from where they were intended, and captured by higher-income groups.

As a result, the neo-liberal approach to water provision and pricing was unsound even on simple economic grounds, because of its failure to cost in eco-social factors such as the penetration of effluent into the water table. Johannesburg's narrow financial-rate-of-return policy would, in turn, fragment city services, thus disengaging civil servants in the water or electricity or waste-removal sectors from those in the health sector, for instance. The destruction of the holism of services provision reflected Johannesburg officials' refusal to identify and recognise major benefits ('public goods' and 'merit goods') that would follow from restructured tariffs and lifeline services such as disease mitigation, gender equity, economic spinoffs and environmental improvements. Moreover, worker and community participation could have been established as integral to services and infrastructure investment so as to maximise the public-good effects of service provision. But without these kinds of provisions, Johannesburg's extreme and debilitating forms of inequality and uneven development could never be reversed.

Saving money – at what cost?

In spite of periodic mass protests, the Igoli 2002 corporatisation of municipal services remained in place. There was no halt to services cut-offs except electricity in Soweto, because local activists intimidated the Eskom national electricity supplier from further disconnections in October 2001 (Bond, 2002; Ngwane, 2003). Indeed the first four months of 2002 (the last available information) witnessed more than 90 000 cut-offs of electricity and water in Johannesburg. The problem of illegal reconnections – an estimated 19 000 – moved inexorably to the inner city. The city's official Democratic Alliance opposition leader Mike Moriarty applauded: 'The cut-offs are good but council has to be ruthless and unforgiving against people who don't pay their bills, or those who reconnect their electricity illegally' (Sunday Times Gauteng Metro, 19 May 2002).

Contrary to the city's claims that 'Services is not the greatest challenge facing Johannesburg in its drive to become a "better" city', the nearly one million people living in informal settlements continued to suffer water apartheid: 65 per cent use communal standpipes, 14 per cent yard standpipes and 20 per cent water tankers. For sanitation, 52 per cent use pit latrines, dug by themselves, 45 per cent chemical toilets, two per cent communal flush toilets and one per cent ablution blocks (Harvey, 2003).

The point of maintaining such low standards so long after liberation in 1994, is to save money. The city and JW are well aware of micro-managerial techniques for lowering the costs of infrastructure and services. One technique is pre-paid water meters, which although declared illegal in Britain after public health problems during the 1990s, are being installed in Johannesburg. The five-year operation termed 'Gcina Manzi' (Zulu for 'conserve water') is aimed at the durable non-payment problems in Soweto, Orange Farm, Ivory Park and Alexandra.

A great deal of money is also lost by JW in providing sanitation to low-income people. The main disincentive to install full sewage is the ongoing operating expense (the 12 litres per flush used in full conventional sewage). According to JW business plans, the company intends to spend R16 million constructing 6500 non-flush pit latrines from 2003–05 in informal settlements. The shallow sewage system is also attractive to the company, because the maintenance costs are transferred to households.

As for the water tariffs, Johannesburg's money-saving technique is to adopt a relatively steep-rising *convex* curve which is vastly more onerous at the second block of consumption than that paid at the end of apartheid. Most townships residents were in the 6–20 kl/month consumption range, so the dramatic increase in their per-unit charges in the second block meant that there was no meaningful difference to their average monthly bills even after the first 6000 litres, whose price is free. The free water promise of the African National Congress during the prior municipal election campaign, which became operative in mid-2001, followed the cholera epidemic and rising community protest. Civil society groups criticised the small amount (6 kl/household/month) and the bias against large households, which could have been ovecome using a per person amount. In contrast, a concave curve that rose more rapidly for high-volume consumption would have more severely penalised the wealthier consumers, assured cross-subsidisation, and probably also have dramatically increased water conservation.

Indeed, the marginal tariff for industrial/commercial users of water actually declines after higher consumption volumes. The desire to diminish cross-subsidisation by corporations to low-income consumers is explicit government policy. A 2003 Department of Water Affairs and Forestry 'Water Resources Strategy' states: 'Government has indicated that equitable share grants, made to municipalities in terms of the annually-enacted Division of Revenue Act, should enable water services authorities to fund the provision of free basic water. The cross-subsidisation of raw water in terms of the pricing strategy, described above, will therefore *not* be implemented, to avoid double subsidisation and to reduce administrative complexity' (Department of Water Affairs and Forestry, 2002). This provision will make it difficult, if not impossible, to make the desperately needed changes from wasteful (if 'higher value') usage of water. The problem here is not merely the importance of the competitiveness of Johannesburg-based companies, and hence their desire for lower water prices. In addition, the distortion of market prices by cross-subsidies is also a deterrent to further water privatisation.

Because of the growing controversy over pricing, particularly in the impoverished Orange Farm township, Suez's problems reached the front page of the New York Times on May 29 2003:

> Officials at Johannesburg Water acknowledged that in communities like these, billing people for water has been like squeezing water from a stone... A veteran of the anti-apartheid movement urges people not to pay. His motto, he said, is 'destroy the meters and enjoy the water. The government promised us that water is a basic right', he said. 'But now they are telling us our rights are for sale' (New York Times, 29 May 2003).

The difficulties in reconciling for-profit water provision and service to low-income people was haunting Suez across the world by 2003. Johannesburg remained a crucial site for defending the company's ambitions, for Suez was also suffering severe problems in Atlanta, Argentina, and the Philippines. As 'The Observer' reported at the outset of the March 2003 Kyoto World Water Forum meeting, 'Many of the biggest private sector water companies are turning their back on previous commitments to work in developing countries':

> Suez, the biggest water company in the world, is reducing its exposure in developing countries by a third. It already had plans to reduce costs by E340 million this year and further E68 million next year and now intends to cut deeper. Not surprisingly in a harsh macro-economic climate, the company now favours 'currency risk-exempt financing', having had its fingers burnt in Argentina and the Philippines (The Observer, 16 March 2003).

In late 2001, Suez was thrown out of Nkonkobe for not serving the low-income section of the community (and did not appeal the cancellation of its contract), and other privatisation pilot projects in Nelspruit and Dolphin Coast faced severe problems (Pauw, 2003). The waning of water contracts was not merely a local phenomenon. According to the World Bank, private sector investments in Third World utilities dropped in 2001 to half the $120 billion level of 1997. 'We have agreed to take the commercial risk, but it is the political risks that kill you', according to Mike Curtin of Bechtel Group (which suffered $25 million in losses in the April 2000 anti-privatisation water revolts in Bolivia). 'My fear is that the private sector is being driven out of the water sector' (Bloomberg, 7 March 2003).

World Bank water advice: commodification and privatisation

Dating back a decade, one institution aimed to reconcile the competing objectives and transmit best international water commodification practices to

Johannesburg: the World Bank. In contrast to the guarantee in South Africa's 1996 Constitution that 'everyone has the right to… sufficient… water', the Bank tends to treat water mainly as a commodity. The main criticism of a free lifeline and rising block tariff offered by the World Bank in 1995 was that it would disincentivise privatisation, since the propensity of a private firm to provide cross-subsidies and a free lifeline is extremely low. Bank staff insisted that sliding-scale tariffs favouring low-volume users could 'limit options with respect to tertiary providers…in particular private concessions [would be] much harder to establish' if poor consumers had the expectation of getting something for nothing (Roome, 1995: 50–51). The Bank's 1999 Country Assistance Strategy for South Africa termed this advice 'instrumental' in the 'radical restructuring' of water pricing policy (see Bond, 2003).

This was standard Bank advice. In addition, the International Monetary Fund drew many water-related issues into its structural adjustment programme conditionalities, whether via the Enhanced Structural Adjustment Facility, Poverty Reduction and Growth Facility or Poverty Reduction Strategy Programme (http://www.challengeglobalization.org; Grusky, 2001). A sample of IMF loan conditions in 2000 revealed that nearly a third contained conditions imposing water privatisation or full cost recovery (Hennig, 2001). Likewise, a February 2003 study by the International Consortium of Investigative Journalists found that over a dozen years, the Bank lent $20 billion to water-supply projects and imposed privatisation as a loan condition in one third of the transactions (Logan, 2003).

The Bank also played an important role in the World Panel on Financing Infrastructure that reported to the March 2003 World Water Forum in Kyoto (www.gwpforum.org/gwp/library/WaterReport.pdf). Chaired by former IMF managing director Michel Camdessus, and with representation from the major regional development banks and the Bank's International Finance Corporation, as well as private financial institutions and water companies, the Panel's recommendations included higher guarantees and other public subsidies for private water investors (Public Services International, 2003).

A final point should be made about the Bank's 'instrumental' influence in South African water pricing policy. If consumers did not pay their bills, Bank staff told Asmal, municipalities needed a 'credible threat of cutting service' (Roome, 1995). As noted above, this was a standard practice in Johannesburg in the post-apartheid era (during apartheid, municipal by-laws against water disconnections were enforced). Tens of thousands of people were disconnected each month in the late 1990s and early 2000s, even if they were behind on their electricity (not water) accounts or rates.

Conclusion: political resistance to water commercialisation

The critique above is widely accepted in South African civil society and even some sectors of government. As a result of the failure of so many water privatisation projects, politicians and technocrats have begun to adjust their formerly pro-partnership rhetoric. By the time of the Kyoto World Water Forum in March 2003, Dwaf's director-general, Mike Muller, was presenting a strong anti-privatisation message in a 'Water 2003' speech. Describing this as a 'clear mandate' from the August 2002 Johannesburg World Summit on Sustainable Development (WSSD), Muller (2003) conceded that, 'We should start by acknowledging key lessons from Johannesburg'. One of these was that 'business as usual will not achieve the goals. We need to acknowledge the constraints and review the paradigms within which we work'.

What, then, had become of the paradigm of water privatisation? Muller observed that 'The pendulum is swinging against too great an involvement of private sector. Resistance to private engagement is the result, in part, of the obvious failure of private initiative to address the core challenge of the unserved'. However, he also recorded the 'vital role for private expertise and resources in providing water services' but warned of the consequences if 'that role is literally forced down the throats of potential beneficiaries'. He worried about giving 'credibility to those who describe private sector engagement as neo-imperialist expansion designed to boost profits of the rich world's service industries'. Muller concluded his argument 'against' privatisation by suggesting that the Bretton Woods Institutions and donor agencies 'cease making private sector involvement a pre-condition for water sector support' and that the OECD countries and their companies should remove water from the General Agreement on Trade in Services and other trade negotiations. The World Bank, IMF, WTO, European Union and United States government did not apparently agree with either suggestion, for pressure continued, notwithstanding an apparent retreat by water companies from the field in many formerly feted pilot projects.

In South Africa itself, only a combination of cholera, popular mass action, and international media exposure has helped to more substantively shift policy towards a more rights-based strategy (as imperfect as that is at present, particularly given ongoing water disconnections, pre-paid meter installations, shallow flush sanitation and pit latrines).[5] In Africa, the Africa Social Forum represents the best hope for a broader, more general campaign to make water a human right, but the network formed only in 2002, and remains ideologically uneven (Bond, 2004).

Even in South Africa, with strong progressive civil society organisations, advocacy for a different public water services strategy has not been easy. It was only on the eve of the Johannesburg WSSD, in August 2002, that Water Minister Ronnie Kasrils invited the South African Civil Society Water Caucus to discuss a variety of problems associated with water/sanitation policy, programmes and projects.[6]

At the August 2002 meeting in Dwaf headquarters, the first such summit with a wide-ranging collective grouping of civil society water specialists since Kasrils assumed office in June 1999, the Caucus' Points of Consensus were presented:

- Water and sanitation are human rights. All people are entitled to have access to water to meet their basic human needs, and rural communities are entitled to water for productive use to sustain their livelihoods.
- Water management must be accountable to communities at a local level.
- We respect the integrity of ecosystems as the basis for all life – both human and nature – with an emphasis on maintaining river ecosystems and groundwater resources.
- We reject the commodification and privatisation of water services and sanitation, and water resources.
- Further, we reject the role of the United States, the other G8 countries and Trans-National Corporations for their role in pushing privatisation and commodification.
- We reject the UN WSSD process and outcomes so far, as nothing more than structural adjustment of the South. We therefore resolve to work together with social movements to realise an alternative vision.
- We reject Nepad and the plans for water in Nepad as not being sustainable. It is structural adjustment by Africa for Africa. In particular we reject the privatisation of water and the hydropower focus. We commit ourselves to building a mass movement for the reconstruction and sustainable development of Africa.
- We undertake to educate and raise awareness and to mobilise communities towards the WSSD.

What the material conditions in South Africa suggest are both that the contradictions in applying New Public Management techniques via private sector firms runs into multiple technical and eco-social contradictions, and that political resistance is not an illogical response. Broad-based coalitions of progressive, democratic forces will be required to contest the kinds of disasters represented by the commodification of water. These coalitions will conjoin the cutting-edge 'militant particularisms', as David Harvey (2001) expresses it, associated with genuine grievances, consciousness-formation and protest.

South Africa is, in this sense, not unusual. Critics of the neo-liberal direction taken by so many states in the developing world, which are evidently so dangerous in the crucial water services sector, might gain inspiration from Johannesburg activists such as those found in the Anti-Privatisation Forum and SA Municipal Workers Union. If they succeed, it will be because common ground is found, and an agenda is established based on the opposite premise to New Public Management, namely that the commercialisation of state services contradicts our most fundamental human rights.

Notes

1. The World Bank's efforts in this area took on far greater intensity beginning with the 1986 launch of the 'New Urban Management Programme', which was further articulated in an important 1991 policy paper that received wide circulation in South Africa through a Bank proxy, the Urban Foundation (World Bank, 1991; and for practical critiques of this approach, see Jones and Ward, 1994 and Burgess *et al.*, 1996).

2. Just at the point that water privatisation was being debated in Johannesburg, Suez subsidiary Dumez was alleged by state prosecutors to have bribed the Lesotho Highlands Water Authority's manager Masupha Sole. The latter allegedly received $20 000 at a Paris meeting in 1991 to engineer a contract renegotiation providing Dumez with an additional R2 million profit, at the expense of Johannesburg water consumers. Johannesburg officials were asked by Samwu to bar Suez from tendering, but they refused (*Business Day*, 5 August 1999; *Washington Post*, 13 September 1999).

3. Although government has disputed the figures, they may actually be understatements. They do not include the millions of rural people who were given water under the full cost-recovery regime put in place with World Bank assistance (via the Mvula Trust) in 1994. According to one government researcher, the majority of projects – 57 per cent – were either 'not working' or 'problematic' according to standards set out in the 1994 Reconstruction and Development Programme (*Business Day*, 1 July).

4. The apartheid-era terminology is used here, not to endorse it, but because this is the way statistics are most readily disaggregated.

5. There were high-profile articles in the *New York Times*, *Washington Post*, *Le Monde Diplomatique*, *London Observer*, *Boston Globe*, *Houston Chronicle*, *Mother Jones*, *L'Humanite* and other outlets supplied by the International Consortium of Investigative Journalists. For documentation, see http://www.queensu.ca/msp under media, where many of the articles are posted.

6. The Caucus had formed in July 2002 explicitly for the WSSD, but many of its members were veterans of national and local water advocacy work. Comprised of 40 organisations as members, the Caucus also drew to its steering committee the premier advocacy groups in the water sector: Earthlife Africa, Environmental Monitoring Group, Network for Advocacy on Water in Southern Africa, the Anti-Eviction Campaign, Rural Development Support Services, Mvula Trust, the Youth Caucus and the South African Municipal Services Union. The Caucus addressed a variety of issues in its own statement of objectives: sanitation, ecosystems, human rights, privatisation and commodification of water, anti-evictions and water cut-offs, rural water supply, urban water issues, the large dam debate, water conservation and demand management, regional and transboundary water issues, labour and the promotion of public services.

15

Latin America: Globalisation, Democracy and State Reform

Ronaldo Munck

'No other region has tried so hard for decades to carry out administrative reforms as has Latin America. And no other has known so many frustrations' (Prats i Català, 1999: 157).

Latin America is currently the world region with the highest levels of income inequality. It also has the dubious privilege of having led the neoliberal 'revolution' under General Pinochet in Chile from the mid-1970s onwards. Today, the issue of state reform in the region is inseparable from the question of democratisation and the reduction of socio-economic inequalities. Under the 'Washington consensus' that prevailed in the 1990s, state reform simply meant 'downsizing' and removing what was seen as state interference in the workings of the free market. Today, the debate on state reform is more complex, with all sides recognising that the 'second generation' reforms, widely seen as needed, will involve restructuring and an improvement in the capacity to govern. Constructing democracy in the era of globalisation for Latin America, as elsewhere, will involve engagement with the contested discursive terrain of 'state reform'.

Context

The contemporary Latin American state emerged out of the crisis of the old agro-export development model following the 1929 international capitalist crisis and the depression of the 1930s. With particular national variations, a policy of import substitution industrialisation began to lessen dependence on the vagaries of the international commodity markets. This was a state-centred matrix of development that involved dynamic and expansionary macro-economic policies and a progressive (if unevenly applied) social policy to bring the mass of the population under the aegis of the new development model. The populist state was to be very different from the oligarchic state that prevailed in the pre-1930 period. The state was to become in the 1950s and 1960s a major provider of employment and source of patronage. Conflict was muted in this way and class conflict blunted. As Peter Smith notes: 'What this tactic created was a dual structure within the state: one for meritocratic advancement and policy-making, the other for patronage' (Smith, 1999: 63). This led to a certain incoherence which to some extent facilitated the neo-liberal offensive which began in the second half of the 1970s, following the 1973 coups in Chile and Uruguay and their 1976 equivalent in Argentina.

The 1980s were widely seen as the 'lost decade' as growth stagnated, the foreign debt mushroomed and the whole import substitution industrialisation model began to crumble. The positive spiral between economic growth and social development was broken. Rightly or wrongly the state-centred matrix that had prevailed since 1930 was blamed for the negative economic and social spiral now emerging across Latin America. The negative features of the old model were now much more apparent: bureaucratisation, patronage and inefficiency came to the fore and the lack of an integrated development strategy became evident. The fiscal crisis of the state made it more or less impossible to regain its social and political legitimacy. The new development model was focussed on privatisation and denationalisation, as well as totally opening up the national economies to global market forces. A new technocrat would emerge in place of the old state bureaucrat as a key agent of the development model and, in many cases, as a direct link with the dominant economic powers as was the case with Chile's 'Chicago Boys'.

State reform clearly did not just begin in Latin America during the 1980s. Indeed, we can trace back major state reforms movements to the 1950s and 1960s, a reform movement only stopped by the brutal military dictatorships of the 1970s (especially in Brazil and the Southern Cone). Peter Spink refers in this regard to how efficiency, effectiveness, good management, and trained staff in the post-war period laid the basis for what would prove to be a major reform period in the early 1960s (Spink, 1999: 101). What we can, however, say, is that the Weberian model of bureaucracy – at the heart of administrative models – was never fully achieved in Latin America where many patrimonialist features subsisted. In this sense, the first wave of 'state reforms' in the 1980s was truly revolutionary, not in any progressive sense, but in its intent to totally restructure the relationship between the state and society. It was in fact the whole society and social policies of the 1930–1975 period that were to be 'reformed' in the 1980s in the interest of a virulent neo-liberal offensive which to some extent prefigured what we now know as globalisation and certainly paved the way for its implementation in Latin America.

First generation

The neo-liberal turn across Latin America was only consolidated in the 1980s, but its origins can be traced back to the brutal military dictatorships that came to power in Chile in 1973 and in Argentina in 1976. The rule of the market was imposed by military force and entailed a severe restructuring or disarticulation of society, and in particular of the working class. Whereas the state had been an agent of social integration during the statist-nationalist period of development (1950s–1960s) it was to now become an agent of social disintegration. From the neo-liberal economists – in the early 1970s only just beginning to climb back from obscurity – the military and their technocratic advisors took the doctrine that state intervention was bad for market-led development. The great irony, of course, is that it took a very strong, not to say coercive, state to reduce the role of the state during this first phase of state reform, if it can be called that in any real sense of the word.

The state was blamed for 'interfering' with the free play of market forces and, in particular, for 'sheltering' vulnerable social groups from its effects. The task of state 'reform' was thus simply to remove as many areas of social and economic life from its remit as possible. In this, privatisation was a key element, as vast swathes of state run enterprises were sold off to private, often foreign, capitalists. Market forces were also introduced within the remaining state sectors in terms of procurement of inputs and services. Many state workers were also simply sacked, based on the assumption that the 'bloated' public sector had always been inefficient. There was not even lip service paid to the need to improve the state sector, with the stress simply on reducing its role, often by brutal, unnecessary and ultimately inefficient surgery. As Oscar Oszlak explains: 'The "ease" with which this initial phase [of state reforms] was carried out depended not only on favourable political-ideological conditions of viability, but on the relative "simplicity" of the reforms posed' (Oszlak, 1999: 86). Chile and Argentina were to be paradigmatic examples of this strategy.

The Chilean state had developed, from 1930 onwards, a wide range of economic and welfare functions. The administrative apparatus of the state had become vast by the 1960s and it had acquired a general reputation for competence and political autonomy. The Pinochet regime, which came to power through a brutal military coup in 1973, '...rapidly eliminated both social and developmental functions [of the state] and dismantled the associated administrative machinery' (Garretón and Caceres, 2000: 48). Then political parties were dissolved by decree, only to be allowed to function again in 1987. Military force should be used to allow market forces free rein. The strong Chilean state sector of the economy was dismantled and privatised, as was the welfare state through 'reforms' that were widely admired in the advanced individualised countries. Social spending was dramatically reduced and taxes were cut back to encourage business development. By the time that democracy was restored in 1990 the Chilean state sector was democratised and disarticulated.

What is most remarkable about the Chilean state reform under Pinochet was not only its brutality but the way it was justified in terms of 'modernisation' by the trans-nationalised economic elite known as the 'Chicago boys'. These US trained economists '...led a vast rationalisation and technocratisation of government arguing that the use of scientific methods should replace the previous irrational and obsolete models of decision-making' (Montecinos, 1998: 130). What was deemed 'irrational' was politics *tout court* insofar as it was seen to have led to a stifling bureaucracy and egregious policy errors, such as import substitution industrialisation. The public sector was deemed the font of all corruption and the cause of debilitating corporatist politics. Technical efficiency was to be everything and market values were to be introduced into all areas of society, including politics. Since the return to democracy in 1990, particularly under the Frei government (1995–2000) a wide-ranging managerial reform of the state sector was carried out in accordance with new public management (NPM) principles, but much of the anti-state sector dynamic remained in the background.

In Argentina the 1976 military coup followed a similar route to that of Chile. While the latter went furthest in privatising social security areas such as pension funds, the selling out of Argentina's state-owned enterprises was the most far-reaching anywhere. This was to include the sale of the country's state oil, energy and telecommunication sectors, the railways, ports and roads and the postal service, as well as the banking and insurance sectors and the main television channels. This process was, ironically, accelerated after the return of democracy in 1982, particularly under the Menem regime (1989–1999). Thus, the 900 000 public sector employees still in post in 1990 were reduced to 300 000 by 1997. This dramatic 'downsizing' was achieved partly through decentralisation with many services such as health and education being devolved to the provinces. With large-scale privatisation of enterprises and services many employees simply changed employer. But a large number of the state sector workers went to swell the ranks of the unemployed and the ill-defined informal sector.

The case of Argentina shows quite clearly that a 'leaner' state is not necessarily a more efficient state and that the ostensibly 'second generation' reforms attempted after 1996 were hardly well placed to effect a dramatic improvement in the workings of the state. Carlos Menem came from the nationalist-populist political tradition (Peronism) but in office throughout the 1990s he implemented a rigorous neo-liberal anti-statist agenda that even the military regime had not taken up to the same degree. Structural adjustment to 'fit' the national economy within the parameters of globalisation had been achieved successfully. Now the state reform had not only to create greater transparency and efficiency but also needed to cope with the increased levels of poverty generated by the new economic model. By the late 1990s, economic growth was faltering and by the end of 2001 the economy virtually collapsed. It is significant to note that in neighbouring Uruguay they had to submit the 1992 Privatisation Law to a plebiscite that led to its rejection by nearly three quarters of the population. There were, indeed, alternatives to neo-liberal state reform/ destruction.

Towards the end of the 1990s the tide had turned against state 'reform' based on crude surgery 'without anaesthetics' – as it was put in Argentina. The turning point was marked by the 1997 World Bank Report 'The State in a Changing World' (World Bank, 1997) which effectively recognised the limits of unregulated markets and the need to 'bring the state back in'. The Inter-American Development Bank's 2000 Report 'Development Beyond Economies', for its part, stressed the 'importance of institutions' also tacitly recognising the limitations of a market only strategy. First-generation state reforms to 'accommodate' Latin America within the neo-liberal globalisation regime would need to be followed by more effective state building insofar as '...good institutions are critical for macroeconomic stability in today's world of global financial integration' (IADB, 2000: 5). The predictability and stability of public institutions was deemed crucial. Urgent institutional reform, according to the Inter-American Development Bank '...should provide clear, widely known, coherent, predictable, credible, and properly and evenly enforced rules' (IADB, 2000: 21). That was the agenda, but what were the results of this strategy?

Second generation

We must first note that there is no clear-cut distinction between so-called first and second- generation state reforms in Latin America. In many ways it was a Gramscian situation where the old had not died but the new had not been fully born either. With that reservation we can proceed to evaluate the post-1995 wave of state reforms, often associated with a consolidation of democracy. The parameters of this phase of state reform were set by the Inter-American Development Bank's belief that:

> To one degree or another, all of the Latin American countries have problems with the rule of law, corruption, and the ineffectiveness of governments in providing essential public services' (IADB, 2000: 7).

Institutional reforms were deemed necessary to 'enhance competitiveness' in the era of globalisation. Reform of the state education sector was also necessary for business reasons as was reform of the judiciary as business leaders demanded more 'reliable and efficient' judiciaries.

The theoretical justification for the second generation or wave of state reforms was in terms of contrasting the bureaucratic and managerial modes of administration. Luiz Carlos Bresser Pereira, Brazil's Minister of Science and Technology during the Cardoso administration articulated this paradigm most clearly. With a long record of Marxist studies of the role of state in the development process and the rise of what he called the 'technobureaucracy' (see Bresser Pereira, 1977: 1981) Bresser Pereira was well placed to develop a theoretical justification for the new managerialism. He traced the emergence of bureaucratic public administration along Weberian lines and its superiority over patrimonial modes of state administration. The failure to achieve a fully-fledged Weberian model of bureaucratic state administration meant that Latin America could 'jump stages' into the new managerial paradigm. This was conceived as more flexible, less hierarchical and more decentralised than the bureaucratic model. The objective, according to Bresser Pereira, was to '…make public administration more efficient and modern, focusing its attention on serving the needs of the citizenry' (Bresser Pereira, 1999: 131). We turn then to how this model was implemented in practice.

Brazil was late to turn in the neo-liberal direction and many features of the nationalist-statist model remained right through the 1990s. However, a severe episode of hyperinflation in 1990 had the same impact as a similar episode in Argentina, namely a turn to economic reform and social adjustment. The perceived dangers of economic meltdown and social disintegration gave added impetus to a critical embrace of the neo-liberal recipes. A special report on public administration by Marxist analyst Regis de Castro Andrade argued, furthermore, that

> The administrative crisis is evinced by low capacity in the formulation, information, planning, implementation and control of public policies. The list of deficiencies in the nation's public administration is dramatic (cited in Bresser Pereira, 1999: 125).

The inauguration of the Fernando Henrique Cardoso administration paved the way for a full-scale managerial reform of the state that achieved considerable consensus within the state apparatus and amongst public opinion. The 'downsizing' element of the Bresser Plan was implemented in full but the overall implementation of managerial reform was inevitably uneven.

The government's privatisation programme did, however, meet severe resistance by traditionalist or nationalist sectors and also, of course, labour groups (although not all of them). On the whole, the trade unions accepted that employees in the public sector and the state-owned companies had enjoyed a relatively privileged position. From outside the organised labour movement, however, the critique of the state reform programme was scathing. It seemed inconceivable that F. H. Cardoso (intellectual font of the dependency theory) could be implementing a neo-liberal programme so assiduously. For Grzybowski, Cardoso's state reform actually '…led to a recentralisation of resources and power and a decentralisation [of the state's] obligations' (Grzybowski, 1999: 160). Privatisation and deregulation had dismantled the state's capacity to intervene in the economy and to promote social reform. It remains to be seen how the Luis Inacio 'Lula' de Silva government, which came into office in 2002, will deal with state reform, given that the Workers' Party had been one of its sharpest critics. Significantly, one of Lula's first measures in 2003 was to seek congressional support for a reform of the public sector pension scheme, deemed by its critics as 'the most generous on the world' and unacceptable if the fight against poverty was to be pursued (The Economist, 2003).

The Mexican case shows, further, how complicated the state reform process in Latin America was, and how it cannot be reduced to a 'technical' procedure. While Mexico did engage in the broad neo-liberal turn from the 1980s onwards, administrative reform was more or less blocked throughout the 1990s. This was largely done through the fusion between the political and bureaucratic elites under the aegis of the PRI (Revolutionary Institutional Party) that had held power more or less continuously from the Mexican revolution until 2000. While the tenets of managerial reform were adapted in the 1990s, the vested interests within the state apparatus could count on political protection by their PRI colleagues in office. As Lawrence Graham explains, while '...in the eyes of Mexican reformers a technocratic revolution was underway... their success in determining macroeconomic policy does not translate into their ability to implement economic and social policy at the grass-roots level' (Graham, 1999: 153–4). Where a state bureaucracy is powerful and embedded as it is in Mexico, reform is by no means straightforward and cannot follow the neat schemas of the international economic organisations.

The Mexican case is also particularly interesting in relation to how non-governmental organisations (NGOs) operate to fill the state sector on many fronts. The state is flexible and porous enough to find room for NGOs to operate within its parameters. One example was the major poverty alleviation programme Solidaridad in the mid-1990s that successfully borrowed from the NGO repertoire of action to displace the more clientilistic patterns that had prevailed. Civil society in this type of scenario is mobilised by a modernising state keen to rationalise its methods. In the era of neo-liberal globalisation and its generalised attack on the state sector we thus also saw the promotion of NGOs in Latin America. After the 1995 earthquake in Mexico, the NGOs became particularly important which also meant the state was more interested in their co-option and the development of hybrid state-NGOs structures and modalities of intervention. This is, then, yet another path that state reform can take.

The managerialist approach to state reform has become the new common sense in this area. One time US Vice-President Al Gore could plausibly talk about 'common sense government' from this perspective. The veritable 'Bible' of this ideology is undoubtedly Osborne and Gaebler's (1993) *Reinventing Government* that not only inspired Al Gore but was also central to many of the Latin American public policy debates. However, there are grave doubts that this particular policy transfer model is appropriate for Latin America. Ted Gaebler himself admitted candidly in interview that 'You have to invent government before you can reinvent it' (Heredia and Schneider, 200: 14). That is precisely the underlying problem when glibly seeking to impose the NPM remedies in Latin America without translation, as it were. With huge social inequalities demanding attention and with clientelism and corruption still rife (see Economic Commission for Latin America and the Carribean, 2000) the managerial model seems to somehow miss the point. To seek technical solutions to political problems is simply not very productive.

Contested terrain

What flows from the above analysis is that 'state reform' in Latin America is a contested discursive terrain. Its meaning is by no means unequivocal, and we should beware of 'applying' universal models to the region. While globalisation (or, more modestly, economic internationalisation) has certainly set the parameters of state reform in Latin America, as elsewhere, this does not necessarily mean that we can refer simply to a 'global revolution' in state sector management as Donald Kettle does:

> Since the early 1980s, a global tidal wave of government sector reform has swept the world. Virtually every government has launched efforts to streamline government and make it more responsive ... Never before in history has such a reform movement moved so far so fast (Kettle, 1999: 41).

Not only is this view unduly benign, but it has a tendency to obliterate national and regional particularities and the path-dependent nature of the 'state reform' process set in its proper political context.

Placed in the political context of the transition to democracy in Latin America during the 1980s and its consolidation in the 1990s the issue of state reform is quite complex. Above all, we need to recognise the ongoing and severe crisis of governability in Latin America that is by no means reducible to the challenges posed by globalisation. The problematic governability thus poses the issue of state reform for a government of progressive hue (Brazil under Lula) as much as for reactionary ones (Argentina under Menem). We can, in this vein, distinguish two possibly quite distinct variants of NPM in Latin America. One is externally imposed as a disciplinary mechanism by the likes of the International Monetary Fund (IMF), while the other is exemplified by the CLAD (Latin American Centre for Development Administration) perspective, for which:

> Rebuilding state capacity is an essential condition for enabling Latin American countries to deal successfully with problems of redemocratisation, economic development and distribution of wealth. In this context,

implementation of Managerial Reform is essential for improving the governance of the State and for enhancing democratic goverability... (CLAD, 1998:47).

On the basis of the second more progressive reading of state reform in Latin America, a new post Washington Consensus is emerging. This is exemplified in the Economic Commission for Latin America 2000 programme:

> Equity, development and citizenship which calls for a new public policy to overcome a crisis of the State that has not been fully resolved, to correct 'market failures' and 'government failures' and, more generally to *build and rebuild institutions*, which is unquestionably one of the more complex challenges now facing the region (ECLA, 2000: 24).

And it is clear that state reform in Latin America is not about technical issues but goes to the core of the development model that will prevail in the region. Efficiency in what has come to be known as the Santiago Consensus (see Munck, 2003) is always matched by concerns with equity and the need to build the institutions and procedures for democratic citizenship. The period of unilateral state reform, imposed from the outside by neo-liberal globalisation, may now be on the defensive but the project of state reform is far from complete. In the years to come Latin America will probably provide interesting experiments in democratic state reform.

Conclusion

In Latin America, as elsewhere in the so-called developing world (see Larbi, 1999), the NPM wave was driven largely by external pressures but these were overlaid on an internal crisis caused by hyperinflation and the perceived exhaustion of the statist-nationalist development model. Certainly in the 1980s some type of state reform was required in Latin America, but the context in which it was carried out – structural economic weaknesses and extreme external pressure – led to a reliance on 'free' market forces which was practically unprecedented. In the 1990s, state reform was accelerated and deepened across the region under the new and somewhat specious banner of 'good government'. However, the contradictions between the goals of institutional change and the imperatives of fiscal adjustment inevitably generated considerable social and political opposition (see Cunha Rezende, 2002). It is the politics of state reform that are rarely studied (but see Hamergreen, 1983; and Tendler, 1997 for useful contextualised research) insofar as NPM is usually conceived in narrowly technical terms which obscure the political context and the various class interests at play.

The introduction of NPM in Latin America is certainly a remarkable story in terms of international policy transfer case studies (see Nickson, 2002) but the results have been very mixed. Certainly few would deny the need for state reform in the region and for the creation of an efficient and reliable public administration. However, what in practice has emerged is a dramatically reduced capacity of the state to protect its citizens from economic insecurity. The collapse of Argentina as a viable entity in 2002 is but the limit case that shows the future for the whole of Latin America if the Santiago Consensus is not eventually adopted. This may well be possible if the tendency, since the turn of the century, for a more progressive and independent stance in Latin America continues against further national and social disintegration. Free markets unrestrained by any social or political regulation will not be able to achieve state reform if the US driven model prevails. In terms of the broader concern with building sustainable democratic institutions and procedures, this dilemma is central and explains much of the current disenchantment (*desencanto*) with 'actually existing democracy' – as has been picked up by opinion polls. The recent rise of leftist and nationalist governments in the region (Brazil, Venezuela, Ecuador, maybe Argentina) points towards the need for 'third-generation' state reforms whose agenda would be less set by the forces behind globalisation (widely discredited by the *débacle* in Argentina) and more by the needs for deepening and broadening the processes of democratisation.

16

Public Administration and the Management of Socio-Economic Development in Developing Countries: Some Trends and Comparisons

Malcolm Wallis

In this chapter, an attempt is made to discuss some of the main trends to emerge in the field of public administration and development in recent years. Whilst this is by no means a comprehensive account, it identifies some directions that seem to be of particular importance. A thread running through this chapter is a concern with two broad concepts. The first of these is a concern with the 'management of development'; that is how managers contribute to the processes, structures and tasks associated with development. Sub-sets of this area would be the management of projects or the management of public health, for example. The second concept is the 'development of management'; that is the ways in which the competence of managers can be enhanced – through human resource policies, for example. These two topics, whilst distinguishable from one another, are also inter-related since the success of development initiatives is partly related to the competence and capacity of the managers and structures responsible for them.

A number of topics are addressed in the chapter. Diverse though these are, the core concern is that existing state performance, in developing countries, does not match the need to promote the elimination of poverty. Around this theme, concepts such as governance, markets, decentralisation and capacity building enter the analysis.

Challenges and diversities

Whilst there are a number of challenges facing the public sector in developing countries, a considerable diversity of experience also has to be noted.

This diversity is reflected in the range of experience analysed by other contributors to this volume. For the purposes of this chapter an overview of these trends will be provided. Realism dictates a more limited objective than the more detailed analysis within other chapters, but an attempt will be made to identify some key themes that are shared by a significant number of the countries we refer to in this text as 'developing'.

The term 'developing countries' will be used here – though many could be seen as moving to a less developed state. They are, in the main, to be found in Africa, Asia, the Caribbean and Latin America. Most of the states with which we are concerned have emerged from colonialism in the second half of the twentieth century, but we need to note diversity and exceptions. Most Latin American states were liberated from Portuguese and Spanish colonial rule in the nineteenth century. Others did not experience formal colonisation at all (for example, Thailand was never colonised), while others (for example Ethiopia) experienced colonisation only briefly. What is also common to the states under review is the pervasiveness of poverty. The chapter will discuss this point in the context of how it affects the way the public sector operates. It will be argued that the poverty question is the most critical one now being faced and that much can be learnt by the review of how the various states have attempted to respond to the fact that large parts of the population live in conditions in which basic needs are not being met effectively.

Also emerging as a theme is the globalisation issue. Whilst this also concerns the developed states, the vulnerability of the developing world in relation to the more powerful states is of particular importance because of, *inter alia*, trade relationships, donor influence and sometimes military action. As far as the state is concerned, there are three general points to which attention must be given. The first is the emergence, in the 1980s, of the idea of 'governance' – and more recently, the more specific 'good governance' (Wolmuth *et al.*, 1998) – that has generated a revived interest in liberal democracy with its supporting elements such as constitutionalism, human rights and accountability. The second is that the new public management has come to be seen as a way of enhancing the capacity of state bureaucracies. Sometimes identified with the notion of 'development management' as distinct from 'public management', this has in recent years manifested itself in various ways, although currently performance management and public private partnerships seem to be the two most prominent (Gasper, 2000). Thirdly, the role of the state in development has come into question.

All the above has, in part, been a result of 'Thatcherism' (in the United Kingdom) and 'Reaganomics' (United States) which spearheaded a renaissance of ostensibly neo-liberal ideology and policy interventions (Hutton, 2002). The latter includes the role of international financial institutions such as the World Bank, the International Monetary Fund (IMF) and the

World Trade Organisation (WTO) which have, particularly in developing states, placed pressure on governments to reduce their involvement in development (especially implementation). The tendency toward marketisation has also manifested itself in a variety of ways. In Bangladesh, India and Pakistan, for example, the systems inherited were originally created by the British, whilst Indonesia's colonial legacy came from the Dutch. In Africa, significant differences can be seen between states depending on whether they were ruled by the British, the French or the Portuguese. In contrast, South Africa's legacy of *apartheid* makes it rather exceptional, in that it inherited some elements from Britain and some from the Afrikaaner dominated government that ruled continuously between 1948 and 1994.

Another aspect of diversity concerns the size of the countries under review. Studies have shown that the administrative systems of small states have distinctive features arising from having small populations and other factors such as vulnerability to intervention by larger states, and economies that are highly dependent on outside forces. There are many such states in the developing world (Baker, 1992; Warrington, 1998). Their populations can often be below one million and are therefore susceptible to being dominated by larger neighbours, and by higher profile developing countries, such as China and India. There are, of course, some difficulties in specifying which states are small and which are not. Take two Asian examples of developed economies. The area of Singapore is a mere 647.5 sq km whilst Hong Kong (part of China but with a significant measure of autonomy) at 1095 sq km is not much bigger. However, their population densities are both decidedly high. Singapore crams over three million people into its area whilst Hong Kong's population is close to seven million (Lam, 2000). What is the impact of 'smallness' on the public sector in such states? Several factors can be noted but it may suffice to suggest just a few. One is that these states tend to be more vulnerable and dependent on external forces than larger states. They are also less self-sufficient. Finally, the lack of scale economies means that the size of public service agencies is also very small. This results in a culture of personal relationships within the bureaucratic hierarchy that is not usual in larger states.

States also vary considerably in the extent to which their economic development can be associated with government intervention. For example, Chiu and Lui (1998) have argued that the success stories in Asia (Singapore, South Korea, Hong Kong and so on) have to be analysed within a framework which acknowledges divergence and complexity and warn against generalised interpretations. In this chapter, this issue is discussed when looking at states and markets since the question of government intervention is linked to the extent to which a state's policies embrace the notion that market forces must prevail. The outgoing Malaysian Prime Minister, Mahathir Mohamad, recently commented on this issue, remarking that it was 'stupid talk' to argue for markets disciplining the state as there were 'a lot of crooks' in the market (*Business Day*, Johannesburg). This comment is particularly interesting as it comes from the leader of a state whose ideology is far removed from socialism.

Political diversity

A few years ago, the influence of national politics, and of ideology, might have been given more weight than is the case now. However, while there has been some evidence of democratisation and stabilisation in the developing world, for example in South Africa, Chile and Angola, many others are far from being democratic (for example, Iraq, Liberia and Zimbabwe). Thus, whilst public sector managers in many states have to fully integrate democratic imperatives into their working lives, in others the focus is on finding the most efficient, effective and economical ways of managing oppression. This was the case in apartheid South Africa where the doyen of Public Administration wrote about the subject as if the fact that the government was racist and excluded the majority of the population from the decision-making process did not matter (Cloete, 1981).

Whilst it is necessary to be aware of the pitfalls of generalisation because of the diversity just mentioned, there is some scope for a discussion that pulls together some critical themes of significance to understanding most of the countries with which we are concerned. Because of the importance of the consequences of state action, our focus is on how 'development management' makes an impact in society. This perspective, in itself, reflects an emerging theme: the importance of assessing management structures and processes in relation to the outcomes that result from them (Van der Molen *et al.*, 2002; Sen, 1999). The themes discussed should not be seen as totally separate from one another, but rather as a variety of inter-related areas of concern. For example, three of the issues under discussion are poverty, capacity building and governance. The question of poverty, however, has to be seen in relation to changing approaches to both governance and capacity building since these can be critical in determining the outcomes of poverty programmes.

Themes in development management

The five themes selected for discussion here are poverty, its implications and relationship to civil society; governance; states and markets; decentralisation and development; and capacity building. These five themes have been selected because they appear to embrace most of the concerns that analysts and leaders are expressing currently. It should be noted that these categories subsume several key issues that might have been highlighted as themes in their own right; for example, corruption is subsumed within the 'governance' theme, whereas privatisation is subsumed within both 'poverty' and 'states and markets'.

Poverty, its implications and relationship to civil society

This is a current theme in debates about development in general, but it also has implications for the field of public sector management that have tended to be ignored. Concern over the level of poverty is rising, particularly in relation to Africa and much of Asia (see, for example, Wolmuth *et al.*, 1998). Developing states now face a dilemma in that they need to take decisive action to respond to conditions related to poverty such as high unemployment and poor or non-existent basic services. Yet, in many such countries there has been a failure on the part of government to successfully implement poverty reduction programmes. The reasons for this record are not as straightforward as might be supposed.

Several points seem to be emerging in relation to the failure to implement poverty programmes. First, there is a growing awareness of the importance of understanding the role of public management in poverty alleviation and taking action accordingly. For example, two leading international associations concerned with the promotion of developmental studies have made this issue the focus for their 2003 conferences (the African Association of Public Administration and Management and the International Institute of Administrative Sciences). Secondly, there is the policy framework to consider. The problem appears to be due to a lack of political will and of the constraints imposed by external factors, which leads to deficient planning and managerial capacity – a point of continuing significance made by critics of development policy from the early 1990s (Evert Vermeer Foundation, 1990). Thirdly, there are formidable challenges arising from the international economic context such as terms of trade and indebtedness. Fourthly, a large part of the problem seems to relate to the performance of government structures. In a participatory poverty assessment survey conducted toward the end of the last decade, the World Bank mentions the following problems often encountered in anti-poverty programmes: formal institutions are largely ineffective and irrelevant in the lives of the poor; corruption directly affects the poor; the poor feel disempowered and humiliated; the collapse of the state increases poor people's vulnerability; the poor confront many barriers in trying to access government services; and there is often collusion or overlap between local governance and the elite (Narayan *et al.*, 2000: 83–84).

Finally, a remedy that is increasingly referred to both in the literature and in policy forums is decentralisation. Some authors have tried to examine closely the extent to which decentralisation is viable as a way of tackling poverty (Bird and Rodriguez, 1999; Belshaw, 2000; Crook, 2003). This suggests a naiveté in arguing that poverty alleviation necessarily benefits from stronger local government since local elites may, arguably, be able to capture the process to serve their own economic and political interests.

In the area of poverty alleviation, it is now accepted by many that governments cannot go it alone. There has to be joint action incorporating institutions outside the realm of the state. Non-government organisations (NGOs) and community based organisations are often referred to as having the potential to contribute in this way, and there are certainly cases of them so doing. In many countries, for example, religious bodies play a growing part in advocacy for change and in the actual implementation of projects. The term 'civil society' has increasingly come into use to depict this sector.

Also outside the formal state, active involvement of donors has been a feature of the past decade or so. These donors embrace the three main categories: the multilaterals such as the United Nations, the bilaterals (national governments) and foreign based NGOs. It is important to see such disparate bodies as the World Bank, the Kellogg Foundation and the Danish agency DANIDA as part of the subject matter in the study of development management and not just as distant observers / benefactors trying to give support. Indeed, such donor bodies may be as much a part of the problem as part of the solution (Belshaw, 2000). For example, work is needed to ensure that the implementation of aid programmes does not become paralysed because of the burdens associated with fulfilling donor requirements. Some donors – notably the European Union – are now investigating this matter. Donor organisations should not be immune from criticisms that are made as a result of these and other inquiries about the effectiveness of poverty alleviation programmes. Another important question to be noted here is whether it is contradictory for donors to support poverty alleviation whilst pursuing economic policies such as structural adjustment that may have the effect of increasing poverty. This point may be made on the role of the World Bank, for example, as it has advocated structural adjustment alongside support for poverty alleviation despite the apparent incompatibility of these two drivers of policy.

A consensus is also emerging about another type of non-state actor, and Public-Private Partnerships (PPP) is another new trend that we have to consider in this account. Closely linked to its forerunner, that is the strategy that advocated various forms of privatisation beginning in the 1990s, this is partly based on the notion that government can be improved by mimicking private sector organisations and management styles. This issue is one that needs to be considered on a broader note since one of its main claims relates to its relevance to dealing with problems facing government more generally. On poverty, the problem to address is whether PPPs can serve the needs of the poor whilst operating in a climate driven by the profit motive and the related notion of users paying for services received. The potential contradiction is apparent here, and limited evidence exists to show that a state can successfully embark on poverty alleviation implemented through PPP approaches. However, some examples from Latin America suggest that this can be instrumental in the alleviation of poverty, and Fiszbein's analysis does provide examples related to sectors such as public health in certain Latin American states to support the idea that a PPP approach can be compatible with state policies to reduce poverty (Fiszbein, 2000: 167).

Governance: a new dimension of public administration

The previous discussion on poverty has raised questions of governance, and, in this section, an attempt is made to show how this relatively new concept has come into prominence in both the study and practice of public administration.

In parallel with the strategies of managerialism and privatisation that rose to prominence in the 1980s, 'governance' has also joined the growing list of key words with which it is apparently necessary to become familiar. As Sing (1999) has noted, governance is not a simple concept to pin down and it would be foolhardy to hope for, or to pursue, a succinct definition which goes to the heart of the matter whilst embracing its multi-faceted nature. Not surprisingly, therefore, there has been worldwide disagreement among academics, officials and political actors of different types, with debates about the extent to which governance should be seen narrowly or more broadly (Theron *et al.*, 2000). Khan (1998), focusing on Bangladesh, rightly takes a broader view than do most analysts by locating the concept in the arenas of markets, international forces and civil society.

A critical point emerging here – and in need of interpretation – is that there are myriad ways in which civil society and government are related. Reference can then be made to a host of examples: ways in which governments can be held accountable to civil society by elections and other means, human rights, constitutions, transparency, anti-corruption strategies and the role of the judiciary.

Governance has been deployed in a normative manner in which it often appears to reflect the main principles associated with liberal democracy as advocated by the West, and the adjective 'good' often qualifies the meaning of governance in this way. However, an attempt has been made to see the concept in a more developmental light. There are at least two ways in which this perspective can be illustrated. First, there is the idea that 'bad' governance hinders development by, for example, siphoning funds into private pockets instead of reaching the planned beneficiaries. Conversely, the good governance model is one whereby procedures are adopted and enforced by which misappropriation of this kind is largely avoided. The second example is the growing emphasis on social and economic rights in addition to those normally associated with the liberal democratic agenda. With a focus on the importance of constitutions, Ndulo (2001) points out that this seems to be of relevance in several parts of Africa. He comments that viable constitutions in Africa have several requirements but one of them is to 'accommodate the general economic and social backwardness that exists in these countries and the consequential need for development on all fronts simultaneously'.

Donors have also been a factor of some importance in making these sort of arguments. The drive for good governance has been a priority for most donors since the 1980s when the World Bank strove for the wide spread adoption of structural adjustment programmes linked to aid. Governance was often strongly featured in this agenda. For example, Ndulo (2001) refers to the World Bank reporting on Africa in 1989. In its view, the crisis of development was closely linked to the crisis of governance and high-lighted the lack of accountability of state officials as one of the main problems in this context.

There are signs of change in some states. Partly, but arguably, because of interventions such as those of the World Bank and other donors and partly because of other factors such as the resurgence and resilience of effective opposition, there has been a shift in much of Africa to the sort of system that is associated with 'good governance' and accountability. Countries such as South Africa, Kenya and Lesotho can be cited here. In Asia, reference can be made to the Philippines, whilst India has for nearly 60 years regularly experienced democratic transitions from being ruled by one party to being ruled by another. Not all states are on this road, admittedly, but the under-lying trend towards freedom (as opposed to formal independence) is clear.

What are the implications of the governance agenda for the administrative systems of developing countries? Several can be noted. Firstly, since 'good' governance means assuring the rights of opposition parties, it follows that the idea of the political neutrality of public servants has to be addressed, especially in situations where changes of government may occur regularly. Secondly, 'good' governance is very much part of the anti-corruption crusade in many countries. This means that codes of ethics, auditing, whistle-blowing and independent investigation of alleged malad-ministration (the 'Ombudsman' role) take on greater salience for practising administrators. The closely related notions of accountability and trans-parency are also growing in importance. This can have many implications but of particular strength is the need to ensure that political representatives are adequately supported when they wish to hold state institutions to account; this means, for example, accurate and timely reporting. In relation to transparency, it has become important to move away from the bureau-cratic obsession with secrecy towards a willingness to open up the affairs of state to more open scrutiny. Thirdly, constitutions are also beginning to be taken more seriously in 'the real world' of public administration. In the past, it was possible to largely ignore issues such as human rights whether lip service was paid to them in the constitution or not. This is much less the case nowadays (Wolmuth *et al.*, 1998). Finally, the related concepts of implementation, service delivery and performance management have come to the fore in many countries.

The new approaches to governance have also made it necessary for bureaucracies to become more developmental in focus. For example, constitutions that make specific reference to social and economic rights clearly make it obligatory for the agencies of government to focus on providing housing, education, health and so on. This remains true even if the state tries to fulfil such obligations through private sector bodies. It is also clear that the empowerment of civil society through elections, community forums and the like creates pressure on the state to ensure that it delivers in response to the demands emerging from such processes. In an interesting analysis, Sen (1999) sees a clear link between freedom and the performance of governments in relation to the important developmental issue of famine. What has also emerged strongly in recent years, and is also a concern pervading Sen's work, is that policies have to be seen in relation to their consequences. There is a sense in which this concern tallies with what is now being said about performance – which is that it moves us towards a more 'outcomes based' way of looking at governance. This shift is not necessarily easy to bring about and a whole paraphernalia of jargon has developed on this issue. However, the central point remains clear in that the performance of public managers and the organisations for which they work will need to be increasingly checked against measurable outcomes such as effects on poverty and the environment.

States and markets

In this section, the question raised is the extent to which there is a balance between the state and market forces. How far should the state retreat from an interventionist role in the economy and allow market dominance? This is a debate, which has mostly been located in Europe and North America and refers to the balance that is sought between the public sector and the private sector. Under capitalism, the concept of the market is central to our understanding of the economy. Under the Thatcher government in the United Kingdom and Reagan in the United States, the 1980s bore witness to a renaissance of the doctrine that the more 'perfect' or 'free' market economies can be, the better it is for society as a whole, even if, in the case of the latter, policies more closely correspond with 'war Keynesianism'. This in turn led to the idea that the balance between public and private sectors should shift in favour of the latter.

The transplant of these policies to the developing world has been controversial. This doctrine generally found expression in developing countries at a somewhat later stage. Often this perspective was propelled by the conditions under which bodies like the World Bank provided financial support to the states that were asking for help, and who were now asserting that the public sectors of debtor countries had become too big. As a result, it was deemed that spending had to be curbed, privatisation encouraged and the users of services had to contribute more. This initiative had far reaching consequences (potential and actual) and placed the World Bank in the controversial position of being accused of exacerbating poverty rather than relieving it (Cornia *et al.*, 1987; Wallis, 1989).

Part of the debate between analysts, from a range of disciplines, has centred on the role of the state in development. Where a degree of development has been attained, how far can this be attributed to the functions performed by the state? Chiu and Lui (1998) argue that a nation's economic performance owes far more to state intervention than the free market advocates would suggest:

> Singapore, for instance, fits the laissez–faire image poorly. The state distributes extensive incentives to foreign investors in strategic sectors, and also provides infrastructural assistance selectively to firms that the state considers beneficial to industrialisation. The state also exercises heavy-handed control over the labour movement and the determination of wages (Chiu and Lui, 1998: 143).

A major theme of these debates is the concept of the developmental state by which the public sector is seen as playing a core role in the transformation of society. Also known as the statist model, this is essentially a critique of the idea that development can be almost entirely market driven. On the contrary, the task of the state is a strategic one in fostering emerging markets in order to contribute to the achievement of national goals. Thus, there is often the assumption that the state and the market can operate in partnership, whereby the former infuses more of the methods and practices of the latter – a theme of the PPP strategy mentioned earlier in this chapter.

It is important to note that those who argue for the developmental state are not arguing for a socialist model in which the role of the state would necessarily be much more pervasive. What they are trying to do is to correct what they see as the naïve view that the state can be ignored almost entirely in the analysis of, for example, the East Asian case. Indeed, some writers with a strong bias towards the private sector implicitly admit that the state's role is in fact significant. Naisbitt's analysis of what he terms the 'Asian renaissance' – part of which is a shift from being 'government-driven to being market-driven' – seems to be in this category (Naisbitt, 1997). There are, perhaps, lessons for developing countries here. Whilst there has been widespread acceptance that the high levels of nationalisation may have been a failure in general, it is important not to throw out the baby with the bath water and assume that states do not matter. As a minimum, it is reasonably clear that states will continue to take responsibility for education and health because of several factors. One factor is that the vast majority of the affected populations will be unable to pay private providers. Another factor is the clear link between levels of health and education on the one hand, and levels of development on the other. So a state in pursuit of development cannot ignore the need to play a core role in provision: and it would be unjust for inequality to be maintained and possibly increased as a result of private sector led policies in these sectors.

What follows from this line of argument is that the state continues to matter. This does not mean that the older style of state dominance needs to be continued or resurrected. An indeed, a measure of private sector involvement, if selective, controlled and planned in full awareness of possible pitfalls, may be a workable strategy for the governments of developing countries to adopt.

Decentralisation and development

Development planning, very much the fashion of the 1960s and 1970s, has been seen as failing for several reasons, one of which was its highly centralised and often undemocratic nature which created a tendency for plans to be unrealistic and lacking legitimacy.[1] It was also noted that local co-ordination was intrinsic to effective implementation of plans but was often very difficult where planning was highly centralised. Conyers and Hills note the frustration that agencies experience when they can only act on the basis of national decisions that may not be made at all, especially where national bodies cannot agree on what should be done (Conyers and Hills, 1984: 222).

The alternative is to decentralise, preferably through elected local government or devolution, according to some such commentators such as Mawhood (1983). However, governments have tended, at least initially, to opt for stronger field administration or deconcentration. This is essentially a strategy in which bureaucrats representing central government departments are posted to districts, provinces and the equivalent and given various forms of enhanced authority. The push for more devolved forms of government came later. Though predating the 'good governance' trend, devolution is clearly linked to it. Moreover, with limited clear evidence of success, it has become a commonly adopted reform in many countries and especially in Africa. The idea is to deepen democracy and make government more responsive to conditions on the ground. In reality, however, decentralisation has foundered. In an overview of Africa, Wunsch (2001) concludes that the strategy has not worked well because resource problems, centralising tendencies, the political preference of local elites, poor design of local institutions and operational difficulties have been bottlenecks of some significance.

A more recent review, whilst rather more optimistic in tone, does not suggest that huge success has been realised in practice (Public Administration and Development, 2003). Crook (2003), for example, argues that decentralisation has generally contributed little to poverty alleviation and has often achieved the opposite. A survey of decentralised governance and poverty programmes covered seven states in Asia and Africa (India, Nepal, Sri Lanka, Uganda, Kenya, Tanzania and Ethiopia) and arrived at only slightly more optimistic conclusions (Belshaw, 2000). It suffices to conclude here that, whilst the overall principle of decentralisation may be worthy of support, there are numerous realities related to factors such as power, lack of resources, capacity, and levels of commitment that are not conducive to effective implementation. A likely scenario is that governments will remain committed to this principle but will tend to maintain large amounts of central control in practice. Others may be more successful in establishing viable locally based systems.

Capacity building

Another trend over the past two decades has been the emphasis placed on capacity building. Originally, this tended to be focussed on government and on training, but in recent years its scope has widened to embrace civil society and other organisations outside of government. It has also moved away from being almost exclusively about training to a perspective that sees capacity as a multi dimensional concept including such important factors as procedures, structures, resources, the management of information technologies and the relationships organisations have with the world outside of themselves.

Taking *information management* as an example, this is now seen as a far more vital factor that it was ten years ago. This is partly because of the growing importance of information technologies as a result of globalisation. However, it is also important for the dissemination of knowledge. The sharing of information through 'alliances' is now being actively promoted. This example also brings out the importance of looking at capacity building through a variety of dimensions or lenses (Ballantyne, 2000).

> This notion of alliances is an increasingly critical part of the capacity building challenge in the information management domain. It recognises that organisations are nowadays unable to achieve all their aims and objectives alone. This is especially true in the information area where the sheer quantity of new knowledge is overwhelming. Scaling up and achieving a necessary critical mass to address a problem or issue is best done through co-operation and partnerships. Here, capacities are mobilised and directed, rather than only being built (Ballantyne, 2000: 2).

As with other issues discussed in this chapter, the increasing recognition of the importance of capacity building, if not donor driven, has been closely linked to technical assistance in several cases. Much of the literature on the subject relates to the donor factor and perhaps it is a healthy sign that capacity assessment is now being applied more intensively to the donor agencies themselves. However, there is a case for in-depth review of donor interventions that might well reveal that the donors themselves have serious capacity gaps that have to be addressed if technical assistance is to meet the expectations attached to it (Land, 2002a). Moreover, some recipient countries have been able to use aid more effectively than others; in order to benefit from the capacity building initiatives of donors, there has to be in place the capacity to use technical assistance well. Botswana is often cited as a country with a record that is comparatively positive, mainly because 'external resources have been integrated into the country's national planning system' (Land, 2002b: 3), and the state's experience of drought relief management demonstrates this point (Wallis, 1990).

Conclusion

This chapter does not claim to be comprehensive; areas such as policy analysis and international administration are only mentioned in passing. HIV-AIDS, an area that has not been discussed at all but is of great significance, must also be mentioned; it needs more attention in the *public administration* discourse than has been the case so far. However, some key trends have been identified and analysed by reference to several countries. I have tried to avoid giving the impression that the experience of development management is the same everywhere – hence the points made earlier about diversity. An important principle that can be stated with some confidence is that there are no formulas to be applied uncritically under all circumstances in all states. What is viable, however, is to carry out situation analyses in the different states, whilst simultaneously bearing in mind the lessons to be derived from elsewhere. Selective application of those lessons may then follow.

Some broad trends that stand out are the growing importance of poverty and governance. What this in turn highlights is that the academic study of Public Administration must avoid intellectual narrowness but see itself as part of a wider project concerned with the role of states in development and in particular in addressing poverty. This involves, as a minimum, the willingness to open up to the fact that other disciplines have much to offer. The problem that the discipline of Public Administration has to confront in many countries has been the tendency to isolate it from the Social Sciences, and especially those with critical traditions. This has been exacerbated by New Public Management approaches as these have contributed to the neglect of fields such as Political Science and Sociology and a growing fraternisation with Business Management. If it fails to correct this imbalance, the usefulness of Public Administration in developing countries will be stifled and its relevance increasingly questioned.

Note

1. A few years ago Birmingham University ran a Masters course with this title. The idea was to argue that the overly centralised states that became such a feature of the 1960s and 1970s were a factor in stalling development.

Conclusion

17
Conclusion: Towards a Revitalisation of the Public?

Geoffrey Wood and Ian Roper

A central theme running through this book is, quite simply, that the public sphere matters. The 'public sphere' is the place where the people at large gather, debate, and choose and recall their representatives. It is characterised by localised selection, reinforced by trust and by shared notions of equity and accountability (Arendt, 1984). In return, representatives of the public sphere should ideally direct the public sector – the bureaucratic and functional arms of government – to realise the concerns and needs of the community and society at large. Any notion of the supremacy and indispensability of the public is difficult to reconcile with conceptions of marketisation, or managerialism. The latter would represent a centralisation of power and the inevitable distortion of political institutions towards autocracy (c.f. Arendt, 1984).

This volume has considered the implications that the ascendant orthodoxy of marketisation, managerialisation and the general scaling down of the public sector has had for the 'public sphere' in a variety of thematic and national contexts. The aim of this chapter is to summarise the issues emerging from this and then to put a more general case for a reinstatement of a revitalised public sphere that has been denied by neo-liberal reform strategies.

Assessing the impact of reform

In chapter 1, six broad threads were highlighted as providing a running theme throughout the book. Five of these will now be reviewed in light of the contributions made by the previous chapters. The sixth thread, which is arguably the core thread, will be the subject of further discussion in the second part of the chapter.

The effects of efficiency savings on the capacity to address social needs

As a broad issue, van den Berg's critique of the core assumptions behind the neo-liberal reform agenda – encapsulated within Public Choice theory – mean that a stable trade off between efficiency and adequate levels of service provision are unlikely to be possible. This is because, as van den Berg points out, Public Choice theory cannot accept that any level of collective provision can ever be justifiable if it is at all possible to provide such services on the basis of individual market based transactions. This is despite there being nothing in Public Choice, that provides any *empirical evidence* as to how private provision of these self-same services would not be subject to *exactly the same* utility-maximising distortions as would the 'self-serving bureaucrat' so derided by neo-liberals. Moreover, even if this anti-collectivist agenda were not set up to rig the choice of balance between 'efficiency' and 'capacity' against capacity, Wood goes on to question the ethics involved in making such trade-offs in the first place – even where such trade-offs are themselves based on a (utilitarian) ethical standpoint. In practice, the effects of the trade-off is demonstrated in the chapter by Harrow, who describes how the disaggregation of service provision has led to a lowering of service quality, with voluntary organisations often being left to 'pick up the pieces'; and by Bond, who finds that the 'reform' of the water industry in South Africa has improved 'efficiency' by transferring the cost from provider to user.

Is the discourse of NPM viable and transportable?

In respect of the viability of New Public Management (NPM), Dibben and Higgins cast doubt on the extent to which this has led to satisfactory outcomes. This is illustrated through the definition of NPM as being a discourse that is dependent on the process of marketisation – manifesting itself through redefining service users as 'customers' and redefining work for service providers through managerialism.

In terms of the transportability of the NPM reform agenda, a general picture emerges that suggests that any notion of convergence along some 'globalisation' rationale is not apparent. Wood, for example, points out that the path that most of Europe has followed has been based on a different model to the Anglo-Saxon neo-liberal path. Similarly, James demonstrates similar patterns to this in terms of collective bargaining practices in Europe. However, while some of the more deterministic assertions about NPM convergence should be rejected, a balance needs to be struck between this in terms of process and outcomes, and the need to recognise that there are common causes in terms of pressures. Otherwise there would be no discussion at all on the notion of the public sector reform debate. In short, therefore, there are similarities and differences.

Interestingly, while Anglo-Saxon countries are generally assumed to be the most exposed to an undiluted neo-liberal reform package, in the two chapters on Canada and New Zealand respectively, Lonti and Verma and Gregory indicate that while the influence of the reform agenda has been significant in both countries, differences are present even here.

Developing countries fare differently. The chapters by Wallis and Munck point to the very different circumstances faced in relation to 'reform' in developing countries in Africa and Latin America respectively, while Liu and Wang characterise the reform process being undertaken in China as, essentially, a hybrid unique to China's own circumstances and historical development.

What is the role of institutions?

The chapter by Hollingsworth underscores the importance of taming the market rather than simplistically following it, since only short term choices can be left to the market, whilst broader developmental questions must be addressed by other forms of co-ordination. Such co-ordination includes sub-national and national level institutions of governance even though such institutions are nested within continental and global regimes. A wide range of contradictory forces are operative at all these levels which makes the future of nations and the global economy difficult to predict, yet opens up historic opportunities, the global hegemony of neo-liberalism notwithstanding. Other chapters point to the role of both grassroots movements (Bond) and trans-national institutions (Wood) in revitalising supportive institutional configurations.

What have the effects of 'reform' been on key stakeholders?

Reform has affected key stakeholders differently. The neo-liberal agenda is preoccupied with value-for-money and the conflation of the public good as being manifested through the eyes of 'the taxpayer'. It should, therefore, be no surprise to find that other stakeholders in the reform process have experienced negative consequences in the attempt to 'redress the balance'. For the public choice advocates this would be seen as a 'good thing' – since organised interests competing for resources are defined seen as being 'the problem' from this viewpoint. The contributors to this volume, however, reach very different conclusions on this point.

Workers providing public services have experienced a variety of pressures, according to Roper, caused by the increasing conflation of 'quality' with 'value-for-money'. Similar negative consequences, in terms of work intensification, are highlighted by Lonti and Verma. Unsurprisingly the natural defenders of public service workers – public service unions – have long been on the rational-choice advocates' 'hitlist'. James points out, however, that while the NPM imperative has increased downward pressure on them, the effects have not been consistent, or as bad, as experienced by *non*-public-service unions. Service users do not fare as well as the reform protagonists claim either, particularly where services address basic needs (rather than aspirational 'wants'), as Bond's chapter amply illustrates in the case of access to clean running water.

How has reform affected the trade-off between efficiency, accountability and democracy?

Of course, no conclusive formula could be proposed to indicate the trade-off between these aspects of the public sphere. However, the evidence presented indicates that, through the pursuit of efficiency, accountability and democracy have been curtailed. This may not be much of a surprise in the West, where reform was predicated upon the 'public choice' rationale of reigning in public expectations of the state to curtail 'government overload'. However, the benefits of reform in developing nations have often been identified – by international institutions such as the World Bank and the International Monetary Fund – as mutually supportive of 'democratic reforms'. The chapters by Baker and Wallis both indicate that this has not been the case and this is echoed in the chapter by Munck, which reminds us how the neo-liberal agenda was introduced on the back of severe curtailments in democracy in Latin America – by those very proponents of market-based liberty.

This leaves us with the primary question raised in chapter 1: within a reform climate dominated by the pervasiveness of minimal government, what is meant by 'publicness', and what remains distinctive about the public sector? The remainder of this chapter will attempt to address this issue.

What remains of the public sphere?

Whilst rapid development can take place under autocracy, a developed and responsive public sphere is closely associated with sustainable economic progress and higher levels of social equity (Przeworski *et al.*, 2000). Yet, how robust is a developed, autonomous and popularly accountable public sphere? Or, does it represent a historical aberration that will inevitably be eroded in the face of market forces or persistent power imbalances?

In classical sociological theory, a close correlation is drawn between economic progress and a developed public sphere. To Weber, the rise of specific patterns of belief system paved the way for more rational forms of economic organisation and associated bureaucratic institutional supports (Weber, 1948).

Again, Durkheim argues that the increased social division of labour results in increasing social interdependence, underpinned by rising organic – or objective – solidarity (Timasheff, 1967; Durkheim, 1933).[1] What both these accounts have in common is that complex forms of economic activity are only possible through the emergence and persistence of general rules providing a basis of certainty in undertaking exchange relations.

Yet, since the 1970s, there has been growing questioning about the desirable nature of the public sphere and the role of the state sector. To neo-liberals, the endemic economic volatility of the past three decades reflects the persistence of market imperfections; further deregulation, centring on minimising the role of the state will provide the impetus for renewed growth. In contrast, more progressive accounts suggest that the speculative excesses of this period reflect the untrammelled power of financial capital; stable growth is contingent on more regulation not less (MacEwan, 1999). The development of the welfare state provided the foundation for unprecedented economic progress and equity (Habermas, 1989); greater social mobility allows for the fullest development of a society's human capital, while social inclusion allows both for improvements in individual material conditions and constantly renewed demand for goods and services.

There is little doubt that, within most of the advanced societies, the present role of the state in society and the manner in which governmental structures are constituted, has come under intense scrutiny; increasingly, there is an assumption that things cannot remain the way they have become. Again, the nature of the two principal alternative roads have become increasingly clear: towards minimalism, or the reconstitution of the public sphere in such a manner as to renew accountability and social inclusion.

Preceding chapters have explored the concept of the public, the consequences of marketisation in pursuit of 'efficiency', the discourse and operationalisation of NPM, the reaction of key stakeholder interests to reform, and possible alternative policy options. In the following pages, we locate debates surrounding the nature of the public within classical socio-economic theory, both as a basis for a summary of the limitations of marketisation, and as a foundation for emerging progressive alternatives.

The experience of neo-corporatism and the highly developed welfare state

The unprecedented social and economic progress of the 1950s and 1960s in the West was contingent on the building of consent both within and between firms, on far reaching social compromises between labour and capital, and firm and community (Giddens, 1981; 2000). A virtuous circle of growth, characterised by positive feedback between increased productivity and higher wages, guaranteed stable aggregate demand whilst limiting inflation (Williams, 2000). The state contributed to sustaining this circle through expanding access to education and training, and supportive social services. Nonetheless, there remained considerable variation in the performance of different economies in the developed world. In general, neo-corporatist economies – examples being Scandinavia, the Low Countries and Austria – seemed superior in terms of generating stable growth rates and in a range of social indicators, such as equity, particularly in relation to their Anglo-American counterparts (Harcourt and Wood, 2003). Arguably, established cultures of collaboration and effective training systems provided a solid foundation for more flexible forms of production (c.f. Sako, 1998;

Dohse *et al.*, 2001). Nor did the success of these systems depend on deals between employee collectives and firms; the state played a central role in underpinning any accommodations, both in terms of encouraging compliance and in bring additional resources to the table. Typically, this would result in the kinds of public policies labour is likely to want incorporated in any deal – centring on the provision of social security and the protection of employee rights – whilst meeting business needs for an effective training infrastructure (Harcourt and Wood, 2003). As a result neo-corporatist countries are characterised not only by relatively strong economic performance – particularly up until the late 1990s – but also highly developed social security and development systems, and, hence, relatively high levels of state employment. Again, the experience of the neo-corporatist countries highlights the importance of the state and public service provision in underwriting economic development.

Economic crises: challenging the public

Since the early 1970s, the global economy has been characterised by mediocre growth interposed with recession, and high volatility. The neo-corporatist economies have, since the late 1990s, tended to perform rather worse than their Anglo-American counterparts. This reflects global over-capacity in manufacturing and volatile demand, forcing ongoing cost-cutting and increasing pressures on countries to institute reforms making Anglo-American-style financial engineering possible (Jurgens *et al.*, 2000). A more insidious weakness has been in the realm of ideas: the ideological hegemony of neo-liberalism has been mirrored by a crisis of confidence in neo-corporatist systems (Harcourt and Wood, 2003; De Angelis, 2000).

Neo-liberalism: contesting the public

In the main, neo-liberal accounts share a notion of the public as being rational profit maximising individuals. There was a close connection between neo-liberal theory and the managerialisation and marketisation of the public sector in the 1980s. This reflected both the hegemony of rational choice theory in economics and political science, and the growing influence of economists committed to an associated methodology that stressed increasingly abstract numerical modelling founded on specific assumptions regarding individual behaviour over more qualitative appraisals of actual social reality.

Neo-liberal policy analysts conceded that individuals might make the 'wrong' decisions through faulty calculations and imperfect knowledge; rationality may in some cases prove elusive (c.f. Feldstein, 1999). Hence, poverty is seen as a lifestyle choice or the product of inappropriate institutional pressures. The neo-liberal individual is not necessarily 'good' or 'perfectable,' but s/he can be encouraged to adopt the enlightened path (Feldstein, 1999). Most contemporary neo-liberal commentators believe that this is only possible through essentially coercive mechanisms, an example being 'tough love' policies that would curtail welfare benefits and force individuals to seek employment, even if the wages and working conditions were not to their liking (c.f. Feldstein, 1999).

Given the inevitable contradictions and distortions that arise from an 'over active' state, Nozick (1984) and Hayek (1984) suggest that the market will operate most efficiently – and wealth will be maximised for the bulk of society – if the state's role is minimalised. Public sector functions should, wherever possible, be outsourced, the state's role, in effect, being reduced to that of enforcer – to secure private property and national security, and to ensure that the 'undeserving poor' are 'encouraged' to pursue their economic interests in a more rational manner. To confirmed neo-liberals, the managerial revolution would thus be an interim stage to subjecting the bulk of government functions to the discipline of the market. Few would, however, contest the enforcer function of the state; this may reflect a deeply seated ideological commitment to the need to secure personal liberty and property, or, simply, the pragmatic acceptance of the inviolability of key vested interests.

Why the public matters: the growing credibility gap

In reality, even the most dedicated proponents of neo-liberalism are quick to call for state interventionism in the face of 'unfair' competition or unexpected shocks (Mellahi and Wood, 2003a). Moreover, as Tilly (1998) argues, persistent or 'durable' inequality reflects clear social divisions, themselves generated through the operation of social organisations, exploitation being the 'pivotal mechanism' through which inequality is generated (Wright, 1999; Wood, 2003). In short, it can be argued that the kind of marketisation envisaged by NPM and the related privatisation of core public services are neither appropriate nor sustainable strategies. Privatisation has, in many cases, proved unsustainable in the absence of additional financial handouts from the 'nanny state'; examples range from the botched privatisation of British Rail to the plight of electrical utilities in both the UK and the United States. In the developing world, unrestrained marketisation has proved generally unpopular and unproductive, offset by very few success stories (c.f. Mann, 2003). In large areas of the developing world, such as tropical Africa, the state lacks sufficient resources to continue to bail out failing privatisation initiatives; this alone underscores the limited transferability of the Anglo-American model of marketisation. A close scrutiny of much vaunted 'model cases' such as Uganda reveals both a continued dependence on foreign aid, and the continued infusion of resources from external sources; in the case of Uganda, the latter has taken the form of the systematic looting of minerals and tropical hardwood from the Democratic Republic of Congo.

The deep social embeddedness of social inequality, and its constant reconstitution by established interests, will result in the continued marginalisation of key segments of society and the strengthening of the hand of others, a mass franchise notwithstanding (Wood, 2003). As C. Wright Mills (1963) notes, the military industrial complex inevitably becomes a powerful lobby, able to call on disproportionate amounts of state resources in comparison to real national security needs, distorting the role of the state and the public sphere. Indeed, marketisation does not necessarily result in reduced state expenditure, but rather such expenditure being diverted in support of powerful vested interests. In the absence of regulation and accountability, the demands of the latter are likely to become increasingly strident, resulting in vulnerable groupings being subjected to a renewed cycle of social exclusion and political marginalisation (Chomsky, 1996). Ironically, whilst the Bush II administration remained an outspoken opponent of neo-liberalism, its massive increases in defence spending and massive overseas deployment have threatened to inflict on the United States the same degree of overspending and overstretch that was the undoing of the Soviet Union (Johnson, 2004).

Why the public matters: economic progress and the public

There is little doubt that the public sphere has come under unprecedented assault; in turn, this has led to the increasing disengagement of the public sector from the public at large. The latter has increasingly been subjected to marketisation and the emergence of an autonomous – and often authoritarian – class of public sector manager, increasingly removed from traditional conceptions of accountability and community service. Yet, the role of the public sphere may be defended on the grounds of both economic efficiency, and in the interests of individual and social actualisation (c.f. Durkheim, 1933; Weber, 1968).

Close accountability and recall, and social inclusion, result in both stronger bonds of organic solidarity, and the legitimisation and durability of norms and rules. As Marsden (1999) notes, whether in the form of legislation or informal practices, rules make for greater efficiency, in that parties to a deal can take much for granted. Within the workplace, employees can count on remuneration and a basic continuity in practices, and employers on an underlying consent (c.f. Marsden, 1999). Where rules are weak, employment relations degenerate into a kind of trench warfare, where the arbitrary exercise of managerial power is matched by overt and hidden resistance. In terms of relations between firms and their customers, weak rules make for opportunism and uncertainty, characterised by the frequent termination of contracts, and endemic disputes over pricing and quality. Again, relations between firms and communities are likely to be characterised by the former seeking to offload as many costs as possible on the latter, in terms of demands on social infrastructures and in dealing with pollution and associated long term costs. This serves to exacerbate existing inequalities, and results in a disproportionate amount of the costs associated with industrial and commercial activity being borne by future generations (Singer, 1995).

In the absence of shared norms, and durable and legitimate rules, exchange is largely made possible by the use of overt power, rather than trust. Whether power is seen as a resource (Arendt, 1963) or an operation (Foucault, 1979), it remains a costly and inefficient mechanism for underpinning exchange relations; it is counter to the inevitable trend in societies towards more advanced and subtle mechanisms of ordering (Foucault, 1979).

It might seem that electronic forms of monitoring employee behaviour within the workplace, complex mechanisms of data interchange binding together supply chain networks, the close circuit television monitoring of downtown areas, grossly intrusive advertising and the compilation of ever more detailed datasets on individual consumer behaviour represent the ultimate realisation of the Benthamite panopticon, of the securing of control through the use of technology (c.f. Poster, 1984). However, as Foucault emphasises, the most advanced forms of social ordering are founded in the realm of ideas and reinforced through social transactions; there are not contingent on the perfection of 'physical apparatuses of capture' (Foucault, 1979; Deleuze and Guattari, 1988).

Why the public matters: competing needs and interests, and the public

Whilst optimistic accounts would argue that societies will naturally tend towards greater fairness and equity (whether through evolution or revolution), as Gumplowicz (1885) suggests, the public is likely to always remain a contested domain between different interests, collectives and classes (Timasheff, 1967). Hence, it is possible for episodic improvements in the human condition to be interrupted through setbacks; there are always 'barbarians' working to put back advances, whether in the hope of reinstating previous forms of dominance or instituting new ones.

As House argues, social change brings about changes in social thinking; the reduction of sharp cleavages in society make it easier to develop objective tools for analysis (Adler, 1966). To Simmel (1981), the rise of the objective *vis-à-vis* the subjective represented a key step in the modernisation process; personal networks and personality based structures of authority are replaced by objective mechanisms for exchange – such as the modern cash economy – and, objective, burcaucratically rational mechanisms of governance.

As Durkheim (1933) cautions, 'forcing individuals to be free' from the restraints of tradition and personal networks can place unbearable strain on the individual. However, it also allows for the strengthening of shared moral values, based on common notions of the *desirable* and can provide the basis for socio-technological progress (Kolb, 1966).

Arguably, it remains possible to develop mechanisms for bridging some of the most durable cleavages in society, building on the common interests and concerns of the majority through active and passive inclusion – in other words, through both a range of participative mechanisms and greater equity in material endowments. As Durkheim (1933) notes, in the absence of organic solidarity, dominant groupings impose an unstable 'forced division of labour'. The latter is incapable of ensuring stability in both the economic and non-economic spheres. These conflicts can be alleviated if the higher occupational bands are not dominated by a single social grouping, and the division of labour is co-ordinated in such a manner as to make for a more functional distribution of talents (Giddens, 1971). This allows individual talents that might have previously remained latent fuller room for actualisation (Giddens, 1971), a point echoed in Rawls' later writings (Rawls, 2001).

As Arendt (1984) suggests, the principle brake on elite domination lies in the polity, and in the development of public spaces open for all to enter. The irreversibility of actions and the unpredictability of consequences acts as a major disincentive to popular participation in public life, encouraging the development of a small elite, although this tendency may be reduced where there is a strong division of powers, which helps mediate and historically ground action (Kristeva, 2001).

Invariably in political life, a disjuncture arises between the top and the bottom, with desires for spatial reach and universality again encouraging the emergence of a political elite far removed from the grassroots. However, it is possible to envisage authority as being vested in each of the layers of a structure of power; in each case, public representatives are accountable to their peers and the collective, authority resting on the confidence of individuals both at community and association level (Arendt, 1984).

A return to the public?

Despite neo-liberal triumphalism, the Anglo-American economies have not been immune to crisis. Much trumpeted booms made possible by financialisation, such as the 'internet revolution' have proved extremely short-lived. The prevalence of incentive driven executive pay has led to a real divergence of interest – between short term but stable maximisation of equity value, and that which is ultra-short term and unstable. The tendency of many managers to opt for the latter has resulted in numerous financial scandals such as the *Enron, Arthur Anderson* and *World.Com* ones. While scandals are the inevitable consequence of any period of speculative excess, those of the early 2000s, it seemed, were not isolated frauds but systemic problems. The heightened mobility of investor capital has led to the tax burden falling on less mobile factors, such as labour and fixed assets (Boyer, 2000). This results in tax becoming more pro- than anti-cyclical, as would have been the case under a Keynesian system (Boyer, 2000).

Growing social inequality characterised by a rising underclass and the stagnation of real wages in most job bands has led to demand being driven by borrowing. As Brenner (2002) notes, the fragility of borrowing-led growth lies in the fact that consumers may, quite simply, lose their nerve, and switch to saving, a situation that would be exacerbated by interest rates increases driven by external shocks. Unlike Japan, the United States does not have the buffer of enormous savings and current account surpluses, to serve as a buffer against a banking crisis (Brenner, 2002). Within Britain and the United States, there is a far closer link between consumer borrowing and house price inflation, than within Western Europe. Whilst additional mortgages may 'unlock' the wealth present in housing stock, it makes consumers – and the economy at large – vulnerable to the vicissitudes of interests rates and property speculation. As Godley and Izurieta (2003) note, debt cannot be an abiding source of growth, unless export demand turns around dramatically.

Hence, it can be argued that the lack of institutional constraints may have opened up new areas of economic activity, but they have not, as yet, proved capable of providing the basis for a stable and coherent growth trajectory. And, whilst 'financialisation' led-growth may be volatile, the social consequences in terms of reduced investment in training and development, and supportive social infrastructures, may make for 'durable inequality', permanently marginalising vulnerable individuals and communities (c.f. Lash, 2000).

Again, whilst Anglo-American model economies have been relatively successful in creating new jobs, many of these have been in those sectors particularly associated with temporary or insecure and low paid work; indeed, a far larger proportion of employees can be found in such jobs than in collaborative systems (c.f. Moody, 1997). Many of the 'new' jobs created have been in outsourced state functions, or, in the case of the United States, within the military-industrial complex (Chomsky, 1996).

Persistent economic crises have led to considerable debate on the role of the state and the public sector in both Anglo-American and neo-corporatist economies. To neo-liberals, further growth can be engendered through the reduction of market 'distortions'. The latter can be brought about through trimming back state functions, privatisation, and the introduction of 'market efficiencies' and the tools of private sector management into residual state functions. More critical accounts have argued that the state needs to be revitalised; the power of large corporations has ensured that democratic accountability has been 'hollowed out' (Anderson, 2000; Hertz, 2001). Voters have increasingly little choice between political parties, whilst reductions in social services have resulted in a growing class of socially excluded.

Hence, any assessment of the role of the public sphere, and of public sector management should be concerned with enhancing popular participation and accountability. In turn, this will help ensure the survival and development of the state as a provider of social services, and help impel new compromises between the state, firms, employees and the bulk of society. Renewal of the public sphere is thus about the revitalisation of democracy, and the development of new forms of social compromise, not only at the point of production, but in communities as well.

Rediscovering utopia: towards a revitalisation of the public

In order to check tendencies towards oligarchy or authoritarianism, a progressive project for revilitalising the public should, as a central objective, seek to make institutions more responsive to the potentially liberating interventions of individuals (Arendt, 1963; Wood, 2003). As noted earlier, traditional forms of social compromise on neo-corporatist lines have been essentially tripartite, involving the state, employers, and those directly involved in the process of production via their collectives, as can be seen from Figure 17.1.

A central strand in the recent literature has been renewed attention on developing alternative perspectives that broaden the base of participation at all levels (c.f. Wallerstein, 1998; Jacoby, 1999; Singer, 1999; Fung and Wright, 2003a; 2003b), echoing Arendt's (1984) earlier writings in this regard. Such initiatives stand in stark contrast to neo-liberal suggestions that continued deregulation represents the inevitable order of nature; the latter vision is essentially ahistorical and discounts the possibility for new

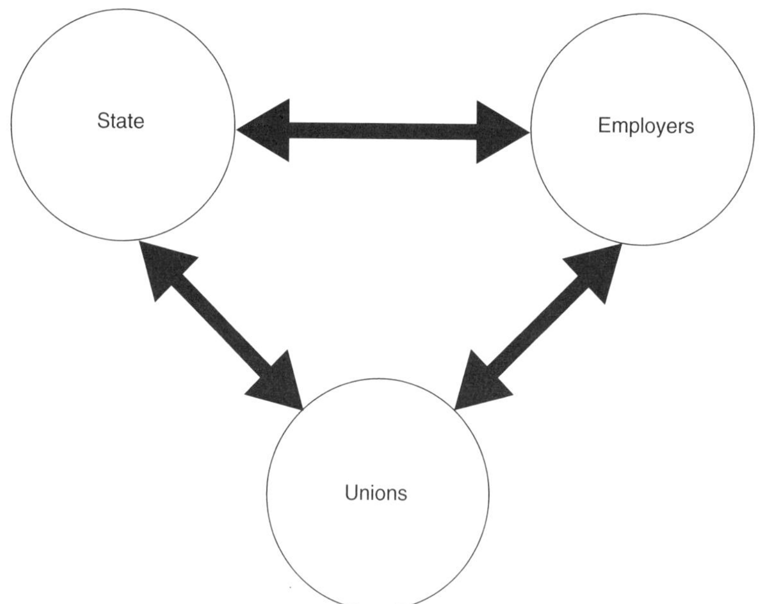

Figure 17.1   Traditional tripartite social compromise

ideas and actions by individuals, communities and their collectives (Soron, 2001). It must be conceded that progressive responses remain fragmented, alternating between wild optimism sparked off by small gains in an age of setbacks, and untoward pessimism.

Nonetheless, there is an emerging consensus around the need to regenerate existing structures for representation and participation both at state and extra-state levels, and for drawing in the growing body of 'outsiders'. The latter are comprised of those in temporary and insecure work, migrants, members of ethnic minorities, and above all, the growing army of the 'poors', the structurally socially excluded (c.f. Desai, 2002). The latter comprise the most marginalised in society, those most marginalised through relentless marketisation, for whom even the act of living becomes increasingly difficult. Traditional neo-corporatist deals inevitably become fragile once a growing body of society finds itself outside of the 'insider' tripartite tent (Casey and Gold, 2000).

Again, the close spatial proximity of workplace and community, and the increasingly visible damage to the biosphere, underscores the interconnected nature of contemporary social and natural life; traditional forms of representation discount the impact that the activities of firms has far beyond the workplace (c.f. Lipietz, 2001). Again, allowing for the inclusion and representation of marginalised social groupings provides an additional check against tendencies towards oligarchy or autocracy; a multiplicity of 'other' voices has the potential to constantly regenerate the polity. Increasingly, established political-economic actors have abandoned efforts to develop meaningful policy alternatives, either defending the present condition as inevitable or hearkening back to earlier 'golden ages'; in contrast, emerging community and grassroots organisations have increasingly been at the forefront of efforts to harness mass dissatisfaction with unrestrained neo-liberalism (Soron, 2001). As Daniel Singer argues, a genuinely progressive alternative should be founded on helping:

> ...people resist the dismal future being prepared for them by their political and economic leaders and acquire the democratic capacity to shape a future more attuned to their needs and aspirations (quoted in Soron, 2001: 212).

Central to more inclusive forms of social pacts is the need to develop alternative forums for social bargaining, and to recognise the role of alternative structures for representation, centring on the role of associations that are neither state nor market, such as employer associations, unions, and civil society groupings. Compromises between such collectives can provide the basis for widely respected rules, and result in workable trade-offs between competing interests and concerns (MacEwan, 1999).

The below figure highlights the manner in which such 'four party' deals might operate (Figure 17.2).

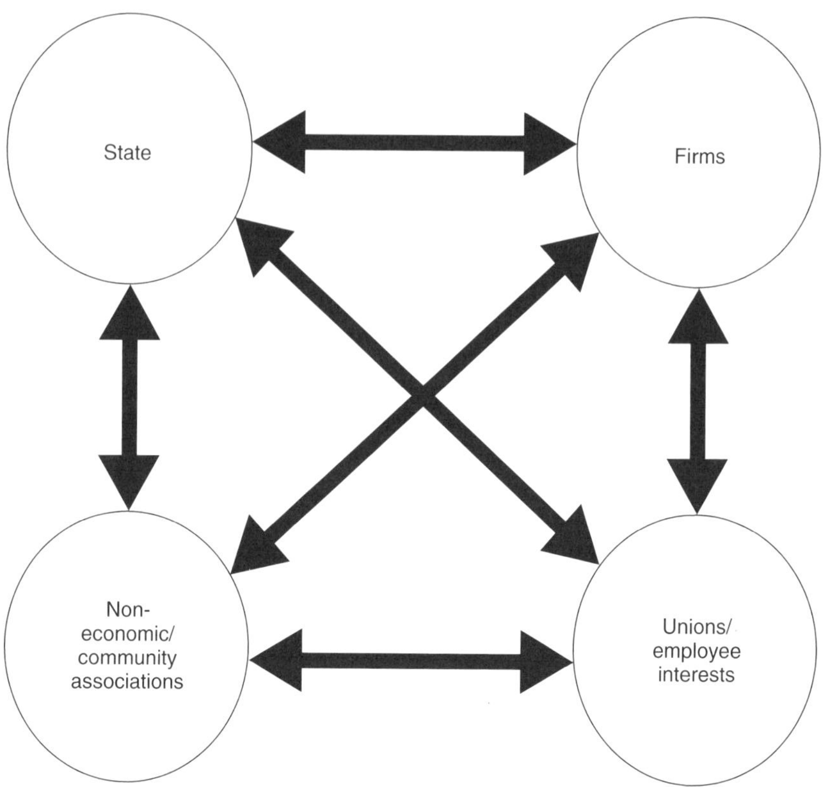

Figure 17.2   Towards a four party compromise

A long tradition in critical thought, most notably that associated with the later Frankfurt school, as well as writers such as Lessing, Benjamin and Arendt (see Benjamin, 1978; Crook, 1991; Jay, 1984; Fung and Wright, 2003a; 2003b) highlights the importance of developing forums for ordinary people to directly participate in decisions that affect their lives both within the workplace and in wider society. Decentralised decision making can be supported by state structures, and the engendering of formal linkages of responsibility (Fung and Wright, 2003b). Habermas (1990) argues that through opening up new opportunities for dialogue – not necessarily confined to the speech act – structures of governance can be rendered more accountable and closer to the needs of the grassroots. The greater richness and detail of social exchanges both facilitate the development and inter-change of knowledge, and allow for the emergence of more sophisticated mechanisms of exchange (Habermas, 1990). Such accounts hold that participation and dialogue should be rather more open ended and with a stronger emphasis on the ultimate goal of advancing social equity than would be suggested by established 'third way' theories. Again, theories of 'empowered participation' place a stronger emphasis on the development of countervailing power at all levels of society (c.f. Fung and Wright, 2003a; 2003b).

Traditional conceptions of social compromises suggest that they are best confined to a particular level; if sufficiently encompassing, the principal negotiating parties have the capacity for 'free-rider' behaviour, and mediate the excessive demands of the grassroots (Olson, 1982). However, it can be argued that such forms of co-operation rarely exist in isolation; rather, greater flexibility can be imparted into centralised deals through an overt or tacit recognition that they are likely to be adjusted, reinterpreted or topped up by more localised bargaining at both firm and community levels, as per Figure 17.3.

In practice, the most durable and best performing examples of social compromise have been those that have been characterised both by regular fluctuations in the degree of centralisation and bargaining practice,[2] and in the persistence of specific institutional features, including 'encompassing organisations' with broad social footprints, and deeply embedded institutional precedents for collaboration (Harcourt and Wood, 2003). Again, specific provision is made for firm level 'top up' bargaining, even if the nature and quality of the latter varies greatly from context to context.

It can be argued that a multiplicity of levels of bargaining is not necessarily destabilising, but can be an inherent strength. By allowing more grassroots participation, formalised structures are likely to prove considerably more dynamic and durable. Collaborative governance at centralised level alone is likely to result in stronger interests, more capable of collective action, capturing weaker groupings; this exacerbates tendencies towards weak feedback loops (from leadership to grassroots) and long lines of accountability and report-back.

The regulation of the individual firm will not necessarily empower workers or communities, unless the latter possess effective countervailing power (Fung and Wright, 2003a). Again, where specific transgressions of

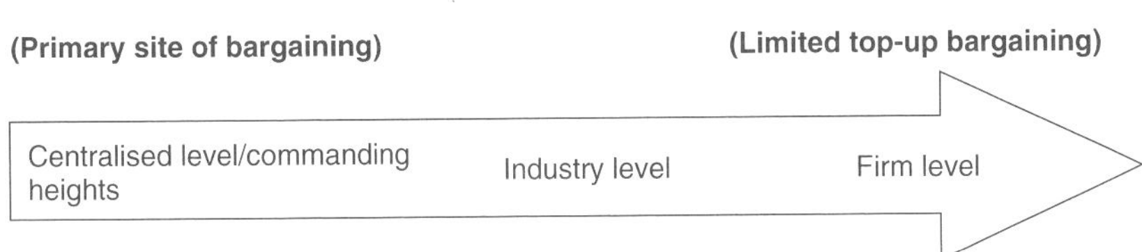

Figure 17.3   Levels of bargaining and compromise under traditional neo-corporatism

individual rights are both widespread and deeply embedded, legal efforts at curtailment are likely to face active opposition or passive non-compliance, necessitating active enforcement (Olson and Kahkonen, 2000: 32). Monitoring of any centralised deals, and local modifications necessitates multiple levels for engagement. Hence, a revitalisation and broadening of neo-corporatism or similar attempts to build social inclusion should, perforce, be multi-level (Mellahi and Wood, 2003b), as per Figure 17.4.

A caveat here is in order. Whilst there is a pressing need to revitalise the public, to reach new social compromises, and to provide a more stable foundation for growth, there remain strong 'negative feedback loops' in favour of the status quo (Sztompka, 1991). The comprehensive social compromises that took place in both compartmentalised and collaborative economies in the 1950s and 1960s were informed by the clear failure of more socially divisive policies in the 1920s and 1930s (c.f. Habermas, 1989). More recently, it was only after a full range of alternatives, including neo-liberalism, had been clearly exhausted, that an accords-based system was established in Ireland (Wood and Harcourt, 2001). A return to genuine social compromise, and/or the institution of a new system of bargained accommodation is contingent on other alternatives being fully exhausted; whilst undesirable, the volatility and speculative 'boomlets' of financialisation reflect a certain systemic vigour, and are undeniably functional to powerful vested interests. Again, whilst renewal and the implementation of progressive alternatives may be necessarily contingent on the status quo being shaken by seemingly irresolvable crises, a severe crisis does not necessarily result in a progressive outcome.[3]

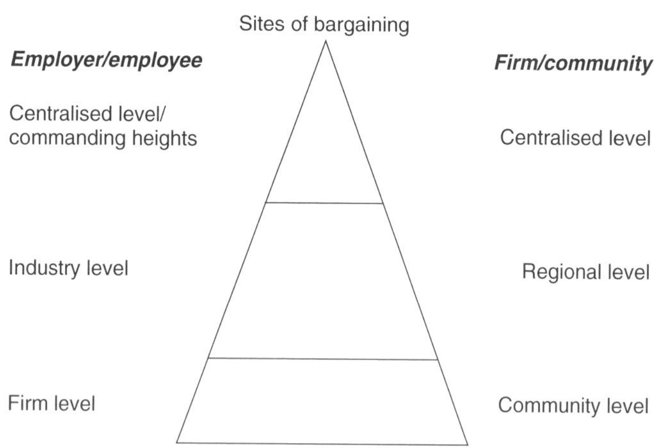

Figure 17.4 Towards multi-level participation and accords?

Conclusion

Democratisation and the rise of the modern welfare state provided the foundation for unprecedented improvements in the material conditions of the bulk of society, and greater room for the actualisation of individuals' skills, aptitudes and talents (c.f. Habermas, 1989; Giddens, 1981). Yet, in the face of persistent economic crises, the role of the public sector – and the vitality of the public sphere – has come under relentless assault from powerful vested economic interests. A persistent crisis of confidence amongst more progressive elements has resulted in, until recently, a dearth of progressive alternatives. Yet, whilst it would be mistaken to call for a 'mummification' of the welfare state of the early 1960s, or an unthinking return to the tools and methods of Keynesianism (c.f. De Angelis, 2000), it can be argued that, drawing on previous experiences, it is both essential and feasible to revitalise the public sphere. Such a revitalisation would include the development of mechanisms for participation and bargaining at all levels of the 'pyramid of authority' (c.f. Arendt, 1963), and a re-energisation of the public sector to provide the social and infrastructural services necessary to underpin a new consensus.

Notes

1. Whilst Weber sees economic progress as being closely associated with the development of specific belief systems, he shares Durkheim's view that economic progress has been linked to rationalisation and the development and diffusion of objective and increasingly legitimate forms of social ordering (Weber, 1968). He also shares Durkheim's concerns about the possibilities for new forms of autocracy and the need for a vibrant and inclusive public sphere. Central to classical sociology is an attempt to explain the experience and life chances of the individual in terms of the wider historical and institutional context (Mills, 1959).
2. Examples being Swedish and Dutch neo-corporatism.
3. It is no coincidence that the 1930s gave birth to both the New Deal and fascism.

Bibliography

AAPAM (2002) *24th Round Table Communiqué*. Maseru, Lesotho: African Association for Public Administration and Management.

Abell, P. (1992) Is rational choice theory a rational choice of theory? In Coleman, J. S. and Fararo, T. J. (eds), *Rational Choice Theory: Advocacy and Critique*. Newbury Park: Sage Publications.

Ackroyd, S. and Thompson, P. (1999) *Organizational Misbehaviour*. London: Sage

Alford, J. (2002) Defining the client in the public sector: A social-exchange perspective. *Public Administration Review*, 62(3): 337–346.

Almond, G. (1991) *Capitalism and Democracy*. Political Science and Politics, 24(3): 467–474.

Andersen, S., Due, J. and Madsen, J. (1999) Denmark: negotiating the restructuring of public service employment relations. In Bach, S., Bordogna, L., Della Rocca, G. and Winchester, D. (eds), *Public Services Employment Relations in Europe*. London: Routledge.

Aoki, M. (1988) *Information, Incentives and Bargaining in the Japanese Economy*. Cambridge: Cambridge University Press.

Aristotle (1952) *Politics*. London: Everyman.

Armstrong, A. (1998) A comparative analysis: new public management – the way ahead? *Australian Journal of Public Administration*, 57(2): 12–26.

Arndt, R. and Jelinek, M. (2001) Public private partnerships in Australia. *Public Management and Policy Association Review*, 15: 10–11.

Arnstein, S. (1969) A ladder of citizen participation. *Journal of the American Institute of Planning*, 35: 216–224.

Arrighi, G. (1997) Globalisation, state sovereignty, and the 'endless' accumulation of capital. Revised version of a paper presented at the conference *States and Sovereignty in the World Economy*. University of California, Irvine, 21–23 February.

Arrow, K. J. (1963) *Social Choice and Individual Values*. New York: Wiley.

Arthur, W. B. (1988a) Self-reinforcing mechanisms in economics. In Anderson, P. W., Arrow, K. J. and Pines, D. (eds), *The Economy as an Evolving Complex System*. Redwood City: Addison-Wesley.

Arthur, W. B. (1988b) Competing technologies: an overview. In Dosi, G., Freeman, C., Nelson, R., Silverberg, G. and Soete, L. (eds), *Technical Change and Economic Theory*. London: Pinter.

Aucoin, P. (1995) *The New Public Management: Canada in Comparative Perspective*. Montreal: Institute for Research on Public Policy.

Aucoin, P. (2002) Beyond the 'new' in public management reform in Canada: Catching the next wave? In Dunn, C. (ed.), *Handbook of Canadian Public Administration*. Toronto: Oxford University Press.

Australian Bureau of Statistics (2001) *Employee Earnings, Benefits and Trade Union Membership in Australia*. August.

Bach, S. (1999) Europe: changing public sector employment relations. In Bach, S., Bordogna, L., Della Rocca, G. and Winchester, D. (eds), *Public Services Employment Relations in Europe*. London: Routledge.

Bach, S. and Della Rocca, G. (2000) The management strategies of public service employers in Europe. *Industrial Relations Journal*, 31(2): 82–96.

Bach, S. and Winchester, D. (2003) Industrial relations in the public sector. In Edwards, P. (ed.), *Industrial Relations: Theory and Practice*, 2nd edition. Oxford: Blackwell.

Bach, S., Bodogna, L., Della Rocca, G. and Winchester, D. (eds) (1999), *Public Service Employment Relations in Europe; Transformation, Modernisation or Inertia?* London: Routledge.

Baker, R. (ed.) (1992) *Public Administration in Small and Island States*. West Hartford: Kumarian Press.

Ball, S. (1993) Education markets, choice and social class: the market as class strategy in the UK and USA. *British Journal of Sociology of Education*, 14(1): 3–20.

Ballantyne, P. (2000) *Information and Capacity Building*. In Capacity. Org. Maastricht: ECDPM.

Bartlett, D., Twineham, J. and Scotland, S. (2002) Local strategic partnerships: lessons from evaluative case studies of urban regeneration in an inner London borough, *British Academy of Management Conference*. London, 9–11 September.

Barzelay, M. (2001) La neuva gerencia pública. Un ensayo bibliográfico para estudiosos latinoamericanos (y otros). Revista del CLAD. *Reforma y Democracia*, 19: 1–31.

Barzelay, M. and Armajani, B. (1992) *Breaking Through Bureaucracy: A New Vision for Managing Government*. Berkeley: University of California Press.

Batley, R. (1999) *The Role of Government in Adjusting Economies: An Overview of Findings*. Birmingham: International Development Department, University of Birmingham.

Baumann, Z. (1993) *Postmodern Ethics*. Oxford: Basil Blackwell.

Baumol, W. J., Panzer, R., Willig, R. (1982) *Contestable Markets and the Theory of Industry Structures*. New York: Harcourt Brace Jovanovich.

Beall, J., Crankshaw, O. and Parnell, S. (2002) *Uniting a Divided City: Governance and Social Exclusion in Johannesburg*. London: Earthscan.

Beaumont, P. (1987) The government as a model employer: a change of direction in Britain? *Journal of Collective Negotiations in the Public Sector*, 16(3): 187–189.

Beck Jorgensen, T. and Bozeman, B. (2002) Public values lost? comparing cases on contracting out from Denmark and the United States. *Public Management Review*, 4(1): 63–81.

Becker, G. (1976) *The Economic Approach to Human Behavior*. Chicago: University of Chicago Press.

Beetham, D. Bracking, S. Kearton, I. and Weir, S. (2002) *International IDEA Handbook on Democracy Assessment*. The Hague: Kluwer Law International.

Belshaw, D. (2000) Decentralised governance and poverty reduction: relevant experience in Africa and Asia. In Collins, P. (ed.), *Applying Public Administration in Development: Guideposts to the Future*. Chichester: Wiley.

Bennell, P. (1997) Privatisation in sub-Saharan Africa: progress and prospects during the 1990s. *World Development*, 25(11): 1785–803.

Bennington, J. (2000) Editorial: The modernisation and improvement of government and public services. *Public Money and Management*, 3(8).

Bent, S., Kernaghan, K., and Marson, B. D. (1999) *Innovations and Good Practices in Single-Window Service*. Ottawa: Canadian Centre for Management Development.

Bird, R. and Rodriguez, E. R. (1999) Decentralisation and poverty alleviation: international experience and the case of the Philippines. *Public Administration and Development*, 19(3).

Blackburn, R. (2002) Symptoms of Euro-denial, *New Left Review*, 18: 131–140.

Block, F. (1990) *Postindustrial Possibilities: A Critique of Economic Discourse*. Berkeley: University of California Press.

Bollard, A. (ed.) (1988) *The Influence of United States Economics on New Zealand*. The Fulbright Anniversary Seminars, Research Monograph 42, Wellington: Institute of Economic Research.

Bollard, A. and Buckle, R. (eds) (1987) *Economic Liberalisation in New Zealand*.

Bolzan, N. and Gale, F. (2002) The citizenship of excluded groups: challenging the consumerist agenda, *Social Policy and Administration*, 36(4): 363–375.

Bond, P. (1992) Redlining Cuts off Jo'burg's Lifeblood. Weekly Mail, 17–23 April.

Bond, P. (2000) *Cities of Gold, Townships of Coal: Essays on South Africa's New Urban Crisis*. Trenton: Africa World Press.

Bond, P. (2002a) *Unsustainable South Africa: Environment, Development and Social Protest*. London: Merlin and Pietermaritzburg, University of Natal Press.

Bond, P. (2003) *Against Global Apartheid: South Africa meets the World Bank, IMF and International Finance*. Cape Town: University of Cape Town Press.

Bond, P. (2004) *Sustaining Global Apartheid: South Africa's Frustrated International Reforms*. London: Zed.

Bond, P. (ed.) (2002b) *Fanon's Warning: A Civil Society Reader on the New Partnership for Africa's Development*. Trenton: Africa World Press and Cape Town, AIDC.

Bond, P., McDonald, D. and Ruiters, G. (2001) *Water Privatisation in SADC Countries: The State of the Debate*. Municipal Services Project, http://www.queensu.ca/msp, October.

Booth, C. and Richardson, T. (2001) Placing the public in integrated transport planning. *Transport Policy*, 8(2): 141–149.

Bordogna, L., Dell'Aringa, C. and Della Rocca, G. (1999) Italy: a case of co-ordinated decentralisation. In Bach, S., Bordogna, L., Della Rocca, G. and Winchester, D. (eds), *Public Services Employment Relations in Europe*. London: Routledge.

Borgmann, A. (1992) *Crossing the Postmodern Divide*. Chicago: University of Chicago Press.

Borins, S. (1995) Public sector innovation: the implications of new forms of organisation and work. In Peters, G. and Savoie, D. (eds), *Governance in a Changing Environment*. Montreal: McGill-Queen's University Press.

Borins, S. (2000) New public management, Canadian style. In Barrows, D. and Macdonald, H. I. (eds), *The New Public Management: International Developments*. Toronto: Captus Press.

Borins, S. (2002a) New public management, north American style. In McLaughlin, K., Osborne, S., and Ferlie, E., *New Public Management: Current Trends and Future Prospects*. London: Routledge.

Borins, S. (2002b) Transformation of the public sector: Canada in comparative perspective. In Dunn, C. (ed.), *Handbook of Canadian Public Administration*. Toronto: Oxford University Press.

Boscarino, J., Alea, S., Ahern, J., Resnick, H., Vlahov, D. (2002) Health service #66 access to psychiatric services in New York City following the September 11th terrorist attacks, *Annals of Epidemiology*, 12(7): 514–514.

Bossert, T. (2000) *Privatization and Payments: Lessons for Poland from Chile and Colombia. International Health Systems Group*. Harvard School of Public Health.

Boston, J. and Dalziel, P. (eds), (1992) *The Decent Society? Essays in Response to National's Economic and Social Policies*. Auckland: Oxford University Press.

Boston, J., Dalziel, P. and St. John, S. (eds), (1999) *Redesigning the Welfare State in New Zealand: Problems, Policies, Prospects*. Auckland: Oxford University Press.

Boston, J., Martin, J., Pallot, J., and Walsh, P. (1996) *Public Management: The New Zealand Model*. Auckland: Oxford University Press.

Bovaird, T., Loeffler, E., and Martin, J. (2002) From corporate governance to local governance: stakeholder-driven community score-cards for UK local agencies? Paper presented to *British Academy of Management*. London, 9–11 September.

Bowie, N. (1991) Business ethics as a discipline: The search for legitimacy. In Freeman, R. (ed.), *Business Ethics: The State of the Art*. Oxford: Oxford University Press.

Bowman, J., Berman, E., and West, J. (2001) The profession of public administration: an ethics edge in introductory textbooks? *Public Administration Review*, 61(2): 194–205.

Boyer, R. (1991) New directions in management practices and work organisation: general principles and national trajectories. Revised draft of paper presented to OECD conference on *Technological Change as a Social Process*. Helsinki, 11–13 December.

Boyer, R. (2001) The great transformation of Eastern Europe: a regulationist perspective. In Jessop, B. (ed.), *Regulation Theory and the Crisis of Capitalism Volume 4 – Country Studies*. London: Edward Elgar.

Boyer, R. and Coriat, B. (1986) Technical flexibility and macro stabilisation. *Ricerche Economiche* XL (October–December): 771–835.

Boyer, R. and Hollingsworth, R. (1997) How and why do social systems of production change? In Hollingsworth, R. and Boyer, R. (eds), *Contemporary Capitalism: The Embeddedness of Institutions*. Cambridge: Cambridge University Press.

Boyer, R. and Orlean, A. (1991) Why are institutional transitions so difficult?, mimeograph CREA, prepared for the conference *L'Economie des Conventions*. Paris.

Boyne, G. (1996) Competition and local government: a public choice perspective, *Urban Studies*, 33(4–5): 703–721.

Boyne, G. (1999) Introduction: processes, performance and best value in local government. *Local Government Studies,* 25(2).

Boyne, G. (2000) External regulation and best value in local government. *Public Money and Management*, 20(3): 7–12.

Boyne, G., Day, P. and Walker, R. (2002) The evaluation of public service inspection: a theoretical framework. *Urban Studies*, 39(7): 1197–1212.

Boyne, G., Gould-Williams, J., Law, J. and Walker, R. (2002) Best value – total quality management for local government? *Public Money and Management*, 22(3): 9–16.

Braverman, H. (1974) Labor and Monopoly Capital. New York: Monthly Review Press.

Brennan, G. and Buchanan J. M. (1985) *The Reason of Rules: Constitutional Political Economy*. Cambridge: Cambridge University Press.

Brennan, G. (2001) Five rational actor accounts of the welfare state. *Kyklos* 54(2/3): 213–234.

Brennan, G. and Buchanan, J. M. (1980) *The Power to Tax: Analytical Foundations of a Fiscal Constitution*. Cambridge: Cambridge University Press.

Bresser Pereira, L. C. (1977) *Estado e Subdesenvolvimento Industrialisado*. São Paulo: Brasiliense.

Bresser Pereira, L. C. (1981) *A Sociedade Estatal e a Tecnoburocracia*. São Paulo: Brasiliense.

Bresser Pereira, L. C. (1999) From bureaucratic to managerial public administration. In Bresser Pereira, L. C. and Spink, P. (eds), *Reforming the State. Managerial Public Administration in Latin America*. Boulder, Colorado: Lynne Rienner Publishers.

Bresser Pereira, L. C. (1999) Managerial public administration: strategy and structure for a new state. In Bresser Pereira, L. C. and Spink, P. (eds), *Reforming the State: Managerial Public Administration in Latin America*. Boulder: Lynne Rienner Publishers.

Breton, A. and Wintrobe, R. (1982) *The Logic of Bureaucratic Conduct: An Economic Analysis of Competition, Exchange, and Efficiency in Private and Public Organizations.* Cambridge: Cambridge University Press.

Broadbent, J. and Laughlin, R. (2002) Public service professionals and the new public management. Control of the professions in the public services. In McLaughlin, K., Osbourne, S. and Ferlie, E. (eds), *New Public Management: Current Trends and Future Prospects.* London: Routledge.

Brook, K. (2002) Trade union membership: an analysis of data from the autumn 2001 LFS. *Labour Market Trends*, July.

Brooks, J. (2000) Labour's modernisation of local government. *Public Administration*, 78(3): 593–612.

Brown, C. (1997) Greater democracy, better decisions. *Consumer Policy Review*, 7(5): 170–173.

Brown, K., Ryan, N. and Parker, R. (2002) New modes of service delivery in the public sector – Commercialising government services. *The International Journal of Public Sector Management*, 13(3): 206–221.

Brown, W., Deakin, S., Nash, D. and Oxenbridge, S. (2000) The employment contract: from collective procedures to individual rights. *British Journal of Industrial Relations*, 38(4): 611–629.

Brown, W., Marginson, P. and Walsh, J. (2003) The management of pay as the influence of collective bargaining diminishes. In Edwards, P. (ed.), *Industrial Relations: Theory and Practice*, 2nd Edition. Oxford: Blackwell.

Bruijn, H. (2002) Performance measurement in the public sector: strategies to cope with the risks of performance measurement. *The International Journal of Public Sector Management*, 15(7): pp. 578–594.

Bruyn, S. T. (2000) *A Civil Economy: Transforming the Market in the Twenty-First Century.* Ann Arbor: University of Michigan Press.

Bryson, C., Jackson, M. and Leopold, J. (1995) The impact of self-governing trusts on trade unions and staff associations in the NHS. *Industrial Relations Journal*, 26(2): 120–133.

Bryson, J. and Anderson, G. (2003) Reconstructing state employment in New Zealand. In Pittard, M. and Weeks, P. (eds), *Rethinking Public Sector Employment in the 21st Century.* Forthcoming.

Buchanan, J. M. (1966) An individualistic theory of political process. In Easton, D. (ed.), *Varieties of Political Theory.* Englewood Cliffs: Prentice-Hall.

Buchanan, J. M. (1977) Why does government grow? In Borcherding, T. E. (ed.), *Budgets and Bureaucrats: The Sources of Government Growth.* Durham: Duke University Press.

Buchanan, J. M. and Tullock, G. (1962) *The Calculus of Consent.* Ann Arbor: Michigan University Press.

Buchanan, J. M. and Wagner, R. M. (1977) *Democracy in Deficit: The Political Legacy of Lord Keynes.* New York: Academic Press.

Buchanan, J. M., Rowley, C. K. *et al.*, (eds) (1987) *Deficits.* New York: Basil Blackwell.

Buckley, P. J. and Casson, M. (1993) Economics as an imperialist social science, *Human Relations*, 46(9): 1035–1052.

Budgen, S. (2002) Chirac redivivus, *New Left Review*, 2(17): 31–51.

Burns, T. and Stalker, G. (1994) *The Management of Innovation.* Revised Edition. New York: Oxford University Press.

Byrne, T. (1994) *Local Government in Britain: Everyone's Guide to How it All Works.* 6th edition. London: Penguin.

Campbell, J. L., Hollingsworth, J. R. and Lindberg, L. (eds) (1991) *The Governance of the American Economy.* Cambridge: Cambridge University Press.

Cardoso, F. H. (1999) Foreword. In Bresser Pereira, L. C. and Spink, P (eds), *Reforming the State. Managerial Public Administration in Latin America*. Boulder: Lynne Rienner Publishers.

Carter, B. and Poynter, G. (1999) Unions in a changing climate: MSF and UNISON experiences in the new public sector. *Industrial Relations Journal*, 30(5), 499–513.

Chandler, A. D. (1962) *Strategy and Structure*. Cambridge: MIT Press.

Chandler, A. D. (1977) *The Visible Hand: the Managerial Revolution in American Business*. Cambridge: Harvard University Press.

Chandler, A. D. (1990) *Scale and Scope: the Dynamics of Industrial Capitalism*. Cambridge: Harvard University Press.

Charich, M. and Daniels, A. (1997) Introduction: Canadian public administration at the crossroads. In Charich, M. and Daniels, A. (eds), *New Public Management and Public Administration in Canada*. Toronto: The Institute of Public Administration of Canada.

Charich, M. and Rouillard, L. (1997) The new public management. In Charich, M. and Daniels, A. (eds), *New Public Management and Public Administration in Canada*. Toronto: The Institute of Public Administration of Canada.

Chase-Dunn, C. (1989) *Global Formation: Structures of the World Economy*. Cambridge: Basil Blackwell.

Chiu, S. W. K. and Lui, T. L. (1998) The role of the state in economic development. In Thompson, G. (ed.), *Economic Dynamism in the Asia-Pacific*. London: Routledge.

CLAD (1998) *A New Public Management for Latin America*. Latin American Centre for Development Administration (www.clad.org.ve)

Clark, B. S. (1998) *Political Economy: A Comparative Approach*. Westport: Praeger.

Clarke, J. and Newman, J. (1997) *The Managerial State*. London: Sage.

Clarke, J., Cochrane, A. and McLaughlin, E. (1994) Mission accomplished or unfinished business? The impact of managerialisation. In Clarke, J., Cochrane, A. and McLaughlin, E. (eds), *Managing Social Policy*. London: Sage.

Clarke, M. (2001) Through a glass darkly: the case of local government, *The Public Management and Policy Association Review*, 14(August): 5–6.

Clarke, M. and Stewart, J. (1992) *Citizens and Local Democracy, Empowerment: a Theme for the 1990s*. London: Local Government Management Board.

Cloete, J. J. N. (1981) *An Introduction to Public Administration*. Pretoria: Van Schaik.

Cochrane, A. (1994) Managing change in local government. In Clarke, J., Cochrane, A. and McLaughlin, E. (eds), *Managing Social Policy*, London: Sage.

Cohen, S. (2001) A strategic framework for devolving responsibility and functions from government to the private sector, *Public Administration Review*, 61(4): 432–440.

Coleman, J. S. (1990) *Foundations of Social Theory*. Cambridge: Harvard University Press.

Coleman, W. D. (1997) Associational governance in a globalising era: Weathering the storm, in Hollingsworth, J. R. and Boyer, R. (eds), *Contemporary Capitalism: the Embeddedness of Institutions*. New York: Cambridge University Press.

Colling, T. (1993) Contracting public services: the management of competitive tendering in two county councils. *Human Resource Management Journal*, 3(4): 1–15.

Colling, T. (1999) Tendering and outsourcing: working in the contract state? In Corby, S. and White, G. (eds), *Employee Relations in the Public Sector*. London: Routledge.

Colling, T. (2000) Personnel management in the extended organisation. In Bach, S. and Sisson, K. (eds), *Personnel Management: a Comprehensive Guide to Theory and Practice* (3rd edition). Oxford: Blackwell.

Colling, T. and Ferner, A. (1995) Privatisation and marketisation. In Edwards, P. (ed.), *Industrial Relations: Theory and Practice in Britain* (1st edition). Oxford: Blackwell.

Common, R. (2001) *Public Management and Policy Transfer in Southeast Asia.* Aldershot: Ashgate.

Commonwealth Secretariat (2003) *Current Good Practices and New Developments in Public Service Management: Malaysia. The Public Service Country Profile Series No. 3.* London: Commonwealth Secretariat.

Cooper, T. L. (1990) *The Responsible Administrator: An Approach to Ethics for the Administrative Role*, (3rd edition). San Francisco: Jossey-Bass.

Cope, S. and Goodship, J. (2002) The Audit Commission and public service: delivering for whom? *Public Money and Management*, October–December: 33–40

Corby, S. (1998) Industrial relations in the civil service agencies: transition or transformation? *Industrial Relations Journal*, 29(3): 194–206.

Corby, S. and White, G. (1999) From the new right to new Labour. In Corby, S. and White, G (eds), *Employee Relations in the Public Services*. London: Routledge.

Corby, S. and White, G. (eds) (1999) *Employee Relations in the Public Services*. London: Routledge.

Cornia, G., Jolly, R. and Stewart, F. (eds) (1987) *Adjustment with a Human Face.* Oxford: Clarendon Press.

Crompton, R. and Jones, R. (1984) *White Collar Proletariat.* London: MacMillan

Crosby, P. (1979) *Quality is Free.* London: McGraw-Hill

Crouch, C. (1979) The state, capital and liberal democracy. In Crouch, C. (ed.), *State and Economy in Contemporary Capitalism*. London: Croom Helm.

Crouch, C. and Streeck, W. (eds) (1996) *Varieties of Capitalism.* London: Pinter.

Cully, M. and Woodland, S. (1997) Trade union membership and recognition. *Labour Market Trends*, June: 231–239.

Cully, M., Woodland, S., O'Reilly, A. and Dix, G. (2000) *Britain at Work: as depicted by the 1998 Employee Relations Survey.* London: Routledge.

Culpitt, I. (1999) *Social Policy and Risk.* London: Sage.

Cunha Rezende, F. de. (2002) Razões da crise de implementação do estado gerencial: desmpenho versus ajuste fiscal, *Revista de Sociologia e Politica*, (November).

Cutler, T. and Waine, B. (1997a) *Managing the Welfare State. Text and Sourcebook.* Place: Berg.

Cutler, T. and Waine, B. (1997b) The politics of quasi-markets. How quasi-markets have been analysed and how they might be analysed. *Critical Social Policy*, 17(2): 3–25

Dalziel, P. and Lattimore, R. (1999) *The New Zealand Macroeconomy: A Briefing on the Reforms.* (3rd edition). Greenlane: Oxford University Press.

David, P. A. (1988) Path-dependence: putting the past into the future of economics, Technical Report No. 533, November 1988, *The Economic Series, Institute for Mathematic Studies in the Social Sciences*, Stanford University.

Dawson, A. (2002) The problem with asylum-seeker dispersal: transitions, structures and myths, *Benefits: a Journal of Social Security, Research, Policy and Practice*, 33(10): 9–14.

Dawson, S. and Dargie, C. (2002) New public management: a discussion with special reference to UK health. In McClaughlin, K., Osborne, S. P. and Ferlie, E. (eds), *New Public Management: Current Trends and Future Prospects*. London: Routledge.

Deakin, N., Smith, P., Thomas, N. and Walsh, K. (1997) *Contracting for Change.* Buckingham: Open University Press.

Deakin, S. and Michie, J. (1997) The theory and practice of contracting. In Deakin, S. and Michie, J. (eds), *Contracts, Co-operation and Competition*. Oxford: Oxford University Press.

Delbridge, R. and Turnbull, P. (1992) Human resource maximisation: the management of labour under just-in-time manufacturing systems. In Blyton, P. and Turnbull, P. (eds), *Reassessing Human Resource Management*. London: Sage.

Deleuze, G. and Guattari, F. (1988) *A Thousand Plateaux*. Minneapolis: University of Minnesota Press.

Deming, W. E. (1986) *Out of the Crisis*. Cambridge: Cambridge University Press.

Denhardt, R. (1999) *The Future of Public Administration: Challenges to Democracy, Citizenship, and Ethics*. pamij.com/99_4_2_Denhardt.

Denhardt, R. and Denhardt, J. (2000) The new public service: serving rather than steering. *Public Administration Review*, 60(6): 549–559.

Desai, A. (2002) *We are the Poors: Community Struggles in Post-Apartheid South Africa*. New York: Monthly Review Press.

DETR (1999) *Local Government Act*. London: Department for the Environment, Transport and the Regions.

DoE (1991) *Competing for Quality: Competition in the Provision of Local Services – A Consultation Paper*. London: Department of the Environment.

Dolowitz, D. and Marsh, D. (1998) Policy transfer: a framework for comparative analysis. In Minogue, M., Polidano, C. and Hume, D. (eds), *Beyond the New Public Management: Changing Ideas and Practices in Governance*. Cheltenham: Edward Elgar.

Domberger, S. and Jensen, P. (1997) Contracting out by the public sector: theory, evidence, prospects, *Oxford Review of Economic Policy*, 13(4): 67–78.

Doner, R. and Schneider, B. (2000) The New Institutional Economics. *Business Associations and Development*. Geneva: ILO.

Douglas, R. (1993) *Unfinished Business*. Auckland: Random House.

Downs, A. (1957) *An Economic Theory of Democracy*. New York: Harper and Row.

DuGay, P. (1994) Making up managers: bureaucracy, enterprise and the liberal art of separation. *British Journal of Sociology*, 45(4): 655–674.

DuGay, P. (1996a) *Consumption and Identity at Work*. London: Sage.

DuGay, P. (1996b) Organising identity: entrepreneurial governance and public management. In Hall, S. and DuGay, P. (eds), *Questions of Cultural Identity*. London: Sage.

DuGay, P. and Salaman, G. (1992) The cult(ure) of the customer. *Journal of Management Studies*, 29(5): 615–633.

Duncan, C. (2001) The impact of two decades of reform of British public sector industrial relations. *Public Money and Management*, 21(1): 27–34.

Dunleavy, P. (1991) *The Bureau-Shaping Model: Democracy, Bureaucracy and Public Choice*, London: Harvester Wheatsheaf. Reprinted in Osborne, S. (ed.), *Public Management: Critical Perspectives*, Vol. 1. London: Routledge, 2002.

Dunleavy, P. and Hood, C. (1994) From old public administration to new public management. *Public Money and Management*, 14(3): 9–16.

Dunleavy, P. and O'Leary, B. (1987) *Theories of the State: The Politics of Liberal Democracy*. London: MacMillan.

Easton, B. (1994) How did the health reforms blitzkrieg fail? *Political Science*, 46(2): 215–33.

Economic Commission for Latin America and the Caribbean (2000) *Equity, Development and Citizenship*. Mexico-City: CEPAL.

Eden, L. and Hampson, F. O. (1997) Clubs are trump: the formation of international regimes in the absence of a hegemon. In Hollingsworth, J. R. and Boyer, R. (eds), *Contemporary Capitalism: the Embeddedness of Institutions*. New York and Cambridge: Cambridge University Press.

Edwards, P. (ed.) (1995) *Industrial Relations: Theory and Practice* (1ˢᵗ edition). Oxford: Blackwell.

Edwards, P. (ed.) (2003) *Industrial Relations: Theory and Practice* (2nd edition). Oxford: Blackwell.

Edwards, P., Collinson, M. and Rees, C. (1998) The determinants of employee responses to quality management: six case studies. *Organisation Studies*, 19(3): 449–476.

Ekelund, R. B. Jr. and Tollison, R. D. (1986) *Microeconomics*. Boston: Little Brown.

Elam, M. (1992) *Markets, Morals, and Powers of Innovation*, unpublished paper presented to the School for Workers, University of Wisconsin: Madison, 6 April.

Elayan, F., Lau, J. and Meyer, T. (2000) Executive incentive compensation schemes and their impact on corporate performance: evidence from New Zealand since legal disclosure requirements became effective. *Working Paper Series 00.22. Department of Commerce, College of Business, Albany*: Massey University, October.

Engberg-Pedersen, L. (1999) *An Analysis of the Poverty Orientation of Current Danish Policies*. Copenhagen: Centre for Development Research.

Escott, K. and Whitfield, D. (1995) *The Gender Impact of CCT in Local Government*. Manchester: Equal Opportunities Commission.

Etzioni, A. (1988) *The Moral Dimension: Towards a New Economics*. New York: Free Press.

Etzioni, A. (2003) Toward a socio-economic paradigm, *Socio-Economic Review*, 1(1): 105–118.

Evensky, J. (2001) Adam Smith's Lost Legacy. *Southern Economic Journal*, 67(3): 497–517.

Fairbrother, P. (2000) *Trade Unions at the Crossroads*. London: Mansell.

Farazmand, A. (1994) The new world order and global public administration. In Garcia-Zamor, J. C. and Khator, R. (eds), *Public Administration in the Global Village*. Westport: Praeger.

Farazmand, A. (2002) Globalisation, privatisation and the future of modern governance: A critical assessment. *Public Finance and Management*, 2(1): 125–153.

Farnham, D. and Horton, S. (1992) Human resources management in the new public sector: leading or following private employer practice? *Public Policy and Administration*, 7(3): 42–55.

Faro de Castro, M. and Valladão de Carvallo, M. I. (2002) Globalização e transformações políticas recentes no Brasil. *Revista de Sociología e Política*, 108: 109–129.

Ferlie, E., Ashburner, L., Fitzgerald, L. and Pettigrew, A. (1996) *The New Public Management in Action*. Oxford: Oxford University Press.

Ferner, A. (1994) The state as employer. In Hyman, R. and Ferner, A. (eds), *New Frontiers in European Industrial Relations*. Oxford: Blackwell.

Financial and Fiscal Commission (1997) *Local Government in a System of Intergovernmental Fiscal Relations in South Africa: A Discussion Document*. Midrand.

Fine, B. (1999) A question of economics: is it colonising the social sciences? *Economy and Society*, 28(3): 403–425.

Fiorina, M. P. (2002) Rational choice in politics. In Smelser, N. J. and Baltes, P. B. (eds), *International Encyclopedia of the Social and Behavioral Sciences*. Amsterdam: Elsevier.

Fiszbein, A. (2000) Public private partnerships as a strategy for local capacity-building: some suggestive evidence from Latin America. In Collins, P. (ed.), *Applying Public Administration in Development: Guideposts to the Future*. Chichester: Wiley.

Fleury, S. (1999) Reforma del estado en América Latina. Hacia donde? *Nueva Sociedad*, 160: 58–80.

Fligstein, N. (2001) *The Architecture of Markets: An Economic Sociology of Twenty-First-Century Capitalist Societies*. Princeton: Princeton University Press.

Florida, R. and Kenney, M. (1991) Transplanted organisations: the transfer of Japanese industrial organisation to the US. *American Sociological Review*, 56: 381–398.

Flynn, N. (1994) Control, commitment and contracts. In Clarke, J., Cochrane, A. and McLaughlin, E. (eds), *Managing Social Policy*. London: Sage.

Flynn, N. (1996) The United Kingdom. In Flynn, N. and Strehl, F. (eds), *Public Sector Management in Europe*. Hemel Hampstead: Prentice Hall.

Flynn, N. (2002) Explaining the NPM: the importance of context. In McLaughlin, K., Osborne, S. and Ferlie, E. *New Public Management: Current Trends and Future Prospects*. London: Routledge.

Flynn, N. and Strehl, F. (1996a) France. In Flynn, N. and Strehl, F. (eds), *Public Sector Management in Europe*. Hemel Hampstead: Prentice Hall.

Flynn, N. and Strehl, F. (1996b) Introduction. In Flynn, N. and Strehl, F. (eds), *Public Sector Management in Europe*. Hemel Hampstead: Prentice Hall.

Ford, R. and Zussman, D. (1997) Alternative service delivery: transcending boundaries. In Ford. R. and Zussman, D. (eds), *Alternative Service Delivery: Sharing Governance in Canada*. Toronto: Institute of Public Administration of Canada.

Foster, D. and Scott, P. (1998) Conceptualising union responses to contracting out municipal services. *Industrial Relations Journal*, 29(2): 137–150.

Foucault, M. (1988) The political technology of individuals. In Martin, L., Gutman, H. and Hutton, P. (eds), *Technologies of the Self: A Seminar with Michel Foucault*. Amherst: University of Massachusetts Press.

Frances, J., Levacic, R., Mitchell, J. and Thompson, G. (1991) Introduction. In Thompson, G., Frances, J., Levacic, R. and Mitchell, J. (eds), *Markets, Hierarchies and Networks: The Coordination of Social Life*. London: Sage.

Fredman, S. and Morris, G. (1989) *The State as Employer: Labour Law in the Public Services*. London: Mansell.

Friedland, R. and Robertson, A. F. (eds) (1990) *Beyond the Marketplace: Rethinking Economy and Society*. New York: Aldine de Gruyter.

Friedman, J. (ed.). (1996) *The Rational Choice Controversy*. New Haven: Yale University Press.

Friedman, M. (1997) The social responsibility of business is to increase its profits. In Beauchamp, T. and Bowie, N. (eds), *Ethical Theory and Business*. Upper Saddle River: Prentice Hall.

Fukuyama, F. (1992) *The End of History and the Last Man*. New York: Free Press.

Gasper, D. (2000) As others see us: Institute of Social Studies, The Hague. In Theron, F. and Schwella, E. (eds), *Public and Development Management*. Bellville: University of Stellenbosch.

Gaster, L. (1995) *Quality in Public Services: Managers' Choices*. Buckingham: Open University Press.

Gauld, R. (2001) *Revolving Doors: New Zealand's Health Reforms*. Wellington: Institute of Policy Studies and Health Services Research Centre, Victoria University of Wellington.

Geddes, M. (2000) Tackling social exclusion in the European Union? The limits to the new orthodoxy of local partnership. *International Journal of Urban and Regional Research*, 24(4): 782–800.

Gerschenkron, A. (1962) *Economic Backwardness in Historical Perspective*. Cambridge: Harvard University Press.

Gibbs, A. (2001) Partnership between the probation service and voluntary sector organisations. *British Journal of Social Work*, 31: 15–27.

Gibelman, M. and Gelman, S. (2002) Should we have faith in faith-based social services? Rhetoric versus realistic expectations. *Nonprofit Management and Leadership*, 13(1): 49–65.

Gilmour, R. and Jensen, L. (1998) Reinventing government accountability: public functions, privatisation and the meaning of 'state action'. *Public Administration Review*, 58(3): 247–57.

Gilpin, R. (1987) *The Political Economy of International Relations*. Princeton: Princeton University Press.

Goldfinch, S. (1998) Remaking New Zealand's economic policy: institutional elites as radical innovators 1984–1993. *Governance*, 11(2): 177–207.

Goldfinch, S. (2000) *Remaking Australian and New Zealand Economic Policy*. Wellington: Victoria University Press.

Goldsmith, A. (1999) Africa's overgrown state reconsidered: bureaucracy and economic growth. *World Politics*, 51: 520–46.

Goldthorpe, J. H. (2000) *On Sociology: Numbers, Narratives, and the Integration of Research and Theory*. Oxford: Oxford University Press.

Goss, S. (2001) *Making Local Governance Work: Networks, Relationships and the Management of Change*. Basingstoke: Palgrave.

Government of Ireland (2000) *Supporting Voluntary Activity*. Stationery Office, Dublin.

Grabher, G. (ed.) (1993) *The Embedded Firm: on the Socioeconomics of Industrial Networks*. London: Routledge.

Graham H, (2000) *Modern China*. London: Penguin Books.

Graham H. (2001) *Buried Treasure: a Study of a Social Services Complaints Procedure*, unpublished MSc dissertation, South Bank University Business, London.

Grant, W. (1997) 'Perspectives on globalisation and economic coordination'. In Hollingsworth, J. R. and Boyer, R. (eds), *Contemporary Capitalism: the Embeddedness of Institutions*. New York: Cambridge University Press.

Graves, F. (1995) *Rethinking Government 94: an Overview and Synthesis*. Ottawa: Ekos Research Associates.

Graves, F. (1999) Rethinking government as if people mattered: from 'Reaganomics' to Humanomics. In Pal, L. (ed.) *How Ottawa Spends 1999–2000*. Toronto: University of Toronto Press: 37–74.

Greater Johannesburg Metropolitan Council (1999) *Igoli 2002 Conceptual Framework*. Johannesburg.

Green, D. P. and Shapiro, I. (1994) *Pathologies of Rational Choice Theory*. New Haven: Yale University Press.

Gregory, R. (1995) The peculiar tasks of public management: toward conceptual discrimination. *Australian Journal of Public Administration*, 54(2): 171–183.

Gregory, R. (2000) Getting better but feeling worse? Public sector reform in New Zealand. *International Public Management Journal*, 3(1): 107–123.

Gregory, R. (2002a) New Zealand: The end of egalitarianism? In Hood, C. and Peters, B. G. (eds), *Reward for High Public Office: Asian and Pacific Rim States*. London: Routledge.

Gregory, R. (2002b) All the king's horses and all the king's men: Putting New Zealand's public sector together again. In proceedings from the *International Political Science Association Committee, Structure and Organisation of Government Research Conference, Knowledge, Networks and Joined-Up Government*. Centre for Public Policy, University of Melbourne.

Grusky, S. (2001) *IMF Forces Privatization on Poor Countries. Globalization Challenge Initiative, www.nadir.org/nadir/initiativ/agp/free/imf/water.htm*

Grzybowski, C. (1999) Desmantelar, desmontar, refundar. Contradicciones e impasses en las reformas del estado. *Nueva Sociedad*, 160: 172–180.

Guess, G. (1997) Transformation of bureaucratic states in Eastern Europe: public expenditure lessons from Latin America. *International Journal of Public Administration*, 20(3).

Habermas, J. (1975) *Legitimation Crisis*. Boston: Beacon Press.

Håkansson, H. and Lundgren, A. (1997) Paths in time and space – path dependence in industrial networks. In Magnusson, L. and Ottosson, J. (eds), *Evolutionary Economics and Path Dependence*. Cheltenham: Edward Elgar.

Halachmi, A. (2002) Performance measurement, accountability, and improved performance. *Public Performance and Management Review*, 25(4): 370–374.

Halligan, J. (1997) New public sector models: Reform in Australia and New Zealand. In Lane, J. E. (ed.), *Public Sector Reform: Rationale, Trends, and Problems*. London: Sage.

Hammergreen, L. (1983) *Development and the Politics of Administrative Reform. Lessons from Latin America*. Boulder: Westview Press.

Haque, M. S. (2001) The diminishing publicness of public service under the current mode of governance, *Public Administration Review*, 61(1): 65–82.

Harcourt, M. and Wood, G. (2003) Under what circumstances do social accords work? *Journal of Economic Issues*. 37(3), 747–767.

Harrison, P., Huchzermayer, M. and Mayekiso, M. (eds), (2003) *Confronting Fragmentation: Housing and Urban Development in a Democratising Society*. Cape Town: University of Cape Town Press.

Harrow, J. (2001) 'Capacity building' as a public management goal: myth, magic or the main chance? *Public Management Review*, 3(2): 209–230.

Harrow, J. (2002) New public management and social justice: just efficiency or equity as well? In McLaughlin, K., Osborne, S. and Ferlie, E., *New Public Management: Current Trends and Future Prospects*. London: Routledge.

Harvey, D. (2001) *Spaces of Capital*. New York: Routledge.

Harvey, E. (2003) *A Critical Analysis of the Decision to Corporatise the Water and Wastewater Services in the City of Johannesburg*. Masters Dissertation, University of the Witwatersrand Graduate School of Public and Development Management, Johannesburg.

Hastings, A. (1996) Unravelling the process of 'partnership' in urban regeneration policy, *Urban Studies*, 33(2): 253–268.

Hayek, F. (1984) Equality, value, and merit. In Sandel, M. (ed.), *Liberalism and its Critics*. Oxford: Blackwell.

Hayes, T. (2002) The non profit sector, government and business: partners in the dance of change – an Irish perspective. *Public Management Review*, 4(2): 257–264.

Hechter, M. (2004) Toward a sociological rational choice theory. In van den Berg, A. and Meadwall, H. (eds). *The Social Sciences and Rationality: Promise, Limits and Problems*. New Brunswick: Transactions.

Hechter, M. and Kanazawa, S. (1997) Sociological rational choice theory. *Annual Review of Sociology*, 23: 191–214.

Heclo, H. (2002) The spirit of public administration. *Political Science and Politics*, 34(4): 689–694.

Heery, E. (1998) A return to contract? Performance related pay in a public service. *Work, Employment and Society*, 12(1): 73–95.

Held, D. (1996) *Models of Democracy* (2nd edition). Oxford: Polity.

Hennig, R. (2001) *IMF forces African Countries to Privatise Water*. 8 February (http://www.afrol.com).

Herrigel, G. (1995) *Industrial Constructions: the Sources of German Industrial Power*. New York: Cambridge University Press.

Hibou, B. (2002) The World Bank: missionary deeds (and misdeeds). In Schraeder, P. (ed.), *Exporting Democracy: Rhetoric vs. Reality*. Boulder: Lynne Rienner.

Higgins, P. and Roper, I. (2002) No room for manoeuvre: does 'best value' provide a better deal for workers in UK local government? *Society in Transition*, 33(2): 266–277.

Hills, J. (1995) *Inquiry into Income and Wealth. Volume Two*. London: Joseph Rowntree Foundation.

Hirsch, P., Michaels, S. *et al.* (1990) Clean models vs. dirty hands: why economics is different from sociology. In Zukin, S. and DiMaggio, P. (eds), *Structures of Capital: The Social Organization of the Economy*. Cambridge: Cambridge University Press.

Hirst, P. and Thompson, G. (1994) *Globalisation in Question: the International Economy and Possibilities for Governance*. Cambridge: Polity Press.

Hirst, P. and Thompson, G. (1997) Globalisation in question: international economic relations and forms of public governance. In Hollingsworth, J. R. and Boyer, R. (eds), *Contemporary Capitalism: the Embeddedness of Institutions*. New York: Cambridge University Press.

Hirst, P. and Zeitlin, J. (1997) Flexible specialisation: theory and evidence in the analysis of institutional change. In Hollingsworth, J. R. and Boyer, R. (eds), *Contemporary Capitalism: The Embeddedness of Institutions*. Cambridge: Cambridge University Press.

Hirst, P. and Zeitlin, P. (1991) Flexible specialisation versus post-Fordism: 'theory, evidence, and policy implications'. *Economy and Society*, 20(1) 1–49.

Hix, S. (1998) The study of the European Union II: the new governance. *Journal of European Public Policy*, 5(1): 36–38.

Hobsbawm, E. (1994) *The Age of Extremes: a History of the World, 1914–1991*, New York: Vintage.

Hoggett, P. and Hambleton, R. (eds) (1987) *Decentralisation and Democracy: Localising Public Services*. Bristol: School for Advanced Urban Studies.

Holiday, I. (1991) The new suburban right in British local government – Conservative views of the local. *Local Government Studies*. 17(4): 5–62.

Hollingsworth, J. R. (1991a) The logic of coordinating American manufacturing sectors. In Campbell, J. L., Hollingsworth, J. R. and Lindberg, L. (eds), *The Governance of the American Economy*. New York: Cambridge University Press.

Hollingsworth, J. R. (1991b) Die logik der koordination des verarbeitenden gewerbs in Amerika, *Kölner Zeitschrift für Sociologie und Socialpsychologie*, 43: 18–43.

Hollingsworth, J. R. and Boyer, R. (eds) (1997) *Contemporary Capitalism: the Embeddedness of Institutions*. New York: Cambridge University Press.

Hollingsworth, J. R. and Lindberg, L. (1985) The governance of the American economy: the role of markets, clans, hierarchies, and associative behaviour. In Streeck, W. and Schmitter, P. C. (eds), *Private Interest Government: Beyond Market and State*. London: Sage.

Hollingsworth, J. R. and Streeck, W. (1994) Countries and sectors: performance, convergence and competitiveness. In Hollingsworth, J. R., Schmitter, P. and Streeck, W. (eds), *Governing Capitalist Economies: Performance and Control of Economic Sectors*. New York: Oxford University Press.

Hollingsworth, J. R., Schmitter, P. and Streeck, W. (eds) (1994) *Governing Capitalist Economies: Performance and Control of Economic Sectors*. New York: Oxford University Press.

Hollingsworth, R. (1997) Continuities and change in social systems of production. In Hollingsworth, R. and Boyer, R. (eds), *Contemporary Capitalism: The Embeddedness of Institutions*. Cambridge: Cambridge University Press.

Holman, O. (2001) Semiperipheral Fordism in southern Europe. In Jessop, B. (ed.), *Regulation Theory and the Crisis of Capitalism Volume 4 – Country Studies*. London: Edward Elgar.

Holmes, S. (1990) The secret history of self-interest. In Mansbridge, J. J. (ed.), *Beyond Self-Interest*. Chicago: University of Chicago Press.

Hood, C. (1991) A public management for all seasons? *Public Administration*, 69(1): 3–19.

Hope, K. and Chikulo, B. (2000) Decentralisation, the new public management, and the changing role of the public sector in South Africa. *Public Management: An International Journal of Research and Theory*, 2(1), 25–42.

Horn, M. (1995) *The Political Economy of Public Administration: Institutional Choice in the Public Sector*. New York: Cambridge University Press.

Hounshell, D. A. (1984) *From the American System to Mass Production, 1800–1932*. Baltimore: Johns Hopkins University Press.

Hughes, O. (2003) *Public Management and Administration: An Introduction* (3rd Edition) Basingstoke: Palgrave.

Huntingdon, S. (1968) *Political Order in Changing Societies*. London: Yale University Press.

Hyman, R. and Ferner, A. (eds), (1994) *New Frontiers in European Industrial Relations*. Oxford: Blackwell.

IADB (2000a) *Beyond the Washington Consensus*. Washington DC: Inter-American Development Bank.

IADB (2000b) *Development Beyond Economics. Economic and Social Progress in Latin America. Report*. Washington DC: Inter-American Development Bank, IADB.

IIAS (2002) *Shared Governance: Combating Poverty and Exclusion*. Brussels: International Institute of Administrative Sciences.

ILPES (1995) *Reforma y Modernización del Estado*. Santiago de Chile: Instituto Latinoamericano del Caribe, de Planificación Economica of Social.

Industrial Relations Services (1997) Historic single-status deal in local government. *Employment Trends*, 639: 5–10.

Ingham, G. (1996) Critical survey: Some recent changes in the relationship between economics and sociology. *Cambridge Journal of Economics*, 20: 243–275.

Ives, D. (1998) Issues concerning the use of 'agencies' in the public sector. Paper presented to *Reform of Public Administration* seminar, February 4, Riga, Latvia.

James, C. (2002) *The Tie That Binds: The Relationship Between Ministers and Chief Executives*. Wellington: Institute of Policy Studies, Victoria University of Wellington.

Jasper, B. (2000) *The Chinese*. London: John Murray.

Jessop, B. (2001) Series preface. In Jessop, B. (ed.), *Regulation Theory and the Crisis of Capitalism Volume 3: Regulationist Perspectives on Fordism and Post Fordism*. Cheltenham: Edward Elgar.

Jodar, P., Jordana, J. and Alós, R. (1999) Spain: public service employment since the transformation to democracy. In Bach, S., Bordogna, L., Della Rocca, G. and Winchester, D. (eds), *Public Services Employment Relations in Europe*. London: Routledge.

Johannesburg (2001a) *Budget 2001–2002: City Development Plan 2001/2002*. Johannesburg.

Johannesburg (2001b) *Johannesburg Metropolitan Council Attitude Survey*. Johannesburg.

Johannesburg Water (2001) *Business Plan*. Johannesburg.

Joldersma, C. and Winter, V. (2002) Strategic management in hybrid organisations, *Public Management Review*, 4(1): 83–10.

Jones, A. (2001) Social responsibility and the utilities, *Journal of Business Ethics*, 3(4): 219–229.

Jones, G. and Ward, P. (1994) The World Bank's 'new' urban management programme: paradigm shift or policy continuity? *Habitat International*, 18(3), 33–51.

Juran, J. (1990) *Juran on Planning for Quality*. London: Collier MacMillan.

Kaye, D. (1995) The importance of information. *Management Decision*, 33(5): 5–12.

Kearney, R. and Hays, S. (1998) Reinventing government, the new public management and civil service systems in international perspective: the danger of throwing the baby out with the bathwater. *Review of Public Personnel Administration*, 18(4): 38–54.

Keller, B. (1999) Germany: negotiated change, modernisation, and the challenge of unification. In Bach, S., Bordogna, L., Della Rocca, G. and Winchester, D. (eds), *Public Services Employment Relations in Europe*. London: Routledge.

Kelsey, J. (1995) *The New Zealand Experiment: A World Model for Structural Adjustment?* Auckland: Auckland University Press/Bridget Williams Books.

Kemp, P., Dean, J. and Mackay, D. (2002) *Child Poverty in Social Inclusion Partnerships, Scottish Executive Central Research Unit*. Edinburgh: Stationery Office.

Kendall, J. (2001) Of knights, knaves and merchants: the case of residential care for older people in England in the late 1990s, *Social Policy and Administration*, 35(4): 360–375.

Kennedy, P. (1987) *The Rise and Fall of the Great Powers: Economic Change and Military Conflict from 1500 to 2000*. New York: Random House.

Kenney, M. and Florida, R. (1988) Beyond mass production and the labor process in Japan, *Politics and Society*, 16: 121–58.

Kenney, M. and Florida, R. (1993) *Beyond Mass Production: the Japanese System and its Transfer to the US*. New York: Oxford University Press.

Keohane, R. (1984) *After Hegemony: Cooperation and Discord in the World Political Economy*. Princeton: Princeton University Press.

Kettle, D. F. (1998) The global revolution: reforming government-sector management. In *Reforming the State. Managerial Public Administration in Latin America*. Boulder: Lynne Rienner Publishers.

Khan, M. M. (1998) Good governance: the case of Bangladesh. *African Journal of Public Administration and Management*, 10(16).

Kickert, W. (1993) Autopoiesis and the science of public administration: essence, sense and nonsense. *Organizational Studies*, 14(2): 61–78.

Kiggundu, M. (1998) Civil-service reforms: limping into the twenty-first century. In Minogue, M., Polidano, C. and Hume, D. (eds), *Beyond the New Public Management: Changing Ideas and Practices in Governance*. Cheltenham: Edward Elgar.

Kim, J., Shakow, A. and Bayona, J. (1999) The privatisation of health care in Peru. *Development*, 42(4): 121–125.

Kindleberger, C. P. (1978) *Manias, Panics, and Crashes: a History of Financial Crises*. New York: Basic Books.

Kirkpatrick, I. and Martinez-Lucio, M. (1995) The uses of 'quality' in the British government's reform of the public sector. In Kirkpatrick, I. and Martinez-Lucio, M. (eds), *The Politics of Quality in the Public Sector*. London: Routledge.

Klinenberg, E. (2001) Dying alone: The social production of urban isolation, *Ethnography*, 2(4): 501–531.

Knickman, J. R. and Snell, E. K. (2002) The 2030 problem: caring for ageing baby boomers, *Health Services Research*, 37(4): 849–884.

Knights, D. (1990) Subjectivity, power and the labour process. In Knights, D. and Wilmott, H. (eds), *Labour Process Theory*. Basingstoke: MacMillan.

Kraft, K. (1998) An evaluation of active and passive labour market policy. *Applied Economics*, 30: 783–793.

Kuitenbrouwer, M. (1996) The Netherlands. In Flynn, N. and Strehl, F. (eds), *Public Sector Management in Europe*. Hemel Hampstead: Prentice Hall.

Lam, N. M. K. (2000) Government intervention in the economy: a comparative analysis of Singapore and Hong Kong. *Public Administration and Development*, 20(5): 397–421.

Lamsa, A. M. (1999) Organisational downsizing – an ethical versus managerial viewpoint. *Leadership and Organizational Development Journal*, 20(7): 345–353.

Land, A. (2002) *Placing Technical Cooperation at the Service of Capacity Development: Emerging Lessons*. In Capacity. Org. Maastricht: ECDPM.

Land, A. (2002) *Taking Charge of Technical Cooperation. Experience from Botswana: a Case of a Country in the Driver's Seat*. Maastricht: ECDPM.

Lane, J. E. (2000) *New Public Management*. London: Routledge.

Lansey, S., Goss, S. and Wolmar, C. (1989) *Councils in Conflict: The Rise and Fall of the Municipal Left*. London: MacMillan.

Larbi, G. (1998) Management decentralisation in practice: a comparison of public health and water services in Ghana. In Minogue, M., Polidano, C. and Hume, D. (eds), *Beyond the New Public Management: Changing Ideas and Practices in Governance*. Cheltenham: Edward Elgar.

Larbi, G. (1998) *The New Public Management Approach and Crisis States*. Geneva: UNRISD.

Lazonick, W. and O'Sullivan, M. (2000) Maximising shareholder value: a new ideology for corporate governance. *Economy and Society*, 29(1): 13–35.

Leach, S., Stewart, J. and Walsh, K. (1994) *The Changing Organisation and Management of Local Government*. MacMillan Press Ltd: Hampshire.

Leadbeater, C. and Goss, S. (1998) *Civic Entrepreneurship*. London: Demos and the Public Management Foundation.

Lechner, N. (1998) La reforma del Estado y el problema de la conducción política. In Revesz, B. (ed) *Descentralización of Gobernabilidad en Tiempos de Globalización*. Lima: Instituto de Estudios Peruanos.

LeGrand, J. (1990) *Quasi markets and Social Policy. Studies in Decentralisation and Quasi-Markets No. 1*. Bristol: SAUS, University of Bristol.

LeGrand, J. (1997) Knights, knaves or pawns? Human behaviour and social policy. *Journal of Social Policy*, 26(2): 149–169.

Levacic, R. (1995) *Local Management of Schools: Analysis and Practice*. Buckingham: Open University Press.

Levine, S. B. and Ohtsu, M. (1991) Transplanting Japanese labour relations. *The Annals of the American Academy of Political and Social Science*, 513 (January): 102–16.

Lewin, L. (1991) *Self-Interest and Public Interest in Western Politics*. Oxford: Oxford University Press.

LGMB (1994) *Quality Initiatives: Directory of Local Government Activity*. London: Local Government Management Board.

LGMB (1995) *Quality Initiatives: Directory of Local Government Activity*. London: Local Government Management Board.

LGMB (1996) *Quality Initiatives: Directory of Local Government Activity*. London: Local Government Management Board.

Light, J. (2000) The World Bank takes more than it gives; an interview on healthcare privatisation in India with Dr. Vineeta Gupta. *CorpWatch*, April 14.

Lipietz, A. (2001) Geography, Ecology, Democracy. In Jessop, B. (ed.), *Regulation Theory and the Crisis of Capitalism Volume 5*. London: Edward Elgar.

Lipson, L. (1948) *The Politics of Equality: New Zealand's Adventures in Democracy*. Chicago: University of Chicago Press.

Liu, J. and Mackinnon, A. (2002) Comparative management practices and training: China and Europe. *Journal of Management Development*, 20(2): 118–132.

Loewe, M. (1990) *The Pride That Was China*. London: Sidgwick and Jackson.

Loffler, E. (2002) in Schedler, K. and Proeller, I. (2002) (ed.), The new public management: a perspective from mainland Europe. In McLaughlin, K., Osborne, S., and Ferlie, E. (eds), *New Public Management: Current Trends and Future Prospects*. Routledge: London.

Logan, M. (2003) Multinationals ride wave of water privatisation. *OneWorld US*, 4 February.

Lonti, Z. and Verma, A. (2003) The Determinants of flexibility and innovation in the government workplace: Recent evidence from Canada. *Journal of Public Administration Research and Theory*, 13(3): 283–309.

Lonti, Z., Slinn, S. and Verma, A. (2002) Can government workplaces be made world-class? Policy challenges for labour and management. *Canadian Labour and Employment Law Journal*, 9(3): 335–359.

Lowndes, V. (1997) Change in public service management: new institutions and new managerial regimes. *Local Government Studies*, 23(2): 42–66.

Lowndes, V. (1998) The dynamics of multi-organisational partnerships: an analysis of changing modes of governance. *Public Administration*, 76(3): 313–333.

Lowndes, V., Pratchett, I. and Stoker, G. (2001a) Trends in public participation: part 1 – local government perspectives. *Public Administration*, 79(1): 205–222.

Lucas, J. (1976) *Democracy and Participation*. London: Penguin.

Lupton, B. S., Fonnebe, V., Sogaard, A. J. and Langfeldt, E. (2002) The Finnmark Intervention Study: Better health for the fishery population in an Artic village in North Norway, *Scandinavian Journal of Primary Health Care*, 20: 213–218.

Lynch, M. (1996) *China From Empire to People's Republic 1900–49*. London: Hodder and Stoughton.

Lynne, L. (1997) The new public management as an international phenomenon: a skeptical view. Reprinted in Osborne, S. (2002) (ed.), *Public Management: Critical Perspectives*. London: Routledge.

Mackerras, C., Taneja, P. and Young, G. (1998) *China Since 1978: Reform, Modernisation and Socialism with Chinese Characteristics*. Harlow: Longman.

Mackintosh, M. (1998) Public management for social inclusion. In Minogue, M., Polidano, C. and Hulme, D., *Beyond the New Public Management: Changing Ideas and Practices in Governance*. Cheltenham: Edward Elgar.

Maddock, S. (2000) Managing the development of partnerships in Health Action Zones, *International Journal of Health Care Quality Assurance*, 13(2): 65–73.

Maddock, S. (2002) Making modernisation work: new narratives, change strategies and people management in the public sector. *International Journal of Public Sector Management*, 15(1): 13–43.

Magnusson, L. and Ottosson, J. (eds) (1997) *Evolutionary Economics and Path Dependence*. Cheltenham: Edward Elgar.

Manning, N. (2000) *The New Public Management and its Legacy*. www1.worldbank.org/publicsector/civilservice/debate1, submitted 10/3/00.

Mansbridge, J. J. (ed.) (1990) *Beyond Self-Interest*. Chicago: University of Chicago Press.

Maor, M. (1999) The paradox of managerialism. *Public Administration Review*, 59(1): 5–18.

Marsden, D. and Richardson, R. (1994) Performing for pay? The effects of merit pay. *British Journal of Industrial Relations*, 32(2): 243–61.

Martin, S. (2002) Best value: new public management or new direction? In McLaughlin, K., Osbourne, S. and Ferlie, E. (eds), *New Public Management. Current Trends and Future Prospects*. London: Routledge.

Martin, S. and Boaz, A. (2000) Public participation and citizen-centred government: lessons from the Best Value and Better Government for Older People programmes, *Public Money and Management*, 20(2): 47–54.

Martinez-Lucio, M. and Blyton, P. (2001) Constructing the post-Fordist state: the politics of labour market flexibility in Spain. In Jessop, B. (ed.), *Regulation Theory and the Crisis of Capitalism Volume 4 – Country Studies*. London: Edward Elgar.

Martinez-Lucio, M. and Stewart, P. (1997) The paradox of contemporary labour process theory: the rediscovery of labour and the disappearance of collectivism, *Capital and Class*, 62: 49–77.

Massey University (1997) *The Role of Government and Work Orientation: International Social Survey Programme*. Department of Marketing, October.

Massey University (2000) *Social Equality in New Zealand: International Social Survey Programme*. Department of Marketing, March.

Masters, M. 1998. Public sector employment in a time of transition. *Industrial and Labor Relations Review*, 51(4): 705–706.

Mathieson, H. and Corby, S. (1999) Trade unions: the challenge of individualism? In Corby, S. and White, G. (eds) (1999) *Employee Relations in the Public Services*. London: Routledge.

Maurice, M., Sorge, A. and Warner, M. (1980) Societal differences in organising manufacturing units. A comparison of France, West Germany, and Great Britain, *Organization Studies*, I: 59–86.

May, R., Walsh, P., Harbridge, R. and Thickett, G. (2003) *Unions and Union Membership in New Zealand*. Annual Review for 2002.

Maynard-Smith, J. (1982) *Evolution and the Theory of Games*. Cambridge: Cambridge University Press.

Mayntz, R. (1993) Governing failures and the problems of governability. In Kooiman, J. (ed.), *Modern Governance*. London: Sage.

McGregor, D. (2001) Jobs in the public and private sectors. *Economic Trends*, 571: 35–50.

McGuire, L. (2002) Service charters – global convergence or national divergence, *Public Management Review*, 3(4): 493–524.

McLaughlin, K., Osborne, S. and Ferlie, E. (2002) *New Public Management: Current Trends and Future Prospects*. Routledge: London.

Mechanic, D. (2002) Socio-cultural implications of changing organisational technologies in the provision of care, *Social Science and Medicine*, 54(3): 459–467.

Meiksins Wood, E. (1997) *Back to Marx*, Monthly Review, 49(2).

Mellahi, K. and Wood, G. (2003) *The Ethical Business*. London: Palgrave.

Menzel, D. C. (2001) Ethics versus evil: Is it before or after midnight in the garden of ethics and evil? *American Review of Public Administration*, 31(3): 340–350.

Miller, C. (1998) Canadian non-profits in crisis: the need for reform. *Social Policy and Administration*, December, 32(4): 401–419.

Miller, G. (1997) The impact of economics on contemporary political science. *Journal of Economic Literature*, XXXV (September): 1173–1204.

Millward, N., Bryson, A. and Forth, J. (2000) *All change at work?* London: Routledge.

Minogue, M. (1998) Changing the state: concepts and practice in the reform of the public sector. In Minogue, M., Polidano, C. and Hume, D. (eds), *Beyond the New Public Management: Changing Ideas and Practices in Governance*. Cheltenham: Edward Elgar.

Minogue, M., Polidano, C. and Hume, D. (1998) Introduction: the analysis of public management and governance. In Minogue, M., Polidano, C. and Hume, D. (eds), *Beyond the New Public Management: Changing Ideas and Practices in Governance*. Cheltenham: Edward Elgar.

Mitchell, W. and Simmons, R. (1995) *Beyond Politics: Markets, Welfare, and the Failure of Bureaucracy*. Boulder: Westview Press.

Moctezuma Barragan, E. and Roemer, A. (2001) *A New Public Management in Mexico: Towards a Government that Produces Results*. Aldershot: Ashgate.

Moist, P. (2001) Privation and public services, Canadian experiences. *Society for Socialist Studies Conference*, Laval University, Quebec City, Canada.

Monroe, K. (ed.) (1991) *The Economic Approach to Politics: A Critical Reassessment of the Theory of Rational Action*. New York: HarperCollins.

Montecinos, V. (1998) Economists in party politics: Chilean democracy in the era of the markets. In Centeno, M. and Silva, P. (eds), *The Politics of Expertise in Latin America*. London: Palgrave Macmillan.

Moody, K. (1997) *Workers in a Lean World*. London: Verso.

Morgan, P. and Allington, N. (2002) Has the public sector retained its 'model employment' status? *Public Money and Management*, January–March: 35–42.

Mossé, P. and Tchobanian, (1999) France: the restructuring of employment relations in the public services. In Bach, S., Bordogna, L., Della Rocca, G. and Winchester, D. (eds), *Public Services Employment Relations in Europe*. London: Routledge.

Mueller, D. (2001) Public choice after 50 years, Bruno Frey after 60. *Kyklos*, 54(2/3): 343–354.

Mueller, D. (2003) *Public Choice III*. Cambridge: Cambridge University Press.

Mueller, F. and Loveridge, R. (1995) The 'second industrial divide'? The role of the large firm in the Baden-Württemberg model. *Industrial and Corporate Change* 4(3): 555–82.

Mulgan, R. (1992) The elective dictatorship in New Zealand. In Gold, H. (ed.), *New Zealand Politics in Perspective* (3rd ed). Auckland: Longman Paul.

Muller, M. (2003) *Water 2003 – What Should be Done: Lessons from Johannesburg and Pointers for the Future*. Speech given at various international fora. Pretoria: Department of Water Affairs and Forestry.

Munck, R. (2003) Neo-liberalism, necessitarianism and alternatives in Latin America. *Third World Quarterly*, 24(3): 495–511.

Murray, M. (forthcoming), City of Extremes: The Spatial Politics of Johannesburg After Apartheid. London: Verso.

Nagel, J. (1998) Social choice in a pluralitarian democracy: The politics of market liberalisation in New Zealand. *British Journal of Political Science*, 28(2): 223–267.

Naisbitt, J. (1997) *Megatrends Asia*. London: Brealey.

Narayan, D., Patel, R., Schafft, K., Rademacher, A. and Koch-Schulte, S. (2000) *Voices of the Poor: Can Anyone Hear Us?* New York: Oxford University Press.

Ndulo, M. (2001) Constitution-making in Africa: assessing both the process and the content. *Public Administration and Development*, 21(2): 107.

Nelson, R. (ed.) (1993) *National Innovation Systems: a Comparative Analysis*. New York: Oxford University Press.

Nelson, R. and Winter, S. (1982) *An Evolutionary Theory of Economic Change*. Cambridge: Harvard University Press.

Neuberger, J. (2001) The Educated patient: new challenge for the medical profession, *Journal of Internal Medicine*, February, 249, S741: 41–46.

Newberry, S. (2002) Intended or unintended consequences? Resource erosion in New Zealand's government departments. *Financial Accountability and Management*, 18(4): 309–330.

Newman, J. (2002) The New Public Management, modernisation and institutional change: disputions, disjunctions and dilemmas. In McLaughlin, K., Osborne, S. P.

and Ferlie, E. (eds), *New Public Management: Current Trends and Future Prospects*. London: Routledge.

Ngwane, T. (2003) Sparks in the Township. *New Left Review*, 22, July–August.

Nickson, A. (2002) Transferencias de políticas y reforma del sector público en America Latina: el caso del New Public Management, Revista del CLAD. *Reforma y Democracia*, 24 (October): 1–15.

Nielsen, H. (1999) *Sector Programme Support in Decentralised Government Systems – a Contextual Donor Challenge*. Copenhagen: Danida.

Niskanen, W. (1971) *Bureaucracy and Representative Government*. Chicago: Aldine-Atherton.

Niskanen, W. A. (1994) Bureaucracy and Public Economics. Brookfield: Edward Elgar.

Norman, R. (2001) Letting and making managers manage: The effect of control systems on management action in New Zealand's central government. *International Public Management Journal*, 4: 65–89.

North, D. (1990) *Institutions, Institutional Change and Economic Performance*. Cambridge and New York: Cambridge University Press.

Nozick, R. (1984) Moral consciousness and distributive justice. In Sandel, M. (ed.), *Liberalism and its Critics*. Oxford: Basil Blackwell.

O'Dea, D. (2000) *The Changes in New Zealand's Income Distribution*. Treasury Working Paper 00/13. Wellington: The Treasury.

O'Hagan, E. (2002) *Employee Relations in the Periphery of Europe: The Unfolding of the European Social Model*. London: Palgrave.

Oakeshott, M. (1983) *On History and other Essays*. Oxford: Blackwell.

OECD (1995) *Governance in transition: Public management reforms in OECD countries*. Paris: OECD.

OECD (2001) *Country study: Canada. Public Service as an Employer of Choice*. Paris: OECD.

Ohno, T. (1989) L'Esprit Toyota, Paris: Masson. In Oliver, N. and Wilkinson, B., *The Japanization of British Industry*. Oxford: Basil Blackwell.

Olowu, B. (1999) Redesigning African civil service reforms. *Journal of Modern African Studies*, 37: 1–23.

Olson, M. (1965) *The Logic of Collective Action*. Cambridge: Harvard University Press.

Olson, M. (1982) *The Rise and Decline of Nations: Economic Growth, Stagflation, and Social Rigidities*. New Haven: Yale University Press.

Osborne, D. and Gaebler, T. (1993) *Reinventing Government*. New York: Plume.

Osborne, S. (2002) Introduction to Volume 3: Multiple Perspectives on Public Management Reform. In Osborne, S., *Public Management: Critical Perspectives*. London: Routledge.

Osborne, S. and McLaughlin, K. (2002) The New Public Management in context. In McLaughlin, K., Osborne, S. and Ferlie, E., *New Public Management: Current Trends and Future Prospects*. Routledge: London.

Ostrom, V. and Ostrom, E. (1971) Public choice: A different approach to the study of public administration. *Public Administration Review*, 31, 203–16, reprinted in Osborne, S. (2002) Public Management: Critical Perspectives. London: Routledge.

Oszlak, O. (1999) De menor a major. El desafío de la segunda reforma del estado. Nueva Sociedad. *Caracas*, 160, 81–100.

Painter, C. and Clarence, E. (2001) UK Local action zones and changing urban governance. *Urban Studies*, 38(8): 1215–1232.

Parekh, B. (1982) *Contemporary Political Thinkers*. Oxford: Martin Robinson.

Parker, M. and Slaughter, J. (1988) Choosing sides: unions and the team concept. *Labor Notes*, Boston: South End Press.

Pauw, J. (2003) *Metered to Death: How a Water Experiment Caused Riots and a Cholera Epidemic*. International Consortium of Investigative Journalists, Washington, February 5.

Pempel, T. J. and Tsunekawa, K. (1979) Corporatism without labor? The Japanese anomaly. In P. Schmitter and G. Lehmbruch (eds), *Trends Toward Corporatist Intermediation*. Beverly Hills, California: Sage.

Perri, 6 (1997) Holistic Government. London: Demos.

Perry, P. and Webster, A. (1999) *New Zealand Politics at the Turn of the Millennium: Attitudes and Values about Politics and Government*. Auckland: Alpha Publications.

Peters, B. (1986) Burning the village: The civil service under Reagan and Thatcher. *Parliamentary Affairs*, 39: 79–97.

Peters, B. and Pierre, J. (1998) Governance without government? Rethinking public administration. *Journal of Public Administration Research and Theory*, 8(2): 223–43.

Petracca, M. (1991) The rational actor approach to politics: science, self-interest, and normative democratic theory. In Monroe, K., *The Economic Approach to Politics: A Critical Reassessment of the Theory of Rational Action*. New York: HarperCollins.

Pfeffer, N. and Coote, A. (1991) *Is Quality Good For You?* London: Institute of Public Policy Research.

Phillips, P. and Stecher, C. (2001) Fiscal restraint, legislated consessions, and labour relations in the Manitoba civil service. In Swimmer, G. (ed.), *Public Sector Labour Relations in an Era of Restraint and Restructuring*. Toronto: Oxford University Press.

Pierson, C. (1991) *Beyond the Welfare State? The New Political Economy of Welfare*. Cambridge: Polity.

Pike, C. (2002) *Managing the Schools Inspectorate: Independent Team Practices and Outcomes*. Unpublished PhD thesis. South Bank University, London.

Piore, M. (2003) Society as a precondition for individuality: critical comments. *Socio-Economic Review*, 1(1): 119–121.

Piore, M. J. and Sabel, C. F. (1984) *The Second Industrial Divide: Possibilities for Prosperity*. New York: Basic Books.

Polidano, C. and Hulme, D. (1999) Public management reform in developing countries: issues and outcomes. *Public Management: An International Journal of Theory and Research*, 1(1): 121–32.

Polidano, C., Hulme, D. and Minogue, M. (1998) Conclusions: Looking beyond the New Public Management. In Minogue, M., Polidano, C. and Hulme, D. *Beyond the New Public Management: Changing Ideas and Practices in Governance*. Cheltenham: Edward Elgar.

Pollert, A. (ed.) (1991) *Farewell to Flexibility?* Oxford: Blackwell.

Pollitt, C. (1993) *Managerialism and the Public Services: The Anglo American Experience* (2nd Edition) Oxford: Blackwell.

Pollitt, C. and Boukhaert, G. (2000) *Public Management Reform: a Comparative Analysis*. Oxford: Oxford University Press.

Pollitt, C., Hanney, S., Packwood, T., Rothwell, S. and Roberts, S. (1997) *Trajectories and Options: An International Perspective on the Implementation of Finnish Public Management Reforms*. Ministry of Finance, Finland.

Port Elizabeth Municipality (1997) *Public Private Partnerships for Municipal Services*. Report by Director: Administration to the Executive Committee, 4 February 1997.

Porter, M. (1986) *The Competition in Global Industries*. Boston, Mass.: Harvard Business School.

Porter, M. (1990) *The Competitive Advantage of Nations*. New York: Free Press.

Powell, W. (1990) Neither market nor hierarchy: the limits of organisation. In Staw, B. and Cummings, L. (eds), *Research in Organisational Behavior*, Vol. 12, Greenwich, Conn.: JAI Press.

Pracher, C. (1996) Germany part II: new models of guidance and steering public administration. In Flynn, N. and Strehl, F. (eds), *Public Sector Management in Europe*. Hemel Hampstead: Prentice Hall.

Prats i Català, J. (1999) Democratic governability in Latin America at the end of the twentieth century. In *Reforming the State: Managerial Public Administration in Latin America*. Boulder, Colorado: Lynne Rienner Publishers.

Public Service Commission of Canada (2000) Canada. Overview of recent public service reforms in Canada, Great Britain, Australia, New Zealand and the United States. http:// www.psc-cfp.gc.ca

Public Services International (2003) *The Report of the World Panel on Financing Water Infrastructure*. Geneva, 12 March 2003.

Purchase, B. and Hirshorn, R. (1994) *Searching for Good Governance*. Kingston: Queen's University, School of Policy Studies, Government and Competitiveness Project.

Putnam, R. (1996) The strange disappearance of civic America. *The American Prospect*, 24: 34–48.

Putnam, R., Leonardi, R. and Nanetti, R. (1993) *Making democracy work: Civic traditions in modern Italy*. Princeton, NJ: Princeton University Press.

Pyke, F. and Sengenberger, W. (eds) (1992) *Industrial Districts and Local Regeneration*. Geneva: International Institute for Labour Studies.

Pyke, F., Becattini, G. and Sengenberger, W. (eds) (1990) *Industrial Districts and Inter-firm Co-operation in Italy*. Geneva: International Institute for Labour Studies.

Rakodi, C. (ed.) (1997) *The Urban Challenge in Africa: Growth and Management of its Large Cities*. Tokyo: United Nations University Press.

Rawls, J. (1984) The right and good contrasted. In Sandel, M. (ed.), *Liberalism and its Critics*. Oxford: Basil Blackwell.

Rawls, J. (2001) *Justice as Fairness: A Restatement*. Cambridge: Harvard University Press.

Redman, T., Mathews, B., Wilkinson, A. and Snape, E. (1995) Quality management in services: is the public sector keeping pace? *International Journal of Public Sector Management*, 8(7): 21–34.

Reid, B. (2001) Partnership and Change in Social Housing. In Balloch, S. and Taylor, M. (eds), *Partnership Working: Policy and Practice*. Bristol: Policy Press.

Reimer, S. (1998) Working in a risk society. *Transactions of the Institute of British Geographers*, 23(1): 116–127.

Repetto, F. (2000) Es posible reformar el Estado sin transformar la sociedad? Capacidad de gestión pública y política social en perspectiva latinoamericana. Revista del CLAD. *Reforma y Democracia*, 16 (Caracao): 1–17.

Report of the Advisory Group on the Review of the Centre (2001) Available on *www.executive.govt.nz/ministers/mallard/ssc*.

Report of the Community and Voluntary Sector Working Party (2001) *Communities and Government: Potential for Partnership*. Wellington NZ: Ministry of Social Policy.

Reports of the Advisory Committee on Labour Management Relations in the Federal Public Service (2000) Identifying Issues. May, 2000.

Republic of South Africa Department of Constitutional Development (1998) *Draft Regulatory Framework for Municipal Service Partnerships*. Pretoria, August.

Republic of South Africa Department of Water Affairs and Forestry (2002) *Draft Water Resources Strategy*. Pretoria.

Reshef, Y. (2001) The logic union quiescence: the Alberta case. In Swimmer, G. (ed.), *Public Sector Labour Relations in an Era of Restraint and Restructuring*. Toronto: Oxford University Press.

Rhodes, R. (1981) *Control and Power in Central-local Government Relations*. Hants: Gower.

Rhodes, R. (1994) The hollowing out of the state: The changing nature of the public service in Britain. *The Political Quarterly*, 65(2): 138–151.

Rhodes, R. (1996) The new governance: governing without government. *Political Studies*, 54: 652–667.

Riccucci, N. (2001) The 'old' public management versus the 'new' public management: where does public management administration fit in? *Public Administration Review*, 61(2): 172–175.

Riker, W. (1962) *The Theory of Political Coalitions*. New Haven, CT: Yale University Press.

Roberts, J. (1987) *Politicians, Public Servants and Public Enterprise: Restructuring the New Zealand Government Executive*. Wellington NZ: Victoria University Press for the Institute of Policy Studies.

Robinson, D. (ed.) (1999) *Social Capital in Action*. Wellington NZ: Institute of Policy Studies, Victoria University of Wellington.

Robinson, J. (2002) Global and world cities: A view from off the map. *International Journal of Urban and Regional Research*, 26(3).

Robinson, R. and Le Grand, J. (eds) (1994) *Evaluating the NHS Reforms*. London: Kings Fund.

Rocha, J. (1998) The New Public Management and its consequences in the public personnel system. *Review of Public Personnel Administration*, 18, 2: 82–87.

Rogers, J. (2002) *Obituary: John Rawls*, Guardian, 27 November.

Roome, J. (1995) *Water Pricing and Management: World Bank Presentation to the SA Water Conservation Conference*, unpublished paper, South Africa, 2 October.

Roper, B. (1997) New Zealand's postwar economic history. In Rudd, C. and Roper, B. (eds), *The Political Economy of New Zealand*. Auckland: Oxford University Press.

Roper, I., Prabhu, V. and van Zwanenburg, N. (1997) (Only) just in time: Japanisation and the 'non-learning' firm. *Work Employment and Society*. 11(1): 27–46.

Rose, J. (2001) From softball to hardball: The transition of labour-management relations in the Ontario public service. In Swimmer, G. (ed.), *Public Sector Labour Relations in an Era of Restraint and Restructuring*. Toronto: Oxford University Press.

Rosenthal, P., Hill, S. and Peccei, R. (1997) Checking out service: evaluating excellence, HRM and TQM in retailing. *Work, Employment and Society*, 11(3): 481–503.

Rowley, C. and Tollison, R. (1988) *The Political Economy of Rent-Seeking*. Boston: Martinus Nijhoff.

Rudd, C. (1997) The welfare state. In Rudd, C. and Roper, B. (eds), *The Political Economy of New Zealand*. Auckland: Oxford University Press.

Rudd, C. and Roper, B. (eds) (1997) *The Political Economy of New Zealand*. Auckland: Oxford University Press.

Sabel, C. (1991) Moebius-strip organisations and open labor markets: Some consequences of the reintegration of conception and execution in a volatile economy. In Bourdieu, P. and Coleman, J. (eds), *Social Theory for a Changing Society*. Boulder, Colo: Westview Press.

Sabel, C. (1992) Studied trust: building new forms of co-operation in a volatile economy. In Pyke, F. and Sengenberger, W. (eds), *Industrial Districts and Local Economic Regeneration*. Geneva: International Institute for Labour Studies.

Sabel, C. and Zeitlin, J. (1985) Historical alternatives to mass production: politics, markets, and technology in nineteenth century industrialisation. *Past and Present,* 108 (August): 133–76.

Safford, J. and McGregor, D. (1998) Employment in the public and private sectors. *Economic Trends,* 571: 22–33.

Saich, T. (1999) *China's Political Structure, China in the 1990s.* Basingstoke: Macmillan.

Saitoti, G. 2002. *The Challenges of Economic and Institutional Reforms in Africa.* Aldershot: Ashgate.

Salinas, F. (2002) Accrual budgeting and fiscal consolidation in the EMU. *Contemporary Economic Policy,* 20(2): 193–206.

Samuelson, P. (1980) The public role in the modern American economy. In Feldstein, M., *The American Economy in Transition.* Chicago: University of Chicago Press.

Sandel, M. (1984) Introduction. In Sandel, M. (ed.), *Liberalism and its Critics.* Oxford: Basil Blackwell.

Sanderson, I. (2001) Performance management, evaluation and learning in 'modern' local government. *Public Administration,* 79(2): 297–313.

Sassen, S. (2001) *The Global City: New York, London, Tokyo.* Princeton: Princeton University Press.

Savioe, D. (1994) *Thatcher, Reagan, Mulroney: In Search of a New Bureaucracy.* Toronto: University of Toronto Press.

Savoie, D. (1995) What is wrong with the New Public Management? Canadian Public Administration, 38(1): 112–121. Reprinted in Osborne, S. (2002) *Public Management: Critical Perspectives.* London: Routledge.

Savoie, D. (1999) *Governing from the Centre: The Concentration of Power in Canadian Politics.* Toronto: University of Toronto Press.

Schedler, K. and Proeller, I. (2002) The new public management: a perspective from mainland Europe. In McLaughlin, K., Osborne, S. and Ferlie, E. (eds), *New Public Management: Current Trends and Future Prospects.* London: Routledge.

Schick, A. (1996) *The Spirit of Reform.* Wellington NZ, State Services Commission.

Schick, A. (1998) Why most developing countries should not try New Zealand reforms. *The World Bank Research Observer,* 13(1): 123–31.

Schick, A. (2001) *Reflections on the New Zealand Model.* Notes based on a lecture at the New Zealand Treasury, August.

Schmitter, P. (1997a) The emerging Europolity and its impact on national systems of production. In Hollingsworth, J. R. and Boyer, R. (eds), *Contemporary Capitalism: the Embeddedness of Institutions.* New York: Cambridge University Press.

Schmitter, P. (1997b) Levels of spatial co-ordination and the embeddedness of institutions. In Hollingsworth, J. R. and Boyer, R. (eds), *Contemporary Capitalism: the Embeddedness of Institutions.* New York: Cambridge University Press.

Schmitter, P. C. and Lehmbruch, G. (eds) (1979) *Trends Towards Corporatist Intermediation.* New York: Sage Publications.

Schneiberg, M. and Hollingsworth, J. R. (1990) Can transaction cost economics explain trade associations?. In Aoki, M., Gustafsson, B. and Williamson, O. (eds), *The Firm As a Nexus of Treaties.* London and Beverly Hills, Calif.: Sage Publications.

Schneider, B. (1998) The material bases of technocracy: investor confidence and neoliberalism in Latin America. In Centeno, M. and Silva, P. (eds), *The Politics of Expertise in Latin America.* London: Palgrave Macmillan.

Schneider, B. and Heredia, B. (eds) (2002) *Reinventing Leviathan: The Politics of Administrative Reform in Developing Countries.* Boulder Colorado: Lynne Reinner Publisher.

Schultz, D. (2002) Civil service reform. *Public Administration Review,* 62(5): 634–637.

Schumpeter, J. (1950) *Capitalism, Socialism and Democracy.* New York: Harper and Row.

Schumpeter, J. (1983) *The Theory of Economic Development.* New Brunswick, NJ: Transaction Books.

Schweers Cook, K. and Levi, M. (eds) (1990) *The Limits of Rationality.* Chicago, IL: University of Chicago Press.

Scott, G. (2001) *Public Management in New Zealand: Lessons and Challenges.* Wellington NZ: New Zealand Business Roundtable.

Scott, G., Bushnell, P. and Sallee, N. (1990) Reform of the core public sector: The New Zealand experience. *Governance,* 3(2): 138–67.

Scott, J. (1991) *Social Network Analysis: A Handbook.* London: Sage Publications.

Scranton, P. (1984) *Proprietary Capitalism: Textile Manufacture at Philadelphia, 1800–1885.* Cambridge and New York: Cambridge University Press.

Segreto, L. (1998) Italian capitalism between the private and public sectors. *Business and Economic History,* 27(2): 455–468.

Shamsul Haque, M. (1995) The contextless nature of public administration in third world countries. *International Review of Administrative Sciences,* 62(3): 315–29.

Shefner, J. (1998) The redefinition of state policies in the social arena: the case of Mexico. In Vellinga, M. (ed.), *The Changing Role of the State in Latin America.* Boulder, Colorado: Westview Press.

Shleifer, A. and Vishny, R. (1999) *The Grabbing Hand: Government Pathologies and Their Cures.* Cambridge, MA: Harvard University Press.

Simeon, R. (2002) Federalism and intergovernmental relations. In Dunn, C. (ed.), *Handbook of Canadian Public Administration.* Toronto: Oxford University Press.

Sing, D. (1999) A governance perspective of public administration. *Administratio Publica,* 9(2).

Singer, P. (1995) *Practical Ethics.* Cambridge: Cambridge University Press.

Skelcher, C. (1993) Involvement and empowerment in local public services. In Flynn, N. (2002) *Public Sector Management.* London: Pearson Education Limited.

Smelser, N. (1992) The rational choice perspective: A theoretical assessment. *Rationality and Society,* 4(4): 381–410.

Smith, A. (1981[1776]). *The Wealth of Nations.* Harmondsworth: Pelican Classics.

Smith, A. and Swain, A. (2001) Regulating and institutionalising capitalisms. In Jessop, B. (ed.), *Regulation Theory and the Crisis of Capitalism,* Volume 4 – Country Studies. London: Edward Elgar.

Smith, M. and Beazley, M. (2000) Progressive partnerships and the involvement of local communities: A framework for evaluation. *Public Administration,* 78(4): 855–878.

Smith, P. (1998) The rise and fall of the developmental state in Latin America. In Vellinga, M. (ed.), *The Changing Role of the State in Latin America.* Boulder, Colorado: Westview Press.

Smith, S. (2000) The ownership solution: Towards a shared capitalism for the 21st century. *Comparative Economic Studies,* 42(3): 130–134.

Sneade, A. (2001) Trade union membership 1999–2000: an analysis of data from the Certification Officer and the Labour Force Survey. *Labour Market Trends,* September: 433–44.

Snidal, D. (1985) The limits of hegemonic stability theory. *International Organisation,* 39(4): 579–615.

Snidal, D. (1991) Relative gains and the pattern of international cooperation. *American Political Science Review,* 85: 701–26.

Sorge, A. (1989) An essay on technical change: its dimensions and social and strategic context. *Organisation Studies*, 10(1): 23–44.

Sorge, A. and Streeck, W. (1988) Industrial relations and technical change: the case for an extended perspective. In Hyman, R. and Streeck, W. (eds), *New Technology and Industrial Relations*. Oxford: Blackwell.

Spink, P. (1999) Possibilities and political imperatives: seventy years of administrative reform in Latin America. In Bresser Pereira, L. and Spink, P. *Reforming the State: Managerial Public Administration in Latin America*. Boulder, Colorado: Lynne Rienner Publishers.

Stace, H. (1998) Janet Fraser – making policy as well as tea. In Clark, M. (ed.). *Peter Fraser: Master Politician*. Palmerston North: The Dunmore Press.

Stanley, P. (1990) Deregulation in the outer metropolitan area. In Bell, P. and Cloke, P. (eds), *Deregulation and Transport: Market Forces in the Modern World*. London: David Fulton Publishers.

State Services Commission (2000) *Declining Government Performance? Why Citizens Don't Trust Government*. Working Paper No. 9. Wellington NZ: State Services Commission.

Statistics Canada (2002) *Perspectives on Labour and Income*, 14(3): 75.

Statistics South Africa (2002a) *Earning and Spending in South Africa*. Pretoria.

Statistics South Africa (2002b) *Database on Expenditure and Income*, 2000. Pretoria.

Steinberg, J. (2001) *Midlands*. Johannesburg: Jonathen Ball.

Stewart, J. and Walsh, K. (1992) Change in the management of public services. Public Administration, 70, 499–518. Reprinted in Bourn, J. (1995) *Public Sector Management, Vol. 2*. Hants: Dartmouth Publishing Company Ltd.

Stillman, R. (1997) American vs. European public administration: Does public Administration make the modern state, or does the state make public administration? *Public Administration Review*, 57(4): 332–338.

Stocker, K., Waitzkin, H. and Iriart, C. (1999) *Health Nutrition and Population Sector Strategy Paper*. Washington, DC: The World Bank.

Streeck, W. (1991) On the institutional conditions of diversified quality production. In Matzner, E. and Streeck, W. (eds), *Beyond Keynesianism: the Socio-Economics of Production and Full Employment*. Aldershot: Edward Elgar.

Streeck, W. and Schmitter, P. (eds) (1985) *Private Interest Government: Beyond Market and State*. London and Beverly Hills, Calif.: Sage Publications.

Streib, G., Slotkin, B. and Rivera, M. (2001) Public administration research from a practitioner perspective. *Public Administration Review*, 61(5): 515–525.

Sutch, H. (1999) The relevance of New Public Management for transition countries. *Public Management Forum*, 5(3): 1–3.

Sutter, D. (1997) Review of William C. Mitchell and Randy T. Simmons, Beyond Politics. *Public Choice*, 91: 421–425.

Swimmer, G. (1995) Collective bargaining in the federal public service of Canada: the last twenty years. In Swimmer, G. and Thompson, M. (eds), *Public Sector Collective Bargaining in Canada: Beginning of the End or End of the Beginning?* Kingston: IRC Press.

Swimmer, G. (2001) Public sector labour relations in an era of restraint and restructuring: an overview. In Swimmer G., (ed.), *Public Sector Labour Relations in an Era of Restraint and Restructuring*. Toronto: Oxford University Press.

Swimmer, G. (2002) Putting the Fryer committee recommendations in context. *Canadian Labour and Employment Law Journal*, 9(3): 313–334.

Swimmer, G. and Bach, S. (2001) Restructuring federal public-sector human resources. In Swimmer, G. (ed.), *Public Sector Labour Relations in an Era of Restraint and Restructuring*. Toronto: Oxford University Press.

Tangri, R. and Mwenda, A. (2001) Corruption and cronyism in Uganda's privatisation in the 1990s. *African Affairs*, 100: 117–33.

Tarantelli, E. (1986) The regulation of inflation and unemployment. *Industrial Relations*, 25(1): 1–15.

Taylor, M. (2002) Social exclusion and the New Public Management: Cause or response? In McLaughlin, K., Osborne, S. and Ferlie, E. *New Public Management: Current Trends and Future Prospects*. Routledge: London.

Teague, P. (1995) Pay determination in the Republic of Ireland: towards societal corporatism? *British Journal of Industrial Relations*, 33(2) 253–273.

Tendler, J. (1997) *Good Government in the Tropics*. Baltimore: John Hopkins University Press.

Terry, M. (2003) Employee representation: shop stewards and the new legal framework. In Edwards, P. (ed.), *Industrial Relations: Theory and Practice*, (2nd ed). Oxford: Blackwell.

The Economist (2003) *The Americas: Lula's great pension battle; reforming Brazil*. April, 5th.

The Evert Vermeer Foundation (1990) *Solidarity against Poverty: a Socialist Program from Holland*. Amsterdam, the Netherlands.

Thiers, P. (2000) Management of public service reform: A comparative review of experiences in the management of programmes of reform of the administrative arm of central government. *Review of Public Personnel Administration*, Columbia, 20(2): 75–77.

Thompson, G. (1992) Network governance, citizenship and consumerism. *Proceedings of the Employment Research Unit Annual Conference*. Cardiff Business School, 9–10 September, 1992.

Thompson, M. (2001) Canadian public sector employment. In Dell'Aringa, C., Della Rocca, G., and Keller, B. (eds), *Strategic Choices in Reforming Public Service Employment*. Houndmills, Basingstoke: Palgrave.

Thompson, P. (1995) (2nd ed) *The Nature of Work*. Basingstoke: MacMillan.

Thompson, P. and Ackroyd, S. (1995) All quiet on the workplace front? A critique of recent trends in British industrial sociology. *Sociology*. 29(4): 615–633.

Tolliday, S. and Zeitlin, J. (eds) (1991) *The Power to Manage: Employers and Industrial Relations in Comparative Historical Perspective*. London and New York: Routledge.

Tomlinson, J. (1988) *Can Governments Manage the Economy?* London, Fabian Tract 524, January.

Tomlinson R., Beauregard, R., Bremner, L. and Mangcu, X. (eds) (2003) *Emerging Johannesburg: Perspectives on the Post-Apartheid City*. New York: Routledge.

Tomlinson, R. (2003) HIV/AIDS and urban fragmentation in Johannesburg. In Harrison, P., Huchzermayer, M. and Mayekiso, M. (eds), *Confronting Fragmentation: Housing and Urban Development in a Democratising Society*. Cape Town: University of Cape Town Press.

Torres, L. and Pina, V. (2002) Changes in public service delivery in the EU countries. *Public Money & Management*, 22(4): 41–48.

Torres, L. and Pina, V. (2002) Changes in public services delivery in the EU countries. *Public Money and Management*, 22(4): 41–48.

Treasury Board of Canada Secretariat (1999) *Results for Canadians*. htpp://www.tbs-sct.gc.ca

Treasury Board of Canada Secretariat (2000) *Managing for Results 2000*. htpp://www.tbs-sct.gc.ca

Treasury, H. M. (2002) Spending Review White Paper. *The Role of the Voluntary Sector in Public Services*. Chapter 30, 159.

Treu, T. (ed.) (1987) *Public Services Labour Relations*. Geneva: International Labour Organisation.

Trevor, M. (ed.) (1987) *The Internationalisation of Japanese Business: European and Japanese Perspectives*. Boulder, Colo.: Westview Press.

Tullock, G. (1965) *The Politics of Bureaucracy*. Washington, DC: Public Affairs Press.

Tullock, G. (1987) Public choice. In Eatwell, J. and Milgate, M., *The New Palgrave: A Dictionary of Economics*. London: Macmillan.

Tullock, G. (1993) *Rent Seeking*. Brookfield, VT: Edward Elgar.

Twombly, E. C. (2002) Religious versus secular human service organisations: Implications for public policy. *The Urban Institute*, 83(4): 947–961.

Udehn, L. (1996) *The Limits of Public Choice: A Sociological Critique of the Economic Theory of Politics*. London: Routledge.

UNDP (1995) Review of the civil service reform programme in Ghana. *Report on a Mission to Ghana*, 19 February–10 March.

US Department of Labour, Bureau of Labour Statistics (2003) *Union Members in 2002*. February 25.

van de Walle, N. (2001) *African Economies and the Politics of Permanent Crisis, 1979–1999*. Cambridge: Cambridge University Press.

van den Berg, A. (forthcoming) Politics versus markets: A note on the uses of double standards. In Breton, R. and Reitz, J., *Globalization and Society: Processes of Differentiation Examined*. Boulder, CO: Westview Press.

van den Berg, A. and Meadwell, H. (eds) (2004) *The Social Sciences and Rationality: Promise, Limits and Problems*. New Brunswick, NJ: Transaction.

van der Molen, K., van Rooyen, A. and van Wyk, B. (eds) (2002) Outcome-based governance: Assessing the results. In Sen, A. 1999. *Development as Freedom*. New York: Knopf Press.

Verma, A. and Lonti, Z. (2001) *Changing Government Workplaces*. Ottawa: Canadian Policy Research Networks.

Voskamp, U. and Wittke, V. (2001) Industrial restructuring in the former German Democratic Republic (GDR): Barriers to adaptive reform become downward development spirals. In Jessop, B. (ed.), *Regulation Theory and the Crisis of Capitalism Volume 4 – Country Studies*. London: Edward Elgar.

Wallerstein, I. (1995) *After Liberalism*. New York: The New Press.

Wallis, J. (2002) Evaluating organisational leadership in the New Zealand public sector in the aftermath of the Rankin judgment. *International Review of Administrative Sciences*, 68(1): 61–72.

Wallis, M. (1989) *Bureaucracy: Its Role in Third World Development*. Basingstoke: MacMillan.

Wallis, M. (1995) The problem of bureaucratic administration. In Fitzgerald, P., McLennan, A. and Munslow, B., *Managing Sustainable Development in South Africa*. Cape Town: Oxford University Press.

Walsh, K. (1995a) *Public Services and Market Mechanisms*. London: MacMillan.

Walsh, K. (1995b) Quality through markets: the new public service management. In Wilkinson, A. and Wilmott, H. (eds), *Making Quality Critical*. London: Routledge.

Walsh, P. (1997) From arbitration to bargaining: Changing state strategies in industrial relations. In Rudd, C. and Roper, B. (eds), *The Political Economy of New Zealand*. Auckland: Oxford University Press.

Walzer, M. (1984) Welfare, membership and need. In Sandel, M. (ed.), *Liberalism and its Critics*. Oxford: Basil Blackwell.

Wang, X. (2002) Assessing administrative accountability: Results from a national survey. The American Review of Public Administration, 32(2): 350–370.

Warrington, E. (ed.) (1998) Public Administration and Development.

White, G. (1993) *Ride White, Riding the Tiger, The Politics of Economic Reform in Post-Mao, China*. Basingstoke: Macmillan.

White, G. (2000) The pay review board system: its development and impact. *Historical Studies in Industrial Relations*, 9(2): 71–100.

White, G. (2001) Adapting the Westminster model: provincial and territorial cabinets in Canada. *Public Money and Management*, 21(2): 17–24.

Whitfield, D. (2002) PPPs – Where will we be by 2010? *Public Management and Policy Association Review*, February, 16, 2–3.

Whitley, R. (1992a) *Business Systems in East Asia: Firms, Markets, and Societies*. London and Newbury Park: Sage.

Whitley, R. (1999) *Divergent Capitalisms*. Oxford: Oxford University Press.

Whitley, R. (ed.) (1992b) *European Markets in Their National Contexts*. London: Sage.

Whitley, R. and Kristensen, P. H. (eds) (1997) *Governance at Work: the Social Regulation of Economic Relations in Europe*. Oxford: Oxford University Press.

Wildavsky, A. (1984) *The Politics of the Budgetary Process*. Boston, Little: Brown.

Wilkinson, D. and Applebee, E. (1999) *Implementing Holistic Government: Joined-Up Action on the Ground*. The Policy Press: Bristol.

Williams, R. (2000) The responsible administrator has the ethics edge. *Public Administration Review*, 60(6): 576-582.

Williamson, A., Scott, D. and Halfpenny, P. (2000) Rebuilding civil society in Northern Ireland: the community and voluntary sector's contribution to the European Union's Peace and Reconciliation District Partnership Programme. *Policy and Politics*, 28(1): 49–66.

Winchester, D. and Bach, S. (1999) Britain – the transformation of public service employment relations. In Bach, S., Bordogna, L., Della Rocca, G. and Winchester, D. (eds), *Public Services Employment Relations in Europe*. London: Routledge.

Wise, L. (1993) Whither solidarity? Transitions in Swedish public-sector pay policy. *British Journal of Industrial Relations*, 31(1): 75–95.

Wise, L. (2002) Public management reform: competing drivers of change. *Public Administration Review*, 62(5): 555–567.

Wood, G. (1997) The delirium of change: giles deleuze's optimistic postmodernism. *Koers*, 62(2): 1–12.

Wood, G. (2003) Participation, state, economy and society. In Burnell, P. (ed.), *Democratization Through the Looking Glass*. Manchester: Manchester University Press.

Wood, G. and Harcourt, M. (2001) The consequences of Neo-Corporatism: A syncretic analysis. *International Journal of Sociology and Social Policy*, 20(8): 1–22.

Woodman, C. (1999) The evolving role of professions in local government. *Local Governance*, 25(4): 211–219.

Woodroffe, J. and Ellis-Jones, M. (2000) *States of Unrest: Resistance to IMF Policies in Poor Countries*. World Development Movement Report.

World Bank (1991) *Urban Policy and Economic Development: An Agenda for the 1990s*. Washington, DC.

World Bank (1995) *Bureaucrats in Business: The Economics and Politics of Government Ownership*. Oxford: Oxford University Press.

World Bank (1997) *World Development Report*. Washington: World Bank.

World Bank (1997) *World Development Report: The State in a Changing World*. Washington DC: World Bank.

World Bank (2002) *South Africa: Monitoring Service Delivery in Johannesburg*. Southern Africa Department, Africa PREM1, April.

Wunsch J. (2001) Decentralisation, local governance and 'recentralisation' in Africa. *Public Administration and Development*, 21(4): 286.

Wunsch-Hitzig, R., Plapinger, J., Draper, J. and del Campo, E. (2002) Calls for help after September 11: a community mental health hot line. *Journal of Urban Health: Bulletin of the New York Academy of Medicine*, 79(3): 417–428.

www.whitehouse.gov/government/fbci/index.html (20.1.2002)

Xu S. (1997) *The Chinese Civil Service System*. Hong Kong: Shangwu Publishing House.

Yeatman, A. (1994) The reform of public management: An overview. *Australian Journal of Public Administration*, 53: 287–95.

Yu, Q. (1998) *Thousands of Jinshi, Yu Qiuyu Collected Works*. Qinghai: People's Publishing House.

Zafirovski, M. (1998) Socio-economics and rational choice theory: specification of their relations. *Journal of Socio-Economics*, 27(2): 165–205.

Zhu, R. (2000) *Report on the Work of the Government by Zhu Rongji, Premier of the State Council* (delivered at the Third session of the Ninth National People's Congress on March 5).

Zhu, R. (2001) *Report on the Outline of the Tenth Five-Year Plan for National Economic and Social Development by Premier Zhu Rongji* (delivered at the Fourth Session of the Ninth National People's Congress on March 5).

Index